The Formation of the Babylonian Talmud

The Formation of the Babylonian Talmud

DAVID WEISS HALIVNI

Introduced, Translated, and Annotated by

JEFFREY L. RUBENSTEIN

OXFORD
UNIVERSITY PRESS

OXFORD
UNIVERSITY PRESS

Oxford University Press is a department of the University of Oxford.
It furthers the University's objective of excellence in research,
scholarship, and education by publishing worldwide.

Oxford New York
Auckland Cape Town Dar es Salaam Hong Kong Karachi
Kuala Lumpur Madrid Melbourne Mexico City Nairobi
New Delhi Shanghai Taipei Toronto

With offices in
Argentina Austria Brazil Chile Czech Republic France Greece
Guatemala Hungary Italy Japan Poland Portugal Singapore
South Korea Switzerland Thailand Turkey Ukraine Vietnam

Published in the United States of America by
Oxford University Press
198 Madison Avenue, New York, NY 10016

Library of Congress Cataloging-in-Publication Data
Halivni, David.
[Mekorot u-mesorot. English]
The formation of the Babylonian Talmud / David Weiss Halivni ; introduced,
translated, and annotated by Jeffrey L. Rubenstein.
p. cm.
Includes bibliographical references and index.
ISBN 978-0-19-973988-2 (hardcover : alk. paper)—ISBN 978-0-19-987648-8
(ebook) 1. Talmud—History.
2. Jewish law—Interpretation and construction.
I. Rubenstein, Jeffrey L. translator, editor. II. Title.
BM501.H35 2013 296.1'25066—dc23
2012039983

1 3 5 7 9 8 6 4 2

Printed in the United States of America
on acid-free paper

Contents

Biography of David Weiss Halivni

DAVID WEISS HALIVNI was born on September 30, 1927, in Poljana Kobilecka, in today's Ukraine. He was ordained in 1943 as rabbi at the yeshivah of Sighet, Romania, at the age of fifteen. When his town was seized by the Germans in March 1944, he was sent first to Auschwitz, and then to the Wolfsberg and Mauthausen concentration camps. He was the only member of his family to survive the Holocaust.

Professor Halivni immigrated to the United States in 1947 and became a naturalized citizen in 1952. He received his B.A. and a medal for excellence in philosophy from Brooklyn College in 1953, his M.A. from New York University in 1956, his Master of Hebrew Literature from the Jewish Theological Seminary in 1957, and his Doctor of Hebrew Literature from the Seminary for his thesis entitled "Fragments of a Commentary on Treatise Taanit" in 1958. Professor Halivni has been awarded honorary degrees from the Jewish Theological Seminary, Haifa University, Lund University, Gratz College, Tel Aviv University, Baltimore Hebrew University, and Bar-Ilan University.

Professor Halivni began teaching at the Jewish Theological Seminary in 1957 and was named Morris Adler Professor of Rabbinics there in 1969. In 1986 he was appointed professor of Classical Jewish Civilization in the Department of Religion at Columbia University, after having previously taught there as an adjunct professor since the 1960s. He has also taught as a visiting professor at the Hebrew University of Jerusalem, Bar-Ilan University, and the Harvard Law School.

In 1995 Professor Halivni was named the Lucius N. Littauer Professor of Classical Jewish Civilization at Columbia University, endowed with a gift from the Lucius N. Littauer Foundation. He is the former president of the American Academy for Jewish Research. Since 1991 he has been the rector of the Institute for Traditional Judaism. He received a grant from the Council of Research in the Humanities (1964), a Guggenheim Fellowship (1970), a Louis Ginzberg Fellowship for Research (1970), and a National Endowment for the Humanities Fellowship (1980). He was appointed as a fellow of the Institute for Advanced Studies at the Hebrew University of Jerusalem (1981) and was a Lady Davis Visiting Professor of Talmud at the Hebrew University in 1984.

In 1985 Professor Halvni received the Bialik Prize, equivalent to the Pulitzer Prize, from the City of Tel-Aviv, Israel. He received the Present Tense Award in 1986 for the best work in the category of Jewish religious thought. He is a member of the executive board of the World Congress for Jewish Studies and a fellow of the American Academy of Arts and Sciences. Professor Halivni was awarded the prestigious Israel Prize in 2008.

His wartime experiences and singular devotion to scholarly study of the Talmud were the subjects of an article in the *New York Times Magazine* ("A Life in the Talmud," September 19, 1977). Eight volumes of his critical commentary on the Talmud, *Meqorot umesorot,* have been published to date. He has written several books on Jewish theology: *Midrash, Mishnah and Gemara* (1986), *Peshat and Derash* (1991), and *Revelation Restored* (1997). He has also written an autobiographical memoir, *The Book and the Sword: A Life of Learning in the Throes of the Holocaust* (1998).

Professor Halivni made aliyah in 2005 and now lives in Jerusalem.

Translation Conventions

THIS ENGLISH TRANSLATION is based on the original publication as the "Introduction" to *Meqorot umesorot: bava batra* (Jerusalem: Magnes, 2007), and the pagination placed in brackets within the text corresponds to that edition. An abridged translation appeared as "Aspects of the Formation of the Talmud," in *Creation and Composition: The Contribution of the Bavli Redactors (*Stammaim*) to the Aggada* (Tuebingen: Mohr-Siebeck, 2005), 339–360, and I am grateful to the press for permitting parts of its use here.

Some corrections have been made to the original Hebrew, including typos, errant references, and other mistakes. Here and there, in consultation with Halivni, I have added clarifying clauses and sentences, introduced minor modifications, and supplied dates for the processes and phenomena described; in these cases the translation departs from the original to a minor degree. I have also provided complete bibliographical information where it is lacking in the original and dates for some of the authorities cited. One paragraph, judged to be a digression, was removed from the text (p. 72; it appears in the annotations), and one long footnote omitted (Part I, n. 79). A postscript, published as the "Introduction" to *Meqorot umesorot: sanhedrin* (Jerusalem: Magnes, 2012), has also been translated and appears as an "Addendum."

The flow of argumentation is occasionally disrupted by minor digressions, due to the incorporation of paragraphs written at a later time and to Halivni's tendency to discuss additional aspects of a source raised in connection with the primary topic. I have marked these digressions with brackets in the text to help the reader follow the main thread of the analysis.

I include a full translation of many of the Talmudic passages discussed by Halivni, and present parallel passages in synoptic columns.

The different sections of the texts have been labeled (A, B, C, etc.) and referenced parenthetically in the translation of the analysis. Halivni presumes an audience with an extremely high level of expertise, including familiarity with much of the Talmud and detailed knowledge of the individual components of each dialectical interchange, and typically suffices with brief and elliptical quotations. I hope that providing the complete passages and indicating the sections to which Halivni refers will enable the reader to follow more readily the analysis without constantly having to consult the original texts, although this will still be necessary in some complicated cases.

I have also provided annotations, indicated by ** in the text. The annotations serve four primary purposes: (1) To provide explanation for complicated issues, especially those that presuppose specialist knowledge or background, and to offer additional clarification where necessary. (2) To supply rabbinic passages that are quoted in part or simply referenced, which Halivni assumes the reader will know (or will consult). (3) To provide references to the writings of other scholars, especially recent scholarship not mentioned by Halivni. And in some cases to provide references to opposing scholarship for the interested reader. (4) To provide cross-references to passages within the text, and to alert the reader to digressions.

Translators often start with a stock introduction that they have attempted to render an idiomatic translation while remaining faithful to the original. In this case the heavy use of technical terminology and specialized Talmudic vocabulary poses an additional challenge: to produce a readable English rather than either a transliteration-saturated gibberish or an impenetrable forest of inscrutable phrases. I have tried to steer a middle course, recognizing that many readers will possess some familiarity with rabbinic literature such that they will prefer to see terms in the original Hebrew or Aramaic, while understanding that others will have little or no familiarity with the specific vocabulary of the discipline. I therefore routinely provide English translations together with parenthetic transliterations, trusting that readers will forgive the annoyance of alien and jarring renditions of familiar expressions, on the one hand, and the eyesore of frequent italics, on the other.

For lack of reasonable English translations I romanize a few terms, including "baraita" and "sugya." "Baraita," which literally means "external, outside," designates a teaching from the Tannaitic era (prior to 200 CE) not included in the Mishnah (hence "external" to the Mishnaic corpus); it felt too barbaric to use something like "external teaching" or "non-Mishnaic Tannaitic tradition" or suchlike. Halivni also uses "baraita" as a collective noun for the compilations of baraitot or the corpus of baraitot available to the Amoraim, which I usually translate as "baraita-collections." "Sugya," which literally means "course, walk," is the standard term for a literary unit of Talmudic discourse (the "course" of a discussion). "Passage" is a fair translation, which I employ at times, but the specific nuances of "sugya" are sometimes not captured by this English equivalent that has a much broader scope. A few other Hebrew words which lack good English equivalents are given in transliteration alone, and brief definitions provided in the general index (e.g., *halitsah*).

The term *setam* is generally translated in accord with its literal meaning, "anonymous, unattributed," sometimes with the accompanying implied noun, "anonymous tradition," "anonymous material," "unattributed passage," "unattributed stratum," and so on. For *setamma degemara* I use "anonymous Talmud." However, Halivni also uses *setam* to refer to the composers of the anonymous material, or in a way that refers somewhat ambiguously both to the composers and their literary traditions. In these cases I sometimes employ "Stammaim" or "Stammaitic," but occasionally resort to "Stam" to retain the connotations of the original term.

Other technical terms and expressions are as follows:

"Reciters" for *tannaim,* the professional memorizers of tradition (not to be confused with Tannaim, the sages from the period of the Mishnah. Reciters functioned throughout the Amoraic period, and perhaps in post-Amoraic times as well).

"Compilers" for *me'asef* and *me'asfim,* the sages who compiled traditions and sugyot, setting them in their present order in the Talmud. Halivni uses the singular, "The Compiler," a collective noun that sounds better in the Hebrew. I use the plural to avoid confusion.

"Transposers" for *ma'avir* and *ma'avirim,* the sages who transferred or transposed material from one passage to another. Again Halivni uses the singular, "The Transposer," as a collective noun, and here too the plural sounds better in English. Similarly, "transpositions" for *ha'avarot,* the material transferred from one location to another.

"Closing" for *hatimah,* literally "sealing." Halivni uses this term for the end of the process by which the Talmud was produced. The Talmud was not "closed" or "sealed" by any formal act or human decision, but came to a close in and of itself, "petering out" we might say, when the Geonim began to produce independent books, circa 770 CE. Even this translation can be misleading, as Halivni claims the Talmud was never strictly closed or sealed, as brief glosses continued to be added even after the "closing" of the Talmud at this time.

"Talmud" for *gemara*, unless the point concerns the Amoraic part of the Talmud, the *gemara* proper, in contradistinction to the Mishnah, in which case the transliterated *gemara* is used.

"Mishnah" (capitalized) is used for the document (the Mishnah of R. Yehudah HaNasi), and "mishnah" (lower case) for an individual mishnah-paragraph. I also use "mishnahs" for the plural, with apologies to purists.

"Medieval commentators," "medieval commentaries," or "medieval jurists" for *rishonim* (literally, "earlier, principal"), the technical term for the leading sages of the eleventh through the fifteenth centuries, the successors to the Geonim.

Acronyms of sages are mimicked in the English and marked by quotation marks, for example, Rashb"a for R. Shlomoh ben Aderet.

All translations of rabbinic texts are my own unless otherwise indicated. The words in brackets are implicit in the original, while those in parentheses I have added as explanation, although the distinction between these sometimes blurs. Translations of biblical passages are from the New Jewish Publication Society translation, although I have freely modified them when needed.

Hebrew translation is phonetic: q = ק, kh = כ, ts=צ, h = ח. I have not differentiated א from ע, ה from ח, or ס from ש except when a philological point is at issue. The *dagesh* is generally not represented.

Names are rendered phonetically except for those with common English equivalents.

Abbreviations

AJSR	*AJS [Association of Jewish Studies] Review*
b.	ben, bar (son of)
DJBA	*Dictionary of Jewish Babylonian Aramaic* (Sokoloff)
HUCA	*Hebrew Union College Annual*
JQR	*Jewish Quarterly Review*
m	mishnah
MLH	*Mavo lenusah hamishnah* (Epstein)
MM	*Meqorot umesorot*
PAAJR	*Proceedings of the American Academy of Jewish Research*
R.	Rabbi
t	Tosefta
TK	*Tosefta kifshutah* (Lieberman)
y	Yerushalmi
ms.	manuscript
mss.	manuscripts

Tractates

Arakh	Arakhin
AZ	Avodah Zarah
BB	Bava Batra
Bekh	Bekhorot
Ber	Berakhot
Bets	Betsah
Bik	Bikkurim
BM	Bava Metsia
BQ	Bava Qamma
Dem	Demai

Ed	Edduyot
Eruv	Eruvin
Git	Gittin
Hag	Hagigah
Hal	Hallah
Hor	Horayyot
Hul	Hullin
Kel	Kelim
Ker	Keritut
Ket	Ketubot
Maas	Maaserot
Mak	Makkot
Meg	Megillah
Meil	Meilah
Men	Menahot
Mikv	Mikvaot
MQ	Moed Qatan
MS	Maaser Sheni
Naz	Nazir
Ned	Nedarim
Nid	Niddah
Par	Parah
Pes	Pesahim
Qid	Qiddushin
RH	Rosh Hashanah
Sanh	Sanhedrin
Shab	Shabbat
Sheq	Sheqalim
Shev	Sheviit
Shevu	Shevuot
Sot	Sotah
Suk	Sukkah
Taan	Taanit
Tem	Temurah
Ter	Terumot
Toh	Toharot
Yad	Yadaim
Yev	Yevamot
Yom	Yoma
Zev	Zevahim

Translator's Introduction

BY JEFFREY L. RUBENSTEIN

THE FORMATION OF *the Babylonian Talmud* is a monumental achievement. The summation of a lifetime of study and scholarship, it is the only comprehensive account of the processes that produced the Babylonian Talmud (= Bavli) written in nearly a century and probably the most inclusive and complete ever. Even a brief glance at the Contents provides a sense of the tremendous scope of this undertaking. It describes the transmission of traditions throughout the generations of sages; assesses the explanation and interpretation of earlier traditions by later masters and of later masters by still later authorities; accounts for the various forms of rabbinic tradition (apodictic statements, brief explanations, dialectical argumentation); provides dates and institutional contexts for the different phases of compilation; delineates the nature, stages, and processes of editing; and explores the roles of all sages who participated in these processes: Tannaim (until 200 CE), Amoraim (200–550 CE), Stammaim (550–750 CE), Saboraim (700–750 CE), Reciters, Compilers, and Transposers. These and other aspects of the formation of the Bavli are illustrated through the penetrating analysis of scores of Talmudic passages. The evidence supporting all of these claims is presented methodically and systematically to set forth a complete account of the Talmud's history and development.

Yet the horizons of *The Formation of the Babylonian Talmud* extend beyond the Bavli itself and include substantive analysis of aspects of the Mishnah, the Jerusalem Talmud (= Yerushalmi), and the halakhic and aggadic midrashim. Not only do these texts supply historical and cultural context but they also set in sharp relief the Bavli's distinctive features and shed light on how and in what ways the Bavli departed from previous rabbinic compilations. The editor of the Mishnah, for example, operated with different purposes and constraints, and therefore treated his sources differently than did the Bavli's editors. The analysis and illustration of these techniques, also accompanied by copious examples, significantly advance our understanding of the nature of the editing of the Mishnah. The Yerushalmi too contains dialectical argumentation, but it differs quantitatively and qualitatively from that of the Bavli. Halivni also provides a methodology for approaching the text critically, detailing the stages through which the student should progress in learning a passage, discerning difficulties, formulating questions, and resolving the problems. We have then not only a major contribution to the development of the Bavli but to rabbinic tradition and literature in general.

A work of this scope and breadth stands out against the trends in rabbinic scholarship over the past forty years. Scholars have shifted away from both general histories covering vast periods of the development of rabbinic Judaism and from inquiries concerning some fundamental questions—such as the date of the editing of the Talmud—on which the evidence is sparse. This is not to minimize the rich and explosive growth in the field, which has flourished with the publication of newly found texts including the full corpus of the Qumran scrolls, the fragments and manuscript leaves recovered from the Cairo Geniza, and additional manuscripts of rabbinic works discovered in libraries around the world. The field of rabbinics has also benefited from significant advances in methodology, both improvements in familiar methods, such as the production of critical editions and textual reconstruction, and the infusion of numerous methods from other disciplines, including literary criticism, anthropology, gender studies, and comparative religion. Yet for all these strides forward the focus of Talmudic scholars has inclined toward more limited and discrete topics: the history of particular laws, the elucidation of problematic passages, the development of a certain theological idea.[1] Even the publication of critical commentaries to chapters of Talmud and tractates of Mishnah, a salutary enterprise of fundamental importance to the future advancement of the discipline, is an endeavor with a relatively restricted scope. In a retrospective assessment of Ephraim Urbach's monumental *The Sages: Their Concepts and Beliefs*, a comprehensive work on rabbinic thought and theology, Yaakov Sussman has observed that after its publication in 1969 "scholarship in this field has disappointed . . . and nothing important and fundamental has been written since."[2] The same might be said for comprehensive accounts of the development and history of the Bavli.

The reluctance to attempt vast and synthetic histories of the Bavli is certainly understandable in view of the formidable challenges entailed. To do so requires proficiency in the "sea of Talmud" in all its length and breadth, its thousands of folios, the variant manuscript traditions, the interrelationships and intertextual connections between its myriads of passages. One must possess exhaustive knowledge of parallel and related passages in the Mishnah, Tosefta, Yerushalmi, halakhic and aggadic midrashim, and in the complete corpus of rabbinic literature with which to compare Bavli traditions so as to reconstruct their development and metamorphoses. A scholar must command the entire post-Talmudic tradition in all its branches and genres, the halakhic codes of the Geonim, responsa, the medieval and early modern commentaries, and historiographical writings across the generations. And one needs the intellectual acumen to master the complexities of the Bavli's dialectical argumentation, to discern the incongruities and inconsistencies in the intricate sequences of nested objections and responses that constitute the signs of development and editing.

For these reasons Halivni's "debate partners" are less contemporary scholars than those of previous generations, especially Isaak Halevy (1847–1914), Jacob Nahum Epstein (1878–1952), and Hanoch Albeck (1890–1972). These giants of the past authored comprehensive and sweeping accounts of rabbinic tradition, the type of grand theories eschewed by more recent scholars. They did not hesitate to make claims about the dating of the Bavli and other rabbinic works, the identity of the editors, the processes and methods of compilation, the relationship of the Bavli to its sources, and other such complex topics. Although their ideas often no longer reflect the scholarly consensus, and while many of their specific proposals have been abandoned, modified, or updated, they remain to some extent the "last word" on the major issues regarding the development of Talmudic tradition. Halevy's *Generations of the Former Sages* (*Dorot harishonim*), in particular, receives close attention, as it covers much of the same territory but reaches significantly different conclusions, and Halivni painstakingly explains why the rival claims should be rejected.[3] The abundant attention directed toward Halevy and his successors, however, does not come at the expense of more recent studies; Halivni builds on the fruits of academic research over the past decades and goes beyond it to produce a comprehensive account of the Talmud's origins and development.

The Formation of the Babylonian Talmud offers a bold synthesis of the history of the Bavli with the supporting evidence for each claim. To be sure, many of the conclusions result from the most subtle and delicate inferences, and from teasing out the implications of slight textual anomalies, irregularities, and inconsistencies. There is a paucity of direct evidence about the major questions of the Talmud's textual development and editing, and sometimes indirect evidence is lacking too. Certainly some of the conclusions must remain in the realm of conjecture or speculation. At the same time, the many thousands of traditions dispersed throughout the over 2,700 Bavli folios contain a wealth of data about the processes by which they were constituted. An outline of the basic stages of development from the articulation of dicta by the Amoraim to the production of the Talmud by its final editors and compilers is actually straightforward: traditions of Amoraic masters were transmitted by students and Reciters from generation to generation, and sometimes combined into dispute-forms with other such traditions; explanatory comments were added by later sages; smaller units of tradition were combined with other units to create more extensive passages (sugyot); sections of tradition were sometimes transposed from one passage to another; the sugyot were contextualized in a tractate in connection with a certain mishnah; and in many cases further transposition of material and glossing took place. This much is clear from the final product, the Talmud as we now find it before us. A much greater challenge is to delineate the details of these stages—how they occurred, the precise dating, the sages involved, the institutional settings, the intellectual parameters, the theological assumptions—and to identify the evidence grounding each point. Through consummate mastery of the Talmud in its entirety together with all of rabbinic literature, and by considering the intertextual relationships among all relevant passages, Halivni ventures to answer these questions that have proved intractable for generations of scholars.

Forced Explanations

The point of departure for Halivni's theory is the issue of "forced explanations." Throughout the Talmud one finds that sources are interpreted in ways opposed to their simple meanings. An Amora often explains a mishnah against the straightforward sense of its language, claiming that it says what it does not seem to say. Later Amoraim in turn offer forced understandings of the traditions of earlier Amoraim, and the anonymous Talmud supplies forced explanations of the traditions of even the latest Amoraim. In addition, the flow of the Talmudic discourse often does not read smoothly, exhibiting gaps and incongruities between questions and their answers or comments and their referents such that the sequence of statements must be read in a "forced" way in order to be understood. Halivni's first volume of Talmud commentary, published in 1969 and entitled *Sources and Traditions* (*Meqorot umesorot*), focused on this problem. Texts were often changed in the course of oral transmission, due to the frailties of human memory, unconscious alterations, and even deliberate emendations, which caused disparities between the "Sources" and their subsequent forms or "Traditions," between the original texts and the way they were received in later times. (There is a double entendre in the Hebrew title, as *maqor* means both "source" and "origin," hence the title contrasts both "sources" and "origins" with later "traditions.") Reconstructing the original sources often solved the problem of the forced explanation: an Amora's explanation of a mishnah, for example, may have been based on a reading that differs from that presented in the Talmud. The Amora's explanation makes perfectly good sense when based on that reconstructed version and only appears forced when juxtaposed with the text as given in the Talmud or in a given manuscript of the Mishnah. Other forced explanations resulted as sources were truncated or abbreviated in the course of transmission, or when their original contexts were lost. In these cases, later sages themselves lacked the requisite information adequately to interpret the source, and the best they could do was to offer a forced explanation to make sense of the version they received. At this time Halivni had not yet realized the implications of this theory regarding the formation and editing of the Talmud as a whole, and he rarely addressed these larger topics. The commentary was dedicated to specific passages and to making better sense of forced explanations scattered throughout the pages of Talmud. But the seeds of a revolutionary understanding had been planted, and more radical conclusions were already entailed in this fundamental insight.

Halivni articulated that "paradigm shift" in his Introduction to the second volume of *Meqorot umesorot*, published in 1975.[4] The Talmud contains two primary layers, two main literary strata, one comprised of attributed statements of the Amoraim, the other of unattributed or anonymous discussion of those Amoraic dicta, hence known as the "anonymous Talmud" (*setam hatalmud*). These strata differ in form and style: Amoraic dicta (*meimrot*) are brief and "apodictic"—a term Halivni borrows from biblical studies, and by which he means both terse and categorical. They typically consist of pronouncements of legal rulings or succinct explanations of an earlier source. The anonymous Talmud, by contrast, is verbose, expansive, and contains the Talmud's intricate and complex dialectical argumentation. It may include series of objections and solutions, rhetorical questions, and contrived and spurious propositions, sometimes extending over a full folio or more. Most important, the anonymous stratum exhibits a high density of forced explanations of the Amoraic dicta upon which it is based. Why? While forced explanations are found among the Amoraim too, the extent and quantity of forced explanations in the anonymous layer—even when predicated on traditions of the latest Amoraim—is striking. These considerations led Halivni to reject the traditional understanding that the two layers are contemporaneous with the attribution or lack thereof indicating individual or communal "authorship": statements were formulated anonymously when they were not associated with any individual sage but emerged from the general discussion of students debating the issue, from "all the members of the academy." He concluded that the anonymous stratum is not contemporaneous with the Amoraic stratum but postdates it. This stratum was not produced by the Amoraim but by later—anonymous—sages whom Halivni called "Stammaim" after the term for the anonymous "*setam*" Talmud. They endeavored to explicate the Amoraic traditions they received but in many cases could not do so satisfactorily and provided forced explanations as the best effort to make sense of traditions from the distant past. The Stammaitic stratum amounts to more than half of the Talmud, as many Talmudic sugyot contain relatively lengthy explanations of the briefer Amoraic dicta or sustained argumentation between two disputing opinions. Halivni had therefore proposed a new theory of the provenance of much of the Talmudic text, and essentially even of the Talmud's composition or "authorship." No longer should the Talmud be attributed to the final Amoraim, the last of the named sages in the Talmud, but to anonymous author-editors who postdated the Amoraic age.[5]

Halivni continued to develop and refine his theory in the Introductions to subsequent volumes of *Meqorot umesorot* (1975, 1982, 1993, 2003), and in his English book, *Midrash, Mishnah, and Gemara* (1986). In these writings he advanced a second major theoretical contribution that pertains to the understanding of the Bavli's dialectical argumentation. The forced explanations found in the anonymous stratum typically appear within the dialectical analysis of an Amoraic dictum, in the course of which interpretations are proposed and rejected, alternatives suggested, and further debate engaged before a conclusion is reached. Why should dialectical analysis be so characteristic of the anonymous stratum and found so rarely among Amoraic dicta? As long as the anonymous stratum was considered contemporaneous with Amoraic dicta, this observation presented no difficulties: debates were typically conducted with many participants, by "all the members of the academy," and consequently formulated without attributions. If the anonymous stratum postdates the Amoraic dicta, however, this difference in form becomes problematic and calls for explanation.

The answer relates to the process of transmission of tradition throughout Talmudic times and to the agents of transmission, the "Reciters" (*tannaim*). They were professional memorizers, men with prodigious memories, who committed earlier traditions to memory and were called upon to recite them before the Amoraim. The Amoraim in turn formulated their own traditions for memorization and entrusted them to the Reciters to be preserved for future generations. Detailed information about these Reciters is frustratingly sparse; some were sages themselves, though most were not; with a few exceptions we do not even know their names. But the fact that Amoraic dicta are marked by such terseness indicates that only the conclusions of their deliberations, the final rulings and explanations of sources, were preserved and memorized by Reciters. The dicta were formulated as briefly and economically as possible to facilitate memorization and accurate transmission. This is not to say that the Amoraim did not engage in dialectical argumentation. Like their predecessors, the sages of the Mishnah, the Amoraim engaged in debate and subjected the traditions they received to dialectical analysis. For the Amoraim, however, dialectical argumentation was a means to an end, a method, a tool used to arrive at the correct understanding of a source, but was not an end in and of itself. And this is indeed typical of law and legal drafting in general. Among Halivni's favorite examples is the United States Constitution, which was debated for months in the Constitutional Convention as the disparate parties argued, deliberated, quarreled, and wrangled over each and every point. In the end they transmitted to posterity the Constitution alone, the conclusion of those debates, and not transcripts of the debates themselves. In other words, the "official transmission," throughout Amoraic times, the corpus of traditions memorized and passed down to the next generation, did not include dialectical argumentation, but only the conclusions of the sages' analysis.

A shift in values involving a change in attitude to dialectical argumentation transpired between the time of the Amoraim and the Stammaim. The Stammaim evidently considered themselves to be living in a post-classical age and to lack the authority of their Amoraic predecessors.

For this reason they ceased formulating traditions with attributions, ceased preserving the names of sages, and began to transmit their traditions in anonymous fashion as a mark of their post-Amoraic provenance and inferior authority. (What precipitated this sense of belatedness is not completely clear; Halivni points to persecutions in the second half of the sixth century.) The Stammaim accordingly dedicated themselves to the analysis and explication of Amoraic traditions. They came to consider dialectical argumentation as an end in itself, an independent value even when not connected to practical law, and also worthy of preservation and transmission. They consequently gave equal attention to minority and discredited opinions, subjecting them too to justification and analysis.

The Stammaim, then, were engaged in a massive project of restitution and reconstruction. Alas, because dialectical argumentation had not been passed down in the "official transmission" of the Reciters, most of it had been lost by Stammaitic times. Fragments of the Amoraic argumentation were remembered by individual sages, but these "survivals" were less reliable than Amoraic dicta as they were not part of the official transmission. We might say that dialectical argumentation was not "canonized," not subject to an authorized and supervised process that guaranteed its accuracy. Each student formulated dialectical argumentation in his own words and later transmitted it to his disciples in his own way. The portions of dialectical argumentation that happened to be preserved therefore contained great variation and many errors. It is this dimension of the transmission process that accounts for the prevalence of forced explanations in the Talmud's anonymous stratum.

This revolutionary understanding of the Talmudic text has become the foundation for all modern critical Talmud study.[6] The first task of the critical scholar attempting to make sense of a Talmudic passage is to distinguish these two literary strata, to separate the Amoraic from the anonymous or Stammaitic layer. But it is important to note that this initial distinction—so appealing and straightforward because of the clear formal markers, the presence or absence of the name of a sage—is only a first step. Halivni's theory devolves primarily from a problem in interpretation—the forced explanation, the lack of a smooth fit between sections of a Talmudic passage—and not from form-critical or literary observations, that is, that some traditions are attributed and others anonymous, or that some are brief and legislative while others are lengthy and interpretive. And the focus on the forced explanation is what distinguishes Halivni's method from that of some earlier critical scholars who began to distinguish the anonymous from attributed layers of the Talmud based on such literary and formal criteria, or due to differences in terminology, notably Julius Kaplan, Hyman Klein, and Avraham Weiss.[7] Indeed, in Halivni's view the Talmud contains not two, but multiple literary strata, as forced explanations are found within the anonymous stratum itself, and not only where anonymous explanations relate to Amoraic dicta. Later Stammaim were confronted with the same problem when interpreting the traditions of earlier Stammaim, and they too resorted to forced explanations when lacking complete information. Thus the primary distinction between the attributed and anonymous strata should not obscure the fact that, for Halivni, each layer comprises numerous sources that can be discerned, distinguished, and dated (at least on a relative basis).[8] The Talmud's many literary strata and their diverse sources testify to a long process of compilation and editing, and a full account of the Talmud's formation must reckon with this evidence.

The Tyranny of "Rav Ashi and Ravina—the end of hora'ah"

The realization that the Talmud's anonymous stratum postdates the Amoraic age and that the dialectical argumentation was reconstructed by later sages led Halivni to a revolutionary conclusion concerning the date of the Talmud's editing. The controversy over this dating derives in large part from what I call the "tyranny" of a brief Talmudic tradition found in BM 86a: "Rav Ashi and Ravina—the end of *hora'ah*." The Talmud contains nothing explicit about its own editing or authorship. This vexing lack of information about the editors of the Talmud, the authoritative source of Jewish law, was clearly a matter of great anxiety that led the medieval commentaries to seize upon this tradition about two of the latter sages as a statement about the Talmud's editors. Rashi comments as follows:

> The end of *hora'ah*—the end of the Amoraim. Until their days the Talmud (*gemara*) had no set order, but when a question was asked in the house of study as to the explanation of a mishnah, or a question about an incident that occurred regarding monetary or ritual law, each and every [sage] stated his explanation. And Rav Ashi and Ravina ordered [*sidru*] the traditions of the Amoraim who preceded them, and arranged [*qavu*] them according to the order [*seder*] of tractates, each and every one with the mishnah that was fitting for it and with

which it was taught. And they propounded the objections that ought to have been raised [*sheyesh lehashiv*] and the responses that were fitting to answer—they and the Amoraim who were with them—and they arranged [*qavu*] everything in the Talmud [*gemara*].

Rashi clearly interprets this tradition in terms of an editing procedure. Prior to Rav Ashi and Ravina there was essentially no text of the Talmud nor any compilation of Amoraic tradition in any form other than the collective memory of the sages as a whole. In the oral milieu of the house of study, each sage articulated from his memory the reasons and justifications that explained a mishnah and that grounded matters of practical law and judicial precedent. Rav Ashi and Ravina (and their colleagues) compiled these traditions, setting them in "order" and "arranging" them according to the tractates of the Mishnah, contextualizing each Amoraic tradition in the appropriate location. In other words, they were the Talmud's compilers and editors. Rashi mentions a second dimension of the activity of Rav Ashi and Ravina, that they "propounded the objections that should have been raised and the responses that were fitting to answer," which refers to the Talmud's anonymous stratum, the unattributed objections and solutions relating to Amoraic dicta. Not only did Rav Ashi and Ravina edit the traditions articulated by their predecessors, the explanations of "each and every" sage, they also produced the dialectical argumentation not specifically attributed to a named master.

Rashi's understanding was shared by other medieval authorities and became the foundation of the traditional view of the Talmud's editing. It has exerted a tyrannical influence on traditional Judaism—still accepted today in the Orthodox and "Yeshivah" worlds—and even upon academic scholarship of the past century. And this despite fatal problems, all discussed at length by Halivni.[9] For one, *hora'ah* means "legislation" or "instruction," and has nothing to do with editing or compilation. Second, the identity of Ravina is problematic. There were two Ravinas, one a junior contemporary of Rav Ashi, the other, known as the "second Ravina," among the latest Amoraim.[10] If Ravina here is the latter Ravina, who died c. 500, why is he mentioned together with Rav Ashi, who died c. 427? (These dates, and almost all basic data concerning the chronology of Talmudic and post-Talmudic sages, derive from Sherira Gaon, c. 900–c. 1000, Head of the Pumbedita Academy.) If it is the contemporary of Rav Ashi, how does one account for the fact that many sages who postdated Rav Ashi are mentioned throughout the Talmud, albeit less often than earlier

Amoraim? Moreover, the Talmud sometimes rejects Rav Ashi's opinions, and occasionally expresses uncertainty as to exactly what he said—which would seem very odd if Rav Ashi himself edited the Talmud. And finally, what is the authority of this tradition itself, and what guarantees its historicity?

Halivni's main reason for rejecting the traditional view of the Talmud's editing, however, is not based on these difficulties but again comes back to the issue of forced explanations. Why did the Stammaim not simply ask the Amoraim about the reasons and explanations for their dicta? Why offer a forced explanation and not appeal to the sage who articulated the statement, or even to his students, for clarification? It must be that the Stammaim lived long after the Amoraic age in a much later historical era such that they had no recourse to the authors of the dicta themselves. The forced interpretations within the Stammaitic stratum itself, passages where later Stammaim provide forced interpretations of the traditions of earlier Stammaim, points to an even later historical age. The formation of the Talmud, its compilation and editing, must be seen as a lengthy and protracted process that continued long after the Amoraic age.

How long? On this question Halivni's thinking has changed over the years. In his first writings on the topic, in *Meqorot umesorot: seder mo'ed* (1975) and *Midrash, Mishnah, and Gemara* (1986), Halivni dated the Stammaim to the era between 427 and 501 or 520, at which point began the era of the Saboraim, the sages mentioned in post-Talmudic sources who lived after the Amoraim and before the Geonim.[11] This dating, interestingly enough, seems to still reflect the influence of the BM 86a tradition, as these dates are those of the deaths of the sages mentioned (as given by Sherira Gaon), the uncertainty of 501 or 520 reflecting the uncertainty as to which Rav Ashi and Ravina are intended.[12] Halivni revised this dating in the Introduction to *Meqorot umesorot: bava metsia* (2003), having concluded that the tradition of "the end of *hora'ah*" should not be seen as a reliable statement of history but rather as an expression of "the adulation of a student who thought that the death of his celebrated master brought an end to *hora'ah*."[13] Emancipated from a dating linked to these sages,[14] and also rejecting Geonic traditions, especially the claims of Sherira Gaon, about the dating of the Saboraic age, Halivni deferred the beginning of the Stammaitic era to c. 550 and its end until c. 600.[15] He also changed his thinking about the Saboraim, now considering them to be Stammaim who lived at the end of the Stammaitic era (600–750). The Stammaitic era could therefore be divided into two: the Stammaitic era proper when the bulk of the dialectical argumentation was produced, and a latter part of the era, the age of the Saboraim, when glosses and minor additions were composed. In the present volume Halivni extends the Stammaitic age until almost the end of the eighth century, until the era when the Geonim begin to compose independent books attributed to individual authors. He also posits a much lengthier Stammaitic era proper (550–700), which necessitates a reduction in the length of the period of the Saboraim, now viewed as the last part of the Stammaitic era (700–750). Only at that point or a little thereafter, c. 770, did sages cease to add their comments within the Talmud and begin to compose "outside" of it. This marks what Halivni calls the "closing" of the Talmud, the final date of redaction or editing. Yet we must understand "closed" (*nehtam*) in a loose sense, as the Talmud was not closed by the decision or agency of any individual or group, nor ever absolutely closed, as glosses and brief additions continued well into the Middle Ages and the era from which our manuscripts date.

Within the lengthy Stammaitic era Halivni delineates several stages of editing and corresponding subperiods. Apart from the Saboraim, who flourished 700–750, there were Compilers (*me'asfim*), those editors who collected sugyot and set them in the present order within the tractates of Talmud, and who also lived toward the end of this era. This late dating of the main part of the Talmud's composition to the late sixth and early seventh centuries, and the final closing to the late eighth century, are among Halivni's most daring and revolutionary claims. A summary of Halivni's views of the chronology of the Talmud's formation, which he presents in different passages throughout his text, is shown in Table I.1

Note that the Compilers are technically Stammaim, as they too are anonymous, so in some respects the Stammaitic/Saboraic period continues until 770. These dates should be taken as approximate, as best guesses, but give a general sense of the various stages of the formation of the Talmud.

Halivni has continually rethought and revised his views on the formation of the Talmud with the publication of successive volumes of *Meqorot umesorot*. We can probably look forward to further minor revisions, even as the main contours of the theory are now firmly established.[16] Let me briefly note here a few areas that deserve some further investigation. Halivni provides comprehensive analysis of the Stammaitic contribution to the halakhic portions of the Talmud but says little about their role in the aggadic sections. Yet aggadah constitutes perhaps one third of the Bavli, and much of it is unattributed. How extensive was the contribution of the

Table I.1 Chronology of the Stages of the Formation of the Talmud

until 200 CE	Era of the Tannaim
200	Editing of the Mishnah
200–450	Main Amoraic period
450–500	Persian persecutions,* decline of Amoraim
500–550	Later Amoraic period, "dwindling" of Amoraim
550	Death of Revai of Rov, the last Amora; end of Amoraic era
550–600	Persian persecutions, beginnings of Stammaitic era
600–700	Main Stammaitic era, composition of sugyot, formation of proto-Talmud
700–750	Later Stammaitic era = Saboraic era: glossing and editing of proto-Talmud; no addition of Amoraic material
730–770	Compilers
770	Closing of Talmud

* Halivni does not mention these persecutions explicitly in his account (except in the Introduction, n. 1). He intends the "years of persecution and sufferings" mentioned in *Epistle of Rav Sherira Gaon*, ed. Lewin, 99, "at the end of the rule of the Persians," which corresponds to 550–589, judging by the context in Sherira's narrative. Sherira states that the sages of Pumbedita came to the "outskirts of Nehardea, to the city of Peroz-Shapur" at this time, which might also imply that the Pumbedita academy was destroyed.

Stammaim to Bavli aggadah, and how can their aggadic traditions be identified?[17] The importance of the ambient Zoroastrian religion and Sasanian (Persian) culture to the understanding of the Bavli has received increased attention in recent years but is hardly mentioned in Halivni's work.[18] Specific legal and cultural influences in such domains as purity law, family structure and lineage aside, did the interpretation, composition, and editing of texts in the Persian world have any impact on the same processes of the Bavli? Did the Arab conquest of the Sasanian empire in c. 630–650 and the gradual penetration of Islam, which occurred during the heyday of the Stammaitic era, influence these processes? Halivni is very cognizant of the oral matrix of the rabbis and the fact that the Talmud remained oral until the ninth century.[19] His emphasis on the critical role of the Reciters in the transmission of tradition and the impact on dialectical argumentation derives in part from this awareness. Yet there has been a great deal of interest lately on the complexities of oral cultures, interfaces of orality and literacy, and mechanisms of textual production and editing in conditions of orality.[20] Some of this work can potentially sharpen our understanding of the formation of the Bavli and the similar dynamics within rabbinic culture.

Another field that has seen great advances in recent years is the collection and collation of textual variants, with the photo-digitization of Talmud manuscripts and their availability through various websites, the "Lieberman Institute's Sol and Evelyn Henkind Talmud Text Databank" which assembles all primary witnesses and early printed editions of the Bavli, and now the publication of the *Thesaurus of Talmud Manuscripts*, a catalog of all known manuscripts and geniza fragments of the Bavli and other rabbinic works.[21] These tools should help determine with greater certainty the correct readings of important Talmudic passages where textual variants make it difficult to reach secure conclusions.[22]

Halivni's contributions to rabbinic scholarship have yet to be fully assessed, and we hope the full English translation will help achieve this desideratum. Certainly all would agree that *The Formation of the Babylonian Talmud* is the most complete presentation of the history and development of Talmudic tradition. The comprehensive theory of the formation of the Talmudic text is accompanied by a corresponding method for analysis, a systematic approach to distinguishing earlier from later sources and reconstructing the development of Talmudic passages.[23] Future scholars undoubtedly will build on Halivni's work to provide a more complete understanding of the many aspects he delineates—the substantial progress in scholarship on rabbinic literature over the past few decades suggests that the field is still in a fertile period of growth. At the same time, it is safe to say that for the foreseeable future *The Formation of the Babylonian Talmud* will be the definitive account of the Bavli and the foundation for all critical study.

Author's Introduction

DAVID WEISS HALIVNI

THIS BOOK ON the formation of the Babylonian Talmud is divided into four parts: (I) The Stammaim, (II) The Editing of the Talmud, (III) Apodictic Transmission and Dialectical Argumentation; (IV) Compilers and Transposers. I discuss these subjects in detail, and provide examples to illustrate the basic issues and different subtopics. These parts do not follow a chronological order but accord with the subjects discussed in the Introductions to the volumes of my Talmudic commentary, *Meqorot umesorot* (Sources and Traditions), in which, apart from the first volume, I described the dating, activity, and contribution of the Stammaim. Here I continue the task of determining the dating of the Stammaim—I revise the view maintained in those previous volumes—and elaborate upon their literary contributions and significance.

I devote a great deal of analysis to the dating and contribution of the Stammaim not only because of their historical importance but mainly due to their role in producing the farfetched questions and forced responses found in the Talmud. The Talmud is full of forced explanations; I was surprised by this phenomenon but found no way to explain it other than to say that those who supplied the forced explanations lacked the complete version of all the relevant sources, or lacked the correct version of the text they were explaining, or lacked the requisite knowledge for understanding the text. Why did they not have access to the sources in their entirety? Because the sages responsible for these explanations lived centuries after those who composed the texts, and over the course of time the relevant sources had been forgotten. I first made this claim in the Introduction to *Seder nashim,* the first volume of my extensive Talmud commentary, *Meqorot umesorot*. Later I realized that most of the forced explanations are anonymous (*setam*), which led me to the conclusion that the Stammaim, who composed the anonymous stratum (*setamot*), flourished long after the Amoraim. If a substantial portion of the Talmud derives from the

Stammaim, then clearly one cannot attribute the editing of the Talmud to the sages Ravina and Rav Ashi, who antedated the Stammaim.

After clarifying the historical era and the scope of the contribution of the Stammaim, I realized that one cannot speak of a general editing but only of a closing (*hatimah*) of the Talmud. I speculated that after the closing of the Talmud, the sages gathered all the sources from the disparate academies—sources that differed in their legal rulings, explanations, and thought processes. These sources were integrated in their current forms, without any substantive changes. At that time sages were not permitted to change Talmudic material or to add their own opinions to the Talmud. Even if they came upon material that was fragmentary and incomplete, they were not allowed to complete it but had to integrate it into the Talmud without comments, and, for the most part, at the end of the relevant passages. The Compilers (*me'asfim*) responsible for this activity lived after the Talmud had been closed and sealed from more elaborate interventions.

And yet the mere fact that the Stammaim lived much later than the Amoraim does not suffice to explain the prevalence of forced explanations in the Talmud. [2] True, as time passes the transmission of tradition deteriorates, and some of it is forgotten—but not to the extent reflected in the quantity of forced explanations found in the Talmud.[1] For this reason, and also on account of other considerations, including the distinctive style and thought process of the anonymous stratum, I concluded that throughout the Amoraic era, as in the Tannaitic era, the anonymous dialectical argumentation—which is the main component of the Talmud—was not transmitted in an official form. Rather, it was reconstructed centuries later by the Stammaim. So it is not surprising that in many cases the Stammaim did not have access to the sources in their entirety. Accordingly, there are two explanations for the forced explanations of the Talmud: first, the vast period of time that elapsed between the Amoraim who formulated the traditions and the Stammaim who explained them, and second, the lack of an official transmission of dialectical argumentation. While these two explanations are not mutually exclusive, they have different implications. It follows from both that the anonymous stratum of the Talmud postdates the Amoraim, and consequently Ravina and Rav Ashi could not have been the Talmudic editors. Yet there is also a fundamental difference between the two. If we assume that the Amoraim, unlike the Tannaim, also transmitted dialectical argumentation, but that the dialectical argumentation found in the Talmud is later and consequently contains forced explanations, then we must conclude that the dialectical argumentation of the Talmud is basically that same Amoraic dialectical argumentation; in some instances, however, parts of it were forgotten over the course of time. Consequently the later interpreters, the Stammaim, could only reconstruct it in a forced manner. Nevertheless, when the text reads smoothly, in a straightforward way, it indicates that the dialectical argumentation is authentically Amoraic. However, according to the second explanation, that there never was an official transmission of dialectical argumentation in the Amoraic period, it follows that the dialectical argumentation now found in the Talmud—whether it reads smoothly or whether it is forced—was composed by the Stammaim. In this case the Stammaim were the first to pass down dialectical argumentation to posterity.

In my opinion, the form of the dialectical argumentation now found in the Talmud is that of the Stammaim. The Amoraim, however, also engaged in dialectical argumentation, on the basis of which they reached their legal rulings—but they did not transmit it to succeeding generations, and it is possible that its character differed from that of the Stammaim. I believe that the content and form of the Talmud that we have inherited derives from the Stammaim, who reconstructed the dialectical argumentation anew and did not merely supplement it in those places where Amoraic tradition was incomplete.

Now the second explanation is far more important and fundamental to the understanding and interpretation of the Talmud, and therefore the order of the book should have been as follows: (I) Apodictic Transmission and Dialectical Argumentation, (II) The Editing of the Talmud, (III) The Era of the Stammaim, (IV) Compilers and Transposers. This order is also chronological, since according to Sherira Gaon, after R. Yehudah HaNasi died—that is, after the editing of the Mishnah and the beginning of the Amoraic era—the sages started transmitting dialectical argumentation too. However, I disagree with this view, and therefore begin my analysis with the Amoraic era in order to demonstrate that there was neither transmission of dialectical argumentation nor a general editing of the Talmud. It was only after Ravina and Rav Ashi that the Stammaim began to reconstruct dialectical argumentation. The period of the Stammaim extended from the period after Rav Ashi (d. 427) and Ravina (d. 500) until the final Compilers who collected the sources but were not permitted to add their own comments to the Talmud (730–770). I include in my discussion of the Compilers analysis of the Transposers [3], whose activity resembled that of the Compilers, as a large percentage of transpositions postdate the closing of the Talmud. At all events, as noted above, the order here follows that of the earlier volumes of *Meqorot umesorot.*

Dialectical argumentation can be divided into a minimum of three categories: (1) questions such as "what is the reason (*mai ta'ama*)?" and "whence are these things derived (*mina hani milei*)?," in which the meaning of the text is clear but its source is unknown; (2) questions such as "what are the circumstances (*heikhei damei*)?," in which the meaning is unclear; (3) questions such as "was it [not] taught in a baraita (*vehatanya*)?" and "there is a contradiction between them (*ureminhu*)," in which both the meaning and source are clear but another source contradicts it. When the answers to these questions are forced, then the answer presumably derives from the Stammaim, whereas the Amoraim had a cogent answer that was forgotten over the course of time. These questions, therefore, are of Amoraic provenance. However, there are some cases when the questions too originate in Stammaitic times, such as when the contradiction derives not from a mishnah or baraita but from local practice; in these cases the entire interchange necessarily derives from the Stammaim. The Stammaim got involved in the sugya not so as to complete a part that was missing due to its being forgotten, but rather they raised the problem because in their time there was an actual question about the issue. These types of cases provide evidence that some anonymous dialectical argumentation did not originate as an attempt to reconstruct forgotten argumentation of the Amoraim.

A good example of this phenomenon is Taan 26b. Mishnah Taanit 4:1 states: "On three occasions during the year the priests 'raise their hands [= pronounce the priestly benediction]' four times on that day, during the morning service, the additional service, the afternoon service, and the service for the 'locking of the gates'—on (1) fast days, (2) on the days of *ma'amadot,* and (3) on the Day of Atonement." The Talmud asks: "But there is no additional service on fast days and at the *ma'amadot*?!" And the Talmud answers: "[The mishnah] has an omission and he teaches thus: On three occasions during the year the priests 'raise their hands' *each time they pray. And on some occasions* four times on that day, during the morning service, the additional service, the afternoon service, and the service for the 'locking of the gates'—on fast days, on the days of *ma'amadot,* and on the Day of Atonement." As I have noted elsewhere, some Talmudic commentators point out that "tTaan 3:1, and especially tTaan 2:4—'On public fast days the priests raise their hands four times during the day, which is not the case of private fasts'—and other sources too imply that the additional service was in fact recited on fast days. This is consistent with the simple reading of the mishnah, and hence there is no need to emend the text as does the Bavli. Now the reason the Bavli objects 'But there is no additional service on fast days and at the *ma'amadot*?!' as if this is an obvious and well-known fact is because at the time of the objection the additional service was not recited on fast days. Thus the objection against mTaan 4:1 derives from the contemporary Babylonian practice. Indeed, according to the Tosefta the additional service was only added on public fast days, not private fasts, and Shmuel claims (Taan 11b) that no public fasts were observed in Babylonia. Hence there never was a practice of reciting the additional service on fast days in Babylonia."[2] The Stammaim responsible for the objection presuppose the Babylonian practice, and therefore emend mTaan 4:1. Yet the question arises: were the Babylonian Stammaim unaware that public fasts were still observed in Palestine? Did they never hear of the Palestinian practice from the sages who traveled to Babylonia? This implies that at the time of the objection it was also not the custom to recite the additional service on fast days in Palestine. The reason they did not recite the additional service on fast days in Babylonia is because such fasts were not authorized by the Patriarch (according to the Yerushalmi); and all fasts not authorized by the Patriarch have only the status of private fast days. The Stammaim responsible for the objection accordingly lived after the Patriarchate had been abolished in Palestine (415 CE), at a time when it was no longer the Palestinian practice to recite the additional service on fast days, and these Stammaim did not know of the custom of earlier times. "They apparently lived several generations after Ravina and Rav Ashi (who are credited with the editing of the Talmud in the traditional view), when the earlier Palestinian practice had been forgotten in Palestine too."[3] This example provides additional evidence that Ravina and Rav Ashi were not the editors of the Talmud, and it also demonstrates that the Stammaim did not only complete Amoraic dialectical argumentation, nor merely reconstruct it, but created some dialectical argumentation anew.

This is a summary of my general argument, "on one foot"; as for the rest—"go and learn."**

The Formation of the Babylonian Talmud

Part I: The Stammaim

MORE THAN THIRTY years ago I proposed that the anonymous stratum of the Bavli—the statements that appear without any attribution, the great majority of which are dialectical—derives not from the Amoraim but from the sages who flourished after them, whom I called "Stammaim," after the Hebrew word *setam*, meaning "anonymous" or "unattributed." I first set forth this thesis in the Introduction to *Meqorot umesorot: yoma–hagiga* (Jerusalem, 1975) and developed it in the Introductions to the volumes of *Meqorot umesorot* (henceforth: *MM*) on the following tractates. With the publication of each volume I supported and elaborated upon the fundamental idea that the anonymous stratum cannot be considered part of the Amoraic corpus of tradition. The Amoraim transmitted to posterity their legal rulings alone, and not the reasoning that led to their rulings. That reasoning remained in the memories of those present in the house of study when the Amoraim explained the sources of their rulings or their interpretation of a mishnah or a baraita (or the statement of earlier Amoraim). The Amoraim transmitted legal rulings to the "Reciters" (*tannaim*), the professional memorizers and official transmitters of tradition, who transmitted them to other houses of study and to students who functioned as Reciters in succeeding generations. And these students transmitted the rulings to their students, and their students to theirs. Such was the official chain of transmission of Amoraic teachings. Dialectical argumentation (*shaqla vetarya*), the reasoning, on the other hand, was not transmitted to Reciters and had no official transmission. Argumentation and reasoning were generally remembered and quoted in the proximate generations but were gradually forgotten after that, and only survived in a fragmentary state.[1] Were it not for the Stammaim who reconstructed and completed [6] the argumentation, it would no doubt have been forgotten completely, just as the argumentation underpinning the Mishnah and baraitot (i.e., the sources of the legal rulings) was completely forgotten.

Thus one fairly can say that the content of the anonymous stratum is not of Stammaitic provenance but is rather a reconstruction of earlier dialectical argumentation formulated in the language and style of the Stammaim.[2]

The Period of the Stammaim

When did the Stammaim begin their activity? I initial believed—or really conjectured (in the aforementioned Introduction to *MM: yoma–hagiga* and in the Introductions to subsequent volumes of *MM*)—that the Stammaim flourished after "Rav Ashi and Ravina—the end of *hora'ah* (BM 86a)," namely, the earlier Rav Ashi and Ravina (c. 430 CE), and continued until the second Ravina (c. 500 CE).[3]** I suggested, "[The Stammaitic period] began with the death of Rav Ashi, and was firmly established with the death of the second Ravina." I accepted the statement "Rav Ashi and Ravina—the end of *hora'ah*" as a historical fact and explained that "the end of *hora'ah*" means the end of the period of *gemara*, as understood by both traditional commentaries and scholars. I therefore concluded that the Stammaim flourished after Rav Ashi and Ravina, after the conclusion of the Amoraic period (c. 430), and before the Saboraic period, which, according to Sherira Gaon, began immediately after the second Ravina (c. 500). Subsequently I realized that the statement "Rav Ashi and Ravina—the end of *hora'ah*" "does not express an historical fact, but rather the adulation of a student who thought that [7] the death of his celebrated master brought an end to *hora'ah*."[4] Consequently in the Introduction to *MM: bava metsia* (2003) I deferred the beginning of the Stammaitic period until after the final conclusion of the Amoraic period, that is, after the latest sage mentioned by name in the Talmud, namely, "Revai of Rov (mentioned in Sanh 43a, according to the reading of R. Hananel)[5] who lived approximately fifty years after the second Ravina, in the middle of the sixth century CE."

The Stammaitic period cannot be dated earlier and equated with the Saboraic era mentioned by Sherira Gaon,** because several of the sages who lived during this time (such as Rav Rehumei, Rav Yosef,[6] Rav Ahai of Be Hatim, and Revai of Rov) are still mentioned in the Talmud, and therefore the period of the Stammaim (i.e., anonymous sages) had not yet begun. It did not trouble Sherira Gaon that the Saboraim included a few sages who appear in the Talmud and were quasi-Amoraim,[7] because the majority of the Saboraim are not mentioned in the Talmud, and the period was named for them. Moreover, most of those Saboraim (viz. the Saboraim named by Sherira Gaon) who are mentioned in the Talmud did not contribute more than occasional dicta and brief explanations akin to those of the Saboraim (viz. the Saboraim of my view). However, if the names of some of these sages appear in the Talmud, we cannot consider them Stammaim, as it is difficult to designate the period in which they lived the "Stammaitic" (anonymous) period. As long as Amoraim existed and are referred to by their names—even if their numbers are extremely small—that period cannot be called the Stammaitic period. The Stammaim began their activity only after there were no longer any Amoraim, about one hundred years after the death of Rav Ashi, c. 550 CE. After Rav Ashi the number of Amoraim began to dwindle, and about one hundred years after his death the Amoraic period ended[8]—and the Stammaitic period [8] commenced.** In my opinion, those sages whom Sherira Gaon calls "Saboraim," the sages not mentioned in the Talmud and who lived after Revai of Rov, belong to the Stammaitic period and contributed to the anonymous stratum of the Talmud. Those sages who lived before Revai of Rov and are not mentioned in the Talmud evidently did not contribute to the Talmud at all. Indeed, even in the Amoraic period we know the names of Heads of Academies who are mentioned in the *Epistle of Rav Sherira Gaon*, but who do not appear in the Talmud itself.[9] We must conclude that they too were not mentioned in the Talmud because they did not contribute to it.

When the Stammaim looked for a means of distinguishing their traditions from those of the Amoraim and for marking the end of that previous era, they could not simply refrain from organizing their traditions into self-contained compilations of rulings and append their traditions to those of the Amoraim. This is because the Amoraim too had not organized their traditions into self-contained compilations (e.g., a kind of Mishnah or baraita-collection) but had appended their traditions to the compilations of the Tannaim. Therefore the Stammaim chose dialectical argumentation as the distinctive style for the expression of their traditions; they reconstructed dialectical argumentation and transmitted it to posterity, a practice that was not carried out during the Tannaitic and Amoraic periods. In addition, we can apply to the Stammaim that which Sherira Gaon said of the Amoraim—that on account of the "decline of the generations"** they were concerned that not all rabbinic masters would be able to reconstruct the argumentation on their own. The Stammaim accordingly reconstructed the argumentation and entrusted it to transmitters so that it be preserved for future generations. They transmitted the argumentation in an anonymous form because neither the Tannaim nor the Amoraim transmitted the argumentation. Hundreds of years later, by the time of the Stammaim, a great deal of it had been forgotten, and they did not know who was responsible for that which remained. Moreover, it was the Stammaim themselves who reconstructed that which was missing. The Stammaim only attributed traditions to Amoraim when they were certain of the Amoraic provenance. And as for the obligations "to use the exact words of one's master" and to speak in the name of one's master—perhaps because everyone knew that the unattributed statements were late, since they were readily identifiable as dialectical argumentation as opposed to the Amoraic teachings formulated in an apodictic manner—the Stammaim no longer took care to indicate the author of the statement.

Moreover, it is possible that the Amoraim did not append their own rulings to Tannaitic traditions so as not to confuse their own words with those of the Tannaim, inasmuch as Amoraic traditions are also formulated in an apodictic manner, which makes it impossible to distinguish between the two. Rav's teachings, for example, are not quoted in the Mishnah even though he was "a member of Rabbi [Yehudah HaNasi]'s assembly" (Git 59a),[10] and is permitted to contradict a baraita ("Rav is a Tanna and disagrees"), and at times even contradicts a mishnah.[11]** Nevertheless, his traditions never entered the Mishnah, because the Mishnah already [9] had been canonized by his time. Thus they did not include even the teachings of a semi-Tanna like Rav so as not to confuse Amoraic with Tannaitic teachings. For this reason there was absolutely no possibility that attributions continue to be preserved in the Stammaitic period, not even a few, just as not a single Amora appears in the Mishnah,[12] as their mere presence would indicate that the previous period had not completely concluded. Accordingly I identified the Stammaitic era as the second half of the sixth century, after the Amoraic period and prior to the Saboraic era.

The Saboraic Era

Placing the Stammaitic period after the final conclusion of the Amoraic period (550–600 CE) led me to defer the era of the Saboraim, who flourished after the Stammaim, to the early Geonic period, and to conclude that some of the Geonim were also Saboraim—an idea that Sherira Gaon rejected (see the Introduction to *MM: bava metsia*). In his opinion, the first Gaon, R. Hanan of Ashiqiyya (who served 589–608), lived after the time of the Saboraim, and no Gaon served in both capacities.

Sherira's view is not at all compelling. "Gaon" was a title received when one became the Head of the Academy, whereas "Stammai" or "Sabora" refers to a sage who contributed to the Talmud, and these need not be mutually exclusive. Sages who never served as Heads of the Academy could have contributed to the Talmud, whereas it is possible that a Head of the Academy did not contribute. Indeed, Sherira refers to Rav Hisda, Rav Ashi, and Rav Revai of Rov as Geonim, which prompted Hayyim Yosef David Azulai to note: "Rav Sherira, in a responsum, even bestows the title 'Gaon' upon an Amora."[13] Why then is it not possible that the earlier Geonim were both Geonim and Saboraim? Moreover, Yehudai Gaon, whose glosses entered the text of the Talmud in greater numbers than any other Sabora, was among the greatest and last of the Saboraim. He too was both a Sabora and a Gaon.

However, I now doubt whether I was correct in stating in the aforementioned Introduction that the Saboraim lived after the age of the Stammaim in the time of the early Geonim, and in limiting the Stammaitic period to the fifty years after the last Amoraim until the first Geonim (c. 550–600 CE). Because Sherira never mentioned the Stammaim and considered Rav Ashi and Ravina to mark the end of the Amoraic period, he was forced to consider all sages who postdate Rav Ashi and Ravina (even if he means the second Rav Ashi and Ravina) as Saboraim, and no longer as Amoraim, even though the names of a few of them are mentioned in the Talmud. However, according to my view that the Stammaim followed the Amoraim, there is no need to postulate two discrete periods, one of Stammaim and one of Saboraim, but rather one period, that of the Stammaim, since the Saboraim were also Stammaim. [10] The Saboraim were the Stammaim who lived in the latter part of the period, when there no longer remained Amoraic material to reconstruct and complete (below I argue that this occurred in the middle of the Stammaitic period). This was also after the Stammaim fully exhausted the production of original dialectical argumentation in areas that lacked any connection to Amoraic statements, which occurred after they had come to recognize its independent value. At this stage the Talmud was almost complete, and all that remained was to add brief explanations and editorial comments—such as "how could he have raised the question at all (*udeqa'arei leih mai qa'arei leih*)," and "as we find it necessary to say later on (*kideva'inan lemeimar leqaman*),"[14] The sages who added these types of statements are called Saboraim, and they essentially closed the Talmud. Nevertheless, the Talmud was not absolutely closed: even after this time additions such as "the law is... (*vehilkheta*)"[15] entered the text from the *Halakhot gedolot*[16] (though not exclusively from there),[17] as did other such glosses.[18] When the Saboraim wanted to circulate their own interpretations, especially in conjunction with rulings that demanded dialectical analysis, they were no longer able to integrate them into the Talmud, since the Talmud was already closed to new dialectical argumentation, and therefore they composed independent books. Such endeavors aptly describe the activity of Yehudai Gaon (second half of eighth century), Aha of Shabha Gaon (c. 680–c. 752), and Shimon Qayyara, the author of the *Halakhot gedolot* (first half of ninth century). They composed independent works, and brief explanations deriving from their writings—in particular those of Yehudai Gaon—entered the Talmud. In sum, the Saboraim were Stammaim who lived in the second half of the eighth century after the Talmud was almost totally closed (*hatuma*) and completed (*hatukha*), and the era of independent books had begun.[19]

This claim will become clearer after an assessment is made of the Stammaitic contribution to the Talmud, in which we can distinguish three different strata. The first stratum consists of sugyot that explicate either a fragmentary or complete Amoraic dictum that is not sufficiently understood, or that explain a mishnah or baraita (or earlier Amoraic dictum) that requires clarification. The Amoraic dicta relate directly to the dialectical analysis, and are formulated as "R. So-and-so said." These Stammaim [11]—apparently the early Stammaim—still possessed traditions concerning the Amoraic dicta they endeavored to explain. The second stratum consists of sugyot that feature the same type of dialectical analysis, but quote the Amoraic dicta from other sources in the form "as R. So-and-so said (*de'amar rabbi ploni*)" or "did not Rav So-and-so say (*ha'amar rav ploni*)," and suchlike. These Stammaim did not possess a tradition that the Amoraic dictum was directly related to the sugya in which they were engaged; they transferred the dictum to the passage from elsewhere. Still later are passages that involve no Amoraic dicta whatsoever and are completely anonymous. The more distant the sugya from Amoraic times, the fewer Amoraic dicta it includes. Sugyot that completely lack Amoraic material are extremely late.

The contribution of the Saboraim was extremely limited compared with that of the Stammaim.[20] The Stammaim are the founders of the Talmud. They created the sugya and bestowed upon the Talmud the character and form so familiar to us. Without the Stammaim, the traditions of the Amoraim would resemble those of the Tannaim as found in the Mishnah and in collections of baraitot—apodictic law with a smattering of dialectical argumentation in minimal quantities. The Stammaim gave to the Talmud its essence and the intellectual attractiveness that distinguishes it from all other literary works. The Saboraim, on the other hand, received the Talmud in an almost complete form; they merely added brief explanations in a few places and appended editorial comments.[21] This literary activity did not require an extended period of time; moreover, they could express themselves by composing other books.

Accordingly, I retract that which I stated in the Introduction to *MM: bava metsia* (2003),[22] that the Stammaitic age lasted for fifty years, from 550–600 CE, and concluded with the rise of the Geonim at the beginning of the sixth century CE, and there followed the Saboraic age, 600–750 CE, about 150 years. I now believe that the Stammaitic was a lengthy period, extending almost 200 years,[23] from the middle of the sixth century (after the entire Amoraic period)[24] until the middle of the eighth century, a relatively protracted time [12] befitting the colossal scope of the Talmud. The Saboraic period, on the other hand, was relatively brief as befits their limited contribution. They flourished at the end of the Stammaitic period, in the second third of the eighth century, after the formation of the sugyot and after the basic form of the Talmud was complete, and they supplemented it with brief explanations. This limited era fits best with the second third of the eighth century, about the time of Yehudai Gaon, Aha of Shabha Gaon and Shimon Qayyara.[25]

I should add that my view follows that of Sherira Gaon in claiming that the Saboraim flourished after the Talmudic era, after the Talmud was almost complete, and that they contributed only minor explanations to the Talmudic text, predominantly to its anonymous portions. However, I disagree as to the periodization of the Saboraim: Sherira Gaon holds that the Talmud, including the anonymous portions, was completed at the time of the second Ravina, at the end of the fifth century, and the Saboraic period began thereafter. Whereas in my view the Stammaim flourished between Ravina and the Saboraim, and the Saboraic period began then—or more correctly, toward the end of the Stammaitic period—in the eighth century, and was a relatively brief period in its length and scope.

And perhaps the Saboraic period should not even be considered as a discrete era. The Saboraim actually mark the end of the Stammaitic period, and they bring the period to its final conclusion. Moreover, although anonymous material pervades and suffuses the Talmud, the Talmud contains no substantive reference to the Saboraim, despite the claims of several scholars. I noted in the Introduction to *MM: bava metsia*, 17, that Sherira Gaon describes the Saboraim as "providing explanations that are close to *hora'ah*" (*Epistle of Rav Sherira Gaon*, ed. Lewin, 69). This description better fits the Stammaim than the Saboraim. For example, Rav Rehumei, Rav Ahai of Be Hatim, and Rav Yosef, who are still mentioned in the Talmud, and whom Sherira Gaon considers as the first of the Saboraim—and we as the final Amoraim—did not engage in "reasoning that is close to legislation"** any more than in legislation itself, and not in dialectical argumentation more than in apodictic law. The Stammaim, however, engaged primarily in "reasoning that is close to legislation" and in dialectical argumentation, and only very rarely in legislation and in apodictic law. Sherira Gaon, I suggested, "transferred the traditional description of the Stammaim to the Saboraim" and confused the Stammaim with the Saboraim. Indeed, his description more appropriately describes the contribution of the Stammaim within the Talmud [13].

It is therefore possible that Sherira Gaon's subsequent observation, "and those sages are called the Saboraim," originally referred to the Stammaim. As noted above, the Stammaim did not engage in formal legislation, but rather in dialectical argumentation, which is a type of "reasoning (*sevarei*) close to legislation"–and the title "Saboraim" (Reasoners) therefore suits them well.[26] Originally the title "Saboraim" was used for those who engaged in "reasoning (*sevarei*) close to legislation," and who flourished for many years after the Amoraic period, that is, to the Stammaim. Later those writers who understood "the end of legislation (BM 86a)" to refer to the editing of the Talmud, including its anonymous portions, transferred the title "Saboraim" from the Stammaim to the sages who lived immediately after the second Ravina (of whom some are still mentioned in the Talmud) and attributed limited literary activity to them. In my view, however, the Saboraim were also Stammaim, and their literary activity was extensive, including the composition of most of the Talmud. This theory proposes a dating similar to that of Abraham ibn Daud, author of the "Book of Tradition" (*Sefer haqabbalah*; chapter 5), who writes that the Saboraic age ended in 689 CE.

And yet the Geonim quote dicta of the Saboraim that do not appear in our texts of the Talmud. If, as we assume, the Saboraim are the same as the Stammaim—why were these dicta not included in the Talmud, which is full of anonymous material? Therefore it is preferable to say that the Saboraim had a distinct status and lived in a separate period that followed the Stammaim, rather than to say that they were included within the

Stammaitic period, even if we defer the conclusion of the Stammaitic period to 200 years after Rav Ashi and Ravina.

In addition: only if we postulate that the Stammaitic period was relatively lengthy can we explain the common phenomenon that a later anonymous passage explains an earlier anonymous passage,[27] and sometimes even has difficulty understanding the earlier passage, failing to provide a satisfying interpretation. The first Stammaitic tradition originated in a much earlier time, and the later Stammaim lacked the information necessary to understand it. A good example of this phenomenon is when the earlier Stammaim state "Whose [ruling] is this? R. So-and-so" (BB 141a) or "Whose [ruling] is this? Not R. So-and-so and not R. So-and-so" (BB 65b) and then the later Stammaim ask, "Which [ruling of] R. So-and-so?" Certainly the earlier Stammaim specified which tradition of R. So-and-so, but this was subsequently forgotten [14] and the later Stammaim no longer knew it.[28] Moreover, in ordinary passages too one can sometimes discern that the latter part of the passage had difficulty understanding the earlier part, though both are anonymous.[29] The latter Stammaim, who lived many years later, no longer knew all the elements of the earlier part of the passage and therefore had difficulty understanding it. The different parts of the passage derive from different eras within the relatively lengthy Stammaitic period.

The Stammaim, it turns out, were not completely anonymous. They flourished from the middle of the sixth century until the latter half of the eighth century, and several of them (certainly not all) were Geonim mentioned by name in the *Epistle of Rav Sherira Gaon* and in *Seder tannaim ve'amoraim*.

Evidence for the Dating of the Stammaitic Period

Because the fundamental difference between the view I propose and the traditional view is the dating of the Stammaitic period,[30] I will set forth at some length the evidence that the Stammaim flourished after the Amoraic age so as to provide compelling support for my claims. I do not base my view solely on the fact that in many instances the anonymous stratum postdates the Amoraim, for one could then propose that in other passages—perhaps in the greater part of the Talmud—the anonymous material is coeval with the Amoraim. Nor is my view based on disparate traditions about this issue scattered throughout the Talmud and post-Talmudic literature. In a literary corpus as vast as the Talmud, such traditions pertain only to the circumstances and time in which they were stated.

In order to be considered absolutely true, they must be validated on the basis of the Talmudic text itself, not only from a few passages, but from numerous passages dispersed throughout the entire Talmud.

Here follow three considerations that apply to the entire Talmud and not to a limited number of passages. I will first state them briefly and go into greater detail below.

(1) Sherira Gaon and the tradition that developed in his wake claim that the Amoraim also transmitted the dialectical argumentation "generation by generation (*dara batar dara*)." According to this view, it is difficult to explain why there are so many places in the Talmud, almost on every single folio, where the Stammaim did not achieve their purpose and were forced to explain Amoraic traditions in an unsatisfying way—this relates to the foundation of critical Talmud study.[31] But the reason for [15] these forced explanations of Amoraic traditions is that the Stammaim lacked the complete version of the sources or the correct order of traditions; in order to complete them or correct the order they had no choice but to offer forced explanations.[32]

(2) Another consideration is that if the Stammaim were contemporaneous with the Amoraim, they should have asked the Amoraim or the students of the Amoraim who were their contemporaries to resolve their difficulties. Indeed, we find a number of cases in which Amoraim ask questions of other Amoraim, but we never find the Stammaim in dialogue with an Amora; the Stammaim do not converse with Amoraim because they postdate the Amoraim.

(3) Moreover, why is the vast majority of questions that precede Amoraic statements formulated anonymously, even when it is almost certain that the Amora intended to answer those questions, such as questions introduced by "there is a contradiction between them (*ureminhu*)," where the Amora answers, "there is no difficulty…(*la qashia*)"? Why is there no mention of the name of the sage who raised the question, as is frequently found in the Talmud where one Amora objects and another Amora—or that same Amora—responds, such as "R. So-and-so raised a contradiction and taught…"?[33] Let me put this issue in different terms: we find some instances where the Stammaim place objections before Amoraic statements, creating the impression that the Amora made his statement because of the objection—but this is actually not the case, as can be easily shown.[34] The Stammaim certainly did not intend to deceive, but assumed that everyone would know that the Amora himself did not make the objection, since it was

formulated anonymously.[35] But if (against our theory) the objections were indeed stated by an Amora, why did he formulate them anonymously?

The most reasonable explanation is that throughout Amoraic times questions and answers were not included with the official transmission of traditions from master to student. Only that which sages happened to remember was preserved, and therefore in the vast majority of cases names are wanting. However the Stammaim, who flourished after the Amoraim, also organized and transmitted the objections and solutions of the Amoraim as part of the official transmission; however, they did not attribute them to the Amoraim—since the Amoraim did not transmit them—but formulated them anonymously in order to underscore that the formulation and style is from the Stammaim themselves, and not from the Amoraim.

Differences between the types of formulations of traditions attested in each Talmudic stratum provide part of the evidence that the Stammaim and Amoraim were not contemporaries.** (The following examples do not follow a logical order but are simply those that come to mind.) And there need not be a parallel phenomenon for each difference attested among the Amoraim; it suffices if we find a particular phenomenon attested among Stammaim and unattested among Amoraim to demonstrate that they [16] were not contemporaries. Most of these examples are taken from *Meqorot umesorot* and can be checked thoroughly by the references provided in the footnotes.

In some cases (albeit rarely) the Stammaim incorporated their own words immediately after "R. So-and-so said" (and similar such formulations), before the beginning of the original Amoraic statement. Two different types of this phenomenon must be distinguished. The first is where anonymous material precedes the "R. So-and-so said," and the anonymous material that follows the "R. So-and-so said" refers back to it. According to the principle that an Amora never refers to anonymous material, it is clear that the material that follows the "R. So-and-so said" is not from the Amora. (In most such instances there is additional evidence that this is the case.) The second type is where no anonymous material precedes the "R. So-and-So said," in which case detailed analysis is required to determine whether the continuation that follows the "R. So-and-so said" is from the Stammaim. An example of the first type is Rav Ashi's statement in Qid 64a:

[A1] (mQid 3:8) [If a man said] "I betrothed my [minor] daughter" [or] "I betrothed her and divorced her while she was yet a minor," and she is still a minor, he is believed.

[A2] [If he said] "I betrothed her and divorced her while she was yet a minor," and she is now an adult, he is not believed.

[B] (Talmud:) What is the difference between the [case in the] first clause [of the mishnah, A1] and the [case in the] second clause [A2]?

[C] In the first clause, it is in his control [to do so]; in the second clause, it is not is his control [to do so.]

[D] Is it not in his control?... Surely... That is no difficulty....

[E] Rav Ashi said: "Do you really think (*tisbera*) that the first clause is in his [the father's] control? Granted it is in his control to betroth her, is it in his control to divorce her? Moreover..."

[F] Rather Rav Ashi said: "In the first clause..."

Rav Ashi's objection [E] is directed at the preceding anonymous answer [C] to the Talmud's question [B]. He points out that first clause too deals with a case that "is not in his control," since it is not in the father's control to effect the divorce of a minor daughter. However, Rav Ashi's objection is so powerful that it is difficult to believe that anyone would intend that answer [C] as a serious explanation of the mishnah, and hence there was no real need for Rav Ashi to undermine it. Clearly, we have here rhetorical argumentation (the rest of the argumentation [D] is borrowed from parallel passages), which is typical of the Stammaim. Rav Ashi did not participate in this interchange, but only provided the final solution [F]; the Stammaim attributed the objection [E] to him.[36]

An example of the second type is when "R. So-and-so objected (*matqif*) to it (or to him)[37]...," are not the words of the Amora but of the Stammaim, as found in several Talmudic passages. The Stammaim wished to explain why this Amora, whose words are quoted in close proximity to the objection with the formulation "Rather, R. So-and-so said...," disagreed with the other Amora, whose statement is quoted previously. I first commented on this phenomenon in *MM*, Pesahim, 454–55. (However I also noted there that "in general one cannot assume that 'R. So-and-so objected...' is not a quotation of R. So-and-so." The formulation "objected [*matqif*] to it" [or "him"] is perhaps not from that Amora,[38] but the content is Amoraic. Therefore I concluded that when we find manuscript variants that read "R. So-and-so said" in place of "R. So-and-so objected" the reading "R. So-and-so said" is earlier.)[39]

The Stammaim also will attribute to an Amora a source for his ruling which was not referenced by that Amora, without disclosing this fact. For example, some instances of the reasoning that follows the phrase "what is the reason?" derive from the Stammaim and not from the Amoraim. And the opposite: in some cases the Stammaim attribute to the Amora an introductory phrase in the first person, which on the surface appears to be the words of the Amora. I refer to the expressions "R. So-and-so says: whence shall I prove it (*mena amina lah*)?"[40] or "R. So-and-so says: [17] whence do you know it (*mena teimra*)?,"[41] which sometimes derive from the Stammaim and not from the Amoraim (though generally this is not the case).[42] The Stammaim conjectured that this was the source of the Amora and formulated their conjecture as if the Amora himself said it. This phenomenon is attested of both Tannaim and Amoraim, and sometimes we find that the Stammaitic conjecture turns into an Amoraic dictum.[43]

Furthermore, there are some very rare cases where the Stammiam quote a question posed by a certain Amora, but before providing the answer of a second Amora they interpolate their own answer and analyze it—and then other, still later Stammaim draw inferences from the analysis of the earlier Stammaim and in turn develop further lines of argumentation. And only after that do the Stammaim quote the response of the second Amora to whom the question was originally posed. An example appears on Bets 36a–b.

[A] Come and hear: One may spread out a mat upon a beehive [on the Sabbath], in the summer because of the sun, and in the winter because of the rain, provided he does not intend to capture [the bees].

[B] Rav Uqba of Meshan said to Rav Ashi: This [ruling] makes sense in the summer, when there is honey [in the hive], but in winter [when there is no honey], what can be said?

[C] [The ruling] is necessary [even in winter] for those two honeycombs [left behind for the bees to eat.]

[D] But those two honeycombs are *muqtsot* (set aside, and cannot be used)!

[E] This is a case when he planned to use them... In that case... This is what he means...

[F] You have explained (the ruling, [A]) in accord with R. Yehudah, who accepts the principle of *muqtsa*. But the final clause, "provided he does not intend to capture the bees" reflects the view of R. Shimon, who holds that an unintentional act is permitted!

[G] Do you really think it is R. Shimon? Did not both Abaye and Rava... Rather... Say rather... That is obvious... You might have thought...

[H] Rav Ashi said: "Does he teach 'in the summer and in the winter'? He teaches 'In summery [days] on account of the sun, and in wintery [days] on account of the rain,' [meaning] in Nisan and Tishrei when there is sun and rain and honey."

The earlier Stammaim provide an answer [C, E] to the question posed by Rav Uqba of Meshan to Rav Ashi [B]. Later Stammaim then object to that answer [F][44] and continue with further argumentation [G]. Only then do we have the answer of Rav Ashi [H], which apparently was stated immediately after Rav Uqba of Meshan questioned him [B]. Why is the passage structured in this way? In *MM,* Betsah, 350 I conjectured that the earlier Stammaim did not know of Rav Ashi's answer; they knew of Rav Uqba's question to Rav Ashi, but not the response, and therefore they provided another answer. (This phenomenon is attested elsewhere.)[45] However, later Stammaim who knew of Rav Ashi's response, and who lived at a time when it was no longer possible to integrate additional material within a sugya but only to append traditions to its end, and also when it was not permitted to add their own contributions,[46] quoted that response at the conclusion of the dialectical argumentation. If this is the case we have further evidence that the anonymous layer should not be attributed to Rav Ashi (see above p. 12 and below p. 92). However, it is also possible that the Stammaim inserted their own answer before that of Rav Ashi instead of placing it after Rav Ashi's answer with the term "and if you prefer, I will say (*i ba'eit eima*)," because Rav Ashi's answer is more fitting, and the Stammaim tend to precede more fitting with less fitting answers; for there is no reason to continue with a less fitting explanation after providing the most fitting one.[47]

Let me now return to general evidence that suggests the Stammaim were not contemporaries of the Amoraim. If the Stammaim and the Amoraim were contemporaneous, and anonymous formulation indicates the consensus (Amoraic) opinion in the same manner as anonymous formulation in the Mishnah—why is the term "anonymous *gemara*" unattested, unlike the term "anonymous Mishnah"?[48] And why do the Stammaim exhibit a tendency to rhetorical argumentation, debating objections whose answers [18] are obvious, a style unattested among the Amoraim? See, for example, Shab 6b: "[The mishnah's ruling] 'In a case of inadvertent transgression he must bring a sin-offering'—this is obvious! It was necessary [to spell it out] because of [the next part of the mishnah:] 'In a case of intentional transgression he is punished by extirpation (*karet*) and stoning.' This too is obvious! Rather it [the mishnah] informs you..." Whoever responded "It was necessary [to spell it out] because of [the next part of the mishnah:] 'In a case of intentional transgression he is punished by extirpation (*karet*) and stoning'" knew that this was not a real answer, and only stated it so as to "increase [discussions of] Torah (*lehagdil torah*)." Similarly, our texts of RH 16a read: "R. Yitshaq said: 'Why do we sound a sustained blast [of the shofar (*teqiah*)] on Rosh HaShana?,'' and the Stammaim thereupon ask: "Why do we sound a sustained blast? The Merciful One said 'Sound a sustained blast'! Rather why do we sound a quavering blast (*teruah*)? The Merciful One said 'Sound a quavering blast!' Rather, why do we sound the sustained blast and sound the quavering blast while sitting and while standing..." Here too whoever answered "Rather why do we sound a quavering blast?" knew that this was not a real answer and stated it only so as to incorporate the case of the quavering blast in the discussion. Likewise in Sanh 3a: "Is not 'full-damages (*nezeq*)' the same [category] as 'injuries (*havalot*)' [so why does the mishnah mention both]? Because he wished to teach [the matter of] 'half-damages (*hatsi nezeq*),' so [he also mentioned full-damages]...'Half-damages' is also the same [category] as 'injuries (*havalot*).'" Again the responder knew that "half-damages is the same [category] as injuries," and only stated "Because he wished to teach [the matter of] half-damages" in order to include half-damages in the discussion.[49] Tosafot Ri"d (Isaiah di Trani, c. 1080–c. 1150) indeed observed: "The nature of the Talmud is to begin by proposing simple solutions that are rejected, and only then to offer the primary solution, in order to expand the argumentation and demonstrate that this is the only way to resolve the issue" (Pes 77a, s.v. *leima*). By "the nature of the Talmud" we should understand "the nature of the Stammaim," as the Amoraim did not engage in rhetoric. Moreover, if the Stammaim were contemporaries of the Amoraim, why are they not concerned with accurate chronology, but quote, for example, "Rather Rabbah bar Rav Hana said in the name of R. Yohanan..." (a second generation Amora) as a response to "Rav Mesharshia objected to him (*matqif leih*)" (a third-generation Amora; Suk 26a and elsewhere)?[50]

So too in some cases the style of the Stammaim differs from that of the Amoraim. For example, I noted that after stating "this was not said explicitly but on the basis of an inference (*lav befeirush itmar ela mikelala itmar*)" the Talmud sometimes asks "and what [difference does it make] if stated on the basis of an inference? (*ve'i mikelala mai*)" but sometimes does not ask this question (*MM*, Megillah, 513–14). This difference points to different circles of sages. The Stammaim who asked "and what [difference does it make] if stated on the basis of an inference?" "belonged to those late circles in which the use of inferences had (already) become common,[51] and consequently they saw no benefit in identifying a dictum that was stated on the basis of an inference. Therefore, when they came upon someone (an Amora) who identified such a dictum, they asked: 'and what [difference does it make] if stated on the basis of an inference?' Those sages (Amoraim) who do not ask 'and what [difference does it make] if stated on the basis of an inference?' belonged to circles in which the use of inferences was uncommon, and consequently they did not ask 'and what [difference does it make] if stated on the basis of an inference?'; they considered this to be an uncommon incident that was worth mentioning."[52] Such differences between the Amoraim and Stammaim would not be attested had they lived in the same era.

[19] Perhaps the strongest argument that the Stammaim were not contemporaries of the Amoraim is their distinctive language. Often we find that the Stammaim employ terms and expressions rarely found among the Amoraim, such as, "What might you have said (*mahu deteima*),"[53] "And if you prefer, I will say (*ve'i ba'eit eima*),"[54] "What does 'and he said' [add] (*mai ve'omer*),"[55] and others. But if the Stammaim were contemporaries of the Amoraim, their masters and their students, one would assume that their modes of expression would be similar.

Similarly, I have periodically noted that the order of Stammaitic material differs from that of the Amoraim. Here are a few examples: "The Stammaim arrange the objections according to the cogency of the objection," and not according to the chronological order [of the speaker];[56] "The Stammaim begin with a weak objection deriving from the end of the last clause, and then proceed to a strong objection deriving from the first clause"; in some cases this is motivated by literary considerations;[57] "the Stammaim arrange the sugya in dialectical form and place objections before the Amoraic statements, even though the Amoraim did not make their statements on account of those objections. And sometimes they add objections that are not substantive."[58]

Some differences between Stammaim and Amoraim are more pronounced. For example: "Stammaitic method is to respond with various solutions, but subsequently to state that the Amora's claim does not require all those solutions. However, this is not the practice of the Amoraim."[59] Similarly, "The Stammaim typically place the strongest objection last. However, each Amora tries to object with the strongest possible objection."[60] "The method of the Stammaim is thus: when the solution to the objection against the first part of the source also resolves the objection against the second part of the source, but the solution to the objection against the second part does not resolve the objection against the first part—they precede the discussion of the second part with that of the first part in order to 'increase [discussions of] Torah.' "[61] The Amoraim did not organize the Talmud in this way; no doubt such differences between the Amoraim and Stammaim demonstrate that the Stammaim postdated the Amoraim, and the organization of the sugya and the Talmudic terminology changed over time. However, it is also possible that terminology and the arrangement of the sugya changed because the Stammaim—unlike the Tannaim and Amoraim—also transmitted the dialectical argumentation to succeeding generations, and this endeavor sometimes required distinct formulations and an order that differed from that used by the Amoraim, who transmitted only fixed laws (*halakhot qetsuvot*) and brief explanations of the Tannaitic sources. Yet I doubt whether this consideration in and of itself suffices to explain the extent of the differences in language and organization between the Amoraim and the Stammaim.

[20] More significantly, the difference between the Amoraim and Stammaim is not expressed only in the terminology, language, style, and arrangement of Talmudic material, but also in the way that the exegetical thought process influenced the halakhah itself—a manner that is difficult to explain according to the assumption that they were contemporaries. I will illustrate this point by an example—by no means unique—chosen because of its great importance and prevalence in the Talmud. When the Amoraim (e.g., R. Yohanan, an early Amora [Shab 140a], and Rava [BB 79b]) do not rule in accord with a mishnah, they say, "This mishnah is an individual opinion." The Stammaim, on the other hand, struggle to accept the mishnah and state, "The mishnah has an omission and he teaches thus (*hasorei mihasra vehakhi katanei*)"; the Stammaim never state, "This mishnah is an individual opinion." I refer in particular to the passage found in Ber 15b and Meg 19b, which discusses mMeg 2:4: "All are fit to read the Scroll [of Esther,] except for a mute, a deranged person, and a minor. And R. Yehudah rules that a minor is fit." The Talmud emends this mishnah and states, "Perhaps [the entire mishnah] is [in accord with] R. Yehudah, and there are two types of minors, and '[the mishnah] has an omission and he teaches thus': 'All are fit to read the Scroll [of Esther], except for a mute, a deranged person, and a minor. *When is this the case? When the minor has not yet reached the age of schooling. But a minor who has*

reached the age of schooling is fit [to read the Scroll of Esther] even ab initio—*these are the words of R. Yehudah. For* R. Yehudah rules that a minor is fit.' " According to the simple reading of the mishnah, there is no need to say that "it has an omission and he teaches thus.... When does this apply...," since the Talmud itself only wonders "Perhaps...," meaning that the problem is not too serious; there is consequently no need to distinguish between a minor who has reached the age of schooling and one who has not. The mishnah simply states that according to the first opinion, a minor is unfit to read the Scroll of Esther, and "R. Yehudah rules that a minor is fit." The disagreement, therefore, is whether a minor is fit to read the Scroll of Esther or not, without any distinction between minors who have reached the age of schooling and those who have not. Tosefta Megillah 2:8 implies the same. The medieval commentators explain that the Talmud states "[The mishnah] has an omission and he teaches thus" and distinguishes between these types of minors in order to explain the entire mishnah in accord with the opinion of R. Yehudah. In the words of Tosafot: "Because we rule in accord with R. Yehudah further on [in this passage], it is preferable to explain [the entire mishnah] to accord with [the view of] R. Yehudah."[62]

The Stammaim constructed sugyot in such a way, although the Amoraim would not have done so. While the Amoraim also explained mishnahs with the term "it has an omission and he teaches thus," they do not do so for the same reasons as the Stammaim, namely, in order to make the mishnah accord with the law. Rather, the Amoraim use this term to explain a mishnah or baraita when the straightforward reading is problematic. For example, Shab 102a commenting on mShab 11:6:

[A1] (mShab 11:6): He who throws and then remembers [that it is the Sabbath] after the object leaves his hand and another person intercepts it, or a dog intercepts it, or it burns up [before landing]—he is not culpable....

[A2] This is the general principle: all [sins] for which the punishment is a sin-offering, one is not culpable unless both the beginning [of the action] and the end [of the action] are done in error....

[B] (Talmud): Then if it lands (and was not intercepted or burnt) he is culpable!

[C] But he remembered (before it landed), and it was taught [in the same mishnah, A2]: "All [sins] for which the punishment is a sin-offering, one is not culpable unless both the beginning [of the action] and the end [of the action] are done in error!"....

[D] Rav Ashi said: "[The mishnah] has an omission and he teaches thus: 'He who throws and remembers [that it is the Sabbath] after the object leaves his hand, or if another person intercepts it, or if a dog intercepts it, or if it burns up [before landing]—he is not culpable. *But if it lands, he is culpable. When is this the case? When he forgot again. But if he did not forget again, then he is exempt. Because* all [sins] for which the punishment is a sin-offering, one is not culpable unless both the beginning [of the action] and the end [of the action] are done in error.' "

Thus Rav Ashi emends the mishnah [D] so that the Talmud's inference [B] from the first clause of the mishnah [A1] does not contradict the subsequent principle [A2]. To this Tosafot comment: "This is not a true [application of the term] 'it has an omission [and he teaches thus],' as the mishnah in its present form can be explained in this manner (and no emendation is required). Rather, Rav Ashi employed the term 'it has an omission' in order to clarify what the mishnah means."[63]

Another example: in Hag 2b, Ravina, and some say Rava, states "it has an omission" in order to resolve a contradiction between mTer 1:2 [21], which rules that those who can hear but not speak or speak but not hear are exempt from the commandment of the priestly tithe (*terumah*), and a baraita (related to tTer 1:2), which rules that they are obligated. Ravina/Rava "emend" mTer 1:2 to refer to the obligation of Appearance (*re'iah*) and explain that the baraita refers to the obligation of Rejoicing (*simhah*)—a standard solution to a contradiction, in the manner of "here we deal with x, there we deal with y," or "this is a case of x, that is a case of y." The Talmud then supports the "emendation" by quoting another baraita of the form "we have also taught thus (*tanya namei hakhi*)." Here too we could say, following the Tosafot quoted above, "This is not a true [application of the term] 'it has an omission and he teaches thus,' as the mishnah (= mTer 1:2) in its present form can be explained in this manner." **

Similarly, in Meil 12b, the Talmud points out a difficulty in understanding mMeil 3:5, which states: "When does this apply? To things dedicated to the altar (*qodshei mizbeah*). But to things dedicated for the upkeep of the temple (*qodshei bedeq habayit*)..." Rav Pappa resolves the difficulty by claiming: "It has an omission and he teaches thus. 'When does this apply? To things dedicated themselves (*qedushat haguf*) to the altar; but if one dedicated the value of the things (*qedushat damim*) to the altar, it is as if he dedicated it for the upkeep of the temple.' " Although Rav Pappa here uses the term "it has an omission and he teaches thus," he does not mean to emend or correct the mishnah, but only to explain it. Here too we do not have a true application of the term as employed by the Stammaim.

Now in three passages, Git 54a, Hul 73a, and Hul 118a, the Talmud itself is uncertain whether the emendation supplied by "it has an omission..." derives from an Amora or from the Stammaim, and after first attributing it to an Amora, the Talmud adds, "and some state it anonymously" (on this term, see below, p. 44). Nevertheless, as a general rule, when an Amora states "it has an omission..." the emendation is required to make sense of the mishnah or baraita. In Hul 73a and 118a Rava states "it has an omission..." in order to explain the baraita, which makes no sense without his interpretation. Without the emendation we would not know how to answer the Talmud's question, "What does this [baraita] mean?" In this case it is necessary to correct the baraita, necessary to say "it has an omission," for without the correction the baraita would be incomprehensible. In Git 54a the emendation supplied by "it has an omission" was omitted from the baraita due to homeoteleuton,** and we find other such cases elsewhere in the Talmud.[64] Only in BQ 14a and 16a do I fail to find a satisfactory explanation for an Amora employing the term "it has an omission..." However, those passages are difficult; I tried to elucidate them in *MM* ad loc., although they remain unclear. At all events, there is a difference between the way Amoraim and Stammaim use the terms "this mishnah is an individual opinion" and "it has an omission and he teaches thus." There should not be differences of this kind were the Amoraim and Stammaim contemporaries.

In addition, the vast majority of the aggadah of the Bavli, which consists of homilies and morals—and not history, metaphysical topics, or lengthy narratives—is attributed, as opposed to the early collections of halakhic midrashim and aggadah, which are anonymous.[65] The reason for this phenomenon deserves due consideration. Perhaps it is because the Stammaim, unlike the Amoraim, did not engage in aggadah and did not transmit it to succeeding generations, just as the Mishnah and the Tosefta did not transmit aggadah and almost omitted it completely (although we know from the collections of halakhahic midrashim that the Tannaim took an interest in aggadah).[66] Both these Tannaitic compilations and the Stammaim had a circumscribed purpose in transmitting material that did not include aggadah. The Mishnah and Tosefta endeavored to preserve the halakhah, which was almost obliterated in the aftermath of the Bar Kochba revolt; therefore they are structured and dominated by halakhah.

The Stammaim, by contrast, attempted to preserve the dialectical argumentation, which was on the verge of being forgotten (just as the dialectical argumentation of the Tannaim was forgotten), since it was not transmitted in an official formulation but was only preserved in the memories of those who had heard it; therefore the Stammaim concentrated on the dialectical argumentation of the Talmud. Neither the Mishnah and Tosefta nor the Stammaim attempted to transmit aggadah, and therefore aggadah finds no place in their literary endeavors.** [22] However, were the Stammaim contemporaries with the Amoraim, it is difficult to believe that the Amoraim would have produced and transmitted aggadah, whereas the Stammaim took no part in it—we have no choice but to conclude that the Stammaim postdated the Amoraim.[67]

Yet perhaps there is no need for all these arguments, as the distinctive language of the dialectical argumentation itself testifies to its belatedness. After the Talmud quotes an unclear dictum—even if it derives from the latter Amoraim who postdated Rav Ashi—the Talmud often begins the dialectical argumentation with language expressing uncertainty, such as "what are the circumstances (*heikhei damei*)...shall we say...rather I would say..." and suchlike, terminology that expresses doubts about the explanation and justification of the dictum. If they had a reliable tradition not only regarding the dictum but also regarding its explanation and justification—if the dialectical argumentation had been transmitted together with the dictum and was contemporaneous with it—why then does the Talmud quote the dictum with certainty but cast doubt on the dialectical argumentation? Now in several passages the Talmud states the justification (including the explanation) with certitude, as part of the dictum itself! Thus there were some instances where they were certain as to the accuracy of the justification, but in the majority of cases, where they ask "what are the circumstances" and suchlike, they were unsure about the reliability of the justification, because they had no authentic tradition.

That the dialectical argumentation, including explanations and justifications, was not transmitted along with Amoraic dicta also accounts for cases when an Amora[68] mentions a Tanna and the Stammaim identify the ruling of the Tanna on the basis of the statement of a later Amora. Originally the first Amora undoubtedly identified the Tanna together with the ruling, but later the ruling was forgotten, and the Stammaim tried to identify it. This phenomenon regularly occurs with a "system (*shita*)," when an Amora combines different Tannaitic opinions into a "system" and lists the Tannaitic rulings on the basis of which he inferred the "system." However, in the course of time those original Tannaitic rulings were forgotten, and the Stammaim later tried to identify them with the help of later Amoraim. See, for example, Qid 48b: "Abaye said: R. Shimon and R. Shimon b. Gamaliel and R. Eliezer all hold that it merely indicates the place to him (*mareh maqom*). R. Shimon—the source we discussed. R. Shimon b. Gamaliel, as we have taught...and Rav Ashi said..." Abaye could not quote Rav Ashi, a later Amora, so it is clear that the Stammaim are responsible for quoting him here. That is, Abaye's dictum ended with "place to him," and the Stammaim quoted Rav Ashi's elucidation of the Tannaitic source containing R. Shimon b. Gamaliel's opinion in their effort to identify the sources Abaye had in mind. Similarly, Qid 62b: "Abaye said: R. Eliezer b. Yaakov and Rabbi and R. Meir all hold that a man may transfer possession of something that does not yet exist. R. Eliezer b. Yaakov—the source we discussed... R. Nahman b. Yitshaq said..." Abaye would not quote R. Nahman b. Yitshaq, who was added here by the Stammaim. Similarly, Sanhedrin 4a: "R. Yohanan said: Rabbi and R. Yehudah b. Roets and the House of Shammai and R. Shimon and R. Akiba all hold that the vocalization of Scripture is authoritative (*yesh em lamiqra*). Rabbi—the source we discussed...and Rav Huna said..." R. Yohanan would not quote Rav Huna, who was inserted into this context by the Stammaim. Moreover, R. Yohanan did not state "the source we discussed," [23] which relates to the tradition of the previous folio, "R. Abbahu ridiculed the statement," as R. Abbahu was among the latter Amoraim.** And it is almost certain that Abaye also did not say "the source we discussed," and nor did the other Amoraim who discerned such "systems." The term "the source we discussed," probably derives from the Saboraim, who engaged in redactional activity.

My fundamental assumption is that throughout Amoraic times, just as throughout Tannaitic times, dialectical argumentation was not transmitted as part of the official tradition. Therefore dialectical argumentation is often truncated. We commonly find that an Amora asks (or objects) to an Amoraic colleague face-to-face ("he said to him"), but the response does not come from the Amora who was asked, but rather from a later Amora or from the Stammaim.[69] The original Amora, when he was asked, undoubtedly provided an answer, or conceded to the objection because he had no good response. However, the Talmud no longer had a tradition as to his answer or his concession. The response was forgotten.[70]

Differences between My Account and That of Sherira Gaon

[24] At this point let me summarize the differences between the traditional account—that of Sherira Gaon—and the account that I propose:[71] According to the traditional view, the anonymous statements of the Talmud are explanations of Amoraic dicta and are coterminous with the Amoraim upon whose traditions they are predicated. Like the anonymous portions of the Mishnah [25], they too were formulated without attribution because all sages agreed that the Amora is to be explained in that way. With the conclusion of the Amoraic period the entire Talmud was completed, including the anonymous statements, the only later additions being brief explanations of the Saboraim (who lived shortly after the Amoraim).[72] In my view, by contrast, the Stammaim who composed the anonymous statements were not contemporaries of the Amoraim but lived long after them. The Stammaim transmitted their teachings without attribution so as not to conflate them with the teachings of the Amoraim, whose period had closed, and to emphasize the difference between Amoraic tradition, which mainly consists of dicta and fixed laws, and Stammaitic tradition, which is predominantly dialectical analysis.[73] The period of the Stammaim—and most of the Talmud is anonymous (*setam*)—extended at least 200 years, from the last Amora until the Geonim who authored books attributed to individuals, such as Yehudai Gaon, Aha of Shabha Gaon, et al. This period extended from the beginning of the sixth century, after the second Ravina, whose traditions are prevalent throughout the Talmud, or from the middle of the sixth century, after Revai of Rov, the last Amora mentioned in the Talmud (once, though not in the manuscripts we possess), until the second half of the eighth century. At that time the sages began to preserve attributions again and resumed the Tannaitic and Amoraic practice of mainly formulating fixed laws without dialectical argumentation, although after the heightened interest in dialectical argumentation in the Stammaitic era they could not completely abandon it or neglect to quote it altogether. Perhaps this point offers some evidence that the period that preceded these Geonic authors was the period of the Stammaim, which was devoted to dialectical argumentation and devoid of apodictic rulings. When the Stammaim felt the need to supplement the Amoraic corpus of apodictic rulings they chose to formulate their own traditions as dialectic argumentation. If, on the other hand, the practice of the period before the Geonic era had been to

transmit apodictic laws together with dialectical argumentation, why did the Geonim themselves specifically choose to formulate apodictic laws?

Thus, contra the consensus view, the Talmud was not completed at the end of the Amoraic period,[74] but rather in the Stammaitic period, at the conclusion of which the Saboraim flourished. However, the Saboraic contribution to the Talmud was minor, limited to matters of editing and suchlike. The Saboraim probably lived only after [26] the Stammaitic corpus of tradition had been completed, and required but editing and brief explanations, a kind of polishing and glossing designed to fill in some lacunae. The Saboraic age accordingly corresponds to about the middle of the eighth century CE.

In passing I wish to point out an additional difference between the traditional view and my view. According to the traditional view, not only was dialectical argumentation transmitted in an official manner, but it was edited at the end (or near the end) of the Amoraic period (together with fixed laws and fixed explanations?) by Rav Ashi and Ravina, whereas according to my view there was no general editing of dialectical argumentation, not even at the end of the Stammaitic period. Therefore, at the end of the Stammaitic period even traditions that were neither reworked nor reconstructed were incorporated into the Talmud. The Compilers (*me'asfim*) were no longer able to add new dialectical argumentation at this late time, yet they possessed raw material with contradictions and inconsistencies which they integrated into the Talmud. See Part II, "The Editing of the Talmud," and Part IV, "Compilers and Transposers."

Because of the importance of this issue, let me note briefly (I will go into greater detail below, p. 43), that the few places where the Talmud quotes early anonymous statements (*setamot qedumim*) and it appears that Amoraim relate to this anonymous material cannot be adduced as evidence against my view. Similarly, the rare cases in which the same dialectical argumentation is anonymous in one Talmudic passage but attributed to an Amora elsewhere is not an argument against my claims. The Stammaim reconstructed the reasons and basis for Amoraic statements, and in most cases they succeeded and correctly understood what the Amora meant to say. Clearly the Stammaim possessed different sources, and the anonymous passages in our Talmud devolve from different academies. Therefore one should not be surprised—statistically it is even necessary—if in some cases the Stammaim of one academy had a source with an attributed tradition and quoted it in the name of the Amora, while the Stammaim of another academy had no explicit Amoraic tradition but accurately reconstructed it and quoted it without attribution. The Talmud indeed states in several passages, "Said R. So-and-so, and some say it anonymously (*kedi*)"—that is, some state this tradition without attribution.[75]

So too cases where an Amora appears to refer to unattributed material are not evidence of the existence of early anonymous statements, for sometimes the Stammaim did not know the reasoning and basis for the Amora's statement. In addition, the Amoraic statements themselves had been transmitted to them in a truncated form. The Stammaim completed the Amora's words, created a context for them, and inferred the reasoning. In order to make the form comparable to other passages and to render the traditions authoritative and reliable, they formulated the (Stammaitic) supplement to the Amoraic dictum with the attribution and the explanatory context for the statement anonymously.[76] In these cases, the Stammaim trusted that future students[77] would know that a portion of the Amoraic dictum had been reconstructed. Moreover, in most such cases there is additional evidence that it was the Stammaim, not the Amora himself, who refer to the anonymous material.

Let me adduce one extreme example to illustrate this point. In Men 55a the Talmud asks about the baraita cited there:

[A1] [Baraita:] "One takes the priestly tithe (*terumah*) from [fresh] figs for pressed figs in a place where it is customary to press figs.

[A2] But one may not take the priestly tithe from pressed figs for [fresh] figs even in a place where it is customary to press figs."

[B] "In a place where it is customary..."—yes (= one is permitted). But in a place where it is not customary—no (= one is not permitted)...

[C] It is obvious that [this must be a case in which] no priest is present. But the final clause [of the baraita, A2] states: "[One may not take] the priestly tithe from pressed figs for [fresh] figs even in a case where it is customary to press [27] figs".... [This implies] that [this must be a case in which] a priest is present.

[D] [Is it possible that] the first clause [= A1] refers to a case where no priest is present and the final clause to a case where a priest is present [A2]?

[E] Yes, the first clause refers to a case where no priest is present and the final clause to a case where a priest is present.

[F] Rav Pappa said: Learn from this that we prefer to give a forced explanation to a Tannaitic source as dealing with two different sets of circumstances rather than attribute it to two different authorities.

Rav Pappa's conclusion, "Learn from this...[F]" appears to be predicated on the words of the anonymous Talmud, "Yes, the first clause refers to a case where no priest is present and the final clause to a case where a priest is present" [E]—thus we seem to have a case where an Amora refers to the anonymous stratum. However, if we scrutinize Rav Pappa's statement, we find that it appears verbatim attributed to Resh Laqish in Qid 63b, and it is impossible that they both independently and autonomously employed the same words (which are uncommon) in the same order. It stands to reason that originally Rav Pappa quoted the statement of Resh Laqish in the manner of the standard Talmudic expression "as Resh Laqish said [elsewhere]," and Rav Pappa's statement was contextualized here as a response to the objection, "[Is it possible that] the first clause refers to a case where no priest is present and the final clause to a case where a priest is present? [D]" (The objections preceding Amoraic statements are almost all unattributed and provide no evidence that the Amoraim related to the unattributed material, as we have noted on multiple occasions.**) The fact that Rav Pappa was originally quoting Resh Laqish was forgotten over the course of time, and Rav Pappa's statement was presented as if he himself formulated it. As a result, the Stammaim were unable to understand the beginning of his statement, "Learn from this"—learn from what? They therefore added to the end of the objection [D] a kind of response, "Yes, the first clause refers to a case where no priest is present and the final clause to a case where a priest is present [E]," and juxtaposed Rav Pappa's statement "Learn from this" with it, that is, learn from this response. However, in reality this was not the case, and Rav Pappa was responding to the objection [D], which was of Amoraic provenance. Rav Pappa employed Resh Laqish's formulation, who said in Qid 63b, "Learn from this [that in R. Yannai's opinion]...." Indeed, in ms. Munich the response [E] does not appear, although it is possible that it was omitted due to homoioteleuton (from the final words of [D] and [E]), as noted by Rabbinowicz in *Diqduqei soferim* ad loc.[78]

The Stammaitic Era and the Closing (hatimat) of the Talmud

Having demonstrated that the Stammaim postdate the Amoraim,[79] I must now determine [28] the period of their activity and show that the Talmud was not closed at the end of the fifth century or the beginning of the sixth century, at the conclusion of the Amoraic era, as is the traditional view, but rather two centuries [29] thereafter, at the conclusion of the Stammaitic era, in the middle of the eighth century. Although no sources point conclusively to the boundaries of the Stammaitic era, it is possible to demonstrate that Stammaitic material contains several strata that testify to the flourishing of several generations of Stammaim, and it stands to reason that this era ended when they began to write other works and attribute them to individual authors, namely, the middle of the eighth century. Below I will bring an example of multiple Stammaitic strata. However, I should first note that we have almost none of the literature composed by the Geonim between the end of the Amoraic era and the era of books attributed to individual authors, such as *Halakhot pesuqot* or *Halakhot qetsuvot* of Yehudai Gaon, the *She'iltot* of Aha of Shabha Gaon, and the *Halakhot gedolot* of Shimon Qayyara. According to the traditional view one has to say either that no literature was composed throughout this period that lasted for more than two centuries,[80] or that nothing of the spiritual treasures composed by the Geonim were preserved[81]–both implausible scenarios.[82] However, according to my view, this was a very fertile period, except that the sages who flourished throughout this era acted not as individual authors but anonymously, as Stammaim, and they are represented in that way throughout the Talmud. They produced the unattributed reconstructions and explanations that comprise the dialectical argumentation, and in this way they bestowed upon the Talmud its distinctive essence and unique character.

Stammaitic Strata

Here I wish to present the Talmud's treatment of a legal topic in which we find four Stammaitic strata that differ one from another in their awareness of the relevant sources. Several medieval authorities assign the earliest of these layers to Huna Gaon of Sura, that is, to the middle of the seventh century CE. I assume that the new material appears in the later strata of a Talmudic passage and was added to earlier strata; for if not, how did later authorities not know what was known to their predecessors? While it is possible in theory that later generations did not know every tradition of earlier sages, the opposite assumption is most reasonable. If my analysis is correct, then the latter layers of the passage outlined below postdate the middle of the seventh century, the century when Stammaitic activity peaked.

[30] I refer to Qid 3b, a passage that Sherira Gaon attributes to the Saboraim,[83] and that several medieval commentaries attribute to Huna Gaon.[84] This synoptic chart (Table 1.1) will facilitate comparisons between the parallel passages:

Qid 3b, sections [e–f], quote a halakhic midrash: "*a writ of divorce (Deut 24:1)*—a writ effects the divorce and no other method can effect the divorce." This midrash also appears in Qid 5a and in three parallel passages (Suk 23b, Eruv 15b, Git 21b), and follows the view of R. Yose the Galilean [F].[85] The Sages, who disagree with R. Yose the Galilean, interpret the words "*a writ of divorce (keritut)*" differently, namely, "something that completely separates (*koret*) him from her" [G]. The midrash here in Qid 3b (also found in Qid 14a), that a woman cannot be divorced through *halitsah* on the grounds that "a writ effects the divorce.... [f]" also follows the view of R. Yose the Galilean, because in the parallel passages the Sages interpret the verb "*and he writes*" to teach that a woman cannot be divorced by means of money: "*and he writes (Deut 24:1)*—she is divorced by means of writing and she cannot be divorced by money [C–D]"—and the Sages would also derive from this midrash that a woman cannot be divorced through *halitsah*. Now it is illogical that the Talmud at Qid 3b would adopt a minority opinion, the midrash of R. Yose the Galilean [F,f], that opposes the teaching of the Sages [G]. Therefore it seems that Qid 3b is earlier and did not know the parallel passages (Qid 5a, Suk 23b, Eruv 15b, Git 21b) which attribute the midrash "a writ effects the divorce and no other method can effect the divorce" to R. Yose the Galielan and not to the Sages [F]. Qid 3b assumes that the Sages too exclude the possibility of effecting divorce through money or *halitsah* based on the midrash "a writ effects the divorce and no other method can effect the divorce" [f]. But there remains a difficulty: why does Qid 3b prefer the midrash "a writ effects the divorce..." and not invoke the midrash "*and he writes (Deut 24:1)*—she is divorced by means of writing and she cannot be divorced by money" [C–D]? Apparently Qid 3b, unlike the parallels, did not distinguish between the words of Deut 24:1 ("*And he writes her a writ of divorce*") so as to interpret "*and he writes*" independently of "*writ*." Accordingly, the passage considered these two midrashim as equivalent; indeed, this is exactly what we find in the Yerushalmi: "*And he writes her a writ of divorce (Deut 24:1)*—she is permitted [to remarry] by a writ (*get*), and is not permitted by *halitsah*" (yYev 5:1, 6d). Therefore when Qid 3b answers: "Scripture states, *a writ of divorce (Deut 24:1)*—a writ effects the divorce... [f]" it also means to include the adjacent word "*and he writes*."

Table 1.1 Synoptic Chart of Qid 3b and Parallels

Suk 23b, Eruv 15b, Git 21b	Qid 5a	Qid 83b	Qid 3b
[A] What is the reason of R. Yose the Galilean?	[a] . . . [should we say] that just as "becoming" (= betrothal) may be by means of money, so "going" (= divorce) may be through money?		
[B] For it was taught: *A writ (Deut 24:1)*. I know only that a writ (= parchment) [may be used to divorce]. How do I know other things too may be used? It teaches *And he writes (Deut 24:1)*—in any form . . .	[b] Abaye said: Should they say: "Money brings (her in to a marriage) and money brings her out (by effecting divorce)! Then the defender (*sanegor*) has become the prosecutor (*qategor*)?" . . .		
[C] As for the Sages, what do they learn from *and he writes (Deut 24:1)*?	[c] Rava said: The verse states, *and he writes (Deut 24:1)*.		
[D] That is necessary [to teach that]: she is divorced by means of writing, and she cannot be divorced by means of money. . . .	[d] She is divorced by means of writing and she cannot be divorced by means of money.		

(*continued*)

Table 1.1 Continued

Suk 23b, Eruv 15b, Git 21b	Qid 5a	Qid 83b	Qid 3b
[E] As for R. Yose the Galilean, how does he learn this conclusion?	As for R. Yose the Galilean, who employs this word ("*and he writes*") for another purpose—how does he derive that a woman cannot be divorced by means of money?		[e] [The mishnah's specification that a woman attains her independence in *two* ways] excludes *halitsah*.... And if I should say that such is the case (that she can be divorced through *halitsah*)?
[F] He derives it from the words *writ of divorce (Deut 24:1)*—a writ effects the divorce and no other method can effect the divorce.	He derives it from the words *writ of divorce (Deut 24:1)*—a writ effects the divorce and no other method can effect the divorce.		[f] Scripture states, *writ of divorce (Deut 24:1)*—a writ effects the divorce and no other method can effect the divorce.
		[H] R. Eleazar b. Azariah answered and said: [The verse says] *divorce (Deut 24:1)*—"something that completely separates him from her." Thus you learn that this is not separation.	
[G] And the Sages? What do they learn from *writ of divorce*? This is necessary to teach [that a divorce must be] "something that completely separates him from her."	[G] And the Sages? What do they learn from *writ of divorce*? This is necessary to teach [that a divorce must be] "something that completely separates him from her."	[G] And the Sages? What do they learn from [*writ of*] *divorce*? This is necessary to teach [that a divorce must be] "something that completely separates him from her."	

It also appears that the passages parallel to Qid 3b (namely Eruv 15b, Suk 24b, Git 21b) did not know the dispute between Abaye and Rava quoted on Qid 5a over the reason that a woman cannot be divorced by money: Abaye claims this law is a logical inference (*sevara*) [b], while Rava derives it from the midrash "*and he writes (Deut 24:1)*—she is divorced by means of writing and she cannot be divorced by money" [c–d]. These three parallel passages continue the discussion of R. Yose the Galilean's opinion [A], in which it is stated that he derives from the words "*and he writes*" that a writ of divorce can be written on any object, not only upon parchment [B], by asking: "As for the Sages, what do they learn from '*and he writes*'" [C]? They answer, "That is necessary to teach 'she is divorced by means of writing, and she cannot be divorced by means of money'" [D]. However, no question is asked with respect to Abaye—who holds that a logical inference is the reason a woman cannot be divorced by means of money and therefore does not require any midrashic teaching [b]—as to what the Sages learn from "*and he writes.*" Moreover, an objection is brought against R. Yose the Galilean as to how he learns that a woman cannot be divorced by means of money, since he interprets the verse "*and he writes*" for another purpose, such that it cannot be used to exclude divorce through money [E]. However, the Talmud does not answer that R. Yose derives it based on a logical inference as does Abaye [F].[86] It therefore appears that these passages did not know of Abaye's opinion [b]; they knew of Rava's opinion, and asked what the Sages would derive from "*and he writes*" according to Rava. The passage at Qid 5a, on the other hand, which knew of Abaye's opinion, opens with an objection against Rava based on R. Yose the Galilean's view: "As for R. Yose the Galilean, who employs this word ('*and he writes*') for another purpose—how does he derive that a woman cannot be divorced by means of money?" [E]. This passage presumably does not object against the view of the Sages, "what do they learn from '*and he writes*'" [as in C] because it was aware of the passage in Qid 3b, and already knew that Rava would explain that the Sages interpret "*and he writes*" to exclude divorce by means of money, and Abaye would say the Sages interpret it to exclude divorce by means of *halitsah* [f].

Now it is clear that the identical anonymous passages found in Eruv 15b, Suk 24b, and Git 21b result from the routine transposition [31] of material from one location to the others, and should be considered the same sugya. Qid 5a, however, which differs, must postdate these three parallel sugyot, since it knew of Abaye's reasoning which they did not [b], as it was added at a later time. Clearly Qid 5a has been influenced by the passage in Eruv 15b, Suk 24b, and bGit 21b, for if not, how can we explain the great similarity between them [sections D,E,F,G]—such a high degree of correspondence could not have developed independently. Yet Qid 3b precedes them all, since it does not know of the dispute between R. Yose the Galilean and the Sages regarding the exegetical basis for the exclusion of divorce by means of money (and *halitsah*) [A–D]. And Git 83b postdates them all, as it transfers only the final section from the three parallel passages (also found in Qid 5a), namely, "and the Sages—what do they learn from *[writ of] divorce (Deut 24:1)*?" [G]. However, the composers of this passage in Git 83b did not realize that this section does not fit the context. For "the Sages" mentioned there include R. Yose the Galilean (since they disagree with R. Eleazar b. Azariah in [H]), while in the parallel passages R. Yose the Galilean disagrees with "the Sages," as pointed out by the medieval commentaries.

If this analysis is correct, then the Stammaim who composed the passage in Qid 3b (the passage attributed to Huna Gaon, who flourished in the middle of the seventh century CE) were the earliest. The Stammaim responsible for the passages in Eruv 15b, Suk 24b, and Git 21b postdated them, still later Stammaim produced Qid 5a, and the latest Git 83b. All this testifies to intensive activity of the Stammaim in the period that postdates Huna Gaon.

Moreover, we find sugyot that do not contradict each other outright but exhibit disparate tendencies, a sign that they were not composed by the same hands. Let us mention the tendency to prefer a legal act (= precedent)—"an act is weighty (*ma'aseh rav*)" or "an act is preferable (*ma'aseh adif*)." Apparently different passages contradict as to whether Abaye takes into account the principle "an act is weighty" (Shab 21a, 126b; BB 83a).[87] Another example: in a single passage the Stammaim respond to R. Yitshaq's inquiry, "Why do we sound a sustained blast [of the Shofar] on Rosh HaShana?" with the question: "Why do we sound a sustained blast [of the Shofar]? The Merciful One said 'Sound a sustained blast [of the Shofar]?!'" (RH 16a). The Stammaim thus assume that the Torah's commandments need no justification, whereas R. Yitshaq believes that they too require a reason. Most likely, these two views reflect different historical eras. Originally both the Tannaim and Amoraim believed that Scripture too required justification. Therefore R. Akiba asks, "For what [reason] does the Torah say to bring the grain offering on Passover?," "For what [reason] does the Torah say to bring the two loaves on Shavuot?," "For what [reason] does the Torah say to pour the water libation on Sukkot?"

(RH 16a, tRH 1:12, tSuk 3:13). Similarly, Rabbah asks: "[For what reason] does the Torah say that, 'One who admits to part of a claim must take an oath'?" (BM 3a). Later, however, in the time of the Stammaim, they no longer thought that Scripture required a reason. Now the Stammaim actually ask that question of R. Yitshaq but do not ask similar questions of the other Amoraic dicta on the same folio of Talmud (RH 16a). While it is possible to distinguish between the dicta, namely, as to why it is appropriate to ask of R. Yitshaq but not of the others, it seems more likely to me that the two halves of the sugya do not come from the same source.[88]

Inasmuch as I touched upon the topic of whether Scriptural commandments require reasons, I will discuss a related issue, that of "interpreting the reason for the verse (*darish ta'ama deqra*)," both on account of its intrinsic significance and also because it demonstrates the late dating of the Stammaim and how their thought processes differed from those of the Amoraim. In ten [32] passages the Talmud, either implicitly or explicitly, invokes the disagreement between R. Yehudah and R. Shimon over interpreting the reasons for verses. The Talmud's source for this disagreement is a baraita about whether one may take a pledge from a wealthy widow. R. Shimon rules that one is permitted to take such a pledge because he interprets the reason for the verse *You shall not take a widow's garment in pledge (Deut 24:17)* as "you must return it to her (in the evening) and thus you will bring her into disrepute among her neighbors" (BM 115a).[89] This reason does not apply to a wealthy widow, as one need not return the pledge every evening. R. Yehudah, who does not interpret the reason for verses, does not distinguish between a wealthy and a poor widow. The Talmud therefore takes the view that all sources seeking the reason for Scriptural commandments should be attributed to R. Shimon (e.g., Yom 42b, Sot 8a, Sanh 16b); for R. Yehudah there is no reason for divine laws. Similarly, the Talmud assumes that whenever a verse provides its own reason, R. Shimon considers that reason superfluous: because we "interpret the reason for the verse," we can derive the reason ourselves, hence its explicit appearance in the verse must be for another exegetical purpose (see Qid 68b and Rashi, ad loc., BM 115a, Sanh 21a).

Yet the baraita of BM 115a offers no proof that R. Yehudah does not "interpret the reason for the verse" or rejects attributing reasons to the dictates of the Torah. Above we noted that R. Akiba and Rabbah—and we could add other sages—"interpret the reason for the verse," and it is implausible to claim that they all side with R. Shimon. Here R. Yehudah in fact disagrees with R. Shimon about returning the pledge of the wealthy widow not because he rejects "interpreting the reason for the verse" in principle, but because he assumes a different reason for this law that applies to poor and wealthy widows alike. It has been noted that Maimonides, in his *Commentary to the Mishnah*, provides two reasons for the prohibition against taking a widow's garment in pledge, the one found in the baraita about bringing her into disrepute among her neighbors, and another relating to "lewdness." The second reason apparently is provided for R. Yehudah,[90] namely [33], that the widow and the lender will bargain about the pledge, and even if he does not return it to her each evening, their interaction will lead to "lewdness," to suspicion of intimacy. Similarly, the reasons given for commandments in Yom 42b, Sot 8a ("so that she not become defiant on account of the other"), and Sanh 16b ("lest the gentiles come and destroy [the whole land]") are accepted by R. Yehudah.** Moreover, I doubt whether R. Shimon actually holds that every reason provided in the Torah is superfluous on the grounds that we could determine the reason ourselves; there are various types of reasons, and I will return to this issue elsewhere.

These considerations lead me to conclude that the resolution of the passage in Git 49b, "[the teacher of the baraita] is R. Shimon who interprets the reason for the verse," is not part of Ravina's original statement there. Likewise in Men 2b the phrase, "for it is R. Shimon who interprets the reason for the verse," was not stated by Rabbah. Both phrases were added to the Amoraic dicta by the Stammaim and accord with their view that Scripture needs no reason. The Stammaim understand R. Yehudah to share this perspective (whereas the opposite can be said of Maimonides: because his philosophical worldview assumes that Scripture has reasons, he attributes to R. Yehudah too a reason why pledges may not be taken from widows). This shift in mentality between the Stammaim and their predecessors indicates that the Stammaim are later, as such differences in thought processes would not take place within a brief time span.

There are also cases of a passage with multiple strata devolving from different times which is identical to a passage in another tractate. Clearly the passage was transferred from one tractate to the other, since it is impossible that two sages would independently formulate the same content and language for a passage that extends over an entire Talmud folio. An example is the passage found in BQ 15a and Ket 41a. The passage undoubtedly is original to Bava Qamma:[91] not only does the issue of half-damages belong there, but the passage begins by analyzing a mishnah in Bava Qamma and only then proceeds to discuss a mishnah in Ketubot.

The passage begins with a dispute between Rav Pappa and Rav Huna b. Rav Yehoshua, continues with unattributed dialectical argumentation, and then concludes by rejecting the opinion that the standard of "half-damages" is a fine *(qenasa)*. This concluded the original Stammaitic passage. At this point a concluding line was added: "and the law is (*vehilkheta*) that half-damages is a fine." This anonymous "law," as is well known, is late; some such "laws" were borrowed from the *Halakhot gedolot*. But then the Talmud continues with an objection: "[First] a rejection [against the opinion] and [then] a law [in its favor]'?" The objection is then answered and the passage continues with some apodictic laws (similar in form to those introduced by "and the law is [*vehilkheta*]"), in the style of the *She'iltot*, and atypical of the Stammaim. It seems that this passage was composed over a lengthy period of time. Initially there was believed to be an objection against the opinion that "half-damages is a fine." Later sages retracted the objection; and after the retraction ("now that you have said that 'half-damages is a fine'") still later authorities—exactly when is unknown—added apodictic laws, such as "if a dog devours lambs . . ." that continue to the end of the passage. At all events, a portion of this passage was added after the Stammaitic era.

Perhaps the finest example of anonymous passages that originated in different periods is the rare case of Sanh 36b. The two Stammaitic strata there each had a different version of mSanh 4:1–2, and yet neither knew that two different versions of the mishnah existed. The mishnah reads:

[A] [mSanh 4:1] . . . In what do monetary cases differ from capital cases?
[B] (1) Monetary cases [are decided by] three judges and capital cases by twenty-three.
[C] (2) . . . (3) . . . (8) . . .
[D] [mSanh 4:2] <In monetary > Cases of impurities and purities they begin with the eldest [judge]; in capital cases they begin from the side.
[E] (9) All are fit to judge monetary cases, and not all are fit to judge capital cases, but only priests, Levites and Israelites that may marry with priestly families.

The Talmudic passage begins: "R. Abbahu said: In ten ways do monetary cases and capital cases differ." The Stammaim then object, "Ten—behold there are nine?," and answer, "There is another, as was taught: 'They do not appoint to the Sanhedrin an elderly man, a eunuch, or a man without children.'" That is, R. Abbahu is not commenting on mSanh 4:1–2, as the mishnah lists only nine ways. Rather, he states the total number of ways that capital cases differ from monetary cases. This is a straightforward and reasonable explanation of R. Abbahu's statement. Yet to this anonymous objection still later Stammaim object, "Behold, it [the mishnah] teaches ten!" that is, how could it be said: "behold there are nine?" And they respond, "Because 'not all are fit to judge capital cases' [E] and '[capital cases by] twenty-three' [B] are one.'" This answer is not satisfying, as it is forced to explain that these two disparate issues "are one" and the same (see the medieval commentaries).[92]

At first I thought—as I wrote in the Introduction to *MM: seder nashim* (19 n. 32)—that whether "there are nine" or "there are ten" depends on the different textual versions of the mishnah: if one includes "in monetary cases" (or just "monetary") before "cases of impurity and purity" in mSanh 4:2 [D, the angled brackets,] as found in our printings of the Mishnah (and the same reading appears in a Yemenite manuscript), then mSanh 4:1–2 contains ten differences between monetary cases and capital cases. If one does not include these words, as found in the Naples printing, then mSanh 4:1–2 contain only nine differences, as that difference as to which judge states his opinion first [D] applies to cases of purity and impurity, not to monetary cases. The version lacking those words was apparently that of the earlier Stammaim, who accordingly objected to R. Abbahu, "Behold, there are nine?" R. Abbahu, however, had the reading of our present editions of mSanh 4:2, which include "monetary," and therefore stated that "In ten ways do monetary cases differ from capital cases." This was also the version of the later Stammaim, who were puzzled by the objection of the earlier Stammaim. Thus the earlier Stammaim did not know that R. Abbahu's version of mSanh 4:2 was that of our current editions, while the latter Stammaim did not know that the version of mSanh 4:2 of the earlier Stammaim was that of the Naples printing and other such witnesses.

However, I subsequently realized that without mention of the words "monetary cases" or "monetary" at the outset of mSanh 4:2 [D] it is inappropriate to discuss "cases of impurity and purity"; for the subject of mSanh 4:1–2 is: "In what do monetary cases differ from capital cases [A]," and if "monetary cases" is not stated first, then the laws of cases of impurity and purity are unrelated to the topic. If so, then one cannot accept the reading of the Naples printing and cannot explain the confusion between nine and ten on that basis. Nevertheless, there undoubtedly existed two versions of this mishnah: one that listed nine differences and one that listed ten. This is because the Talmud explicitly states "nine" and "ten," even if it is not clear which clause was lacking in the version that contained nine differences. The same conclusion emerges from the Yerushalmi, which comments: "We taught nine"—implying that some sages taught ten (ySanh 4:2, 22b). Thus it appears that R. Abbahu's version of the mishnah contained ten differences, whereas the earlier Stammaim only knew the version that listed nine; they therefore objected to R. Abbahu and provided a reasonable response. The latter Stammaim, however, were unaware of a version of this mishnah with but nine differences, and were therefore forced to explain that "'not all are fit to judge capital cases' [E] and '[capital cases by] twenty three' [B] are one." A passage such as this could not develop unless the earlier Stammaim postdated R. Abbahu, and the latter Stammaim lived long after the earlier Stammaim, after the existence of different versions of this mishnah had been forgotten.

I have discussed the issue of different—and even contradictory—Stammaitic strata at length in order to illustrate the comprehensive and intensive activity of the Stammaim, and to demonstrate that their activity continued for hundreds of years after the Amoraim. Stammaitic teaching is not all of one cloth—their origins are diverse and they had access to many sources. Some differences developed over the course of time, and some differences were there from the beginning on account of their disparate origins, and over the years different approaches also emerged. The vast time span is not only responsible, in some cases, for causing the different versions of the Mishnah, baraitot, and Amoraic dicta [35] to be forgotten such that the Stammaim had to resort to forced explanations in order to understand them, but also for the fact that later Stammaim sometimes were not well acquainted with the explanations of the earlier Stammaim, and therefore struggled to make sense of them.[93]

Let me also add that contemporary scholars of the Yerushalmi have demonstrated conclusively[94] that the Bavli did not know the Yerushalmi. But if Rav Ashi and his academy were the editors of the Bavli, and if they lived after the closing (*hatimah*) of the Yerushalmi[95] at a time when we can assume that sages "traveled up and down [from Babylonia to Israel]"—how is it possible that they were not influenced by the Yerushalmi and did not know it? However, according to my view that the Bavli came to a close in the Stammaitic era more than 300 years after the closing of the Yerushalmi, it is not surprising that the Bavli did not know the Yerushalmi, since some Geonim and medieval jurists knew almost nothing of it. Yet these arguments are tentative, and I concede that, based on the same logic, the earlier observation that Sherira Gaon and his successors knew nothing of the Stammaim or at least do not mention them would raise some doubt about the relatively late dating of the end of the Stammaitic period and also of the closing of the Talmud to approximately 150 years before Sherira Gaon (c. 900–1000 CE).

The evidence for the late dating of the Stammaim—evidence scattered throughout the entire Talmud—is diverse, direct, and of different types. Some of it was presented above and some will be presented below. But evidence for the dating of the end of the Stammaitic period derives exclusively from passages comprised of multiple strata of Stammaitic material that accrued over the course of several generations,[96] and its precise date cannot be known. I consider the second half of the eighth century CE as the most likely date. It should also be noted that the medieval commentaries were aware of the existence of multiple Stammaitic strata that derive from different times. R. Zerahia Halevi (1125–1186), author of the *Sefer hamaor,* comments on a baraita of the form "there is a teaching that accords with him (*tanya kevateih*)" that follows a "refutation (*tiuvta*)": "This was an extraneous tradition that the Saboraim discovered after the closing of the Talmud, and they included it in the Talmud" (commentary to Alfasi, *Pesahim,* #771). Concerning the term "and the law is (*vehilkheta*)" that follows a refutation (*tiuvta*), as found in Eruv 11a, Eruv 16b, Ket 41b and BQ 15b, Abraham b. Nahmanides writes: "Earlier sages did not know this response and concluded the passage with a refutation; subsequently, later authorities came up with a response, but they did not want to reject the conclusion of the earlier sages" (Bets 25a, quoting Tosafot; also noted by Nahmanides to Nid 45a). The same could be said of "if you prefer, I will say (*i ba'eit eima*)" following a refutation (Shab 20b, Git 28a, Zev 85a) and of "shall we say that [the Amoraic dispute] is like the [dispute among] Tannaim (*leima ketana'ei*)" following a refutation (Git 53b, Sanh 27a, Tem 25b). That which follows the refutation is much (generations?) later than the refutation, since they were no longer able to remove the refutation from the Talmud. The same applies to the case of "resolve it as we taught initially. And if you prefer, I will say..." (BB 110b). The response, "And if you prefer, I will say..." was added after the "resolve it as we taught initially..." had been fixed in the Talmud.[97] All these examples illustrate the existence of later strata; nevertheless, the precise date of the end of the Stammaitic period remains a matter of conjecture.

Having summarized my conclusions, I will now devote a few words to my methodology. My fundamental assumption is that there are forced explanations scattered throughout the Talmud, but that these should not be accepted [36], and other explanations should be found. (I described the nature and definition of forced explanations in the Introduction to *MM*: *seder nashim*.) Forced explanations derive from the fact that the interpreter did not have access to the sources in their entirety, or did not know the correct textual version, or lacked the original sources—and he had no choice but to resort to a forced explanation to complete that which was missing; had he possessed the original sources, he would not have offered a forced explanation. Why did he not have access to the original sources? Because the interpreter lived many years after the sage whose dictum he was explaining. These sources consisted of anonymous explanations, mostly dialectical argumentation, which were not handed down as part of the official transmission of tradition; therefore the sages knew only that which happened to be remembered. Over the course of time the dialectical argumentation became tainted with both additions and omissions, and later sages reconstructed it by conjecture, and often they could do no better than to offer a forced explanation. Methodologically, it is critical to distinguish the teachings of the Stammaim from those of named Amoraim, whose teachings appear in apodictic form, typically fixed laws, and were handed down in the official transmission.[98] Similarly, it is important to determine exactly what sources lay before each interpreter, for only in that way can we understand why he gave a forced explanation of the passage.[99]

I also assume that the Talmud contains many contradictions, as the medieval commentators sensed. These contradictions devolve from the fact that the Stammaim drew from various rabbinic academies, which apparently pursued their studies independently. The Talmud had no general editor to reconcile the sources and harmonize the contradictions between them; they remained in their extant states and were included in the Talmud by the Compilers. These Compilers flourished at the end of the Stammaitic period, after the commencement of the Saboraic age, when the Talmud was closed to dialectical argumentation and to the continued development of sugyot, and therefore it was impossible to remove the contradictions and inconsistencies. Brief explanations, however, never ceased entering the Talmud even after the Saboraic age, as evidenced by the variant readings attested in our manuscripts. Differences between variant readings are sometimes due to the fact that one manuscript includes a brief explanation, while another omits it, which indicates that the explanation derives from a relatively late time. These observations have significant implications regarding the formation of the Talmud; above all they demonstrate that Rav Ashi was not the editor of the Talmud and that the anonymous stratum reached completion hundreds of years after the Amoraic era,[100] in the middle of the eighth century CE—and not, as per the traditional view, in the middle of the fifth or the beginning of the sixth century CE. Indeed, in my opinion there never was a general editing of the Talmud.

In general I recommend that a sugya be analyzed in five stages:

First stage: Study the sugya with the medieval commentaries and selected later Talmudic commentaries (*aharonim*)—each tractate has a different selection of later Talmudic commentators whose commentaries are important.

Second stage: Then examine the text being explained by the Talmud (a mishnah, baraita, or Amoraic dictum) to see whether the Talmud's explanation fits the language of the text without being forced, that is, without adding or removing any words.

Third stage: If the Talmud's explanation fits the text—there is no explanatory problem. However, if the Talmud's explanation does not fit the language of the text, then one must determine whether the Talmud's explanation indeed [37] raises a real question that requires a response. By this I mean to exclude non-serious questions of the "scriptural support *(asmakhta)*" type,** as well as rhetorical questions whose goal is to clarify structural matters or provide some elucidation unrelated to the legal issue, the form of the clarification being that of a question and answer.

Fourth stage: If the difficulty is indeed a serious question deserving an answer, then one must examine the parallels to the passage to see if the version of the text (*girsa*) is accurate; one must check mishnah citations found in other sources; check parallels to a baraita in the halakhic midrashim and in the Tosefta; compare Amoraic dicta in other passages in the Bavli or Yerushalmi.

Fifth stage: If we find that the text is correct and yet the Bavli's explanation seems forced, then we must assess the reasoning that led the interpreter to offer the explanation in case the cause resulted from historical factors or from the lack of the requisite information.

This method of analysis differs from the traditional approach in two respects. Traditional methods of study attempt to eliminate the difficulty such that the text appears clear-cut, straightforward, and unproblematic. The critical method, on the other hand, emphasizes the difficulty and makes no attempt to remove it; rather, the critical method accounts for the source and cause of the difficulty. Whereas the traditional method is oriented "forward" and adds to the received text, the critical method looks "backward" and attempts to understand the sources of the text's development.

Opposition to the critical method in certain circles possibly stems from the discomfort at recognizing difficulties in the text and resolving the problems based on historical or philological considerations. The same perspective should have led to opposition to the assessment of manuscript variants too, as perforce only one reading can be correct. And in fact, were it not that the medieval commentaries including Rashi routinely observe, "our texts read. . . . ," this opposition would have extended to consideration of variant readings too.

Concerning variant readings, however, we should apply the principle "both these and those are the words of the living God."** Just as we do not think of the House of Shammai or Abaye as mistaken in cases where the law does not accord with their views, so too variant readings and forced explanations should not be considered errors but rather attempts to find the truth.

Early Anonymous Passages

The claim that the Stammaim are late does not entail that *every* (emphasis on *every*) anonymous (*setam*) passage is not of Amoraic provenance, nor should historical conclusions be derived on this basis. I have already explained that the dialectical argumentation of the Amoraim was not transmitted as part of the official transmission nor preserved for future sages. Rather, parts of it happened to be remembered by the sages who heard it, and these were transmitted to future generations without being verified or updated. Now the more distant the memory of the tradition is from its source, the more its accuracy is open to question. After the Amoraic period the Stammaim verified and corrected whatever remained in their collective memory, and they meticulously filled in whatever was missing. Clearly some materials of Amoraic provenance remained, but the attributions were lost, rendering them anonymous in form (*setam*). It seems that anonymous statements that successfully reconstruct Amoraic memories precisely as they had existed in Amoraic times are early, even though their formulation and style derive from the Stammaim [38].

How does one identify early unattributed traditions? How does one distinguish later from earlier anonymous material?

Here I am not dealing with older traditions transmitted without attribution, brief narratives and praises that glorify the Amoraim, akin to stories, which are commonly found throughout the Talmud. Nor do I refer to anonymous comments that an Amoraic dictum "was not said explicitly but on the basis of an inference (*lav befeirush itmar ela mikelala itmar*)." A tradition of this type, which contradicts an attributed statement, even though it is formulated anonymously, undoubtedly dates to the same time as the tradent or shortly thereafter. (In the case of unattributed stories, some are contemporaneous with the protagonists, and some are from a short time later.) I deal here with explanations and statements resembling explanations that appear in the Talmud without attribution, whose origins antedate the Stammaitic period. How can these be detected? Let me point out some of the external indications by which one can identify unattributed traditions that originate in, and perhaps even antedate, the Amoraic period. These indications in and of themselves are not an absolute guarantee, and in most cases there are also additional reasons that emerge from analysis of the passage itself supporting the early dating for the unattributed traditions. A combination of external markers and internal evidence from the passage provides a firm foundation for the early dating. I will list the indications and divide them into different categories. I will also distinguish those whose early dating is evident, or almost evident, based on a straightforward reading of the Talmud itself, from those whose early dating can only be recognized by analysis of, and inferences from, the passage. Whether these early anonymous statements are evident or discerned by inference, their existence cannot be doubted.

External Signs of Unattributed Statements

(A) "And Some State It Anonymously (*ve'amri lah kedi*)"

In about fifteen places the Talmud states, "R. So-and-so said, and some state it anonymously (*kedi*)," that is, some sages transmit the statement in the name of an Amora, and some say an unknown Amora made the statement; in other words, they transmit it without attribution.[101] This expression appears both in connection with the earlier Amoraim such as R. Yehoshua b. Levi (Hor 8a), and in connection with the latter Amoraim, such as Rav Pappa (BM 2a, and commonly with Rava). Statistically speaking, it is clear that many names of the tradents of dicta would have been forgotten over the course of time, and these dicta were thereafter transmitted anonymously, without attribution. The number of such anonymous traditions in the Talmud certainly exceeds the fifteen instances in which there were conflicting traditions as to whether the tradent of the dictum was an Amora or an anonymous sage (*stammai*). If we assume that in these fifteen instances the attribution to the Amora is correct, then the alternative tradition forgot the name and transmitted the early material anonymously. Presumably phenomena of this type were more widespread, namely, that the name of the Amora was forgotten and yet the Talmud does not say explicitly "and some state it anonymously." In other words, names of tradents were forgotten not only in cases where we have a disagreement and one line of tradition transmits the source with attribution and a second line transmits it anonymously, but it is also possible that the tradent's name was forgotten in cases where we only have an unattributed source. (I have noted elsewhere that the difference in manuscript variants between an Amoraic attribution and the lack of attribution is more commonly found with Abaye than other Amoraim, for which I have no explanation.)[102] In these cases too the style and formulation derive from the Stammaim, who molded the dictum and integrated it into the larger context. [39]

At first glance it would seem that cases where the dictum is attributed to an Amora in one passage and appears unattributed in another passage are also types of this phenomenon, and could be described with the term, "and some state it anonymously." For example, a dictum attributed to Rabbah in Eruv 38b appears without attribution in Bets 4a; a dictum attributed to Rav Pappa in Suk 50b–51a appears without attribution in Arakh 11a; a dictum attributed to Rav in Ket 84a appears without attribution in Bekh 52b.[103] These cases are similar to those introduced by the expression "and some state it anonymously," except that the difference in attribution appears in two different passages, whereas the cases of "and some state it anonymously" are mentioned in a single passage. However, the phenomena are similar only if the two dicta share identical content; but if the content is not identical, then the Stammaim transferred the content of an attributed dictum, but they did not mention the tradent in the second passage because they were modifying the dictum for a different purpose. And even if the content is in fact identical in two passages, it is possible that the Stammaim originally added some words to the attributed dictum, and therefore they omitted the name in the second passage; and still later, after the closing of the Talmud, the words added by the Stammaim were transposed back to the attributed dictum such that they now appear to be identical, even though that was not the case originally (see "Transposers and Types of Transpositions" in Part IV). Thus it is possible in the aforementioned case of Suk 50b–51a that Rav Pappa's original dictum consisted only of "[This dispute is] similar to a Tannaitic dispute (*ketana'ei*)," up to the word "and do you really think so (*vetisbera*)," and he was responding to Rav Yosef's claim that R. Yose b. R. Yehudah and the sages disputed whether the essence of the [Levite] music was singing or musical instruments. The remainder of the dictum, from "and do you really think so" to the end, was not stated by Rav Pappa but was transferred there from Arakh 11a (where it refers to the mishnah), and derives from the Stammaim.**

Let me add that two other types of seemingly parallel passages, one attributed and the other anonymous, where the content is not identical, provide no evidence that the Amora quotes an earlier anonymous dictum: instances of Amoraim stating "as we taught" and "as we rejected" in reference to an anonymous teaching quoted earlier in the passage.** In such cases the Amoraim originally could have articulated the teachings and rejections themselves, and later the Stammaim rearranged the presentation of the traditions to make for a more logical order, and then sufficed with placing abbreviated references "as we taught," "as we rejected" in the mouths of the Amoraim (and Rasha"l [Solomon Luria] says as much in his comments to Hul 76b). The phrasing indicates that this is indeed the case, for if the Amoraim were referring to anonymous traditions appearing earlier in the passage, they would have said, "as *they* taught," "as *they* rejected." The forms "as *we* taught," and "as *we* rejected" imply that the Amoraim themselves were the ones who taught and rejected. In sum, a teaching attributed to an Amora in one passage but appearing anonymously and without attribution elsewhere does not conclusively demonstrate that the anonymous passage is of Amoraic or post-Amoraic provenance.[104] [40]

(B) "The Master Stated (*amar mar*)"

In several passages the Talmud introduces a dictum with the term "the master stated" (or "did the master state?," "as the master stated," and suchlike), and although this is a type of anonymous formulation, elsewhere the dictum is attributed directly to an Amora. See, for example, Ket 19a: "As the master stated: Nothing takes precedence over the saving of a life..."

This dictum is attributed to R. Yohanan in the name of R. Shimon b. Yehotsadaq in Sanh 74a, while in Ket 19a it is anonymous, without the attributions. It seems that the dictum appears without attribution in Ket 19a because it is not quoted in its entirety; the Amora stated more than is quoted in Ket 19a, and therefore it was not considered appropriate to attribute to him a briefer form of the dictum. A fine example of this phenomenon appears in Mak 9b: "But behold, they did not warn him! The teacher of this mishnah is R. Yose b. R. Yehudah..." In Mak 6b Rav Pappa asked this very question of Abaye, and Abaye answered him; but because their interchange is abbreviated in Mak 9b, their names were omitted.[105]

(C) Combination of Different Opinions into a Dispute

In some Talmudic passages the Amoraim quote a dispute with the phrase "according to the one who said (*leman de'amar*)." By their time the disparate opinions had been combined into a dispute, even though originally the disputants did not disagree with one another face-to-face. There are some cases where the disputants indeed disagreed face-to-face, and such phrases as "R. So-and-so explained it in accord with R. So-and-so's view" testify to this fact.** However, in most cases it is more reasonable to assume than an anonymous student heard the different opinions from the Amoraim and subsequently combined them and formulated them as a dispute. In some cases they later forgot who said what, so the Stammaim transmitted the dispute in the form "one said x and the other said y."[106] This form is also attested among the Amoraim. A good example appears in Shab 52a: "R. Yirmiah b. Abba (the earlier sage of this name, the student of Rav and Shmuel) said: Rav and Shmuel disagree: One said...and the other said.... Rav Yosef said: You can conclude that Shmuel was the one who said...Abaye said to him: The opposite! You can conclude..." [41]. Already in the first generation after Rav and Shmuel (the time of R. Yirmiah b. Abba, and certainly before the time of Rav Yosef, in the second Amoraic generation), they had combined the different opinions into dispute form, and they already no longer recalled who said what. Who is responsible for this? Who combined the conflicting opinions into one tradition? We do not know. They were combined by an anonymous sage who did not connect his name to this activity. Elsewhere I referred to them as "anonymous combiners (*hastammaim hametsarfim*)"; they combined conflicting opinions into disputes, and concurring opinions into one united view, "the two of them said (*amri tarvaihu*)."[107] Perhaps for this reason Amoraim subsequently did not hesitate to claim "they do not disagree" in order to break apart the combination of the opinions into a single view. (The term "they do not disagree" is generally Amoraic, although it is Stammaitic when it precedes the phrase "the one master [rules] according to his place and the other master [rules] according to his place.") The Amoraim knew, or at least suspected, that the (purported) disputants themselves had not formulated their opinions as a dispute, hence the dispute form was unreliable and could be changed.

It should be noted that these "combiners" were not completely passive. They did more than simply combine two conflicting opinions into a dispute; they actually influenced the formulation of the dicta themselves. A number of times in the Talmud we find that the combiners arranged the Amoraic disputes in the atypical order. For example, they put Resh Laqish before R. Yohanan and truncate R. Yohanan's statement, omitting that which was already articulated by Resh Laqish (see Qid 79b, Sanh 15b and 16b)—the same way the Mishnah and baraitot formulate traditions as, for example, "...and R. So-and-so exempts." R. So-and-so originally said more than "exempt," but they omitted from his words what was already stated in the first opinion. The combiners employed this atypical arrangement because in these cases Resh Laqish limits the scope of the mishnah or baraitot and explains, for example, "they only taught this in a case of...," "[the source] applies only...," and suchlike, whereas R. Yohanan expands the scope of the ruling and states "even [in the case of]..." and suchlike; the combiners formulated the tradition with the limitation preceding the expansion.[108] The addition of the word "even (*af*)" creates the impression that R. Yohanan was aware of Resh Laqish's limitation and glossed his statement, although this is unlikely because of their relative ages, as R. Yohanan was senior to Resh Laqish.

[The same phenomenon is sometimes found in the Mishnah and among baraitot, where the editor combined different sources and added to the second opinion the word "even."[109] Let me quote one example from mGit 5:1: "Damages are paid from [42] land of the best quality, and a creditor from medium quality, and a woman's marriage contract from the lowest quality. R. Meir says: Even (*af*) a woman's marriage contract [is paid] from medium quality." In contrast, there is a baraita that reads: "A woman's marriage contract [is paid from land of] the lowest quality, these are the words of R. Yehudah. R. Meir says: From medium quality." The editor of the Mishnah, who combined the law "a creditor from medium quality" with the ruling of R. Yehudah that the marriage contract is paid from the lowest quality, then added the word "even" to R. Meir's statement that a marriage contract is paid from medium quality (as found in the baraita)—as if R. Meir was aware of R. Yehudah's ruling that the marriage contract is paid from land of the lowest quality.**]

However, later sages sometimes question (with the technical term, "it was asked of him [*ibaya lahu*])" whether R. Yohanan intended to limit the ruling like Resh Laqish, and their uncertainty indicates that they failed to discern that this dispute was formulated so as to mention the expansion before the limitation. If R. Yohanan had meant to limit the ruling, he ought to have been mentioned before Resh Laqish. I refer to Sanh 24b, where the Talmud deals with the dispute in mSanh 3:2 between R. Meir and the Sages as to whether a litigant who states "I trust my father [to serve as a judge]" can retract or not. The Talmud begins with Resh Laqish, who states that the dispute applies "Before the verdict has been issued. But after the verdict has been issued, they [R. Meir and the Sages] agree that he may not retract. And R. Yohanan said: The dispute is after the verdict has been issued." The Talmud then continues: "It was asked of him: [Does R. Yohanan hold that] the disagreement [between R. Meir and the Sages] is only after the verdict has been issued, but before the verdict has been issued they both agree that he cannot retract? Or perhaps [R. Yohanan holds that] they [R. Meir and the Sages] disagree in both cases [both before and after the verdict has been issued.]" However, had R. Yohanan meant that R. Meir and the Sages disagree only after the verdict has been issued, then he too would have limited the mishnah accordingly, and there would have been no reason to mention his opinion after that of Resh Laqish.[110]** A similar analysis can be applied to AZ 68a, where the Talmud first quotes the opinion of Ulla: "Ulla says: They [R. Meir and R. Shimon] disagree in a case where the mixture is [first] improved [by the addition of a forbidden substance] and then is worsened. But where it is [first] worsened and then improved, they [R. Meir and R. Shimon] agree that it is permitted. And R. Yohanan says: they disagree in the case where it was first worsened." The Talmud continues: "It was asked of him: Does he [R. Yohanan] hold that the disagreement [of R. Meir and R. Shimon] is in the case 'where it was first worsened and then improved' but in the case 'where it was first improved and then worsened' they [R. Meir and R. Shimon] agree that it is forbidden. Or perhaps in both cases [R. Yohanan holds that] they disagree?" Here too this question is problematic, for if R. Yohanan held that the disagreement was only in the case "where it was first worsened and then improved," then he too limits the disagreement, and there is no reason to first quote the opinion of his student Ulla.[111] We have to conclude that the sages who queried, "it was asked of him" lived hundreds of years after the "combiners" and were no longer aware of their conventions in presenting disputes. This too is evidence that Rav Ashi and Ravina were not the editors of the Talmud, as they certainly would have been aware of the conventions of the combiners and would have resolved the query.

In passing let me note that, if R. Yohanan held that "they disagree in both cases" in these passages (Sanh 24b and AZ 68a), why do they directly attribute to him only the case of "after the verdict has been issued" in bSanh 24b—"R. Yohanan said: the dispute is after the verdict has been issued"; and in AZ 68a only the case of "where it was first worsened"—"R. Yohanan said: they disagree in the case where it was first worsened." The reason must be that the sages who queried "it was asked of him" held that one could explain the expressions "after the verdict has been issued" and "where it was first worsened" as if they included the word "even" (i.e, "even after the verdict has been issued"; "even where it was first worsened"), as found numerous times in the Talmud. [43]

Internal Markers of Anonymous Dicta

(A) Brief Explanations (*nimuq qal*)

A brief explanation added to a mishnah, baraita, or dictum of an early Amora probably accompanied the text from the beginning and is contemporaneous with the text. For example, "'[The father] is entitled to anything she (= the daughter) finds [mKet 4:4]'—because of [i.e., to avoid] resentment" (Ket 46b–47a). The comment "because of resentment" is not necessarily Stammaitic; it is possibly Tannaitic and was transmitted together with the mishnah. Even reasoning in Aramaic is arguably early. See, for example, Shab 147b: "One does not go upon a wrestling ground [on the Sabbath]... What is the reason? On account of sinking [into the clay]"; and so too Sanh 25a, "'Pigeon-trainers' [mSanh 3:3]... It has been explained as [one who says,] 'If your pigeon bests mine [in a race].'" This is not a Stammaitic gloss but an explanation that accompanied that mishnah. The Mishnah was always studied with the justifications for its rulings (in Hebrew or Aramaic), and for this reason the Talmud refers to this explanation in Sanh 25a as "according to the one who explains (*leman de'amar*) [the mishnah in this way]" (Sanh 25a). However, the Talmud would not refer to a Stammaitic interpretation in this way. Therefore when Rav

Nahman (BQ 116b) and R. Shimon b. Elyaqim (BQ 117b) say of mBQ 10:5: "We interpreted it [as a case] where he showed [the field to the thieves]," they are not referring to the Stammaitic question about the mishnah, "How should this be understood?... (BQ 116b)," and answer "[This is a case] where he showed [the field to the thieves]"; rather these Amoraim refer to the brief explanation of the ruling that accompanied the teaching of the Mishnah even in Tannaitic times. It is possible that the verb "we interpreted (*ve'okimna*)" was not stated by these Amoraim but derives from the Stammaim who placed the anecdotes about the Amoraim after the explanation of the mishnah, integrating these anecdotes with their explanation. Indeed, in both of these places ms. Hamburg reads "We hold (*veqayma lan*)" in place of "We interpreted."[112]

(B) Questions Preceding Amoraic Responses

The content of the questions and objections that precede the responses and solutions of the Amoraim is entirely or partially Amoraic, even if the style and formulation are Stammaitic. And the Amoraim indeed relate to this content in their responses and answers. There are, however, exceptions, when the Stammaim lacked a tradition about the question or objection and had to infer it themselves, as the medieval commentaries have observed.[113] When an Amora responds, "There is no difficulty. This [clause of the mishnah] is R. So-and-so; that [clause] is R. So-and-so," or suchlike, he was certainly responding to the very objection that the Stammaim formulated and placed before his statement. So too in the cases of the term, "There is a contradiction between them (*ureminhu*)," which presents a contradiction between two Tannaitic sources; the content of this question is Amoraic although it is formulated anonymously. Let me bring another example from Sanh 17a. The anonymous objection (before R. Abbahu), "In the end, a majority of two for a guilty verdict is impossible," is one of the Talmud's most cogent objections, and R. Abbahu's response, "[A majority of two] is only possible when they add [two] judges," was not originally an answer to this anonymously formulated objection but to a similar objection that he himself had raised. Nevertheless, the objection is not attributed to R. Abbahu, because only apodictic law and brief explanations were passed down in the official transmission of the Amoraim, and not objections and questions, not even simple questions in the form "what is the reason?" and "whence these words (i.e., what is the source of this ruling?)" These types of explanations apparently were attached [44] to a source, to a mishnah or a baraita, albeit without reasoning and justifications. The Talmud transmitted these separately from the Mishnah, and sometimes added reasoning or justification in very abbreviated form and without attribution. The few passages that state "R. So-and-so raised a contradiction and resolved it" were probably not handed down in the official transmission by the Reciters, but in a kind of private transmission by the sages who heard the objections and responses, even though the Amora did not ask them to preserve it. Perhaps this insight helps explain the difference between "R. X said," and "R. Y said that R. X said."[114] The first reached us through the official transmission, whereas the second reached us through another Amora who was his student.

(C) Attributed Scriptural Interpretations (*derashot*) That also Appear Anonymously

Scriptural interpretations (*derashot*) that are anonymous in one passage and attributed elsewhere perhaps belong to this category of early anonymous material, as the sages were not always punctilious about quoting scriptural interpretations with attributions. A nice example is Sanh 59b: "That [= the repetition of the commandment to circumcise] comes to permit [circumcision on] the Sabbath: *on the [eighth] day (Lev 12:3)*—and even on the Sabbath." The Talmud does not mention that this scriptural interpretation is from R. Yohanan and is quoted in his name in Shab 132a. In Sanh 59b the scriptural interpretation answers an objection against R. Yose b. R. Hanina, R. Yohanan's disciple, who certainly would have known his master's interpretation. Similarly, the passage continues: "But behold, [the commandment to] reproduce and multiply…that comes to teach that anything [prohibited] by a vote requires another vote to abrogate it." Rav Yosef propounds this scriptural interpretation in Bets 5a, where he also says, "Whence shall I prove it (*mena amina lah*)," implying that he is the first to proffer this interpretation. Sanh 59a, however, does not quote the interpretation in his name. Thus it appears that the sages did not meticulously preserve attributions of scriptural interpretations, and this may explain why there is so much unattributed material among the halakhic midrashim, which largely consist of scriptural interpretations. It should also be noted that some scriptural interpretations attributed by the Talmud to Amoraim, and not only those that appear anonymously, are attested in the halakhic midrashim. See, for example, Qid 68a: "Rav Pappa said.… *If a man has two wives, one loved and the other unloved (Deut 21:15)*. Is any wife unloved before the Omnipresent?"

This interpretation appears without attribution in *Sifre Deuteronomy* #215 (ed. Finkelstein, 248). However, in this case it is possible that the Talmud attributed the interpretation to Rav Pappa because he adds a comment before quoting the interpretation, namely, "Regarding those [relationships] prohibited by a negative commandment, it is stated explicitly" (Qid 68a). More significantly, there is a lengthy scriptural interpretation in Naz 40a involving a proof based on "the common element (*hatsad hashaveh*)," akin to Stammaitic dialectical argumentation—yet Rabbah b. Mesharshia refers to its tradent as "this Tanna." Rabbah b. Mesharshia's reference troubled the commentator Samuel b. Joseph Strashun (Rasha"sh): "This matter requires consideration, because all this seems to be [45] the dialectical argumentation of the members of the academy." But in fact a scriptural interpretation can be of Tannaitic provenance, even if transmitted anonymously and without attribution, and despite containing some Aramaic words.

(D) Brief Explanations That are Scriptural Interpretations

Above we noted that brief explanations are possible instances of early anonymous material. This is especially true when the brief explanations are also scriptural interpretations. An interesting example is found in Taan 17a, parallel at Sanh 22b, which quotes a baraita containing three laws: "A king cuts his hair every day," "A high priest [cuts his hair] every Sabbath eve," "An ordinary priest [cuts his hair] every thirty days." In Taan 17a R. Abba b. Zavda quotes the verse "Let your eyes behold a king in his beauty (Isa 33:17)" as the reason that a king cuts his hair every day,[115] whereas Rav Shmuel b. Yitshaq proffers the reason for the second law, that the high priest cuts his hair every Sabbath eve, "Because the priestly divisions (*mishmarot*) change then." The reason for the third law, that an ordinary priest cuts his hair every thirty days, is not ascribed to an Amora but appears anonymously: Taan 17a appends an addendum: "This is derived [by a scriptural analogy (*heqesh*)] from 'hair' [*pera*, Ezek 44:20], 'hair' [*pera*, written] in connection with the Nazirite [Num 6:5]," while Sanhedrin 22b also quotes the verse in full before the scriptural analogy, "They shall neither shave their heads nor let their hair (*pera*) go untrimmed (Ezek 44:20)." Now this verse alone suffices to explain the law; it was originally transmitted together with the mishnah without any Amoraic attribution—here you have a brief explanation that is a scriptural interpretation. However, the scriptural analogy (*hekesh*) is not a brief explanation but was added later, as can be seen from Rav Pappa's question to Abaye: "I could say [that the verse means] not to let [their hair] grow long at all (i.e., not even for a month)." Had Rav Pappa known the scriptural analogy, he would never have asked this question. (The medieval commentaries already found Rav Pappa's question problematic; Tosafot's answer is extremely forced, as one cannot equate "they should cut their hair on the 29th" with the words "not let [their hair] grow long at all"; see the comments of Rasha"l.) We must conclude that Abaye and Rav Pappa did not know of the scriptural analogy (*heqesh*)—their source quoted the verse from Ezek 44:20 alone. That verse is also the basis for Ravina's question to Rav Ashi, "Who stated [this law] before Ezekiel came?" However, with the sequence of traditions as now found in the Talmud, Ravina's question appears to be based on the scriptural analogy to the case of the Nazir, and thus Rashi comments: "Before Ezekiel came—and created the scriptural analogy." Thus this passage developed in three stages: first there was the verse from Ezek 44:20 alone, without the scriptural analogy based on the word "hair," and on the basis of the verse itself Rav Pappa objected to Abaye, "I could say [that the verse means] not to let [their hair] grow long at all." Later, they added the scriptural analogy that follows the verse—this is the state of the passage as found in Sanh 22b. Finally, they omitted the verse and quoted the scriptural analogy alone—as we find in Taan 17a.

In sum, an anonymous dictum, and even more so an anonymous scriptural interpretation (*derashah*), cannot be considered late and of Stammaitic provenance unless it is both unattributed and consists of dialectical argumentation with objections and solutions that do not directly impact the law. Amoraim never transmitted these types of anonymous dicta to succeeding generations, and it was the Stammaim who reconstructed them and preserved them throughout the Talmud. They collected dialectical argumentation from the collective memory of the sages and filled in the missing parts themselves. [46]

Why Did Previous Chroniclers and Authors Fail to Mention the Stammaim?

The question must be asked: why did previous chroniclers ignore the Stammaim?[116] If I am correct that the Stammaitic period lasted more than 200 years, from about the mid sixth century to the second half of the eighth century, and that the Stammaim composed or at least formulated the dialectical sugyot that analyze apodictic rulings throughout the

Talmud, how is it that "we drink their waters" (most of the Talmud is unattributed material) and yet "we do not know their names"?** How is it possible that the very fact of their existence, to say nothing of their historical period and intellectual contribution, were not mentioned at all by the Geonim and their successors? These later authorities mention, dispute, and identify the Saboraim whose contribution, at the end of the Stammaitic period, consisted only of brief explanations, while they completely efface the Stammaim, the architects of the Talmud? Astonishing!

My explanation is that the Geonim and their successors understood the Talmudic statement "Rav Ashi and Ravina—the end of *hora'ah*" (BM 86a, and they understood "*hora'ah*" as *gemara* or Talmud) as a historical fact. In addition, they may have felt theological pressure to confer upon the Talmud, including its anonymous dialectical argumentation, the authority of Rav Ashi. Rav Ashi, the leading Babylonian Amora of the fifth century, restored the crown of Torah to the academy of Mata Mehasia, located near Sura, from which it had departed since the time of Rav Hisda. He served as Head of the Academy for sixty years and reviewed the Talmud in two cycles, "the first cycle and the second cycle" (BB 157b).[117] If Rav Ashi was the "end of the Talmud," then he was also the "end" of the anonymous material. Dialectical argumentation perforce concluded with his demise, which left no place for a Stammaitic era after the Talmud. Indeed, the expression "anonymous Talmud (*stamma degemara*)" does not appear among the Geonim; it is prevalent, rather, among the Ashkenazi authorities, such as Tosafot and Asheri (1250–1327). The Saboraim, however, who contributed but a few brief clarifications and did not produce "legislation," did not need the veneer of authority of Rav Ashi and Ravina.

Now the role of Rav Ashi as "the end of anonymous material (*sof setamot*)" can be understood in two ways: Rav Ashi as the editor of the Talmud, including the anonymous material that predated him, or Rav Ashi as the author of the anonymous material.[118] This question was already debated by the medieval commentators. Tosafot, for example, [47] rule according to the Stam's interpretation of the Mishnah against Rav Aha bar Yaakov on the grounds that "the anonymous Talmud (*stamma deshas*) rules thusly, and this is Rav Ashi[119] who edited the Talmud, and he is the later [sage], so the law follows him in disputes with Rav Aha bar Yaakov" (who lived much earlier; Tosafot, Shab 9b, s.v. *tisporet*). Tosafot reasons that the anonymous layer derives from Rav Ashi ("this is Rav Ashi,") and its authority is equivalent to that of Rav Ashi.[120] Yet Asheri cites Tosafot and disagrees with them: "The first reason [i.e., the Stam's explanation] was not articulated by

Rav Ashi. Rather, when the members of the academy debated the matter, they encountered a difficulty, and they had no choice but to resolve it with a forced explanation in order that they not leave the academy still in dispute, and subsequently Rav Aha bar Yaakov provided a satisfactory reason." For Asheri, Rav Ashi plays no role in formulating the anonymous material of the Talmud.[121] This stance also emerges from his comment: "The law follows Rav Ashi [opposing Mar Zutra] since the anonymous Talmud [accords with him]..., and also because Rav Ashi was greater in knowledge and status than Mar Zutra" (*Pisqei harosh* to Bava Metsia, chapter 1, #40).[122] If Rav Ashi composed the anonymous stratum, then it cannot also serve as proof that the law accords with him. For Asheri, then, Rav Ashi merely edited or arranged the anonymous Talmud. Apparently he understood the statement "Rav Ashi and Ravina—the end of *hora'ah*" in the same manner as did Sherira Gaon: anonymous statements, or at least a good portion of them, predate Rav Ashi; they too were transmitted "generation by generation," until eventually Rav Ashi edited them just as he edited Amoraic dicta. But he did not compose them, and therefore they lack his imprimatur.

The later Talmudic commentators disagree along similar lines. Avraham Even Ezuz, *Lehem abirim* (Venice, 1605), to BM 33b, explains Rashi's comment, "Rami bar Hama objects to it—he is taken aback by the mishnah's ruling," as follows: "[Rashi understands the objection to be directed against the mishnah] because it is impossible that Rami bar Hama objects to the words of the Talmudic editors (= the anonymous Talmud), Rav Ashi and Ravina, who were among the latter sages."[123] However, Solomon Algazi, *Yavin shemua* (Venice, 1639), Section 2, to *Halikhot olam* (by Jeshua b. Joseph Halevi [1490]), disagrees with Even Azuz, since even "before Ravina and Rav Ashi there existed Talmud... just as there existed Mishnah before R. Yehudah HaNasi. Just as R. Yehudah HaNasi edited the Mishnah, so Ravina and Rav Ashi collected all the arguments of the earlier Amoraim who debated in the academy." Either way, whether Rav Ashi composed the anonymous dicta (so Even Azuz) or whether he edited them (so Algazi), the traditional view believed that no anonymous dicta [48] were formulated after the editing of the Talmud. Therefore it is no surprise that chroniclers neglected to mention the Stammaim; they identified them with Rav Ashi or with his predecessors.

One troubling issue remains to be addressed. Sherira Gaon possessed archival documents from which he drew detailed information about the order of generations of Amoraim—most of which we also know from the Talmud itself—and about the details of the generations of the Geonim—concerning which we are totally dependent on the *Epistle of Rav Sherira Gaon* and *Seder tannaim ve'amoraim*. He both quotes these documents by name and relates details about them, and also at times adduces other oral traditions unknown to us. It is difficult to understand why none of these sources even hints at the existence of the Stammaim, the architects of the Talmud.

However, close examination of Sherira's quotations from archival materials reveals that they are accurate with respect to the places and dates that the Geonim were appointed Heads of Academies, lived, flourished, and died, but inaccurate as to their contribution to the Talmud, namely, who was a Stammai and who a Sabora.** The title "Gaon" was given to the Head of the Academy; his appointment was recorded in the archives in writing and publicized orally in order that it be universally and perpetually known. Yet the extent of a sage's activity—of his contribution to the formation of the Talmud—is an assessment rendered not during the Gaon's lifetime, but only after he completed his life's work and was compared to his predecessors and successors. Therefore these archival sources contained nothing about the contribution of the Stammaim to the formation of the Talmud. That assessment was made by chroniclers who retrospectively evaluated the sage's contribution and placed him in a certain period. When the archival sources were being written they did not record who contributed and who did not contribute, who was a Stammai and who was a Sabora; these were later judgments expressing a subjective opinion.

I base my account exclusively on internal analysis of the Talmud itself. Anonymous material comprises the basic structure of the sugya, objecting and responding, building and destroying, and reaching conclusions. In some cases brief explanations that do not add much to the content of the sugya were also appended. These explanations were added toward the end of the Stammaitic period, when the sugya was almost complete and lacked only explanatory glosses. They were added by sages who lived at the end of the period, who are called "Saboraim" after this type of activity ("explanations" = *hesberim*).** The Stammaim who produced the Talmudic sugyot were not called Saboraim, but preceded them. The Stammaim created the sugya and the Saboraim subsequently explained that which remained to be clarified.

Explanations of Amoraic Dicta Understood as the Amora's Own Words

At this stage it is appropriate to note that the medieval commentaries routinely attribute to the Amora himself the anonymous comments that explain his statement. For example, Rav states, "Washing one's hands and feet in hot water in the evening is voluntary, but I say it is commanded" (Shab 25b). The Stammaim then ask, "What is the [nature of this] commandment?" and answer, "As Rav Yehudah said in the name of Rav (or Shmuel): Thus was the custom of R. Yehudah b. Ilai. On the Sabbath eve they would bring him a basin full of water, and he would wash his face, hands and feet." I noted that this answer is problematic: "How can they (the Stammaim) bring a proof as to whether it is voluntary or commanded from a custom?," and conjectured that Rav himself was referring to a different source, not to the custom of R. Yehudah b. Ilai (see *MM*, Shabbat, 80). Now the reading of the *She'iltot* omits "What is the [nature of this] commandment?," which would then render the answer "As Rav Yehudah..." as the continuation [49] of Rav's statement. With this reading one cannot claim that Rav was referring to a different source, and my question has no solution. Thus the *She'iltot*, by omitting the question of the Stammaim, wrongly attributes a connection made by the Stammaim directly to the Amora himself. If one objects that examples of this phenomenon from the *She'iltot*, which was composed close to the Stammaitic period, are not probative, let me adduce an example from R. Hananel (d. 1053). In his commentary to Shev 32a, R. Hananel quotes the Talmudic passage as follows: "R. Yohanan said, 'You can even say the [source follows the view of the] sages. What circumstances are we dealing with? When he retracts within the time of an utterance.... Each one [retracts] within the time of the utterance of his fellow." The statement "You can even say..." cannot be the verbatim words of R. Yohanan, as in its Talmudic context the dictum counters Rav Hisda's explanation, "Who is [the authority behind] this [view]? R. Yose the Galilean," and Rav Hisda postdated R. Yohanan. Therefore it must derive from the Stammaim. Moreover, R. Yohanan did not say "Each one [retracts] within the time of the utterance of his fellow," as Ravina articulates this statement in the Talmud. Thus R. Hananel, who knew well that these explanations of both the Stammaim and Ravina ("You can even say...," "Each one [retracts] within...") were not in fact the words of R. Yohanan, nevertheless attributes them to R. Yohanan himself. (See too Ket 32b: "R. Yohanan said: You can even say that this is a case when his sister is a maiden"—which counters Ulla's explanation on Ket 31a. Ulla was a student of R. Yohanan, so this too must be from the Stammaim.[124] Similarly, other instances of "You can even say" and suchlike are from the Stammaim.) Another example: when the anonymous Talmud explains, "The one master holds... and the other master holds...," the medieval commentaries routinely spell out the names of the Amoraim in their quotation, "R. So-and-so holds...," thus ascribing the explanation of the Stammaim directly to the Amoraim themselves (see *MM*, Bava Qamma, 451 n. 4).

This phenomenon is even attested within the Talmud itself, for example, in Ket 17b: "For Rav Huna said: One may not acquire a minor's property through presumption (= usucaption; *hazaqa*)." Rav Huna did not state this explicitly; rather Rava inferred as much from Rav Huna's statement in BM 39a: "Rav Huna said.... Rava said: Infer from it (*shma minah*) that one may not acquire a minor's property through presumption." Tosafot to BM 39a and other commentaries call attention to this phenomenon, although their interest is motivated by the Talmud's objection, "Does Rav Huna come to inform us of a Tannaitic teaching?"; after all, Rav Huna himself "was not dealing" with the case of "acquiring property through presumption." At all events, this phenomenon of attributing the explanation of an Amora's statement to the Amora himself is extremely common and generally not worthy of special attention due to its prevalence. See too Ned 6a: "But behold, Abaye said, 'I rule even according to R. Yehudah'? He [Abaye] retracted." Abaye did not explicitly state that he ruled according to R. Yehudah; rather, the Stammaim explained his statement that way in Ned 5b: "Abaye could say to you: 'I rule even according to R. Yehudah.'" Nevertheless, the Talmud states, "He [Abaye] retracted."[125] Similarly, in BQ 43b, "Did not Resh Laqish say [50], 'For example, when he set fire to the body of the slave'?" Resh Laqish made no such statement; the Stammaim offer this as a response to an objection against Resh Laqish on BQ 22b, asserting: "Resh Laqish could say to you: what is the case here? When he set fire to the body of the slave."

R. Yehudah HaNasi frequently adopted the same policy in his editing of the Mishnah, for example, mKet 3:3: "R. Akiba says: there is a fine for [intercourse with] her (a maiden who was betrothed and divorced), and the fine goes to her." However, the baraita in Ket 38b quotes R. Akiba as, "There is a fine for [intercourse with] her, and the fine goes to her father." This leads to the conclusion that R. Akiba only said "There is a fine for [intercourse with] her." R. Yehudah HaNasi added "and the fine goes to her" to R. Akiba's words in mKet 3:3, whereas the transmitter of the baraita added "the fine goes to her father"—the formulation of both the mishnah and the baraita make it appear that R. Akiba himself articulated those words.[126] This too is apparently the case of the very first mishnah in Tractate Berakhot. Rabban Gamaliel did not state that the time for reciting the evening Shema lasts "until the rise of dawn," but rather, "the entire night." However, R. Yehudah HaNasi, consistent with his opinion that night ends at dawn,[127] quoted Rabban Gamaliel in that mishnah as if he mentioned dawn. By contrast *Avot d'Rabbi Natan* follows the opinion of R. Eleazar b. R. Shimon, who holds that night ends with cockcrow, and therefore quotes Rabban Gamaliel as stating that one recites the Shema "until cockcrow" (version A, chapter 2; version B, chapter 3). The Tosefta too reads "They engaged in the study of the laws of Passover the whole night, until cockcrow (tPes 10:8)"; this too accords with the opinion of R. Eleazar b. R. Shimon. R. Yehudah HaNasi would have formulated this tradition as "[they engaged in the study of the laws of Passover] the whole night, until the rise of dawn."

Hence it is no wonder at all that in Sherira Gaon's opinion anonymous material derives from the Amora himself, and the Amora is explaining his own view, or that it derives from Rav Ashi. Either way, Amoraic authority attaches to the anonymous stratum, as it appears that it devolves from the Amoraim. Accordingly, one should not be surprised that Sherira Gaon fails to mention the Stammaitic era. In his view, anonymous traditions are also from the Amoraim. Indeed, for Sherira Gaon the anonymous statements of the Talmud, like those of the Mishnah, are more authoritative than attributed statements, as they point to the consensual view as opposed to an attribution that indicates an individual opinion. In his words: "If all the sages received a certain tradition [51] and together stated it, and no one stated it first, then it was formulated anonymously" (*Epistle of Rav Sherira Gaon*, 64). And he continues: "If all of the sages stated the same tradition together, it was formulated as '*kedi*'" (= anonymously, without any attribution (p. 66; see above, p. 44).

Such is the view of Sherira Gaon, yet we have argued that this was not the case. The Stammaitic era—including the Saboraim, who lived at the end of the era—was a separate period. The Stammaim flourished after the Amoraim, from the middle of the sixth century to the middle of the eighth century, from the time of the last Amora mentioned in the Talmud until Yehudai Gaon, author of the *Halakhot pesuqot*, and Aha of Shabha, the author of the *She'iltot*, in whose time there begin to be independent books attributed to individual authors. We have received very little legal material from this period; the first Gaon from whom we have responsa—though very few—is Rav Sheshna (also known as Rav Mesharshia bar Tahalifa), who lived at the end of the seventh century. It is unlikely that the Stammaim produced nothing. They produced a great deal—but their contributions were incorporated into the anonymous stratum of the Talmud.

The foregoing implies that the proper method of attaining a comprehensive understanding of a Talmudic passage is first and foremost to distinguish the Amoraic and Stammaitic strata. One must distinguish linguistic shifts (Hebrew vs. Aramaic), shifts in person (first person, second person, third person), and different styles. Because hundreds of years may have separated the Amoraim from the Stammaim, we must ascertain whether the Stammaim possessed complete sources, and whether their explanations accurately reflect the meanings of Amoraic dicta without adding, detracting, or changing them. In this matter the medieval commentaries are very helpful, as they were sensitive to awkward and poorly fitting explanations, even if their fidelity to the Talmud and efforts to remove the awkwardness frequently produced unsatisfying answers. If the explanation of the Stammaim does not fit the Amora's statement, then we must endeavor to find an alternative possibility by using different manuscript variants and parallels, where these exist. If we are unable to find the correct version of the dictum, we must postulate a new explanation by analyzing the Talmudic sugya, an explanation that better fits the words of the Amora. And of course, if possible, we must explain why the Stammaim did not explain the statement in that way.

Part II: The Editing of the Talmud

[52] I HAVE attempted to demonstrate that anonymous traditions, the unattributed sections of the Talmud, are not contemporaneous with the Amoraim but postdate them and therefore were not edited by the Amoraim. Here I endeavor to show that the anonymous dialectical argumentation never was subjected to an editing process but simply came to a close in and of itself.[1] Only Amoraic dicta and brief explanations went through a type of editing by the Amoraim themselves. The Amoraim debated an issue until they reached a conclusion, then formulated it in a succinct and concise manner, typically in Hebrew, and finally transmitted it to the "Reciters" (*tannaim*), the transmitters of tradition. Sometimes students combined the concise and succinct Amoraic dicta and explanations with the opinions of other Amoraim and created disputes, and in some cases they subsequently forgot who said what such that the dispute was transmitted in an anonymous manner, "One said x and one said y." Even if Amoraic material did not undergo an editing process proper, it nevertheless was subjected to a type of editing. Anonymous dialectical argumentation, however, was not even subjected to this minimal form of editing but only to reconstruction, explanation, and arrangement as a sugya.[2]

Here I wish to clarify that when I speak of "editing" ("editors," etc.; Hebrew: *arakh*), I refer to the assessment of the accuracy of statements. An editor examines whether statements were in fact made and whether they were transmitted reliably according to the accepted criteria. If he finds that traditions have been corrupted, he has the authority to change, omit, or completely reject them. An editor bears responsibility for the accuracy of the content. Now according to the traditional view, Rav Ashi and his colleagues carried out such an assessment of Amoraic statements and explanations: "They completed, improved, and clarified, clarification upon clarification... to clarify and elucidate each and every tradition and to be exacting about the accuracy of the attribution."[3] In my opinion, it was only the Amoraic stratum, and not the entire Talmud, that was edited in this way. The majority of the Talmud, namely, the anonymous stratum, was reconstructed but not examined as to its accuracy.

Now clearly, according to the modern conception of editing, when an editor "selects the items, chooses the style, determines the order and form and suchlike"[4] but does not control the content, in this sense the Talmud too was edited. "Compilers" determined the order and form,[5] while the Saboraim established the style (if such a notion applies at all).[6] The Saboraim added brief explanations and types of [53] annotations, such as "as we find it necessary to say later on (*kideva'inan lemeimar leqaman*)," "as we say in general (*ude'amrinan be'alma*)." Both the Compilers and the Saboraim lived at the end of the Stammaitic period (700–750/770 CE), hundreds of years after Rav Ashi; clearly, then, no editing was carried out by Rav Ashi and his colleagues.

The main evidence that the Talmud never went through an editing process—either by Rav Ashi or by anyone else, an editing that encompassed the entire Talmud and reconciled the contradictions and inconsistencies of its various parts—is the contradictions and forced argumentation that can be found on almost every Talmudic folio. Contradictions can be found not only between different tractates (see, for example, Yom 72a, "Is it written, *[The hem for the priestly garments] not be torn (Exod 28:32)*," and Sanh 21a, "*He shall not have many [wives]* such that *his heart not go astray (Deut 17:17)*"; BM 53b, "the Sages did not distinguish..." and Sanh 113a, "and do the Sages make an edict..."; see the medieval commentators ad loc.),[7]** and not only between different passages in the same tractate—which one could explain by conjecturing that the editors forgot what was written in the other passage—but even on the very same folio, in which case it is impossible to claim the contradictions were not discerned.[8] If Rav Ashi edited the Talmud, why did he not remove the contradictions?[9] Furthermore, the medieval authorities often comment on "contradictory sugyot"[10] [54], although I have not found them objecting that if Rav Ashi and Ravina were involved in the editing of the Talmud, why did they not reconcile these sugyot?[11] The medieval commentators consider these contradictory sugyot as analogous to such terms as "there are some who say (*ika de'amri*)" and "another version (*lishna aharina*)," where the Talmud itself leaves both versions of a passage intact and does not reconcile them. However, the commentators, and especially the Tosafists, raise many objections regarding other types of contradictions, but their solutions are forced and unsatisfying. If one does not wish to resort to forced explanations, one must conclude that the contradictions result from the fact that these anonymous passages devolve from different academies and were incorporated into the Talmud at a time when it was no longer possible to reconcile them; these types of contradictory sugyot are unlike the contradictions connected to the terms mentioned above, and they cannot be reconciled as per the strategies of the medieval commentaries. Moreover, if there had been a Talmudic editor, it is difficult to imagine that he would not have reconciled the contradictions, or at least would not have noted that his sources contained contradictions. Reconciling contradictions occurs within the sugyot of the Talmud, since each sugya had a type of editor, but not between disparate sugyot. The different sugyot were studied in different academies, so they sometimes remained inconsistent and divergent.

Contradictions in the Talmud

Contradictions and inconsistencies are prevalent throughout the Talmud, dispersed through all tractates.[12] [55] It is impossible to quote them all; therefore I will begin with one example that threads its way through different passages and disparate tractates, and then I will adduce examples of contradictions found on the same folio. When contradictions are found on the same folio it appears at first glance that the two sources comprising the sugya complement each other; but after probing the matter they appear to be contradictory sources that conflict with one another. (I use the term "contradictory" sources against the claim of Malakhi b. Jacob HaKohen, *Yad malakhi*, #497, citing Betsalel Ashkenazi, *Shita mequbetset*, BM 9a [though I could not find the reference in Ashkenazi's commentary there]: "The term 'contradictory sugyot' only applies to sugyot found at a distance from one another, but not close together.") [56] I focus on contradictions and not forced explanations, because contradictions are less subjective, and it is implausible to claim that the editors were unaware of them.

(A) Contradictions across the Talmud

Let me begin by examining the statement of R. Eleazar HaKappar, "A Nazirite is called a sinner." Does this apply only to an impure Nazirite or also to a pure Nazirite? In Naz 3a the Talmud explicitly states: "Even according to R. Eleazar HaKappar, who said that a Nazirite is a sinner—these words apply only to an impure Nazirite... but a pure Nazirite is not called a sinner." However, later in that same tractate, Naz 19a, the Talmud quotes the full statement of R. Eleazar HaKappar, namely, that a Nazirite is called a sinner because he deprives himself of wine, and then objects, "But it (the verse) is written of an impure Nazirite, and we hold that it applies even to a pure Nazirite?" This contradiction recurs in other passages throughout the Talmud, in some cases almost explicitly, and in some cases implicitly. Thus in Sot 15a the Talmud objects: "If so then the Nazirite's sin-offering"—also brought by the pure Nazirite at the completion of the time of his vow—"should also require libations, since it is not brought on account of sin?" And the Talmud responds, "He holds like R. Eleazar HaKappar who said that a Nazirite too is a sinner." Clearly, the Talmud here considers a pure Nazirite too to be a sinner. In Taan 11a the Talmud claims that Shmuel, who stated "Anyone who fasts is called a sinner," holds like R. Eleazar HaKappar. This implies that R. Eleazar HaKappar refers also to a pure Nazirite, and the Nazirite's sin is depriving himself of wine. This conclusion follows too from Talmudic passages at Naz 22a and BQ 91b.[13] However, in Ker 26a, the Talmud objects: "Then a Nazirite in doubt [as to whether he has become impure], after Yom Kippur intervenes, should not bring a sacrifice?!"—as his sacrifice does not atone for a sin—and then immediately objects, "And what can be said for R. Eleazar b. HaKappar, who holds that a Nazirite is called a sinner?" The Talmud explains, "[He brings a sacrifice] to permit eating consecrated food (*qodashim*)," or, according to a different reading, "To allow him to resume his Nazirite vow in a pure state." In either case, the response only works for an impure Nazirite, although the objection applies equally to a pure Nazirite. Therefore we must conclude that the Talmud here assumes that R. Eleazar HaKappar holds that only an impure Nazirite is called a sinner.[14] Now it is interesting that this passage in Ker 26a is identical to Shevu 8a up to the final response, and since it is nearly impossible that two individuals would independently formulate the same statements in the identical order, it appears that the passage in Ker 26a was taken from Shevu 8a (see p. 89, example c). Clear proof for this claim is that in Ker 26a Rav Oshaya mentions the verse "*for* all of *their* sins (Lev 16:21)" with reference to the atonement effected by the day of Yom Kippur—whereas the verse in the Torah that speaks of the Day of Atonement reads "*from* all of *your* sins (Lev 16:30)." But in Shevu 8a the context is the goat of Yom Kippur, and there the verse indeed states "*for* all of *their* sins (Lev 16:21)." Therefore the sugya of Ker 26a was borrowed from Shevu 8a,[15] and nevertheless [57] the responses to the objection against the view of R. Eleazar HaKappar differ in the two passages.[16] It is possible that Shevu 8a—as opposed to Ker

26a—assumes that R. Eleazar HaKappar holds that a pure Nazirite too is considered a sinner, and therefore it could not accept the response found in Ker 26a, which dealt only with an impure Nazirite, and gave a different response.[17]

This contradiction apparently devolves from the fact that not all sources possessed the baraita of R. Eleazar HaKappar in its complete form. Some sources only had a partial tradition of R. Eleazar HaKappar's view, namely, the brief dictum that a Nazirite is called a sinner. Had they possessed the entire baraita, they would have known that the reason was "because he deprives himself of wine"—and this reason applies to a pure Nazirite too. Those who possessed the brief dictum alone—which was widespread and well known[18]—conjectured that his reason was the verse, *And make expiation on his behalf for the sin that he incurred through the corpse (Num 6:11)*, which deals with an impure Nazirite; consequently they reasoned that R. Eleazar HaKappar spoke only of an impure Nazirite.

The anonymous stratum of Ker 26a seems to have reasoned along these lines. Note that it only knew the baraita attributed to R. Shimon b. Yohai (quoted in that passage prior to the discussion of the Nazirite) in the form borrowed from Shevu 8a, that "a parturient (*yoledet*) is a sinner," and not in its entirety, as quoted in Nid 31b, "Why does the Torah say that a parturient must bring a sacrifice?..." The full baraita states explicitly that the purpose of the parturient's sacrifice is not, as claimed in Ker 26a, "to permit her to eat consecrated food" but to atone for her sin. Likewise, the purpose of the sacrifice of the Nazirite is not, as claimed by Ker 26a, "to allow him to resume his Nazirite vow in a pure state" but to atone for sin.[19]

If there had been a Talmudic editor, such contradictions would not be found in the Talmud, as he would have removed them.

(B) Contradictions on the Same Folio

At this point I bring examples of contradictions found on the same folio. Some of them are types of "deficiencies of knowledge," as not only do the anonymous passages contradict one another, but one Stammaitic author knew that which his colleague did not; had he possessed that information, he would not have said what he said. Such cases cannot be considered as types of "there are some who say (*ika de'amri*)" or "another version (*lishna aharina*)," for the editor of the sugya quoted both anonymous passages as an integral part of the redaction. Because contradictions of this sort are lesser known, I will provide a number of examples,[20] [58] the first from two sugyot found on Sanh 16a and a related sugya from Sanh 18b:

Sanh 16a (first sugya):

[1A] [Citation from mSanh 1:5] "And not the high priest" [i.e., the high priest may not be judged in a lower court, but only in the court of 71].

[1B] Whence is this derived? Rav Ada bar Ahava said, "*Every great matter shall be brought to you (Exod 18:22)*—the matters of a great man."

[1C] They objected: "*Great matter (Exod 18:22)*, this means a difficult matter. You say it means a 'difficult matter'? Perhaps rather it means the 'matters of a great man'? [No.] Because it says, *The difficult matters they would bring to Moses (Exod 18:26)*, therefore it must mean 'difficult matter.'"

[1D] He [Rav Ada b. Ahava] held according to this Tanna, who taught, *Great matter (Exod 18:22)*, the matters of a great man. You say it means the matters of a great man? Perhaps it means "a difficult matter"? Because it says *the difficult matter (Exod 18:26)*—behold, "difficult matter" is already stated. How then do I interpret *great matter*? The matters of a great man.

Sanh 16a (second sugya)

[1E] R. Eleazar asked: The [goring] ox of the high priest [who kills a man]—how many [judges are required]? Do we compare it to [the judges necessary for] the execution of its owner (the high priest, hence 71 judges) or to the execution of the owner in general (i.e., a typical owner of a goring ox, not the high priest, hence 23 judges)?

[1G] Abaye said: Because he (R. Eleazar) asked about his ox (of the high priest), it implies that he (R. Eleazar) is certain about (other) monetary cases (of the high priest, that they are not brought before the court of 71, but of 23).

[1H] Is this not obvious? [No.] Because it is written *every great matter (Exod 18:22)*, you might have thought that this includes every matter of the great person (= the high priest, including monetary cases, is to be brought before the court of 71). Therefore he [Abaye] informs us [otherwise].

Sanh 18b:

[2A] [Citation from a baraita, cited above]: "The high priest who violates a positive or negative commandment [behold he becomes like a layman for all matters]."

[2B] Is this not obvious? [No.] Because . . . and Rav Ada bar Ahava said, "*Every great matter shall be brought to you (Exod 18:22)*—the matters of a great man." I might say this includes every matter of the great man (is to be brought before the court of 71). Therefore it [the baraita] informs us [otherwise].

[2C] Perhaps that is so [that the verse includes all matters of the high priest, which are to be brought before the court of 71]?

[2D] [No.] Is it written "The matters of a great (man)"? Rather, "*great matter*" is written—a great matter in its literal sense[21] (such as a capital crime, is to be brought before the court of 71, but not other monetary cases.)

The second sugya of Sanh 16a and the sugya of Sanh 18b contain similar analyses of Exod 18:22 [1H vs. 2B]. However, in Sanh 18b the Talmud continues with an objection [2C], whereas in Sanh 16a the Talmud does not raise this objection.[22]

It would seem that the Stammaitic authors derived different information from their different sources. The Stammaim of the second sugya at Sanh 16a knew only the first baraita of the "objection" cited above in the first sugya [1C], which interprets "Great matter" of Exod 18:22 as "difficult matter." According to this baraita, "great matter" cannot mean "matters of a great man." For this interpretation appears only as the alternative possibility—"Perhaps rather it means the matters of a great man? [No]"—and therefore the Stammaim do not object, "Perhaps that is so" here, as that is not the conclusion of the baraita. Consequently the Talmud in Sanh 16a only employs that interpretation of the verse as the alternative possibility, namely, "you might have thought..." [1H]. However, the Stammaim of Sanh 18b also knew (or only knew, see below) the second baraita quoted in the first sugya of Sanh 16a in response to the objection, namely, "He held according to this Tanna who taught, "*Great matter (Exod 18:22)*, the matters of a great man..." [1D]. Here this interpretation of "great matter" in terms of the "matters of a great man" is the conclusion of the baraita, and therefore the Talmud at Sanh 18b objected "Perhaps that is so" [2C].

At this point it should be clear why the anonymous stratum of Sanh 18b mentions Rav Ada b. Ahava in its inference based on the mishnah [2B], and the anonymous stratum of the second sugya of Sanh 16a does not mention him [1G]. The Stammaim responsible for this section of Sanh 16a did not know of R. Ada b. Ahava's dictum, but only of the baraita that opposes him (that interprets "great matter" as "difficult matter" [1C]), whereas R. Ada b. Ahava's statement is based on the second baraita, "He held according to this Tanna..." [1D]. The Stammaim responsible for this sugya of Sanh 16a did not mention Rav Ada b. Ahava because its context is the clause of mSanh 1:5, "And not the high priest" [1A], whereas the baraita alone explicates the verse, *Every great matter shall be brought to you (Exod 18:22)* [1D]. However, the Stammaim of Sanh 18b transferred the interpretation of the verse quoted in the baraita to various other laws, for example, the law of a high priest who violates a positive or negative commandment, and therefore quoted the baraita [2B]. The same can be said of Rav Matneh (Sanh 15b–16a), who quotes Rav Ada b. Ahava but not the baraita [1D], and does not state "Did we not teach . . . ?" Rav Matneh learned from Rav Ada b. Ahava's statement [1B] how to understand mSanh 1:5, even though Rava Ada b. Ahava did not explicate that section of mSanh 1:5, "One may not judge a tribe . . . ," but only the clause about the high priest [1A].** However, it is possible that the anonymous stratum of Sanh 18b also knew the first baraita (which interprets "great matter" as "difficult matter" [1C]), but rejected it, and therefore did not want to answer the objection, [59] "Perhaps that is so . . ." [2C], with the response that the baraita stating "behold he becomes like a layman for all matters" (tSanh 4:2 [2A]) holds like the first baraita (interpreting "great matter" as "difficult matter"); it therefore provided a different response [2D].

It turns out that there were three distinct anonymous strata, and each one had different information: the Stammaim who explained, "He held according to this Tanna . . ." (in the first sugya of Sanh 16a [1D]), knew both baraitot and the dictum of Rav Ada b. Ahava [1B, 1C, 1D]; the Stammaim who reasoned, "You might have thought . . ." (in the second sugya on Sanh 16a, [1H]) did not know the second baraita [1D] or the dictum of Rav Ada b. Ahava [1B]; these two sugyot are quoted in succession on Sanh 16a, on the same folio, one after another, as the Compilers juxtaposed them. In contrast, the Stammaim of Sanh 18b knew the second baraita [1D] and the dictum of Rav Ada b. Ahava [1B, 2B], and it is unclear whether they did not know of the first baraita or rejected it [1C].

Sanh 45b provides a second example of this phenomenon:

[A1] Shmuel said, "If the hands of the witnesses are amputated, he [the criminal] is exempt. What is the reason? We require, *Let the hands of the witnesses be the first against them (Deut 17:7)*, and they have none." . . .

[A2] But according to this, if the witnesses were without hands from the outset, in this case too they would be invalid?

[A3] There [Shmuel's case] it is different, as the verse states, *Let the hands of the witnesses (Deut 17:7)*—the hand that was already there.

[B1] But do we require a verse be carried out as written? Has it not been taught: "*The assailant shall surely [*mot yumat*] be put to death; he is a murderer (Num 35:21)*. I only know this of the [means of] death prescribed for him? How do I know that if you cannot execute him with the death prescribed for him, then you execute him with any [means of] death that you are able? The verse teaches *the assailant shall surely [*mot yumat*] be put to death*—in any way (*mikol maqom*)."

[B2] There it is different, as the verse states *he shall surely [*mot yumat*] be put to death (Num 35:21)*.

...

[C1] Mar Qashisha b. Rav Hisda said to Rav Ashi: "Do we not require a verse [be carried out] as written? Did we not learn: If one of them [his parents] was without hands or mute or lame or blind, then he does not become a stubborn and rebellious son, as is said, *They shall take hold of him (Deut 21:19)*, which excludes those without hands [= mSanh 8:4]. What is the reason? Is it not because we require a verse to be carried out as written?"

[C2] No, there it is different, as the entire verse is superfluous.

Mar Qashisha b. Rav Hisda's objection is problematic [C1]:[23] where did he find a source stating that we do not require a verse be carried out as written, against which he objects by citing mSanh 8:4? One cannot say that Mar Qashisha objects to the anonymous stratum's "initial assumption" (*hava amina*) of the objection against Shmuel, the attempt to prove from the baraita introduced by "Has it not been taught..." that we do not require a verse be carried out as written [B1]—because "this is not the way of the sugya" (so Solomon Luria [Rash"al] ad loc.). Indeed, it is not the style of the Talmud to object in this way, and an Amora certainly would not object to the "initial assumption" of the anonymous stratum. So against whom did Mar Qashisha object?

It therefore seems that, while our sugya appears to be a single sugya [B1–C2], in fact two contradictory sugyot that did not know one another were combined. One is wholly anonymous [B1–2]; the other begins with the objection of Mar Qashisha to Rav Ashi [C1] and continues anonymous [C2]. Originally Mar Qashisha's objection was against the baraita from which the anonymous stratum objects to Shmuel in the previous sugya, "How do I know that if you cannot execute him with the death prescribed for him, then you execute him with any [means of] death that you are able? [B1]"—implying that one does not require that a verse be carried out as written. Against this baraita Mar Qashisha objected from mSanh 8:4, "If one of them [his parents] was without hands...he does not become a stubborn and rebellious son, as is said, *They shall take hold of him (Deut 21:19)*, which excludes those without hands" [C1]—proving that one requires a verse be carried out as written. Mar Qashisha did not know of the anonymous discussion of Shmuel's dictum [B1], nor the response, "There it is different, as the verse states, *He shall surely [*mot yumat*] be put to death (Num 35:21)*" [B2], as this explanation would also answer his objection.**

We might even conjecture that Rav Ashi offered this very response to Mar Qashisha's objection [B2], and the response to Mar Qashisha's objection that now appears in the second sugya [C2] was not stated by Rav Ashi, but by the Stammaim, who also did not know the response of the Stammaim of the previous sugya [B1–B2]. Proof that this response ([C2], which implies that "we require a verse be [carried out] as written,") is not from Rav Ashi is that according to its logic, if a verse is *not* superfluous, then "we do not require [60] the verse be [carried out] as written." Yet Rav Ashi himself requires that a verse be carried out as written in Sot 27a, and rules that a "[suspected adulteress who is] lame or without hands does not drink, as is written, *He shall make the woman stand before the Lord...and place upon her hands the meal offering (Num 5:18)*." Tosafot and other medieval commentaries to Sot 27a point out this difficulty. However, if we explain that Rav Ashi responded to Mar Qashisha as now found in the unattributed response of the first sugya [B2], and therefore "we do not require a verse be [carried out] as written," then his scriptural interpretation in Sot 27a coheres with his view here, as in all places where the verse does not state "he shall surely (*mot yumat*) be put to death" or suchlike, we require that the verse be carried out as written.**

Now it is possible that the Stammaim responsible for the first sugya knew Rav Ashi's response but did not quote it in Rav Ashi's name, because Rav Ashi did not originally state it as an answer to Shmuel. The Stammaim who composed the second sugya did not know Rav Ashi's dictum in Sot 27a and therefore offered a different response. What about the Combiners (*metsarfim*) who juxtaposed these two sugyot [B1–B2 vs. C1–C2] in this way? It is possible that they lacked the original context of Mar Qashisha's objection, namely, the baraita, "How do I know that if you cannot execute him...[B1]," and they therefore integrated Mar Qashisha's objection without any real context. It is also possible that they did not notice the contradiction between the sugyot, and after they combined them together, they relied on the baraita, "How do I know that if you cannot execute him ... [B1]" quoted in the first sugya, also to provide context for the objection of Mar Qashisha with which the second Stammaim begin their sugya [C1]. Here we have a case of both a contradiction within a single passage and also of Stammaim who did not know of Rav Ashi's opinion (found in Sot 27a)—providing yet more evidence that Rav Ashi was not the editor of the anonymous stratum.

A third example is the contradiction between the first and second parts of the passage explicating mGit 8:1 at Git 78a. An outline of these passages together with the parallel at BB 85b is as follows:

Git 78a, first part:

[1A] [He who throws a bill of divorce to his wife, and she is within her house or within her courtyard—she is divorced. If he threw it to her when she was in his house or his courtyard, even if he is with her in bed—she is not divorced (= mGit 8:1)].

[1B] Rava said: This mishnah applies only if it is his bed, but if it is her bed, then she is divorced. It has also been taught thus: R. Eliezer says: In his bed—she is not divorced. In her bed—she is divorced.

[1C] And is she divorced if it is her bed? This is a case of "vessels of the purchaser in the domain of the seller"! Infer from this that "vessels of the purchaser in the domain of the seller" acquire possession for the purchaser? (Since the bed, belonging to the wife [= purchaser], though in the domain of the seller [= husband], apparently acquires possession for the wife, as it effects the divorce.)

[1D] No! ....

Git 78a, second part:

[2A] Into her lap or into her basket—she is divorced (= mGit 8:1):

[2B] Why? [This is a case of] "vessels of the purchaser in the domain of the seller"! Rav Yehudah said Shmuel said: "For instance, if the basket is hanging from her."

[2C] And so R. Eleazar said R. Oshaya said: "For instance, if the basket is hanging from her." And R. Shimon b. Laqish said: "Even if it [the basket] is tied to her, although not hanging from her." Rav Ada b. Ahava said: "For instance, if the basket is resting between her legs." Rav Mesharshia b. Rav Dimi said: "For instance, if her husband is a seller of baskets."

BB 85b:

[3A] Rav Sheshet asked of Rav Huna: "Vessels of the purchaser in the domain of the seller"—does the purchaser acquire possession or not?

[3B] He said to him: "You learn it [from this]: 'If he threw it [a bill of divorce] into her lap or into her basket—she is divorced (= mGit 8:1).' "

[3C] Rav Nahman said to him: "Why did you resolve this [question] from that which has been beaten with one hundred measures (= arguments) to one? For Rav Yehudah said Shmuel said: 'This is [a case] where the basket is hanging from her.' "

[3D] And R. Shimon b. Laqish said: "Even if it [the basket] is tied to her, although not hanging from her." Rav Ada b. Ahava said: "For instance, if the basket is resting between her legs." Rav Mesharshia b. Rav Dimi said: "For instance, if her husband is a seller of baskets."

The first part of the sugya states "'If she is in his bed—she is not divorced. If she is in her bed—she is divorced.'... Infer from this[24] that 'vessels of a purchaser in the domain of the seller acquire [possession] on behalf of the purchaser' " [1B–1C]. This implies that the law of "vessels of a purchaser in the domain of the seller" is not known with certitude. However, the second part states: "'[If a husband throws a bill of divorce into her lap] or into her basket—she is divorced (mGit 8:1).' Why?[25] This is a case of 'vessels of a purchaser in the domain of the seller' " [2B]—as if it is obvious that the "vessels of a purchaser in the domain of the seller" do not confer possession to the purchaser.[26] It appears that these two passages derive from different sources. Now in BB 85b–86a, Rava concludes that the "vessels of a purchaser in the domain of the seller do not confer possession to the purchaser," so it is according to his view that the second part of Git 78a states, "Why?..." [2B], that is, why does that mishnah state that if a man throws a bill of divorce into his wife's basket she is divorced, since this is a case of "vessels of a purchaser in the domain of the seller," and Rava holds that the purchaser does not acquire possession. On the other hand, the proof in the first part, "Infer from this... [1C]," follows the Amoraim who reject Rava's proof in BB 86a, and where the question of whether "vessels of a purchaser in the domain of the seller" confer possession to the purchaser remains unresolved.[27] For this reason the first part in Git 78a states, "Infer from this" [1C], while the second part states, "Why?" [2B]. The Compiler combined them together.

Now the Talmud's discussion at Git 78a [2B–2C] that follows "[If he throws her a bill of divorce] into her lap or into her basket" [2A] is constructed from a combination of the statements of Rav Huna, Rav Nahman, and the anonymous stratum of BB 85b [3A–3C]. Rav Sheshet asks Rav Huna whether [61] the "vessels of the purchaser in the domain of the seller" acquire possession or not [3A]; and Rav Huna answers him by quoting mGit 8:1, "If he throws her [a bill of divorce] into her lap or into her basket—she is divorced" [3B]. In response to Rav Huna's proof, Rav Nahman quotes the comment of Rav Yehudah in the name of Shmuel limiting the scope of the mishnah: "This is a case where the basket is hanging from her" [3C].[28] (Note that in BB 85b, Rav Nahman only quoted Shmuel's dictum; the rest of the dicta quoted there, namely, those of Rav Ada b. Ahava and Rav Mesharshia b. Rav Ami [3D], were not quoted by Rav Nahman but by the Stammaim, as Rav Nahman lived a generation before them [and the Rav Ada b. Ahava who appears there is the second sage of this name.]) Although the sugya at Git 78a [2A–2C] is constructed out of the words of Rav Huna and Rav Nahman, it does not mention their names, since it does not quote them verbatim. The same policy underpins the use by the Stammaim of the term "the master said (*amar mar*)" to introduce dialectical argumentation; they introduce a dictum without attribution when the quotation is not verbatim.

However, the Talmud, according to our readings, changed the original formulation of Shmuel's statement in Git 78a, "For instance, if the basket is hanging from her" [2B], and nevertheless attributed it directly to him. For originally, Shmuel apparently stated, "This is [a case] where the basket is hanging from her" [3C] directly on mGit 8:1, just as we find in BB 85b, and as is typical of the term "This is [a case] (*vehu*)." Shmuel made his statement independently of Rav Sheshet's question to Rav Huna in BB 85b [3A]; Shmuel held that "vessels of a purchaser in the domain of the seller" do not confer possession to the purchaser and therefore interpreted the mishnah's ruling as applying to a case where the basket was hanging from her. But if the basket was resting on the ground, it does not confer possession to her. This is the meaning of the term "This is [a case]"—only in that case, but not in other cases. However, the other Amoraim who add comments to Rav Huna's response to Rav Sheshet in BB 85b [3D] were uncertain about the law of "vessels of a purchaser in the domain of a seller," and therefore had reservations about Rav Huna's answer. Consequently they employ the term "For instance (*kegon*)" [3D], meaning that it is possible that the woman acquires possession of the document, but not certain. However, in Git 78a the Talmud also employs the term, "for instance (*kegon*)" to introduce Shmuel's dictum [2B], even though it quotes the dictum in response to the objection, "Why? This is a case of 'vessels of a purchaser in the domain of the seller'" [2B] and not directly on the mishnah, its original context. Here we would have expected the Talmud to introduce Shmuel's statement with "the master said (*amar mar*)," as Shmuel is not quoted verbatim: this discrepancy again indicates that the Talmud lacked a general editor.

Apparently, the Compilers were confronted by two sources: one source asked, "Infer from this that the vessels of a purchaser in the domain of the seller acquire [possession] on behalf of the purchaser?" with respect to a bill of divorce thrown into the wife's bed [1A–D]. However, this source did not deal with the case of a bill of divorce thrown into her lap or basket, because its composers were aware of the dicta in BB 85b of Rav Sheshet, Rav Huna, Rav Nahman, and perhaps the Stammaim too [3A–C]. A second source dealt with the issue of a bill of divorce thrown into a woman's lap or basket [2A–C], which was transferred to Git 78a from BB 85b, albeit with some changes. This discussion, as in BB 85b, does not address the case of a bill of divorce thrown into the bed. The Compilers, however, combined the two sources together: they juxtaposed the first part of the sugya [1A–C], which deals with the issue of the bed, with the second part [2A–C], which deals with her lap and basket.

The fourth example, from Sanh 23a, differs in certain respects from the preceding examples:

[A1] [mSanh 3:1] Monetary cases [are tried before a court of] three. This party chooses one and the other party chooses one, and the two together choose another one—these are the words of R. Meir.

[A2] [Talmud:] Why does "This party choose one [court] and the other party choose one [court]?" Three judges suffice! This is what it means: If this party chooses a court, and that party chooses a different court (such that they don't agree on the court), then the two together choose another (mutually acceptable) court.

[A3] Is even a debtor able to reject (the judges selected by the creditor)?

[A4] As said R. Yohanan [below]: "This was taught of the Syrian courts." Here too it was taught of the Syrian courts, but not of experts.

[A5] Rav Pappa (some texts read: Rava) said: "You could even say it applies to experts; for example to the courts of Rav Huna and Rav Hisda, since he [the debtor] can say to him [the creditor]: 'Am I causing you any trouble? (since they are close together).' "

[A6] We learned in the Mishnah: "But the Sages say, 'The two judges choose another one.' " If it is as you say, [that the mishnah means that they choose] a court, then would a court, after they reject it, go and choose another court? And also, how do you explain "This party chooses one and the other party chooses one" (which implies that each indeed makes the choice)? Rather, this is what it means: After this party chooses one judge and that party chooses one judge, the two [litigants] together choose another one. What is the advantage of doing it in this way? They said in the West (= Israel) in the name of R. Zeira: "Since this party chooses one judge, and that party chooses one judge, and the two together choose another, a true judgment will be rendered."

[B1] [Citation from mSanh 3:1] "This party may reject the judge selected by that party, and that party may reject the judge selected by this party."

[B2] Does he have the right to reject judges?

[B3] R. Yohanan said: "This was taught of the Syrian courts, but not of a court of experts."

Note that the Talmud quotes responses of both R. Yohanan and Rav Pappa in the discussion of the first clause of mSanh 3:1 [A4–A5]. In the discussion of the second citation of mSanh 3:1[B1], the Talmud quotes the same response of R. Yohanan [B3 = A4]. However, Rav Pappa's response is not quoted here, even though it is more fitting than in the context above [A5], namely, that only in the case of the "courts of Rav Huna and Rav Hisda" [62] is one party permitted to reject the other's selection. In the discussion of the first clause of mSanh 3:1 [A1], they transferred R. Yohanan's response [A4] from the discussion of the latter clause [B3], as indicated by the introductory formula, "As said R. Yohanan." However, they failed to mention Rav Pappa even though his explanation is more appropriate than in the discussion of the first clause of the mishnah [A5], as the first clause deals with a debtor [A1], and the second citation with the judges [B1]. I have no better explanation than to suggest that the Talmud did not know of Rav Pappa's explanation when it discussed the second citation, although it knew of it when it discussed the first clause. In my opinion, Rav Pappa actually commented only upon the second citation, not the first clause, and the "As said" stated in reference to R. Yohanan in the first clause [A4] in fact also applies to Rav Pappa [A5]. His response too—and not only the comment of R. Yohanan—was transferred from the discussion of the second citation. In order to apply Rav Pappa's comment to the first clause, it was necessary to create the impression that he explained the mishnah according to the Talmud's initial assumption, that the mishnah's ruling "this one [litigant] selects..." means "this one selects a court..." [A2]. This explanation opposes the simple language of the mishnah (as the Talmud itself asks, "In addition, how do you explain 'This party chooses one and the other party chooses one'" [A6]), opposes that which was "stated in the West" in the name of R. Zeira (the earlier R. Zeira) [A6], and opposes logic. We should rather explain that Rav Pappa interpreted this first clause of the mishnah as per the conclusion of the Talmud [A6], that "this party chooses" refers to choosing a judge, and commented on the second citation alone [B1]. The statement attributed to him on the first citation of the mishnah [A6] is a transposition (*ha'avarah*). So why was his comment not quoted in the discussion of the second citation? We have to conclude that the Talmudic editors who dealt with that citation did not know of it.

The fifth example beautifully illustrates a glaring local contradiction between two consecutive anonymous passages. Hul 95a states, "Rav said: Meat that disappeared from sight is forbidden." The Talmud debates this ruling, and concludes, at the bottom of the folio, that Rav did not make this statement "explicitly (*befeirush*)," but rather it was attributed to him "from an inference (*mikelala*)." The inference, however, provides no proof regarding the question of meat that disappeared from sight, since Rav's statement pertained to the "the market of the idolators" (Hul 95b). The Talmud confirms that this was indeed a mistaken inference: "You know this from that which he [Rav] said to them, 'Forbidden [meat] is common there,'" namely, in the market of the idolators. Elsewhere, however, Rav might not have prohibited meat that disappeared from sight. At this point the Talmud asks, "Then how did Rav [ever] eat meat?" Now it is clear that whoever asked this question either was not aware that Rav never stated the prohibition explicitly, or he knew that Rav did not state the prohibition explicitly and that it was derived from an inference, yet did not know that the inference was problematic. Similarly, we find in BB 24b that the Talmud objects: "Behold, Rav said, 'Meat that disappeared from sight is prohibited.'" This passage too was not aware that Rav never made this statement explicitly and that it was attributed to him based on an inference that subsequently was rejected. In Hul 95a–b contradictory sources were combined and juxtaposed in succession. Had there been a general editor of the anonymous passages, he indubitably would have reacted to the contradiction.

The sixth example features a sugya constructed from two anonymous passages that do not contradict each other but clearly derive from disparate sources; because of the similar content the disparate sources were integrated into one sugya: Eruv 81b–82a:

[A] Rav Yehudah said Shmuel said: The law follows R. Yehudah (in mEruv 7:11, who states, "When does this [= that one may give money to a wine-seller or baker to acquire an *eruv*] apply? To the *eruv* of Sabbath-boundaries but not to the *eruv* of courtyards.")

[B] Rav Aha b. Rava said to Rav Ashi: "'The law [follows R. Yehudah]'—this implies there is a disagreement. But did not R. Yehoshua b. Levi say: 'Whenever R. Yehudah says "When (*eimatai*)?" and "In what circumstances (*bameh devarim amurim*)?" he is simply explicating the words of the Sages?' "

[C1] But do they not disagree? Behold, we have learned (mEruv 7:7, cited at Eruv 80b): "If they [the number of residents] increased, he must add [to the food] and grant them acquisition, and he must make the declaration [again]."

[C2] That is in the case of a courtyard between alleys (but not a regular courtyard).

[C3] But did not Rav Shizvi say that Rav Hisda said, "This means that R. Yehudah's colleagues disagree with him?"

[D] <He said to him:> But do you oppose one Amora with another Amora (*gavra agavra ka rameit*)? One master holds that they disagree, and one master holds that they do not disagree.

Between Rav Aha b. Rava's question [B] and the response [D] the Stammaim interpolated and questioned R. Yehoshua b. Levi's claim, bringing an objection from mEruv 7:7 [C1]. The Stammaim then reject this argument [C2] such that Rav Aha b. Rava's question stands.[29] Here [63] is the proper place to respond, "Do you oppose one Amora with another Amora?" [D]. However the Stammaim do not do so, but rather continue to object by quoting the dictum attributed to Rav Shizvi in the name of Rav Hisda, which contradicts R. Yehoshua b. Levi's claim [C3]. At this point we find the response, "But (some texts read 'He said to him') do you oppose one Amora with another Amora?" [D]. Here it is unclear to which sages the "one Amora with another Amora" refers: R. Yehoshua b. Levi and Shmuel (as Rashi explains), which would have to be the case if one reads "He said to him," that is, Rav Ashi said to Rav Aha b. Rava; or R. Yehoshua b. Levi and Rav Shizvi quoting Rav Hisda, in which case the Stammaim, and not Rav Ashi, reply "Do you oppose one Amora with another Amora?"

We are apparently dealing with two sources: one source transmitted the question Rav Aha b. Rava asked of Rav Ashi and his response, "Do you oppose one Amora with another?" [B,D]. If the correct reading is "He said to him," then Rav Ashi obviously responded to his colleague, whereas if the reading is "But," then apparently Rav Ashi's answer had been forgotten[30] and the Stammaim reconstructed it on their own. A second source transmitted the objection of the Stammaim against R. Yehoshua b. Levi's claim based on Rav Shizvi's statement together with the response "Do you oppose one Amora with another?" [C3, D]. Obviously, this answer was preceded by the rhetorical question, "Do they not disagree? Behold, we have learned..." [C1]. Over the course of time the two sources were amalgamated, and we received one sugya which begins with Rav Aha b. Rava's statement and continues with Stammaitic material; it is unclear whether the response "Do you oppose one Amora with another?" is from Rav Ashi or whether the Stammaim reconstructed Rav Ashi's response. I would assume that the reading "He said to him" [D] is a later addition, as a scribe probably believed the dialogue between the Amoraim continued and therefore added "He said to him."[31] Therefore it seems that the correct reading is "But." If so, then Rav Ashi's response was forgotten, and the Compilers, instead of simply quoting "Do you oppose one Amora with another?" [D] as a response to Rav Aha b. Rava's question, integrated the entire Stammaitic sugya [C1–C3], and also added the Stammaitic sugya that follows immediately on Eruv 82a: "[Let us return to] the full text (*gufa*): R. Yehoshua b. Levi said...."

[If I may digress briefly from the primary topic of "Contradictions on the same folio," I would like to continue the analysis of this passage, Eruv 81b–82a. In the subsequent sugya on Eruv 82a, and in the parallel in Sanh 24b–25a, the Talmud objects to R. Yehoshua b. Levi's claim, "Whenever R. Yehudah says 'When?' and 'In what circumstances' he is simply explicating the words of the Sages," on the basis of tSanh 5:2, where the Sages disagree with R. Yehudah. There R. Yehudah states, "When [is this the case, that a gambler and certain other occupations are not valid witnesses, because they take money based on a 'stipulation (*asmakhta*)']? If he has no other occupation, but if he has another occupation, he is valid." The Sages, on the other hand, hold that whether or not he has another occupation, he is not a valid witness. The Talmud responds that R. Yehudah stated this ruling in the name of R. Tarfon, who said "The vow of a Nazirite must be unambiguous," but that R. Yehudah himself does not disagree with the Sages. This answer is difficult, and the medieval commentaries were perplexed at the relevance of a Nazirite's vow to a stipulation. It is more plausible that R. Yehoshua b. Levi intended his claim, "Whenever R. Yehudah says 'When?' and 'In what circumstances?' he is simply explicating the words of the Sages," to apply only to the first authority of a mishnah (*tanna qamma*), who is apparently an early sage with whom R. Yehudah would not disagree. However, another Tannaitic authority, a contemporary of R. Yehudah, can disagree with R. Yehudah's explanation of the first opinion of the mishnah (or with that opinion itself), and therefore can hold that there is no difference as to whether he has another occupation or not—this is indeed the position of the Sages of tSanh 5:2. It is even possible that the wording of Rav Shizvi, quoting Rav Hisda, supports this conclusion, "This means that R. Yehudah's colleagues disagree with him" [C3]. If Rav Shizvi, quoting Rav Hisda, disagrees with R. Yehoshua b. Levi and holds like R. Yohanan that the term "In what circumstances" always disagrees with the previous comment, then it is clear from mSanh 3:3 itself, which states, "R. Yehudah says: In what circumstances...," that the Sages disagree with R. Yehudah. There is no need to adduce support from a single mishnah. It appears, then, that Rav Shizvi, quoting Rav Hisda, [64] also holds like R. Yehoshua b. Levi, that R. Yehudah, when he employs the terms "When," and "In what circumstances," does not mean to disagree with the first opinion of a mishnah but to explicate it. However, in this one case, mEruv 7:7, Rav Shizvi, quoting Rav Hisda, holds that the Sages disagree with R. Yehudah.

Indeed, elsewhere I have noted similar examples in the Mishnah that do not use the terms "When" or "In what circumstances," and yet the Tannaim are explicating the first opinion.[32] For example in mShab 2:1 the first opinion stating that one may not light Sabbath lamps with tallow is immediately followed by: "Nahum the Mede says: One may light with melted tallow." He could have stated: "In what circumstances? In tallow that was not melted. But one may light with melted tallow." The mishnah then adds: "But the Sages say," that is, they disagree with Nahum the Mede, and hold that according to the first opinion, "It is all the same whether [the tallow is] melted or not melted—he may not light."[33] Thus both Nahum the Mede and the Sages explicate the first opinion. If this explanation is correct, then we can say that the Stammaim incorrectly reconstructed Rav Ashi's response to R. Aha b. Rava in Eruv 81b [D]. He did not state, "Do you oppose one Amora with another Amora?" but responded in the same manner as R. Shizvi, quoting Rav Hisda, that in mEruv 7:7 the Sages indeed disagree with R. Yehudah ("R. Yehudah's colleagues disagree with him," C3), and Shmuel rules against these Sages when he states, "The law follows R. Yehudah." If this reconstruction of Rav Ashi's original answer is correct, we have yet more evidence that Rav Ashi was not the editor of the Talmud. And perhaps this distinction between R. Yehudah's use of the terms "When" or "In what circumstances" with reference to an earlier authority (whom he means to explicate) as opposed to a contemporary (with whom he may disagree) is what the Talmud meant with its response, "That [opinion] was R. Yehudah quoting R. Tarfon", that is, that R. Tarfon is an earlier authority with whom R. Yehudah is explicating, not disputing.]

This is the appropriate point to refer to the indices of the volumes of *Meqorot umesorot*, s.v. "combination (*tseiruf*)," in particular "combination of contradictory passages" and "combination of contradictory sources." A considerable portion of those cases deal with baraitot and with the Mishnah, which underwent a kind of editing.[34] Amoraic traditions, however, were not subjected to a similar editing process. As for Stammaitic traditions: there were Compilers (*me'asfim*), but their function differed from editors and redactors.[35] The Yerushalmi (yEruv 1:7, 19b) already mentions a baraita that went through an editing process:

> It was taught: Everything that contains the breath of life may be used as a wall, but not as a side-post [for the *eruv*]. These are the words of R. Meir... R. Yose said: There were two Reciters [*tannaim*] (for the ruling of R. Meir.) He who said "may be used as a wall," holds it may be used as a side-post. He who says "it may not be used as a side-post," holds it may not be used as a wall. (This reading follows the emendation found in *Sha'arei torah erets yisra'el*; cf. Lieberman, *Hayerushalmi kifshuto*, ad loc.)

That is, this baraita is a combination of two contradictory versions of R. Meir's ruling: according to one version R. Meir ruled that living entities may neither be used as a wall nor as a side-post; according to a second version R. Meir ruled that they may be used both as a wall and as a side-post. The baraita in its current form begins with a part of the latter version (that they may be used as a wall), and concludes with a part of the former version (that they may not be used as a side-post).[36]**

The references in those indices include not only baraitot but also similar cases involving Talmudic passages. Perhaps we should include among these examples of "combinations of contradictory passages" that of AZ 68a, where the Talmud states: "[The question] stands (*teiqu*)," and immediately thereafter, "Come and hear" (see Tosafot, s.v. *teiqu*), and that of Tem 25b, "[Shall we say...] it is a refutation of R. Yohanan? It is a refutation. Shall we say... is a dispute between Tannaim..." [65].[37**] Here, however, I will discuss another example, at once more general and more complicated, which is in fact the first example I commented upon in *MM*, Nazir, 428–29. I observed that in Naz 62a we find a:

> combination of disparate sources without an appropriate transition. That is, the dialectical argumentation is constructed from two sources without sufficient editing. In one source they asked: Why did the Torah write *a man (Lev 27:2)* in connection with vows of valuation? And they answered: to include "[a youth] who can discriminate (*mufla*) and is close to [becoming] a man." The response to this answer is: "This is well for the one who says that [a youth] who can discriminate and is close to [becoming] a man [may vow] according to Scriptural authority. But for the one who says that [a youth] who can discriminate and is close to [becoming] a man [may vow] according to rabbinic authority, why is the verse, *When a man explicitly vows (Lev 27:2)* necessary? To include 'an idolator [youth] who can discriminate (*mufla*) and is close to [becoming] a man.'" In another source they asked: Why did the Torah write *a man (Lev 27:2)* in connection with vows of valuation? And they gave the same answer, to include "[a youth] who can discriminate (*mufla*) and is close to becoming a man." To this answer they then asked: "This is well for the one who says that the verse, *[Speak to the] Children of Israel (Lev 27:2)* teaches that Israelites can be the subject of vows of valuations... But for the one who says that the verse, *[Speak to the] Children of Israel (Lev 27:2)* teaches that Israelites may make vows of valuation... then even a one-month-old baby can be the subject of a vow of valuation. Why then is the verse, *When a man explicitly vows (Lev 27:2)* necessary? Rav Ada bar Ahava said: To include an adult idolator..." In keeping with this second source they subsequently asked: "Now why is the verse *When a man explicitly vows (Lev 27:2)* necessary in connection with vows of the Nazirite?" Over the course

> of time the two sources were combined and juxtaposed together—and this caused the difficulties with the passage.

It is possible that Sanh 24a-b provides a similar example: On Sanh 24a the Talmud quotes Rava as: "The disagreement (between R. Meir and the Sages in mSanh 3:2, concerning whether one who accepts a disqualified judge for his case may subsequently retract) is in [a case where the defendant says] 'I will pay you,' but [if the plaintiff said] '[My claim] is remitted to you' they both agree that he cannot retract." Now on Sanh 24b Rava is quoted as: "If he accepted a relation or one disqualified [from serving as judge or witness], he may retract before the final verdict, but after the final verdict he may not retract." In the continuation of the passage the Talmud relates that they asked Rav Nahman b. Yaakov: "Teach us, our Master: Is the disagreement (between R. Meir and the Sages in mSanh 3:2) before the final verdict or after the final verdict, and with whom does the law accord?" He answers, "The disagreement is after the final verdict and the law accords with the Sages." Rav Ashi then states: "They sent to him (Rav Nahman b. Yaakov) thus: 'Is the disagreement (between R. Meir and the Sages in mSanh 3:2) over 'I will pay you' or '[My claim] is remitted to you,' and with whom does the law accord?" And he answered back, "The disagreement is over 'I will pay you' and the law accords with the Sages." The Talmud then notes, "Thus they taught in [the Academy of] Sura." However, if Rav Nahman b. Yaakov, Rava's primary teacher, was asked about both issues and responded by clarifying the law—what new element did Rava subsequently add by issuing his ruling? It seems that "the Academy of Sura" and Rav Ashi disputed not only what question was asked of Rav Nahman b. Yaakov, but also what Rava said. According to Rav Ashi they asked Rav Nahman b. Yaakov about the case of "I will pay you" or "[My claim] is remitted to you," whereas Rava made his ruling on the issue of the final verdict. According to the Academy of Sura, on the other hand, they asked Rav Nahman b. Yaakov about the issue of the final verdict, whereas Rava stated the law about the issue of "I will pay you" or "[My claim] is remitted to you." The Talmud, however, combined both questions asked of Rav Nahman b. Yaakov and both answers as if they complemented one another, whereas in reality they disagree with one another.

These and many similar examples demonstrate that the Talmud had no general editor who reconciled contradictions, worked out discrepancies, unified passages, or removed inconsistencies in order to render the Talmud consistent in style and content. However, each independent sugya in and of itself was corrected and edited, although we still find sugyot that were constructed from contradictory sources and were not subjected to sufficient editing; the examples above provide ample testimony to this phenomenon.

"Rav Ashi and Ravina—the End of hora'ah"

[66] Beginning with Sherira Gaon (c. 900–1000 CE), though attested even earlier, writers frequently adduce the statement in BM 86a, "Rav Ashi and Ravina—the end of *hora'ah*," and understand it as establishing that Rav Ashi and Ravina were the editors of the Talmud.[38] "The end of *hora'ah*" is interpreted in terms of the end of the *gemara*, though this is in fact not the case. The meaning of *hora'ah* in hundreds of instantiations throughout the Talmud is consistently apodictic law and not the dialectical argumentation that comprises the essence of the Talmud. On the contrary, since the passage does not refer to the "end of the Talmud" but rather "end of *hora'ah*," it implies that Rav Ashi and Ravina did not conclude the *gemara* or Talmud, but only the period of *hora'ah*, the period of practical law.[39] The composition of the Talmud, however, did not cease in their days but continued thereafter, perhaps even mostly thereafter. Isaak Halevy and those who follow in his wake cite Ber 5a (cf. Ker 13b), "*To teach them* (lehorotam; Exod 24:12)—this refers to Talmud," in order to prove that Talmud is *hora'ah*. But this is a mistake: forms of the infinitive such as "to teach them" or other verbs derived from the root *YRH* can be used for *gemara*, but *hora'ah* as a noun does not mean *gemara*, namely, dialectical argumentation, but rather apodictic law. Moreover, the verb "to teach them" (*lehorotam*) in the verse "*which I have written to teach them*" (Exod 24:12) is completely inappropriate for "talmud," which is characterized by traditions that are not written. See yPeah 2:6, 17a: "R. Zeira [said] in the name of Shmuel: One does not learn from laws (*halakhot*), nor narratives (*haggadot*), nor supplements (*tosafot*), but from the talmud." The continuation of the passage reads: "R. Hanania said in the name of Shmuel: One does not learn from the *hora'ah*." Thus "talmud" is not *hora'ah*. Furthermore, this tradition about Rav Ashi and Ravina should not be relied upon, as it appears but once in the entire Talmud, in an aggadic context, namely, a quotation from "The Book of Primordial Adam."[40]** No one knows who made this statement, nor why it was stated, nor whether history subsequently confirmed or contravened the claim.

[67] More important, the expression "the end of *hora'ah*," does not connote compilation (*siddur*) or editing (*arikha*) but the final place on a list, namely, that Rav Ashi was the last with respect to *hora'ah*;[41] it does not mean that he edited, elucidated, or clarified that which was stated before him. Rav Sherira and his followers apparently attributed the editing of the Talmud to him (though not explicitly; see below) because they drew an analogy between "Rav Ashi—the end of *hora'ah*" and "Rabbi [Yehudah HaNasi] and R. Natan—the end of Mishnah," which is mentioned in the same Talmudic tradition;[42] and R. Yehudah HaNasi, as is well known, was the compiler of the Mishnah. Therefore they inferred that Rav Ashi too was the compiler of the Talmud (its editor). However, they overlooked R. Natan, who, according to the best of our knowledge, had no role whatsoever in the compilation of the Mishnah; he is mentioned together with R. Yehudah HaNasi because these two sages were among the last Tannaim mentioned in the Mishnah. So too Rav Ashi and Ravina (the first) are mentioned together because they were among the last sages to engage in *hora'ah* (whatever the meaning of *hora'ah*), and not because they were editors of the Talmud. Now Sherira Gaon attributes the end of *hora'ah* to Rav Ashi and Ravina, following the Talmudic tradition, but he then writes: "even though there was no *hora'ah* proper. . . ."; it is only later, in the generation of R. Yose (a Sabora), that Rav Sherira explains, "the 'end of *hora'ah*' occurred during his days, and the Talmud was completed." And the author of *Seder tannaim ve'amoraim* says nothing at all about Rav Ashi and Ravina (the first), and says of the second Ravina: "in the year 811 (= 499 CE), Ravina, 'the end of *hora'ah*,' passed away, and the Talmud was completed." While their views are not completely clear,[43] it appears that they identified "the end of *hora'ah*" with the end of the *gemara* in the sense of editing. Nevertheless, I do not consider this conclusion necessary. Some medieval jurists even identified the anonymous stratum of the Talmud with Rav Ashi on account of this tradition and used this as a criterion for halakhic decisions: if the anonymous stratum disagrees with an Amora, the law follows the anonymous stratum because it possesses the authority of Rav Ashi.[44] However, it is difficult to link the "end of *hora'ah*" with the issue of the author of the anonymous stratum, and likewise problematic to connect the "end of *hora'ah*" to the editing of the Talmud. Thus the entirety of the Talmud itself offers no compelling evidence that Rav Ashi was its editor:[45] "end" implies neither "editing" or "compilation," but only determines a point in time.

[68] Moreover, the statement "Rav Ashi and Ravina—the end of *hora'ah*" should not be taken as a historical fact but as an expression of a

student's veneration of his master, albeit an idealization that was not realized over the course of time. In the Introduction to *MM: bava metsia*, 12, I connected this statement with the statement of Rav Aha b. Rava that compares Rav Ashi with R. Yehudah HaNasi: "From the time of Rabbi [Yehudah HaNasi] until Rav Ashi, Torah and prestige (*gedulah*) were never found in the same place" (Git 59a, Sanh 36a). The Stammaim object to this: "Behold, there was Huna b. Natan?" and respond, "Huna b. Natan was subservient to Rav Ashi." In parallel fashion, the Stammaim follow the statement concerning Moses, "From the time of Moses until R. Yehudah HaNasi Torah and prestige were never found in the same place" with the objection: "No? Behold, there was Joshua!" However, they do not object to the claim about R. Yehudah HaNasi, "Behold, there was..." because after R. Yehudah HaNasi there was no sage comparable to him. Now it stands to reason—so I stated in the aforementioned "Introduction"—that Rav Aha b. Rava referred to Rav Ashi because he considered Rav Ashi "the end of *hora'ah*," the conclusion of an era, analogous to R. Yehudah HaNasi who was "the end of Mishnah." Huna b. Natan, however, was not "the end of *hora'ah*," hence the objection, "Behold, there was Huna b. Natan?" is out of place. Similarly, the objection to the claim about Moses, "Behold, there was Joshua?" is out of place, since Joshua did not bring the Torah down from heaven, nor take part in the writing of the Torah, nor end an era. Why then do the Stammaim object, "Behold, there was Huna b. Natan?" and "Behold, there was Joshua?" It appears that the Stammaim lived long after Rav Ashi and experienced the continuation of *hora'ah*, and accordingly did not consider the uniqueness of Rav Ashi to be that he marked the end of *hora'ah*, but rather that he served as Head of the Academy for sixty years and had many disciples.** Similarly, the uniqueness of Moses was not considered his role in bringing the Torah down from heaven but that he led the people. Therefore the Stammaim considered Huna b. Natan comparable to Rav Ashi, as Huna b. Natan also had access to the royal court (*karov lamalkhut*; Tosafot, Sanh 36a, s.v. *veha*), and they considered Joshua comparable to Moses. However, they rejected the analogy because Rav Huna b. Natan did not hold the same rank as Rav Ashi but was subservient to him. Rav Aha b. Rava considered Rav Ashi to be "the end of *hora'ah*," and perhaps he really was the end of *hora'ah* at this time (whatever we take the expression to mean). However, as time passed material continued to be added to Rav Ashi's *hora'ah*, and the Stammaim who lived after Rav Aha b. Rava (perhaps long after him) no longer knew that there was anyone who considered Rav Ashi to be the end of an era, and therefore they thought that Rav Aha b. Rava had mentioned Rav Ashi because of his greatness, and they ventured to compare Rav Huna b. Natan to him.

Indeed, we find a number of statements in the Talmud that are true only of specific periods, although the Talmud [69] quotes them as if they apply to the entire Talmudic era. For example, Sanh 17b: "[The formula] 'They sent from there (= The Land of Israel)' refers to R. Yose b. R. Hanina (or, according to a second opinion, to R. Eleazar)." Yet Zev 87a states: "They sent from there: The law follows Rav Yosef"—and Rav Yosef postdated R. Yose b. R. Hanina and R. Eleazar. Clearly, R. Yose b. R. Hanina sent instruction to the diaspora in his time. After his death someone else took his place, but the Talmud does not mention the names of those who lived in subsequent generations: it included the original dictum and left it in that state. Were there a general editor of the Talmud, he probably would have commented on this issue.

Forced Responses about Statements of Rav Ashi

Furthermore, in some cases the Stammaim have difficulty explaining statements of Rav Ashi—among the greatest of the later Amoraim, and to whom the traditional view attributes the editing of the Talmud—because they did not know Rav Ashi's version of the Mishnah, or because they did not know the reasoning underpinning his view, or because they did not correctly identify his original statement.[46] This phenomenon would not occur, certainly not to such a great extent, were the Stammaim contemporaries of the Amoraim and Rav Ashi the editor of the unattributed stratum of the Talmud. The medieval commentaries were aware of the forced explanations and attempted to resolve the difficulties,[47] but they frequently end up transferring the difficulties from the statements of the Amoraim to those of the Stammaim.[48] Even if we hold like I. Halevy [70] that Rav Ashi and his school began the task of editing the Talmud, which continued for nearly seventy years until the second Ravina and still later,[49] and that his successors occasionally corrected Rav Ashi's statements or disagreed with him—it is difficult to believe that the Stammaim would misunderstand Rav Ashi if the Stammaitic stratum was in fact edited by Rav Ashi or by his school. Rav Ashi's successors would certainly have had accurate knowledge of his traditions. In addition, why would they have needed seventy years to edit sugyot that had taken shape during a period of less than 200 years, from the time of Rav until Rav Ashi, if other Amoraim also had detailed traditions as to the dialectical argumentation?

Here are examples where the Stammaim have difficulty explaining Rav Ashi's statements:

(a) According to Ned 60b: "Rav Ashi emended the mishnah... and on that basis resolved the question.... However, it is hard to imagine that Rav Ashi would delete a letter from a mishnah, and then make conclusions from the deletion solely on the basis of the weak objection 'why was it necessary to state?'"[50**] Therefore, I concluded that Rav Ashi did not emend the mishnah but rather his version of this mishnah read that way. His successors, however, did not know that version, and therefore "they had no explanation other than to say that Rav Ashi emended the mishnah." If the authors of the anonymous stratum did not know Rav Ashi's version, clearly they were not contemporaries of Rav Ashi, nor did they live in the following generation, and nor were they members of Rav Ashi's school who collaborated with him in editing the Talmud.

(b) In Eruv 12a, the anonymous stratum does not know the correct reasoning grounding Rav Ashi's explanation of R. Shimon b. Gamaliel's ruling in a baraita. Rav Ashi appears to proffer a forced explanation of R. Shimon b. Gamaliel's position in order that R. Shimon b. Gamaliel not contradict the statement of "a student in the name of R. Ishmael in the presence of R. Akiba." But this motivation is not sufficient. It is easier to say that R. Meir (the student quoting R. Ishmael) and R. Shimon b. Gamaliel disagree. In *MM*, Eruvin, 26 I explained that "Rav Ashi offered this explanation of R. Shimon b. Gamaliel so as to resolve the internal tension between R. Shimon b. Gamaliel's rulings in the two halves of the baraita."

(c) In Ker 26a the Talmud questions R. Shimon b. Yohai: "If that is so, then a parturient of doubtful status (*safeq yoledet*), after Yom Kippur intervenes, should not bring (a bird as sin-offering), as Yom Kippur makes atonement for her." Two responses are quoted: "[Yom Kippur atones] for *all sins (Lev 16:21)*, not for all cases of impurity," and that "the sacrifice functions to permit her to eat consecrated food (*qodashim*)." According to both responses, the sacrifice does not function to atone but to purify her from the state of impurity, to permit her to eat consecrated food. Now this is stated explicitly in mKer 6:7 (which appears on Ker 25b). Rav Ashi reacts to the second response: "We too learned thus (*af anan namei tanina*), 'A woman who is liable to bring a bird as sin-offering for a doubtful case, and Yom Kippur intervenes, is obligated to bring it after Yom Kippur, because it permits her to eat sacrifices.' " Rav Ashi is quoting mKer 6:7, and therefore should have said "It was also taught thus" or "It was taught in accordance with him." The term "We too learned thus" never is used when the source states verbatim what it is adduced to support, and certainly not when the objection ("If that is so, then a parturient of doubtful status, after Yom Kippur intervenes, should not bring [a bird as sin-offering]") refers to the same mishnah (as Rashi comments: "why does the mishnah [= mKer 6:7] teach that she should bring [a sin-offering]?"). For it is inappropriate to use the term, "We too learned thus," when the solution derives from the same source as the difficulty. We must conclude that originally Rav Ashi's statement was based on the objection in Shevu 8a, that a parturient, after Yom Kippur intervenes, does not need [71] to bring a sacrifice because the goat of Yom Kippur atones for her. Rashi explains Rav Hoshaya's response, "[Yom Kippur atones] for *all sins (Lev 16:21)* not for all cases of impurity," that "the parturient's sacrifice does not function to atone, but to purify her from the state of impurity to eat consecrated food." It is with respect to this response of Rav Hoshaya, which deals with a parturient of certain status (*vaday*), that Rav Ashi brings proof from mKer 6:7, which deals with the sin-offering of a bird for a parturient of doubtful status. Here it *is* appropriate to say "We too learned thus." Rav Ashi apparently was not troubled by the objection that appears in both tractates, "And what would R. Shimon b. Yohai, who rules that a parturient is also a sinner, respond?" because Rav Ashi thought that R. Shimon b. Yohai considered the parturient's sacrifice analogous to the sacrifice for a "useless oath (*shevuat bitui*)." This is implied from R. Shimon b. Yohai's statement in Nid 31b: "At the time when she kneels down to give birth, she impulsively swears that she will never have sex with her husband again, therefore the Torah obligates her to bring a sacrifice," in order to atone for her oath (and according to ms. Munich of Nid 31b, it is Rav Ashi who raises the objection "Moreover, she must bring a sacrifice on account of the oath")—and the goat for Yom Kippur does not atone for the sin of a "useless oath."[51] Nevertheless, both the anonymous stratum of Shevu 8a and that of Ker 25b thought that one could raise this objection against R. Shimon b. Yohai (that the goat sacrificed on Yom Kippur should atone for the parturient's sin), and they provided different responses. The anonymous stratum of Shevu 8a responds, "R. Shimon b. Yohai follows his own reasoning, as he said, 'it [= what the goat for Yom Kippur atones for, which does not include the sin of the parturient] is determined by its own text.' " The anonymous stratum of Ker 25b responds, "to permit her to eat consecrated food." But it is not fitting to follow either of these responses with, "We too learned thus." The term does not fit Ker 25b for the reason noted above, and it does not fit Shevu 8a because R. Shimon b. Yohai disagrees with the first opinion on whether a parturient's sacrifice atones for sin (R. Shimon b. Yohai ruling that it does)—and it is inappropriate to state "We too learned thus" in the case of a Tannaitic dispute. Rather, one would have to say "the source disagrees with R. Shimon b. Yohai" or suchlike. For this reason Rav Ashi's statement is not quoted at all in Shevu 8a.[52] However, the anonymous stratum in Ker 25b, for whom there is no disagreement between R. Shimon b. Yohai and the first opinion, apparently did not realize that the term "We too learned thus" in Rav Ashi's statement is not fitting; they preserved their source and retained the original wording.

It turns out that the sugya at Ker 25b originates in Shevu 8a but disagrees with that original sugya on several points. According to Ker 25b, the responses to the objections against R. Shimon b. Yohai still make it possible to quote Rav Ashi's statement (which was originally responding to R. Hoshaya). Moreover, the sugya at Ker 25b, as opposed to Shevu 8a, did not discern that the wording of Rav Ashi, "We too learned thus," is not fitting and quoted it verbatim. A development such as this could only take place several generations after Rav Ashi, and therefore one cannot attribute the editing of the Talmud to Rav Ashi or his school.

More significantly, Rav Ashi's statement in Git 4a, "Who is this (the Tannaitic authority of mGit 1:1)? It is R. Yehudah," makes it clear that he did not know the conclusion of the passage at Git 4b that "Rabbah also accepts Rava's [reason]." The medieval commentaries were confounded by this problem: "Behold, since Rav Ashi was a later sage, and he certainly must have known the conclusion of the passage that 'Rabbah also accepts Rava's [reason],' why then did he give the forced explanation [72] that aligns the mishnah with R. Yehudah's view?" (So Tosafot, Git 3a, *s.v. man*; and Rashb"a, ad loc.) In addition, this conclusion contradicts the beginning of the passage: "What is the reason (that mGit 1:1 rules that one must say, 'It was written and signed in my presence')? Rabbah says, "Because they (Jews from distant lands) are not well-versed [with the principle] 'for her name' (*lishmah*; that a bill of divorce must be written specifically for that woman)," since the issue of witnessing applies both to the writing and the signing (Git 2a–2b). And without this understanding of the witnessing applying to both, there is no place for the question that Rav Ashi answers, "Who is the Tannaitic authority who holds that [a bill of divorce] must be both written and signed 'for her name'" (Git 3a–3b)?[53] Thus it is clear that the conclusion of the passage, that Rabbah also accepts Rava's reason, derives from the Stammaim. Rav Ashi lived before their time and knew neither their contribution nor their conclusion to this passage.** (Similarly, the Stammaitic author of the statement on Git 5b against whom it is objected, "Do you really think so [*vetisbera*]? But behold, Rabbah also accepts Rava's [reason]" also did not know the conclusion, that Rabbah accepts Rava's reason:[54] this objection was made by later Stammaim against earlier Stammaim.)[55]

Disagreements between Rav Aha and the Second Ravina

The most compelling evidence that the Talmud was never subjected to a real process of editing, by which I mean the clarification and elucidation of Amoraic dicta, derives from a simple and extremely obvious question: If Rav Ashi and his academy, including Ravina—who was apparently the greatest among Rav Ashi's colleagues, as he is mentioned together with Rav Ashi (in BM 86a, as "the end of *hora'ah*")—edited the Talmud, then why does the Talmud contain a number of disagreements between Rav Aha and the second Ravina (or between their contemporaries and even between sages who slightly postdated them) introduced by the phrase "one said...and one said....," which means that they no longer knew which sage stated which ruling?[56] How did it happen that the editors [73] themselves did not know that which they themselves said,[57] that which took place in their own academy? (And one would have to say that disagreements of this type attributed to their successors were added to the Talmud at a still later date.) It is not possible to claim (as does I. Halevy, *Dorot harishonim*, vol. 3, section 1) that it was the first Ravina who disagrees with (the earlier) Rav Aha, and that he was not a member of Rav Ashi's academy, and therefore Rav Ashi lacked precise knowledge of Ravina's rulings. This possibility is precluded by the passage in Yev 11a:

> Rav Ashi holds like Resh Laqish...Ravina holds like R. Yohanan... Rav Aha and Ravina disagreed: one said [this case involves a transgression subject to punishment] "by extirpation" (*karet*), and one said [the transgression is of] "a positive commandment" (i.e., they did not know who said what). He who said 'extirpation' holds like Resh Laqish; he who said 'a positive commandment' holds like R. Yohanan.

If Ravina "holds like R. Yohanan" and "he who said 'a positive commandment' holds like R. Yohanan," then Ravina was the one who stated "a positive commandment" and who held which opinion easily could have been determined. Clearly the Ravina who disagrees with Rav Ashi (and holds like R. Yohanan) is not the same Ravina who disagrees with Rav Aha. The Ravina who disagrees with Rav Ashi is the first Ravina, and the Ravina who disagrees with Rav Aha is the second Ravina.[58]**

Moreover, this disagreement between Rav Aha and Ravina in Yev 11a contains multiple strata. In Pes 74b and Hul 93b the Talmud states: "Throughout the entire Torah, Rav Aha rules strictly and Ravina leniently, and the ruling accords with Ravina for leniency, with these three exceptions (raw meat, eggs, and jugular veins), in which Rav Aha rules leniently and Ravina strictly, and the ruling accords with Rav Aha for leniency." Various Talmudic passages, however, disagree over this general principle; the sugyot in Sot 25a ("it stands to reason that the law follows the one who says that it [the husband's warning] cannot be retracted"), AZ 33b ("the ruling accords with the one who forbids"), and AZ 75b ("the ruling is that it [a glazed vessel] is treated according to its final state" and requires immersion) do not accept it.** And apparently the sugyot in Yev 39b, Hul 8b, and Hul 46b also do not acknowledge this general principle, as in these three passage the Talmud concludes "And the law is... (*vehilkheta*)." Had they accepted this principle, "It would not have been necessary to rule explicitly that the law follows the lenient opinion. They would have known by applying the general principle that the law accords with the lenient position."[59]

It therefore appears that originally there were two different traditions concerning disagreements between Rav Aha and Ravina. Both taught "Rav Aha and Ravina disagreed: one said... and one said...," an expression that demonstrates that the disagreement was not formulated during the time of Rav Aha and Ravina, but only at a later time when they no longer recalled who said what. One tradition transmitted the disagreement in this form ("one said... and one said...,") without determining with which view the law accords (as reflected in Yev 39b, Hul 8b, and Hul 46b); the final ruling was set in later times (as indicated by the term "the law is" [*vehilkheta*], which is known to be a later addition to the Talmud). The second tradition added to the presentation of the disagreement the general principle that "Throughout the entire Torah, when Rav Aha rules strictly... with these three exceptions... and the ruling accords with Rav Aha for leniency." Later the two traditions were amalgamated, such that

Pes 74b and Hul 93b first quote the statement "Rav Aha and Ravina disagree [in the cases] of raw meat, eggs, and jugular veins," and then adduce the general principle determining the law, which derives from the other tradition.[60]**

These strata obviously were not composed during the time of Rav Aha and Ravina, who were members of Rav Ashi's academy [74]—if indeed there even existed such an institution**, which is actually unattested in Talmudic sources[61]—but many years thereafter. It was the Stammaim who integrated these strata into the Talmud long after the time of these sages. The unattributed term "The law is (*vehilkheta*)" demonstrates that these passages are late. However, there is a temporal gap between Sot 25a and the other aforementioned passages. In those passages the law is determined without justification, with the typical formulation "The law is (*vehiklheta*)," the standard terminology found in legal codes that postdate the Stammaim.** Yet Sot 25a uses the term "it stands to reason (*mistabra*)" and proceeds to adduce a baraita as proof, demonstrating that this passage derives from Stammaitic times, when the Stammaim were engaged in the production of dialectical argumentation.[62]

The same question can be asked, even more tellingly, about the disagreement between Rav Aha and Ravina in Hul 57a–58a. They disagree explicitly over a point of law, and there is no uncertainly as to their opinions: "Rav Aha holds like Rav Aha b. Yaakov.... Ravina does not hold like Rav Aha b. Yaakov." However, they also disagree over Amemar's statement and response to Rav Ashi's question. According to Rav Aha, Amemar stated: "As to the eggs of a wounded [bird, *tereifah*]: the first clutch is forbidden. Successive clutches are cases of multiple causality (*zeh vezeh gorem*), and are permitted." Rav Ashi objects to Amemar on the basis of a baraita: "They [the Tannaim] agree about the egg of a wounded [bird] that it is forbidden, because it grew within something forbidden," and therefore no distinction obtains between the first clutch and successive clutches. Amemar responds to Rav Ashi: "That is a case of [the bird becoming pregnant through] friction with the ground," but in a case where a healthy male bird inseminates the hen, successive clutches are permitted. The subsequent discussion—which is entirely anonymous—explains that Rav Aha holds that a wounded animal is capable of giving birth, and therefore he distinguishes between the first clutch ("since the egg was already within her womb when she was wounded") and subsequent clutches. Ravina, however, taught that Amemar stated: "Those eggs of the first clutch of a wounded animal of doubtful status must be left aside. If it subsequently lays eggs, then we permit them." Ravina holds that a wounded animal is incapable of giving birth, and if the animal subsequently lays eggs, then it cannot be a wounded animal. But "if not, [the eggs] are forbidden." After Rav Ashi objects to Amemar on the basis of the baraita, "They [the Tannaim] agree about the egg of a wounded bird, that it is forbidden, because it grew within something forbidden" (the same objection that he posed, according to Rav Aha's version), Amemar responds to Rav Ashi (different from his response, according to Rav Aha's version): "That applies only to the first clutch," which is forbidden, as Rashi explains, "because it is mixed with her sinews and accounted as her body."[63]

Now the disagreement between Rav Aha and Ravina over the legal ruling can be attributed to their different assessments of the pertinent legal considerations. The interchange between Rav Ashi and Amemar, however, is a historical fact. Of Rav Aha and Ravina's conflicting versions of this interchange one could say that which Rav Dimi said when informed that Rabbah bar Hana quoted R. Yohanan differently than he did: "Either he is a liar or I am a liar!" (Yev 55b). Is it plausible that editors would make a mistake of this type?

If these two Amoraim, Rav Aha and Ravina, were members of the school of Rav Ashi and editors of the Talmud, how could they not have known the exact statement of Amemar against which Rav Ashi objected [75] on the basis of the baraita? How did they not know what Amemar responded? Why did they disagree over his response?[64] This example, however, is no different from other such examples throughout the Talmud, attested both among early and later Amoraim. Students transmitted their masters' words in different formulations, each one believing that he had heard thus. Talmudic editors certainly would have clarified the correct version of the tradition by consulting their colleagues and checking the tradition of the "Reciters," the professional memorizers and transmitters of tradition; however, Rav Aha and Ravina were not among the editors of the Talmud, and they act much like all other Amoraim.[65] They transmitted that which they believed they had heard; they were limited to their own schools and did not always have the opportunity to clarify the tradition and to validate it by checking with others. One can assume that often they did not even know that another version of the tradition existed, even if the tradition was transmitted by prominent authorities such as Rav Aha and Ravina.

For this reason I do not explain the disagreement between Rav Aha and Ravina in BB 95a in the same manner as the Talmud (see *MM*, Bava

Batra, 174–75): "It was asked of him: What [is the law when the seller says: I sell you] 'a cellar of wine' and [the buyer] does not say to him 'For a dish'? Rav Aha and Ravina disagreed: One said, '[The buyer] must accept [ten casks of sour wine for every hundred].' And one said, '[The buyer] need not accept [ten casks of sour wine for every hundred].'" The Talmud's explanation is that "The one who says '[The buyer must] accept [ten casks of sour wine for every hundred]'" emends the baraita quoted above, which seems to contradict his view, and claims, "The teaching has an omission and he teaches thus," a desperate solution proposed only when there is no other possibility. In addition, according to this explanation, the objection of Tosafot and others remains cogent [76], namely, why Rav Zevid of the school of R. Oshaya, also quoted above, did not explain mBB 1:6 as a case "When he said to him 'I am selling you a wine cellar'" without further specification (*setam*), that is, "Without saying to him, '[I require this wine] for a dish.'"[66] This explanation appears explicitly in tBB 6:6: "One who sells a cellar to his fellow without further specification—this is the case concerning which they stated [in mBB 6:1], 'He must accept ten sour jars for every hundred.'" Therefore I explained the disagreement between Rav Aha and Ravina in this way: "The one who says '[The buyer must] accept [ten casks of sour wine for every hundred]'" follows mBB 6:1 which states, "[One who sells] a wine cellar (without further specification)—[the buyer] must accept ten casks of sour wine for every hundred." By contrast, "The one who says, '[The buyer need] not accept [ten casks of sour wine for every hundred]'" made an inference from the addition to this ruling made by Rav Zevid of the school of R. Oshaya: "[If he said,] 'I sell you *this* cellar,' then he must give him wine that is all good,"[67] and concluded "This is the cellar about which our Sages taught in our Mishnah (= mBB 6:1)";[68] but if he said "I sell you a cellar," without clarifying "*this* [cellar]," the buyer need not accept ten casks of sour wine for every hundred. (This inference is the opposite of that stated in the Talmud.) Thus mBB 6:1 and Rav Zevid of the school of R. Oshaya disagree about the case of a cellar when no further specification is made. But the Talmud did not offer this explanation, apparently because it did not want to produce a disagreement between the Mishnah and the school of R. Oshaya.

Now if Ravina was the editor of the Talmud and it came to a close at that time, how did the Talmud not know the correct explanation of Ravina's opinion?

I have insisted repeatedly that reliable historical evidence for the formation of the Talmud cannot be based on an explicit statement, since "your guarantor needs a guarantor,"** and one must always suspect that such a view is only an individual opinion. We must rely rather on that which emerges by implication from the Talmudic text. Based on the Talmudic text itself we would not conclude that Rav Ashi (and his academy) was the editor of the Talmud. In this regard Rav Ashi differs from R. Yehudah HaNasi, insofar as we know on the basis of the Mishnah itself that R. Yehudah HaNasi and his court had a hand in the redaction of the Mishnah. Evidence for this derives from the fact that the Mishnah mentions no Tanna who lived after R. Yehudah HaNasi,[69] whereas the Talmud mentions dozens of Amoraim who lived after Rav Ashi. On the contrary: from the Talmud itself it can be concluded that the anonymous portions of the Talmud are later than the attributed statements, and that the Talmud contains contradictions, and that the anonymous stratum itself is comprised of multiple layers, which point to a lengthy and late era for the formation of the Talmud.

In sum, the impression left by the activity during the period between Rav Ashi and the latter Ravina and the succeeding generation is a far cry from the consistent and continual editing suggested by the expression "Rav Ashi and Ravina—the end of *hora'ah*." This expression in no way should be understood as meaning that Rav Ashi and Ravina together edited the Talmud, especially the anonymous portions. This period does not differ from the previous Amoraic periods. I find no difference as to the formation of the Talmud, nor in the manner of expression.[70] [77] We find, for example, that the Talmud objects against Rav Ashi too, and even against Mar b. Rav Ashi, "They responded (*meitivei*)," and answers by correcting the original language of the dictum with the term "But if it was said, it was said thus,"[71] a phrase that expresses doubt as to the accuracy of the corrected version ("if it was said"—but not with certainty).[72] If Rav Ashi had been the editor, then certainly his students, the members of his academy, would have known the correct version of his and his son's statements. Moreover, the medieval commentaries already observe that sometimes the Talmud—after responding "[the latter clause] comes to explain [the earlier clause]"—asks as to the purpose of the superfluity,** although sometimes the Talmud does not ask this question.[73] Rav Ashi is among those who ask about the superfluity (BB 104a), and if he had been the editor, we would expect consistency, that is, that the Talmud would ask this question in every place. (However, the case at BB 104a is actually insufficient proof, as the usage of the expression "[the latter clause] comes to explain [the earlier clause]" here differs slightly from the typical usage.

Here it essentially means "which case"—"in which case is [the expression] 'a *beit kor'* [of land] considered equal to [the expression] 'about a *beit kor*' "—and it is possible that Rav Ashi only asks in this case about the superfluity, but in other cases he too would not be sure whether to ask or not.) Finally let me turn to *MM*, Bava Qamma, 357 ff., where I demonstrated that close to twenty times the Talmud resolves a contradiction concerning a mishnah [78] or baraita with the explanation, "He holds like him in one respect and disagrees with him in one respect." Likewise, I have provided a number of examples showing that "The typical Talmudic sugya opposes interpreting sources along the lines of 'He holds like him in one respect and disagrees with him in one respect.' " Had there been a general editor of the Talmud, we would not find such blatant inconsistencies.

Rav Ashi indeed served as Head of the Academy for sixty years, apparently a longer tenure than other Amoraim known to us. But there is no evidence that throughout this lengthy period of activity he changed or deviated from the modes of study of his predecessors. True, some sugyot conclude with statements of Rav Ashi—but we find the same of other Amoraim, even if not in the same quantity.[74] Yes, many Amoraim turned to Rav Ashi with questions, and some of them are not mentioned in any other context**—but in this respect too he is not unique, as other Amoraim were asked questions too. At all events, these considerations are unrelated to the issue of editing, and one cannot adduce them as proof that the Talmud came to a close with Rav Ashi and his academy.[75]

Rabbana Ashi, the Closing and Editing of the Talmud

There are two Talmudic passages that refer to Rav Ashi with the title "Rabbana"—"the court of Rabbana Ashi" (Ket 22a, Sanh 30a). This is the same title given to Nehemia and Uqba, "the sons of Rav's daughter."[76] Rav's grandsons served as exilarchs and apparently were called "Rabbana" on account of this office.** Rav Ashi, however, was not the exilarch, as Rav Huna b. Natan was the exilarch at that time, and yet Rav Ashi is called "Rabbana." This title was not given him because he was the editor of the Talmud, as it does not accompany his name throughout the Talmud, and is never given to his companion Ravina. What then is the meaning of the title "Rabbana" that is twice bestowed on Rav Ashi?

First of all, we must address the issue that troubled the medieval commentators: why is Rav Ashi mentioned in that passage (Sanh 30a = Ket

22a)? Why choose him? What is the relationship between Rav Ashi and the content of the passage, cited here from Sanh 29b–30a?

[A] There was written in a certain deed of acknowledgement (*odita*): "A memorial of the words" but it was [otherwise] completely the language of a court [document], except that it did not contain the [standard] phrase, "We were in a session of three, and one is no more."—Ravina thought to say: "This is the case to which Resh Laqish referred" (who is quoted above in the previous passage.)

[B] Rav Natan b. Ami said to him: "It was stated thus in the name of Rava: In any such case we are concerned that the court has made an error."

[C] Rav Nahman b. Yitshaq said: "And if there is written in it: 'A court,' no more is necessary."

[D] Perhaps it was a presumptuous court, in accord with Shmuel. For Shmuel said: "Two who rendered judgment—their judgment is valid, but they are called a presumptuous court."

[E] [No, this is a case when] there was written in it: "The court of Rabbana Ashi."

[F] Perhaps the sages of Rav Ashi's school hold like Shmuel?!

[G] [No,] there was written in it: "And Rabbana Ashi told us [to write the document]."

Now, R. Hananel does not even mention Rav Ashi in his comments to Sanhedrin, whereas Rashi contradicts himself. In Ket 22a he states that the Talmud mentions Rav Ashi because "He was the Head of the Academy of Matta Mehasia in the time of Rav Nahman b. Yitshaq whose statement is being discussed"; in Sanh 30a he claims: "Rav Ashi is mentioned because his court was supreme in the days of Ravina, and the two of them edited the *gemara* of the Babylonian Talmud . . . and these dicta were stated during his time and incorporated into the Talmud." However, Rashi's two explanations are flawed. Rav Nahman b. Yitshaq did not live at the time of Rav Ashi; according to the *Epistle of Rav Sherira Gaon* he died almost seventy years beforehand.[77] In Sanh 30a Rashi mentions Ravina because that passage (unlike Ket 22a) begins with a statement of Ravina [A]. However, the continuation of the passage, "Rav Nahman bar Yitshaq said . . ." [C]—which is then explained by the reference to "the court of Rabbana Ashi" [E]—is not predicated on Ravina's statement [79] (as Ravina lived after Rav Nahman b. Yitshaq, and it is unlikely that this is the earlier Ravina), but rather on Rava's words: "Rav Natan bar Ami said to him [Ravina]: Thus Rava said, 'In any such case[78] we are concerned that the court has made an error' " [B]. Likewise the Talmud's objection to Rav Nahman b. Yitshaq's statement, "Perhaps it was a presumptuous court..." [D], and the response to this objection [E], are the continuation of the explication of Rav Nahman b. Yitshaq's statement [C], and are not the words of Ravina. So too the response to the second objection [F], namely: "Rabbana Ashi told us [to write the document]" [G], is a continuation of the discussion of Rav Nahman b. Yitshaq's statement. If so, why did the Talmud specifically choose Rav Ashi, and even add the honorary title "Rabbana" to his name?

It seems that the Stammaim disagreed with Shmuel's ruling that "Two who rendered judgment—their judgment is valid, but they are called a presumptuous court" [D]. Even though Rav Nahman ruled like Shmuel (above, Sanh 5b),[79] the Stammaim ruled against him,[80] and supported their ruling with the stature of Rav Ashi, that is, if Rav Ashi had ruled in accord with Shmuel, they too would not have ruled against Shmuel. Therefore the latter generations of Stammaim[81] integrated the objection from Shmuel's statement, and then rejected it on the grounds that "There was written in it: 'The court of Rabbana Ashi' " [E]. For in the later Stammaitic times Rav Ashi was considered a great decisor, as he was praised as the greatest Amora, and it was said of him: "From the time of Rabbi [Yehudah HaNasi] until Rav Ashi Torah and prestige (*gedulah*) were never found together in the same individual" (Git 59a, Sanh 36a). In order to increase his stature the Stammaim added here in Sanh 30a (= Ket 22a), and only here, the title "Rabbana." In their times, that is, in Geonic times, this title was bestowed upon the greatest sages, even those who were not exilarchs.[82] This provides additional evidence that the anonymous passages of the Talmud are late and may even originate in Geonic times; indeed, that Rav Ashi is called "Rabbana" is unattested in Amoraic sources.

I accordingly conclude that the Talmud was not edited (*ne'erakh*) but came to a close (*nehtam*). It did not come to a close by virtue of a decision of an assembly, nor because of a consensus, but rather came to a close in and of itself. In fact, it was completed twice. The first time, after about the fifth century, after the second Ravina and Rabbah Tosfa'ah [80], when legislation and apodictic rulings diminished and the period of the Amoraim ended. And a second time, long after the Amoraim, almost 250 years later, when dialectical analysis decreased and the period of the Stammaim ended. Throughout the first period, the Amoraim, like the Tannaim, transmitted to succeeding generations the apodictic rulings alone; throughout the second period the Stammaim also transmitted the dialectical analysis that accompanied the apodictic rulings. At the time of this second closing, there developed the practice of attributing books to individual authors, such as *Halakhot pesuqot* (of Yehudai Gaon?), *She'iltot* (of Aha of Shabha Gaon), and *Halakhot gedolot* (of Shimon Qayyara), which contain both legislation and dialectical argumentation, although not in equal proportions. The proportion of each depends on the time of composition and purpose of the work.

Most anonymous sugyot, when considered in and of themselves, are worked over, that is, the content has been analyzed from different points of view, and Amoraic statements, sometimes transferred from one place to another, have been integrated into complex argumentation so as to bestow a dialectical form upon the sugya. However, there are some sugyot that are not reworked and consist merely of an association of Amoraic dicta with a thin contextual setting, and some lack this too. However, when one analyzes sugyot comparatively, it is evident that the Talmud was never subjected to a general editing process.[83]

The assumption that the Talmud never went through a general editing is indispensable for the critical method I employ, which frequently explains Amoraic dicta and baraitot and even occasionally Mishnaic passages differently than do the Stammaim. These critical explanations are based on additional sources or fragmentary sources. Had the Talmud been edited, and especially had the Talmud been edited by Rav Ashi and his school, these other sources would have been available to him, and he would not have expounded earlier traditions in the same way as the Stammaim. However, the Stammaim lived long after the period of the Amoraim, and it is possible that they no longer knew all of the sources. Thus the method of Talmudic study (critical or traditional) cannot be detached from the issue of the history of the formation of the Talmud, and one cannot pursue the former independent of the latter or vice versa, as they are interdependent: our view of the formation of the Talmud impacts our method of study and how we understand the text, while our understanding of the text confirms the cogency of our view of the Talmud's formation. Whoever focuses on only one of these issues and neglects the other is prone to misunderstand the Talmud or to arrive at incorrect historical conclusions, for these two subjects are interconnected.[84]

[81] Before concluding the discussion of the editing of the Talmud, I should explain why the reconstruction of dialectical argumentation took

place during the Stammaitic era and not during Amoraic times. Let me first, however, distinguish between editing and reconstruction. An editor's purpose is to clarify and elucidate the content, to explain that which seems to be obscure, to delete that which is incorrect, to reconcile contradictions, to harmonize passages, and to determine their literary forms—however, an editor does not change the text itself. The text arrives at an editor almost intact and only requires corrections. This type of editing, a comprehensive editing of the whole Talmud, did not take place even in Stammaitic times. They did not scrutinize the entire Talmud in order to reconcile all of its parts. They collected dialectical argumentation but did not harmonize it, for the purpose of reconstruction is to collect the fragments that have been passed down in an incomplete state, to complete them, to identify Tannaitic or Amoraic contexts, and to attach dialectical argumentation that serves as their underlying reasoning—even if it is rhetorical and artificial and has only a stylistic function—or at least that serves as a possible explanation. The dialectical argumentation of the Talmud was not edited but reconstructed. Editing generally takes place during the time of the composer of the text, and it helps him improve and perfect his composition, whereas reconstruction takes place many years after the analysis of the original, when only a fragment remains, the greater part having been forgotten.

My fundamental assumption is that one or two academies were the dominant forces in establishing the content and organization of rabbinic study in the Stammaitic era, such that it was feasible for them to carry out the reconstruction (contra I. Halevy, who claims that in Amoraic times rabbinic academies were concentrated under one overarching authority—what he calls the "general academy"; see *Dorot harishonim,* chapter 64 ff.).[85] I accept the view that in Amoraic times the rabbinic schools were more academic than the Geonic academies, that is, that in Amoraic times itinerant students did not come to learn for but limited periods of time as they did in the Geonic era, nor did cohorts of students rotate after a brief time at the academy, nor did the head of the school suffice with a brief explanation of the topic and limit himself to introducing the subject and stating the conclusions.[86] In the Amoraic setting, when academies were dispersed in many locations, there was no opportunity to [82] reconstruct the fragmentary traditions that were passed down. Such a task requires a center in which all known traditions are collected, such that they can all be examined and organized into general sugyot. A center of this type existed in the Stammaitic era and in early Geonic times.[87]**

The Editor of the Mishnah and His Role in Editing

The role and function of the editor of the Mishnah also require clarification. It cannot be doubted that R. Yehudah HaNasi played a leading role in the editing of the Mishnah, since several passages in the Talmud refer to him as the Mishnah's editor.[88] However, one cannot know exactly how much he contributed to our Mishnah, nor how much of our Mishnah derives from him. The problem is exacerbated by the fact that on several occasions the Talmud raises the possibility that "our mishnah does not accord with Rabbi [Yehudah HaNasi]" and concludes that a mishnah does not follow R. Yehudah HaNasi's view,[89] and also by the fact that R. Yehudah HaNasi is mentioned very infrequently in the Mishnah compared with his younger contemporaries such as R. Yehudah, R. Shimon, and R. Meir. R. Yehudah HaNasi, together with other editors, undoubtedly influenced our Mishnah; it is conceivable that his role as the Mishnah's editor was to determine the topic that he and his court ("Rabbi's assembly [*minyana derabbi*]"; Git 59a) would discuss at that particular session, and that he selected the participants who engaged in dialectical analysis, and then they subsequently decided on the ruling. When the Tannaim disagreed, R. Yehudah HaNasi and his colleagues adjudicated the law by assigning different degrees of authority: if the law in the mishnah is formulated as an anonymous ruling without any disagreement, it possesses the highest authority. If the law is formulated as an anonymous ruling with which one sage disagrees, it has a lesser degree of authority. If the law is formulated as a disagreement among Tannaim followed by "and the Sages say," it possesses a still lower degree of authority. Perhaps R. Yehudah HaNasi and his court instituted the principles of adjudication utilized by the Talmud for settling disagreements between Tannaim.** The sages of R. Yehudah HaNasi's court, apparently, made decisions by following the majority, and R. Yehudah HaNasi's opinion did not outweigh the majority. Sometimes they voted against R. Yehudah HaNasi and formulated as the anonymous ruling of a mishnah an opinion with which he disagreed.

Thus we find Rav Yosef explaining: "The mishnah is [according to the view of] R. Yehudah HaNasi, and he formulated it in accord with [the views of both] Tannaim: he formulated the law of awareness [of sin through impurity] according to R. Ishmael; he formulated the law of oaths according to R. Akiba" (Shevu 4a). Thereupon Rav Kahana clarifies to Rav Ashi that Rav Yosef did not mean that "R. Yehudah HaNasi formulated (edited) according to [the views of both] Tannaim but did not himself agree, but rather that R. Yehudah HaNasi ruled according to his own reasoning." It is not clear whether Rav Kahana disagrees with Rav Yosef, in that Rav Yosef held that R. Yehudah HaNasi did not think thus, or whether Rav Kahana is explaining Rav Yosef's view, such that Rav Yosef too thinks that "R. Yehudah HaNasi ruled according to his own reasoning." The same is true of the parallels to this passage (RH 7b, Meg 9b, Hul 84a, Hul 104a), assuming they indeed derive from Rav Yosef and are not simply transpositions.[90] At all events, these sources recognize the possibility that R. Yehudah HaNasi did not agree with an anonymous mishnah, as the very fact that Rav Kahana needs to state that R. Yehudah did not disagree recognizes that such a possibility exists. [83] On the other hand, we find that R. Yohanan, for example, claims that "R. Yehudah HaNasi[91] agreed with the view of R. Meir in the law of 'it and its young' (Exod 23:19) and attributed it to 'the Sages' (which is less authoritative than had it been formulated as an anonymous opinion) and [R. Yehudah HaNasi] agreed with the view of R. Shimon in the law of covering the blood (Lev 17:13) and attributed it to 'the Sages'" (Hul 85a).** In that same passage the Stam considers an anonymous mishnah as having been given its anonymous formulation by R. Yehudah HaNasi.[92] R. Yehudah HaNasi was the living spirit of the Mishnah and perhaps was also responsible for editing it after the halakhah had been decided, and therefore the Mishnah was attributed to him.

A separate question concerns the extent to which editors passed on earlier opinions without change or modification. The term "the (earlier) mishnah was not changed from its [original] form (*mishnah lo zazah mimqoma*)" (Hul 32b and parallels) does not mean that the editor "did not change the language of his predecessors, but transmitted what he received verbatim."[93] Rather, it means that in cases where the editor changed his mind, he nevertheless left the earlier mishnah intact and did not delete it.[94] Indeed, the editor of the Mishnah frequently changed the original language of his sources, especially that of the disputing opinion. Originally the disputant certainly said more than one word, such as "obligated" or "exempt," "pure" or "impure," "permitted" or "forbidden," but the editor abbreviated this statement to one word. In some cases he summarizes the disputant's ruling and does not quote it in its original form, for example: "Abba Shaul says, 'The reverse is the law'" (*hiluf hadevarim*; mGit 5:4).[95] Abba Shaul did not actually say, "The reverse is the law"; rather the editor of the Mishnah formulated his words in this way. A similar phenomenon is found with baraitot, except there we also find the expression, "R. So-and-so reverses (*mahlif*)." But there is no substantive difference between these formulations; this is one of the variations between the language of the Mishnah and of baraitot that has no bearing on the content.[96]

[84] In some cases an Amora states of a mishnah: "A contradiction (*tavra*)! He who taught this [clause], did not teach that [clause]"; the terminology of the Yerushalmi is "Two [different] students taught it," or "They are two." However, I have shown that "There is not necessarily an internal contradiction in the mishnah. Rather, the clauses of the mishnah derive from disparate sources."[97] I supported this claim on the basis of Pes 37b, where R. Eleazar states: "A contradiction! He who taught this [clause], did not teach that [clause]" about mHal 1:6 (= mEd 5:2): "Dough-paste (*me'isa*): The House of Shammai exempts [from dough-offering] and the House of Hillel obligates [in dough-offering]. Dumplings (*halita*): The House of Shammai obligates [in dough-offering] and the House of Hillel exempts [from dough-offering]." This Mishnah does not contradict itself, and one need not necessarily interpret it in terms of "A contradiction! He who taught this [clause], did not teach that [clause]" (in yHal 1:6, 58a: "Two different [students] taught it.") One could easily explain that The House of Shammai holds "the upper [substance] prevails," and therefore if one pours the flour upon the scalding water, as in the case of dough-paste, it is exempt from the dough-offering. But dumplings, when one pours the scalding water upon the flour, are obligated in dough-offering. The House of Hillel, on the other hand, holds "the lower substance prevails," and therefore dough-paste is obligated in the dough-offering, but dumplings are exempt.[98] However, R. Eleazar claims, "A contradiction! He who taught this [clause], did not teach that [clause]," because originally the clauses were indeed taught by different authorities, as evidenced by the baraita quoted in that same passage: "R. Ishmael b. R. Yose said in the name of his father: Both are exempt. Others say: Both are obligated." The editor of the Mishnah decided, on the basis of his own reasoning, that the House of Hillel obligated dough-paste in the dough-offering in accord with R. Yose (in mEd 5:2), since this is one of the disagreements that R. Yose lists where the House of Shammai rules leniently and the House of Hillel stringently; and he decided that the House of Hillel exempts dumplings from dough-offering in accord with the views of R. Meir (the tradent of mEdduyot Chapter 4) and R. Yehudah (mEd 5:1), as this case was not listed among those where the House of Shammai rules leniently and the House of Hillel rules stringently; consequently the House of Shammai obligates both dough-paste and dumplings in dough-offering, and the House of Hillel

exempts both. Despite the fact that neither R. Yose nor R. Yehudah agrees with this view (since R. Yose holds that dough-paste is obligated in the dough-offering, and the same applies to dumplings, while R. Yehudah holds that dumplings are exempt from the dough-offering, and the same applies to dough-paste), R. Eleazar states: "A contradiction! He who taught this [clause], did not teach that [clause]," meaning that in the earlier mishnah-collection from which the editor took the source that appears in our Mishnah, it was indeed the case that "He who taught this [clause], did not teach that [clause]."[99] Thus even in cases where an Amora claims: "A contradiction! He who taught this [clause], did not teach that [clause]," the Mishnah's editor played a role.

Similarly, the editor of the Mishnah sometimes omitted a part of the statement of the dissenting opinion, thus creating the impression that the sage who dissents does not disagree with the part that was omitted, when in truth [85] he disagrees with it too. The editor of the Mishnah (or the tradent of a baraita), however, did not consider the omitted portion authoritative enough to be included even as an individual opinion. I commented on this phenomenon on several occasions. For example, the first opinion in mBets 5:4 holds: "A woman who borrows from her neighbor spices, water or salt for her dough—these are limited [on the Sabbath to domains] where both of them may go." The mishnah then continues: "R. Yehudah exempts water, as it has no substance." This implies that R. Yehudah concedes that salt "has substance." The Talmud objects on the basis of a baraita that states: "R. Yehudah says that water and salt are annulled (*beteilin*) [when mixed with dough or cooked food]," which implies that salt does not "have substance," and answers the objection by distinguishing between salt of Sodom (which is hard, hence not annulled, and "has substance") and salt of Istria (which is soft, hence it is annulled, and "has no substance"; Bets 39a).[100] However, it is more reasonable to assume that R. Yehudah originally ruled about both water and salt as in the baraita: "Water and salt may go on the Sabbath wherever the borrower may go, because they have no substance" (Bets 39a). However, the editor of the Mishnah did not deem R. Yehudah's opinion about salt having "no substance" worthy to include even as an individual opinion, and therefore omitted that part of R. Yehudah's ruling.[101] Similarly, we find in mQid 1:4: "Large cattle are acquired by delivery (*mesirah*) and small cattle by lifting; these are the words of R. Meir and R. Eliezer. And the Sages say: small cattle are acquired by pulling (*meshikhah*)." Thus the Sages ostensibly agree with the opinion of R. Meir and R. Eliezer that large cattle are acquired by delivery. Yet a baraita states: "And the Sages say: this (large cattle) and that (small cattle) [are acquired] by pulling" (Qid 25b). There is no need to assume mQid 1:4 and the baraita disagree over the Sages' opinion as to how large cattle are acquired. Rather, this mishnah and the baraita agree that the Sages said that both types of cattle are acquired by pulling; they disagree as to the practical law: the baraita rules completely in accord with the Sages and quotes their original statement, whereas the editor of the Mishnah agreed with the Sages only in the case of small cattle, but disagreed with their ruling regarding large cattle, and therefore did not include that part of the Sages' opinion in mQid 1:4.

[86] Therefore, one need not accept the Talmud's explanation when it claims of a mishnah, "The entire mishnah is [the opinion of] R. So-and-so, and it has an omission (*hasorei mihasra*)." Rather, the mishnah should be understood in the same way I explained above, that originally the Tanna stated both rulings, but the editor of the Mishnah accepted the first ruling as authoritative (and therefore formulated it anonymously) and treated the second ruling as an individual opinion (and therefore retained the attribution to the Tanna). This explanation is only possible if the first and second rulings are distinct, and do not contradict each other, and are also not equivalent. If the rulings contradict each other, then one cannot claim that one Tanna originally stated both. If they are equivalent, then it would not make sense for the editor of the Mishnah to have distinguished between them and to quote one ruling as the anonymous Mishnah and the other as an individual opinion. However, if they are distinct then one can claim that the difference provided sufficient justification for the editor of the Mishnah to formulate them differently. I have analyzed such cases in detail in *MM*, Bava Qamma, 359; and *MM*, Bava Batra, 169, and provide additional references.**

To this point I have discussed changes to the original formulation of a source caused by omission.[102] The omission produces a disjunction between the clauses, which is liable to cause a misunderstanding of the law and of the proper explanation.[103] In other cases an editorial addition causes the disjunction.[104] In still other cases the disjunction results from the editor having combined two opinions, creating the impression that they were in dialogue with one another, when in fact they were not; each sage originally stated his opinion independently. Let me bring one straightforward example from tBik 1:2:

> He who acquires one tree within his fellow's field: He brings [first-fruits to Jerusalem] but does not recite [the first-fruit liturgy],

> because he does not own the land—these are the words of R. Meir. And the Sages say: He neither brings [first-fruits to Jerusalem] nor recites [the liturgy].

The reasoning attributed to R. Meir, "because he does not own the land," explains [87] why the bringer of first-fruits does not recite the liturgy, a ruling with which the Sages agree, and on which there is no dispute. Thus it is clear that R. Meir was not originally relating to the Sages' ruling, and his reasoning does not contrast with theirs. Rather, R. Meir's reasoning here underpins his own ruling in mBik 1:6: "He who acquires two trees within his fellow's field. . . . R. Meir says: He brings and recites." However, one who acquires only a single tree does not recite, "because he does not own the land." Thus the editor of the Toseftan baraita combined the opinions of R. Meir and the Sages as if they were disputing in this way.[105]

The editor of the Mishnah also made other types of substantive additions to the original statements of the Tannaim. Not only did he add connective words such as "also (*af*),"[106] but even explanatory phrases relating to the law as he himself understood it, yet without indicating his own contribution. In some cases the editor of a baraita opposed the changes to a Tannaitic dictum introduced by the editor of the Mishnah: he therefore added his own explanatory phrases to the original words of the Tanna, albeit in a manner that counters the Mishnah's editor's reformulation. All these interventions to the original dictum illustrate the significant contribution of the editor to the formation of the Mishnah.[107] I also am not certain whether the editor of our Mishnah was faithful to the sequence of rulings originally formulated by the Tanna, or whether the editor followed a sequence of his own choosing. See ySuk 2:8, 53b: "He (the editor of the Mishnah) saw that they (the elders of the House of Shammai) were older than them (the elders of the House of Hillel) and placed their opinion first (in formulating disputes between the Houses in the Mishnah.)"** Yet the sages of the House of Hillel themselves did not quote the rulings of the House of Shammai before their own rulings when formulating traditions.[108] Tannaitic statements were transmitted to us by way of the editors and were edited according to the needs and formulations of those editors.

Accordingly, the general principle attributed to R. Yohanan in Hul 32b and Hul 116b, "The mishnah was not changed from its [original] form (*mishnah lo zazah mimqomah*)," does not apply to the entire Mishnah but only to the sections of Mishnah to which R. Yohanan referred, primarily to mHul 3:1. But as far as the rest of the Mishnah is concerned, we might well say that "the mishnah *was* changed from its [original] form."[109] The Stammaim, however, apparently considered this principle to apply to the entire Mishnah and employed it even when it was not necessary to explain a mishnah in this way, for example, when it was equally possible to explain the mishnah along the lines of "this and there is no need to say that (*zo ve'ein tsarikh lomar zo*)" (see Yev 30a, Yev 32a).**

It is worth adding that the Talmud at times claims, "This informs you of the extent of R. So-and-so's [ruling]," meaning that the tradent of the first opinion formulated his ruling in a manner that emphasizes the extent of his disputant's position. For example, in BB 97a the Talmud analyzes mMaas 5:6, "He who makes wine from grape-skins, and puts water into a measure, and then finds 'an equal measure' [of liquid], is exempt [from tithing it]. And R. Yehudah declares him liable." The Talmud initially infers that the dispute [88] concerns "an equal measure," but if one finds a quantity greater than an "equal measure," the first opinion too would declare him liable to tithe it. The Talmud subsequently rejects this inference and states: "They also disagree over a quantity greater than an 'equal measure,' and the fact that he disagrees over an 'equal measure' is to inform you of the extent of R. Yehudah's ruling." That is, the first opinion stated "and then finds 'an equal measure' "—even though he himself ruled that one who finds a quantity greater than "an equal measure" is also exempt from tithing it—in order to emphasize the distinctiveness of R. Yehudah's ruling. This explanation seems strange, and we should rather suggest that it was not the tradent of the first opinion who formulated his own words in this way, but rather the editor of the Mishnah changed them in order to inform us of the extent of R. Yehudah's opinion. If this is correct, then we have another case of the editor of the Mishnah changing the original language of his sources.

(The Talmud's explanation—that the tradent of the first ruling in the Mishnah formulated his ruling in such a way as to illustrate the extent of his disputant's ruling—appears forced.[110] And indeed, no Amora ventures an explanation of this type except for Abaye in Yom 30b. In that passage Abaye asks Rav Yosef whether the Sages agree with Ben Zoma and "The reason that they mentioned the leper was to inform you of the extent of R. Yehudah's ruling, or whether the case of a leper differs in that he is accustomed to his state of impurity."** Thus Abaye entertains the possibility of a dispute formulated so as "to inform you of the extent of R. So-and-so's [ruling]," but Rav Yosef rejects that explanation. It is unclear whether Rav Yosef holds that such explanations should always be rejected or only refers to that case. Perhaps too the Talmud in BB 97a, mentioned above, is only expressing a theoretical rejection, a remote possibility.)

In some cases the editor of the Mishnah (and the editors of baraitot) quotes the opinion of a sage and then returns to that same opinion with the term, "For R. So-and-so would say (*shehaya rabbi ploni omer*)" or "For R. So-and-so says (*sherabbi ploni omer*)." It is worth inquiring as to the function of these repetitions. Elsewhere I discussed the nature of these two terms and classified them into three types[III]:

(1) These terms are used to supply reasoning and justification for statements stated previously in the name of that sage. For example, mZev 1:4: "For an animal sacrifice can be rendered invalid by [errors] in [any one] of four things: slaughter, receiving [the blood], conveying [the blood to the altar], throwing [the blood]. R. Shimon rules it valid [if an error occurred] in conveying [the blood]. For R. Shimon would say: An animal sacrifice is impossible without slaughter, and without receiving [the blood], and without throwing [the blood], but is possible without conveying [the blood], since it can be slaughtered next to the altar." The expression, "For R. Shimon would say," introduces the reasoning of R. Shimon who "rules valid [a sacrifice when an error occurred] in the conveying [of the blood]."

(2) These terms function as an introduction to a source of a ruling stated previously. The sage originally stated the source, and the editor of the Mishnah attributed to that sage a ruling on the basis of that source. For example, mMikv 3:1: "A ritual pool (*mikveh*) lacking forty *seah* [of water], into which fell three *log* [of drawn water], and [the pool] was then divided into two, is invalid, since an invalid classification has [already] been placed upon it. And R. Yehoshua declares it valid. For R. Yehoshua would say: Any pool lacking forty *seah* of water, into which fell three *log* less a *kartov* [of drawn water], is valid, since it lacks [the full] three *log* [of drawn water]." The latter statement of R. Yehoshua provides no explanation at all for his initial ruling. Rather it is a generalization of the law underpinning the specific case of a pool divided into two pools that relates to all cases of pools lacking forty *seah*. This generalization, apparently, is the source of R. Yehoshua's initial ruling.

(3) In some cases the terms "For R. So-and-so would say" and "For R. So-and-so says" neither supply reasoning nor provide the source of a ruling. For example, [89] mGit 2:2: "If it [a divorce document] was written during the day and signed at night, it is invalid. R. Shimon declares it valid. For R. Shimon used to say: All documents written by day and signed at

night are invalid, with the exception of divorce documents." In such cases I suggested that the editor transmitted "the sage's words verbatim. If the editor of the Mishnah found two parallel dicta of a certain sage, even if the same reasoning underpins them both, he neither combined them nor formulated them as one dictum, because the sage himself did not do so."

In some cases when the Mishnah repeats the same ruling in two different contexts the Talmud asks: "What does he inform us? We learned it (*mai qamashma lan tanina*)" or "We learned on another occasion (*tanina hada zimna*)." For example, to mBer 7:4, "Three who ate together are not permitted to separate [and say grace on their own]," the Talmud objects, "What does he inform us? We learned on another occasion, 'Three who ate together are obligated to summon [each other and say grace together] (Ber 50a).' "[112] In most of the cases where the Talmud makes this type of objection the content is indeed repeated but the formulation is not identical, and it appears that the rulings derive from different sources. Thus mKet 4:1 rules: "The seduced maiden (*na'arah shenitpatetah*)—her 'shame' and her 'blemish' go to her father, and her fine goes to her father. But the 'pain' goes to the violated maiden (*tefusah*)." The Talmud objects, "What does he inform us? We learned on another occasion (= mKet 3:4): The seducer pays three types [of compensation] and the rapist four. The seducer pays 'shame' and 'blemish' and a fine. The rapist adds to these 'pain' " (Ket 42a). I noted that the terminology "raped (*anusah*)" derives from the school of R. Akiba, and the terminology "violated (*tefusah*)" originates in the school of R. Ishmael;[113] therefore it is plausible that the repetition of the content results from the different sources.[114]

**[In this context let me point out that the Bavli at times asks "Does R. So-and-so [state] the same [ruling] as the first opinion?" (Shab 24b; Git 4a; RH 29b, where we have: "Do the Sages [state] the same [ruling] as the first opinion?").[115] However, the Bavli never suggests that R. So-and-so and the Sages disagree over how to interpret the first opinion and that the mishnah in fact contains three names but only two opinions. The Bavli refrains from this suggestion because, were this the case, there would have been no reason for R. Yehudah HaNasi, the editor of the Mishnah, to include the first opinion at all, as it contributes no discrete position to the legal dispute. Yet in other passages the Talmud does not ask this question, and Tosafot point out that this is because it is possible to explain that the second and third opinions disagree over the interpretation of the first opinion, that is, that in these cases there are three names but only two opinions.[116]

According to the logic of these Talmudic passages, R. Yehudah HaNasi included the first opinion to show us the source of the disagreement even though it has no [90] bearing on the law itself. Again we confront a discrepancy between Talmudic passages, between the Stammaim, over the degree to which R. Yehudah HaNasi refrained from harmonizing his sources. This provides additional evidence that there was no general editing of the entire Talmud.

Finally, it is worth adding that on several occasions the Stammaim or the later Amoraim respond to a dispute between early Amoraim or even a dispute between Tannaim in baraitot, "They do not disagree." However, I have only found two places in which this response is applied to Tannaitic disputes contained in the Mishnah: the dispute between R. Yehudah and the Sages in mBM 3:8, and the dispute between R. Eleazar b. Azariah and the Sages in mMen 13:6. In these two passages the Talmud states, "They do not disagree. The one [rules according] to his place, and the other [rules according] to his place (BM 40a; Men 107b)." On the surface it is difficult to say "they do not disagree" when the editor of the Mishnah formulated the opinions in the standard dispute form, with the phrase "R. So-and-so states."[117] (And this cannot be compared to an Amoraic dispute formulated as "It was said... [*itmar*]," as we do not know who combined the two Amoraic opinions into this dispute form.)[118] But it is possible that the explanation, "The one [rules according] to his place, and the other [rules according] to his place," clarifies that the two Tannaim disagree over the formulation of the ruling, although they do not disagree over its substance, and therefore it is indeed appropriate to formulate the opinion as "R. So-and-so states." Nevertheless, this explanation does not work in Pes 3a, where the Talmud claims, "They do not disagree. The one [rules according] to his place, and the other [rules according] to his place," as the Talmud initially cites an objection by Mar Zutra—"Mar Zutra responded: One who miscarries on the eve of the eighty-first day..."—which demonstrates that Mar Zutra thought that Rav Huna and Rav Yehudah also disagreed over the substance of the law.]

Differences between the Closing (hatimah) of the Mishnah and of Baraitot and the Closing of the Traditions of the Amoraim and Stammaim

The period of the Stammaim concluded when the "creative" powers of the Stammaim ceased, when they finished explicating the dialectic argumentation of the Amoraim that had been transmitted to them.[119] The period of the Amoraim was completed when their explanations were attached to mishnas and baraitot and their legal rulings and dicta combined with these sources; however, the creative power of the Amoraim did not cease. There were always new legal rulings and novel explanations, and, apparently, the closing of the Amoraic era should be attributed to external factors (see below). The number of Amoraim dwindled until there were no more. We know of the end of the Amoraic period from the *Epistle of Rav Sherira Gaon*. The end of the Stammaitic period, on the other hand, I infer happened as described above.

[91] However, a different factor was responsible for the conclusion of the Tannaitic period: the status and authority of R. Yehudah HaNasi caused the Tannaitic period to come to an end with the closing (*hatimah*) of his Mishnah. The baraitot attributed to R. Hiyya and R. Oshaya** and the "Mishnah of Bar Qappara" also were closed at that time—these collections had some connection to the Mishnah of R. Yehudah HaNasi, as implied by Nid 62b: "If R. Yehudah HaNasi did not teach it, how did R. Hiyya know it?" The Tannaitic period concluded almost immediately after the time of R. Yehudah HaNasi and his students; the Amoraic period, however, continued several decades after Rav Ashi. The Amoraim dwindled out little by little until none remained, apparently on account of a plague that struck at the beginning of the sixth century[120] and due to "the persecution instituted by Yazdegard" in 499 CE, according to the *Epistle of Rav Sherira Gaon* (ed. Lewin, 96–97), in which some sages were imprisoned and killed.** Similarly, the Stammaitic period apparently did not conclude all at once, but gradually, when they completed, or felt that they had completed, the reconstruction of dialectical argumentation and the explanations of Amoraic traditions; many minor insertions, however, were added thereafter.[121] I am not speaking here about copyists or scribes who emended the text, believing that they were restoring the original readings—these never ceased. I refer to explanatory insertions, which clearly were not part of the original but were added to make the text easier to understand.[122]

Moreover, it appears that R. Yehudah HaNasi's approach differed from that of his predecessors, including "The Mishnah of R. Akiba" (mSanh 3:4), "The Mishnah of R. Eliezer b. Yaakov" (Eruv 62b and parallels), "The Mishnah of R. Natan" (Ket 93a, Tem 16a) and even "The Mishnah of Bar Qappara" (BB 154b, AZ 31a): all these sages expressed their own opinions, whereas the Mishnah of R. Yehudah HaNasi does not express his opinion, but rather the accepted, normative, and dominant opinion. Therefore we find a number of instances when the Mishnah opposes R. Yehudah HaNasi's opinion, "The mishnah is not in accord with R. Yehudah HaNasi" (Eruv 35a, RH 19b etc.); and therefore R. Yehudah HaNasi is not mentioned very often in the Mishnah. More important, even though the Mishnah was compiled by R. Yehudah HaNasi, the Talmud will ask, "Shall we say this mishnah is not in accord with R. Natan?" who disagrees with R. Yehudah HaNasi, and the Amoraim struggle to explain the mishnah in accord with R. Natan too (Qid 64a). Even if we venture the unconvincing suggestion that the Amoraim are not really claiming that the mishnah contains the opinion of R. Natan, that is, they do not mean that the mishnah was stated by R. Natan, but rather they mean that the mishnah's ruling can be reconciled with R. Natan's view under the circumstances that they describe (and even if this is the case elsewhere)—in Qid 64a this suggestion is not plausible.

In sum, the Mishnah was produced by the court of R. Yehudah HaNasi and is therefore not called "The Mishnah of R. Yehudah HaNasi," but rather "our Mishnah." The members of the court established the law according to their opinion, even if R. Yehudah HaNasi disagreed with them. This procedure resulted from R. Yehudah HaNasi's [92] goal of creating a Mishnah that would be the culmination of all mishnah-collections, a Mishnah that would include all the valid opinions from all other mishnah-collections, and not simply his own opinions. However, this did not prevent him from selecting the Mishnah-collection of R. Meir, according to the tradition of R. Meir's teacher R. Akiba,[123] as the basis of "our Mishnah," the communal Mishnah. The status of R. Yehudah HaNasi, the participation of his court in the editing of the Mishnah, and his policy of conceding to the majority opinion contributed to the ascendancy of "our Mishnah," and resulted in the closing of the age of the Tannaim, the compilers of the Mishnah.[124]

Therefore a student proficient in a single tractate of the Mishnah, perhaps even in a single chapter, has a sense of the form and style of the entire Mishnah, as these are almost consistent throughout the whole Mishnah. I emphasize "almost" because there are nonetheless a few stylistic differences within the Mishnah, for example, quotations from the Bible: some tractates lack even a single quotation and some are replete with quotations. In addition, most tractates lack argumentative interchanges, that is, cases when one party responds once or multiple times after the other party objects to his opinion. But extended debates of this type appear in mPes 6:2 (between R. Eliezer and R. Akiba), mKer 3:9 (between R. Yehoshua and R. Akiba), mYad 4:3 (between R. Eleazar b. Azariah and R. Tarfon), and in a few others. In contrast, one who is proficient in the stammaitic stratum of a single tractate of the Talmud, and certainly if he is only proficient in the stammaitic stratum of a single chapter of Talmud, has no reliable knowledge of the form and style of the entire Talmud: the stammaitic stratum differs not only from tractate to tractate but even within the tractates themselves, from chapter to chapter and even from folio to folio.

In speaking of these stylistic differences in the stammaitic stratum I do not mean the types of distinctions noted by the medieval commentators, such as their observation that a certain Talmudic passage makes an inference from the language of the Mishnah whereas another passage does not make the same type of inference.[125] This manner of variation is also attested in the Mishnah itself, as Tosafot noted: "In some places he (the Reciter of the Mishnah) teaches 'There are' (*hen*, as in 'There are four new year days' [mRH 1:1] and 'There are four primary categories of damages' [mBQ 1;1]) and in other places he does not teach 'There are' " (Tosafot, RH 2a, s.v. *arba'a* and BQ 2a s.v. *arba'a*). Similarly, I am not referring to such phenomena as when a baraita contains material omitted in a parallel mishnah; in some cases the Talmud asks "Why does our Reciter (= the Reciter of the Mishnah) not teach thus (as found in the baraita)," and in some cases it does not ask this question. When the Talmud [93] has a good response it makes this observation and asks the question, and when it has no good response it neither notes the difference nor asks about it.[126] A similar comment is quoted in *Halikhot olam* in respect to the phrase, " 'All (*kol*)'—what does this add (to the items mentioned in the mishnah)": "Regarding all passages where they teach that the word 'All' is for exposition (*derashah*), that is, to add something that was not known previously... sometimes it [the Talmud] expounds it and sometime it does not expound it."[127] I am referring rather to the progression of thought of the sugya, which differs from passage to passage. For example, in some passages the Talmud states "He taught [some matters] and omitted [others] (*tanna veshayar*)" and then asks, "What [else] did he omit [besides] this omission?" and in other passages it does not ask this question.[128] In some cases the Talmud states, "It was not stated explicitly but derived from an inference" and continues "What [difference does it make] if stated on the basis of an inference?" and sometimes it does not continue with this question.[129] Sometimes the Talmud states "It is [merely] an explanation (*peroshei ka mefaresh*)" and then asks "What is the purpose of the repetition?" and sometimes it does not.[130] In some cases Amoraic statements appear in chronological order and in some cases they are presented in a different order.[131] In addition, the logic of the sugya differs from passage to passage, and objections raised by the Stammaim in one passage are not always raised in other passages, and so too responses offered in one passage are not always offered elsewhere.

Therefore it appears that the Mishnah had a single editor—or one school, namely, R. Yehudah HaNasi and his court—and he edited it on the basis of earlier sources, most of which he quoted verbatim. The Talmud, on the other hand, was composed by different Stammaim from different academies in different times; they reconstructed the Talmud on the basis of fragmentary sources and without an official interpretive tradition (and each group of the Stammaim only in a partial manner). The contradictions in the Mishnah[132] do not vitiate this claim, because they—unlike contradictions in the Talmud—are not indicative of different editors, but of different degrees of legal authority. Certain medieval commentators observed [94] that an anonymous opinion in the Mishnah that follows a dispute between an anonymous and an individual opinion (*setam ve'ahar kakh mahloqet)* is more authoritative than an anonymous opinion without any dissenting opinion.[133] And one can argue, on the basis of mEd 1:5, that a less authoritative ruling is easier for a later court to annul. Perhaps contradictions in the Mishnah, even when both sources are anonymous, indicate that the court of R. Yehudah HaNasi was unable to decide, and were about evenly split, so they included both opinions in order that their successors could rely on their own views and adjudicate between them.[134] However, the anonymous passages in the Talmud do not have equivalent authority, and the contradictions among them indicate that they originated in different academies and were later assembled by various compilers, but no general editor harmonized the contradictions.

Part III: Apodictic Transmission and Dialectical Argumentation

[95] MY FUNDAMENTAL claim is that Amoraic explanations and apodictic rulings were transmitted in a systematic and precise manner, whereas the unattributed dialectical argumentation of the Talmud was reconstructed in later times. I touched on this idea here and there in my discussion of the formation of the Talmud, but I did not explicate it sufficiently, nor trace its history, nor support it with evidence. In this Part, I consider it in detail, outline its development, and anchor it in the sources.

The Development of Dialectical Argumentation in the Halakhic Midrashim, in the Yerushalmi and in the Bavli

At first, during the era of the Tannaim, there was no official transmission of dialectical argumentation.[1] Only apodictic law and brief explanations were transmitted to "Reciters" (*tannaim*), the official transmitters, those who transmitted traditions from generation to generation. However, the reasoning underpinning these laws and explanations was not transmitted; some of it was retained by chance in the memory of sages but was forgotten over the course of time. Shortly thereafter, at the beginning of the Amoraic era in the Land of Israel, they began to transmit the dialectical argumentation too, albeit in stages. First the halakhic midrashim were edited (c. 250 CE);[2] these involve a sort of dialectical argumentation in that they contain legal debates, arguments such as "you say it is so or is it not rather thus" that culminate in the demonstration that the logical argument fails and proof must be adduced from the biblical sources of the law. However, because halakhic midrashim were not taught together with the Mishnah—even though the Mishnah was derived from them by abbreviating their contents—the dialectical argumentation was not transmitted and not preserved with the same punctiliousness devoted to the Mishnah, and as time passed parts of it were forgotten.[3] After that, a different category of dialectical argumentation, namely, objections, responses, and dialogue between Amoraim, was redacted in association with the Mishnah and preserved together with it. About a century after the editing of the halakhic midrashim, the "Order of Damages of the Yerushalmi (*yerushalmi neziqin*)," "the Talmud of Caeserea," was edited; however, it contains a relatively small amount of dialectical argumentation (c. 350 CE).** About fifty years thereafter, the Talmud Yerushalmi of the other tractates was edited (c. 400 CE), with a greater quantity of dialectical argumentation and more complex content, but still not the same level of dialectical argumentation as that of the Bavli, of the [96] Stammaim, neither in quantity nor quality: dialectical argumentation in the Land of Israel continued to be secondary to legal rulings and Amoraic dicta.

Throughout these times no change in the transmission of dialectical argumentation took place in Babylonia; the change occurred only after the Amoraic era during the age of the Stammaim. Up to this point the Amoraim added explanations and apodictic dicta to a mishnah or baraita and entrusted them to transmitters. But they did not transmit the dialectical argumentation,[4] which remained in the memory of students and suffered from omissions and imprecisions. This is how I understand the expression, "Did you fix it in the *gemara*?" (Eruv 32b).[5] In that passage R. Hiyya b. Abba, R. Asi, and Rava b. Natan transmitted to Rav Nahman the explanation of a mishnah together with the corresponding dialectical analysis. Rav Nahman praised their explanation, "Right! (*yishar*)," and they in turn asked him, "Did you fix it in the *gemara*?," that is, they questioned whether the explanation—not the underlying analysis—was included in the official transmission. Rav Nahman responded, "Yes," and the Talmud brings proof: "It was also stated (that it was transmitted as follows): Rav Nahman said that Shmuel said: Here [in this mishnah] we are dealing with a tree that stands in the public domain, and he intends to make his Sabbath-abode below [ten handbreadths], and the authority of the Mishnah is R. [Yehudah HaNasi] who holds . . ."** The term "It was also stated" quotes only the explanation, not the analysis. This establishes that the analysis grounding the explanation, the dialectical argumentation, was not transmitted in the official transmission of the *gemara*. It remained etched in the memory of the audience of that generation, but was forgotten over the course of time, and was lost to succeeding generations.

It is important to emphasize that the difference between apodictic rulings and dialectical argumentation, both in the Land of Israel in the Tannaitic era and in Babylonia in the Amoraic era, is not manifest solely in the manner of transmission—by expert transmitters or through individual memories—and in the completeness of the content—by proficient transmitters or fragmentary memory—but also in the degree of reliability of the transmitted material. Before an Amora transmitted his dictum to a transmitter, he investigated and verified it; edited, refined, polished, and formulated it (for the most part) in Hebrew.[6] The dialectical argumentation that survived in the memory of a given sage, on the other hand, was sometimes articulated only in order to save it from oblivion. It was marshaled as material for debate, as a type of conjectural argument that was open to refutation; but it was not edited, nor verified against the sources, nor passed down with full understanding of the content, nor with polished formulation. Consequently it is open to doubt whether the dialectical argumentation comprises an accurate expression of the ideas of the sage to whom it is attributed, and therefore the Talmud rejects dialectical argumentation more easily than it rejects attributed dicta.[7]

[97] Even among the apodictic rulings, the legal decisions (*halakhot pesuqot*), there are several cases in which an Amora corrects the words of the "Reciter,"—"The Reciter (*tanna*) recited before him"—and then the Reciter asks the Amora, "Should I strike it out," should I delete the dictum because it was not transmitted correctly? However, in the Talmudic era, during the period of the Stammaim, hundreds of years after the Amoraim, the number of "deletions," continued to increase, and many of the apodictic rulings and brief explanations were not accurate. Therefore the Talmud itself will emend apodictic rulings. For example, BM 8a: "Rava said, 'Now that you have said that a "Because argument (*migo*)" is acceptable: in the case of a deaf-mute and a normal person who lift up a lost object, because the deaf-mute acquires it, the normal person acquires it.' " The Talmud objects to this claim and emends it: "Rather I will say: the deaf-mute acquires it; the normal person does not acquire it." Subsequently the Talmud rejects this formulation too and emends further: "Because the normal person does not acquire it, so the deaf-mute does not acquire it."[8]

In some cases an Amoraic dictum is formulated as an explanation of a mishnah, but in reality it is an apodictic ruling, as I have noted on several occasions. Let me quote here the comments of R. Nissim b. Reuben Gerondi (Ra"n), Ned 85b: "Shmuel does not disagree with Rav over the explanation of the mishnah, as he certainly concedes to Rav.... He only disagrees over the law, as Rav understands the mishnah to accord with the view of R. Meir...whereas he (Shmuel) thinks that the law follows the Sages." In other cases the Talmud initially understands an Amora as referring to a mishnah or baraita, and then it rejects the Amora's explanation of the mishnah and asks, "In accord with whom?" is the Amora ruling?—and responds that the Amora rules in accord with another Tanna and was not referring to that mishnah at all. For example, in Git 72a (cf. Git 81b): "Rav Huna said, 'And she must perform *halitsah*,' " referring to the proximate mishnah (mGit 7:3). The Talmud then asks: "Inasmuch as a subsequent case [in the mishnah states] 'and she must perform *halitsah*],' one infers that in the first case (where it does not state 'she must perform *halitsah*') she is also eligible for levirate marriage? The mishnah accords with the opinion of the Sages, and Rav Huna follows the opinion of R. Yose." In incidences of this type we must say that the initial transmission of the dictum was inaccurate.

Above (p. 58), I presented three examples in which a Stammaitic explanation or response became a part of the dictum of the Amora itself, and was then quoted as if the Amora himself said it. This occurs with dialectical argumentation, but I have not encountered a single case of an explanation or response of the Stammaim turning into a legal ruling.[9] In such a case the Stammaim would have had to utilize a term such as "R. So-and-so holds (*qasavar rabbi ploni*)," and the claim "holds" would have had to be attached to an Amora's name—I have not found a single explicit case of this type.[10] However, it is possible that something similar took place in BM 22b:

> [One who finds] sheaves in the public domain—these belong to him [= the finder; mBM 2:1]. Rabbah said: This applies even to something that has a sign [that identifies it]. Therefore Rabbah holds that a sign that is liable to be trampled [and destroyed] is not considered a sign. Rava said: This [ruling] only applies to something that has no sign [that identifies it]. But if it has a sign—he must proclaim [the lost object in public]. Therefore Rava holds that a sign that is liable to be trampled [and destroyed] is [nevertheless considered] a sign.

The term "holds" indicates that Rabbah and Rava did not disagree explicitly over a "sign that is liable to be trampled," but that the Stammaim formulated their opinions in this way. Hence the continuation of the Talmudic passage—"There are some who teach this tradition as an independent [disagreement]: A sign that is liable to be trampled [and destroyed]: Rabbah states: It is not considered a sign. And Rava states: It is considered a sign"—may provide an example of "R. So-and-so holds..." that turned into an attributed legal ruling. Some evidence for this claim derives from the dictum attributed to Rav Zevid in Rava's name: "If you should think that the first authority holds that a sign that is liable to be trampled [and destroyed] is not considered a sign..." (BM 23a).[11] I emphasize "some" because it is possible that Rav Zevid is referring to the formulation, "There are some who teach this tradition as an independent [disagreement]," and that it was indeed an autonomous tradition in this form. And perhaps a related phenomenon obtains in [98] Nid 29a: "Let us say that they disagree over [the dictum] of Shmuel.... There are those who teach this tradition as an independent [argument]...." The "independent" formulation of the tradition, that is, the direct attribution of the dictum to Shmuel, resulted from the Stammaim proposing "Let us say that they disagree over [the dictum] of Shmuel."[12]

In addition, the Talmud sometimes states, "This was not stated explicitly but on the basis of an inference," that is, that the source of that apodictic ruling was not transmitted by an Amora to the transmitter, to the Reciter. Rather, "one who saw [the incident]"—one who was present when the Amora made a practical ruling—transmitted this ruling; however, it is possible that the ruling would be otherwise in differing circumstances.[13] Yet in Shevu 21a the "inference" is not derived from an incident, but from a logical deduction, a type of explanation, and nevertheless the logical deduction was transmitted like an apodictic ruling.[14]** Perhaps this is what the Talmud means by "but on the basis of an inference"—that this is not a typical apodictic ruling, and is not all that reliable. I have even found one case where an Amora explains a mishnah (or a baraita), and the explanation includes a ruling, and later the ruling was separated from the explanation and was transmitted independently as an apodictic ruling attributed to that Amora. This case admittedly depends on the analysis of Sanh 17a: "And R. Abbahu said: In a case when they add judges, they make a 'balanced court' (= a court with an even number of judges) ab initio." The Talmud objects, "This is obvious (*peshita*)!," and responds that R. Abbahu's point is that "The one (judge) who says, 'I do not know'—it is as if he were not present, and if he says something, we do not listen to him." (Then the court, which originally had twenty-three judges, now would have twenty-four, as the judge who said "I do not know" is ignored and two judges were added, leaving a "balanced court.") This explanation of R. Abbahu's dictum appears forced, for if R. Abbahu meant that "The one who says 'I do not know'—it is as if he were not present," he should have stated this explicitly. Perhaps, then, the answer to the Talmud's objection, "This is obvious," is that this ruling of R. Abbahu became separated from his explanation of the mishnah quoted earlier in that same passage, and became an autonomous dictum. Mishnah Sanhedrin 1:6 states, "An adverse (= guilty) verdict requires a majority of two," and the Talmud responds that a court of twenty-three judges cannot produce a majority of two. R. Abbahu explains: "It is impossible to have (an adverse verdict with a majority of two) except by adding [judges]." That is, if one judge says that he does not know, then they add two more to produce a "balanced court," and in these circumstances there may be a majority of two. Originally, R. Abbahu stated only his explanation of mSanh 1:6, which entails by implication the ruling that adding judges may result in a "balanced court." This ruling subsequently became separated from the explanation and turned into an independent ruling that was attributed to R. Abbahu as an apodictic law, and it was to this that the Talmud objects, "This is obvious!" However, an alternative explanation of R. Abbahu is possible, namely, that his point is that even the Tannaim who hold that a "balanced court" is not permitted (above Sanh 3b [*Mekhilta, Mishpatim*, chap. 16, ed. Horowitz-Rabin, p. 304] and 13b [*Sifra, Vayyiqra*, chap. 6, ed. Weiss, p. 7a]) concede that a "balanced court" can result from adding judges. If this is his point, the objection "This is obvious!" is still somewhat appropriate, as mSanh 5:5 states as much.

In this context let me quote at length from my Introduction to *MM: bava metsia*, 23, that sometimes apodictic rulings also change, but as a result of different processes: "Apodictic rulings, interpretations (*oqimta'ot*), and explanations of the Amoraim also underwent a process of change and transformation. The many discrepancies between the apodictic dicta of the Bavli and their parallels in the Yerushalmi provide evidence for this fact (even if the content is similar, the formulation almost always differs), as does the different technical terminology found in parallel passages in the two Talmuds, phenomena analogous to 'There are those who say (*ika de'amrei*),' and 'Another version (*lishna aharina*),'** and also disputes between Amoraim over the dictum of another Amora. Because only one of the conflicting versions can be the *ipsissima verba* of the Amora, the other version perforce resulted from changes to the original statement. [99] It is also possible that an Amoraic dictum transmitted in different ways resulted from the Amora himself changing his mind: 'In the morning he said thus and in the evening he said thus.' The transmitters passed down his words accurately, but one transmitted what he stated in the morning, and the other transmitted what he stated in the evening. Certainly such retractions are to be found among the typical differences in the traditions brought by Amoraim who 'went up and went down,' transmitting traditions between the Land of Israel and Babylonia, such as, 'When Rav Dimi came [back from the Land of Israel], he said: Thus said R. So-and-so...' and 'When Ravin came [back from the Land of Israel], he said: Thus said R. So-and-so...'

However, I doubt whether such retractions can account for a significant amount of these differences. Most differences in formulations of Amoraic dicta should be attributed to errors in hearing—one student was convinced that he heard it thus, and another was convinced that he heard it otherwise—and not to the speaker changing his mind."

However, all of these types of changes are the exception.** The vast majority of apodictic rulings were preserved in the language and form that the Amora transmitted to the Reciter, and were transmitted in apodictic form (whether as a ruling or an explanation) from the start.** Not so the dialectical argumentation. It was not transmitted to the Reciter initially, and lingered as fragmentary memories without authentication and verification by officials.

All this changed with the Stammaim. They reconstructed the dialectical argumentation, collected the fragments of traditions, and completed the omissions themselves, and then they united the reconstructed argumentation to the apodictic dicta and transmitted it to the transmitters. When transmitters could not handle the vast amount of tradition, they resorted to writing.[15] The reconstructed dialectical argumentation included two types: that which had been accepted and became part of the reasoning underlying the Amoraic dictum or apodictic explanation, and that which had been rejected and refuted and was stated only as "what one might have thought," that is, so that a later sage not venture this explanation.[16] The first type was better preserved because the reasoning explained the dicta and the apodictic explanations passed down by the transmitters [100]—the dicta functioned to preserve the accompanying dialectical argumentation. But the Stammaim also reconstructed the second type, even though they—unlike the Amoraim—were fully aware that this dialectical argumentation had been refuted and that the dictum could not be supported dialectically; nevertheless, its historical value was not diminished.

Prior to the Stammaim the sages engaged in dialectical argumentation only in order to resolve questions about new laws and explanations. Dialectical argumentation was associated with the Mishnah and with Amoraic dicta, but had no independent worth. The Stammaim, however, considered even the dialectical argumentation that was refuted and rejected to possess significant value, and they developed it to the best of their abilities, treating it as a goal in and of itself, even when it was not directed toward resolving problems.

However, because the Stammaim integrated fragments of the Amoraic dialectical argumentation into their own dialectical argumentation, they produced a different type of dialectical argumentation from that which circulated in Amoraic times. In Amoraic dialectical argumentation, earlier parts are completely independent of latter parts and are not influenced by what follows; whereas in Stammaitic dialectical argumentation, the beginning of the reconstructed material is influenced by subsequent parts and is structured so as to pave the way for the continuation—for the Stammaim were aware of the continuation before they began to reconstruct the lacunae and from the start prepared a place for the parts they filled in. Similarly, the Stammaim sometimes incorporated into their dialectical argumentation sections the original forms of which they could not reconstruct successfully and which did not fit the sugya well. As a result, there are some passages where the logical thread of the dialectical argumentation is incoherent, the smaller units do not follow or mesh or combine together well, and the sugya contains details that were already expressed in another way, or are obvious,[17] or are out of place. Why so? Because the Stammaim aspired to incorporate as much Amoraic dialectical argumentation as possible, and found no other way to integrate it into the relevant sugya.

Here I present an example of three sugyot that all quote the same apodictic dictum, but only one of them knows the dialectical argumentation related to that dictum: Yevamot 20a–b, Yevamot 61a, and Sanhedrin 18b–19a. An abbreviated version of Yevamot 20a–b is as follows:

[A] A widow with a high priest (performs *halitsah* but may not enter into levirate marriage; mYev 2:3)

[B] He (the authority of the mishnah) learns decisively (*qa paseiq vetanei*): there is no difference between [a widow] after marriage and [a widow] after betrothal. This makes sense [regarding a widow] after marriage, as it is a case of [violating] a positive commandment (i.e., the high priest is commanded to marry a virgin) and a negative commandment (i.e., that the high priest is commanded not to marry a widow); and a positive commandment (i.e., to perform the levirate marriage) does not override both a negative and a positive commandment. However, [regarding a widow] after betrothal, it is merely a negative commandment (i.e., against marrying a widow, as she is still a virgin). Let a positive commandment come and override the negative commandment!

[C] Rav Giddel said in the name of Rav: The verse states, *His brother's widow shall appear before the elders at the gates (Deut 25:7)*. There was no need to state *his brother's widow* (again, since the first half of the verse states, *But if the man does not want to marry his brother's widow*). What does [the repetition of *his brother's widow*] teach? There is a case of *his brother's widow* who is eligible for *halitsah* but not for levirate marriage. And which is that? These are the marriages forbidden by negative commandments.

[D] I could say rather that these are marriages forbidden.... The verse states.... If that is so...

[E] [20b] Rava objected: [A woman] prohibited on account of a commandment or a [rule concerning] holiness, with whom the levir had intercourse or performed *halitsah*....

[F] He [Rava] objected and he solved it....

[G] Rava objected:

[The baraita states]: A man with crushed testes or with a cut member, or a man-made eunuch, or an elderly man—they either perform *halitsah* or enter into levirate marriage. How so?

[G1] If they died, and were survived by brothers who had wives, and the brothers arose and issued a *ma'amar* to their widows, or gave them a divorce document, or performed *halitsah*—their deeds take effect. And if they had intercourse with them, they acquired them as wives.

[G2] If the brothers died, and they [the maimed or elderly men] issued a *ma'amar* to their widows, or gave them a divorce document, or performed *halitsah*—their deeds take effect. If they had intercourse with them, they acquire them as wives, but they may not retain them, as it states, *No one with crushed testes or a cut member shall be admitted to the congregation of the Lord (Deut 23:2)*.

[G3] If you should think that those forbidden by a negative commandment of Scriptural authority (*de'oraita*) may perform *halitsah* but may not enter into a levirate marriage, why then "If they had intercourse with them, they acquire them [as wives]" (and similarly, why should the high priest not enter into levirate marriage with a woman widowed after betrothal)?

[H] Rather Rava said: A woman widowed after betrothal is also forbidden [to the high priest] by both a positive and negative commandment...

[I] What would you say then of the cases of a woman of illegitimate birth (*mamzeret*) or a *netinah*? It is written, *They shall be holy to their God (Lev 21:6).*

[J] If so, [all negative commandments] throughout the entire Torah can be considered both positive and negative commandments, as it is written, *You shall sanctify yourselves (Lev 11:44).*

[K] Rather Rava stated: A widow after betrothal is [forbidden] as a preventative measure on account of a widow after marriage.

[L] What would you say then for the cases of woman of illegitimate birth (*mamzeret*) or a *netinah*? It is a preventative measure.... But in that case...Then it is a preventative measure...

[M] Rather Rava stated: The first act of intercourse [with the woman widowed after her betrothal] is [prohibited as] a preventative measure against a second act of intercourse [with her, which would then lack a positive commandment to take precedence over the negative commandment].

[N] It was also taught thus (*tanya namei hakhi*): If they (the men prohibited in the baraita above, [G1]) had intercourse with them, they acquire them [as wives]. This applies to the first act of intercourse, and they may not retain them (the wives) for a second act of intercourse.

[O] Subsequently Rava—others say Rav Ashi—said: What I said was not a [valid] statement (= [M]), for Resh Laqish said: In all cases where you find a positive and negative commandment, if you can uphold both of them, well and good. If not, the positive commandment overrides the negative commandment. Here too (i.e., the case of the widow after betrothal and the high priest), it is possible [for the high priest] to perform *halitsah*, and thereby to uphold both the positive commandment (to perform levirate marriage or an act of *halitsah*) and the negative commandment (not to marry a widow).

[P] They objected: "If they, had intercourse with them, they acquire them [as wives] (= G2)."

[Q] This is a refutation [of Rava] (i.e., his answer at [O], as the women are acquired as wives, and thus the positive commandment overrides the negative commandment even when you can uphold both of them).

Mishnah Yevamot 2:3 states that the High Priest may not perform levirate marriage [A]. The Talmud raises the difficulty: why can the high priest not engage in levirate marriage with a woman widowed after her betrothal, for only a negative commandment prevents this union, and the positive commandment of performing the levirate marriage should take precedence over the negative commandment [B]. Rav Giddel in the name of Rav answers that the verse, *His brother's widow shall appear before the elders at the gates (Deut 25:7)*, teaches that a woman widowed after her betrothal also may not enter into a levirate marriage with the high priest [C]. Rava then objects to this on the basis of the baraita which states "If they had intercourse with them, they acquire them [as wives]," that: "If you should think that those forbidden by a negative commandment of Scriptural authority may perform *halitsah* but may not enter into a levirate marriage, why then, 'If they had intercourse with them, do they acquire them [as wives]'" [G3]. He therefore offers a different answer: "The first act of intercourse [with the woman widowed after her betrothal] is [prohibited as] a preventative measure against a second act of intercourse [with her, which would then lack a positive commandment to take precedence over the negative commandment]" [M]. The Talmud then states: "It was also taught thus (*tanya namei hakhi*): If they had intercourse with them, they acquire them [as wives]" [N]. Clearly, whoever added, "It was also taught thus...," only knew of the apodictic part of the previous sugya, Rava's explanation [M], but not the dialectical argumentation, namely, Rava's objection on the basis of the baraita [G3], even though Rava proposed his explanation because of that very objection. For it is not fitting to bring support for an Amora and to state "It was also taught thus" [N] when that Amora himself makes the inference from that very baraita.**

[101] Similarly, in the continuation of that sugya, the Talmud objects to Rava, "They responded: 'If they had intercourse with them, they acquire them [as wives]...'" and concludes: "A refutation [of Rava]" [P–Q]. This perplexed the medieval commentaries: "Rava himself raised an objection from this baraita, and now they refute him from it?!"[18] The composer of the latter part of the sugya, who composed the section from "It was also taught thus" [N] onward, did not know of the reasoning—the objection devolving from the baraita [G1]—on the basis of which Rava made his statement [G3]. He had heard Rava's explanation from the Reciters, and they had only transmitted the apodictic traditions without the dialectical argumentation. The composer of the first part of the sugya [A–M], on the other hand, knew of Rava's explanation from the "survivals," the fragments

of tradition that remained in the memories of students, which included Rava's objection on the basis of the baraita.

Likewise, just as the passage in Yev 20b from the "It was also taught thus" [N] did not know the dialectical argumentation (the section, "Rava objected" [G]), so too the passages in Yev 61a and Sanh 19a did not know of this dialectical argumentation (see Table 3.1).

Sanh 18b–19a certainly did not know the dialectical argumentation, as it quotes Rava's solution ("The first act of intercourse is [prohibited as] a preventative measure..." [W]) without mentioning his name, and also includes the section "It was also taught thus" [X], which, as noted above, does not fit after "Rava objected..." ([G], attested in Yev 20b). Yet even Yev 61a, which does not include the "It was also taught thus," also did not know of the dialectical argumentation found in Yev 20b. The unattributed response, "The first act of intercourse is [prohibited as] a preventative measure..."[T], without its attribution to Rava [as at M], indicates that the Stammaim who formulated it here knew the passage in Yev 20b, where Rava retracted and admitted, "That which I stated was not valid...."[O]. These Stammaim nevertheless quoted Rava's dictum (without the attribution), despite the fact that the Talmud in Yev 20b objects against him: "They objected: 'If they had intercourse with them, they acquire them [as wives]...'" [P] and then concludes: "A refutation [of Rava]" [Q]. True, Rava retracted, but the baraita supports his position, and therefore these Stammaim quoted his dictum without mentioning his name [T].[19] However, if the composers of this passage had known the section, "Rava objected..." [G], they would not have accepted the refutation against him (since Rava himself adduces that baraita from which he is ostensibly refuted), and they would have figured out an answer for him (and also quoted the response in his name). The answer would have been something along the lines of that proposed by the post-medieval commentaries, that according to Rava, even though levirate marriage does not override the prohibition against the high priest marrying a woman widowed after her betrothal because "*halitsah* is an option," nevertheless, "If they had intercourse with them, they acquire them [as wives]." The fact that the composers of Yev 61a accepted the refutation of Rava ([P], as indicated by their omitting his name) indicates that they did not know the section "Rava objected..."[G].

However, it stands to reason that the composers of Sanh 18b-19a would not have stated "It was also taught thus" [X] in the absence of a disagreement. If Rava's explanation is the only explanation of the mishnah, then

Table 3.1 Yev 61a and Sanh 18b–19a

Yev 61a	Sanh 18b–9a
[R] mYev 6:4: A high priest whose brother died—he performs *halitsah* and does not enter into levirate marriage.	[U] (mSanh 2:1): [The high priest]...performs *halitsah* and they perform *halitsah* with his wife, and they enter into levirate marriage with his wife, but he does not enter into levirate marriage [with his brother's wife], because he is forbidden to marry a widow.
[S] He (the authority of the mishnah) learns decisively (*qa paseiq vetanei*): there is no difference between [a widow] after marriage and [a widow] after betrothal. This makes sense [regarding a widow] after marriage, as it is a case of [violating] a positive commandment (i.e., the high priest is commanded to marry a virgin) and a negative commandment (i.e., the high priest is commanded not to marry a widow); and a positive commandment (i.e., to perform the levirate marriage) does not override both a negative and a positive commandment. However, [regarding a widow] after betrothal, it is merely a negative commandment [i.e., against marrying a widow, as she is still a virgin]. Let a positive commandment come and override the negative commandment!	[V] He (the authority of the mishnah) learns decisively (*qa paseiq vetanei*): there is no difference between [a widow] after marriage and [a widow] after betrothal. This makes sense [regarding a widow] after marriage, as it is a case of [violating] a positive commandment (i.e., the high priest is commanded to marry a virgin) and a negative commandment (i.e., the high priest is commanded not to marry a widow); and a positive commandment (i.e., to perform the levirate marriage) does not override both a negative and a positive commandment. However, [regarding a widow] after betrothal, it is merely a negative commandment [i.e., against marrying a widow, as she is still a virgin]. Let a positive commandment come and override the negative commandment!

(*Continued*)

Table 3.1 Continued

Yev 61a	Sanh 18b–9a
[T] The first act of intercourse [with the woman widowed after her betrothal] is [prohibited as] a preventative measure against a second act of intercourse [with her, which would then lack a positive commandment to take precedence over the negative commandment].	[W] The first act of intercourse [with the woman widowed after her betrothal] is [prohibited as] a preventative measure against a second act of intercourse [with her, which would then lack a positive commandment to take precedence over the negative commandment].
	[X] It was also taught thus: If they went ahead and had a first act of intercourse with them, they acquire them [as wives], and they may not retain them (the wives) for a second act of intercourse.

the mishnah itself supports his position, and there is no need to adduce support from a baraita. Therefore it seems that, while the composers of Sanh 18b–19a did not know of Rava's objection [G], they did know the midrashic interpretation of Rav Giddel in the name of Rav, "*His brother's widow shall appear before the elders at the gates (Deut 25:7)*..." [C], and they adduced the "It was taught thus..." [X] to counter this interpretation.

Thus the sugyot of Sanh 18b–19a and Yev 61a offer an example of a sugya that quotes the apodictic conclusion of the dialectical argumentation, "Rava said: The first act of intercourse is [prohibited as] a preventative measure..." [T,W], which was originally stated after Rava's objection and attempts to find other explanations [as in Yev 20b, G–L]. But the sugya continues without awareness of the underlying reasoning, namely, the objection [102] on account of which Rava stated his solution. This must be because the objection [G], the dialectical argumentation, and Rava's apodictic statement [M] were not transmitted through the same channel of transmission.

At this point I wish to illustrate—on the basis of this very sugya, Yev 20a–b—my aforementioned claim, that in some cases the progression of the argumentation of the Stammaim is not coherent. Consider sections [H] through [L] in the extract presented above. Against Rava's second answer [K], which apparently resolves the objection against the cases of the woman of illegitimate birth (*mamzeret*) and the *netinah* [I], the Talmud makes exactly the same objection, "What can be said then of the case of a woman of illegitimate birth or a *netinah*?" [L]. Moreover, according to the Stammaitic dialectical argumentation [I], the objection against Rava's first answer [H], pertains only to the cases of the woman of illegitimate birth and the *netinah*; there is no objection to the case of the widow after betrothal, as it involves a positive commandment and a negative commandment, and is therefore not superseded by the commandment of levirate marriage.[20] Why then does the Talmud subsequently state in Rava's second answer, "Rather Rava stated: A widow after betrothal is [forbidden] as a preventative measure on account of a widow after marriage..." [K], since the case of the widow after betrothal had been resolved? We must conclude that the dialectical argumentation is artificial: it functions solely to explain why Rava answered, "The first act of intercourse [with the woman widowed after her betrothal] is [prohibited as] a preventative measure against a second act of intercourse" [M], rather than the other two answers ([H] and [K]), namely, primarily because these two answers do not satisfactorily address the cases of the woman of illegitimate birth and the *netinah.*** The Talmud could have accomplished this task in another manner: for example, it could have provided Rava's third answer at the outset, and then continued with the form "Let him rather say (*leima*)...," providing Rava's first and second answers, and explaining why they do not resolve the issues. This is indeed how the Talmud proceeds in many places, but here it preferred to provide the possible alternative answers in Rava's name and then to reject them. It is preferable to understand the genesis of the sugya in this way than to say that each of Rava's first two answers was refuted for different reasons, but the Stammaim did not know those reasons, and therefore substituted this artificial argumentation. For if so, then we have to say that the Stammaim, not knowing the objection against Rava's first answer,[21] repeated against this answer the objection against Rava's second answer (i.e., the objection based on the "woman of illegitimate birth or a *netinah*" [I], [L]), unaware or unconcerned that Rava's second answer should be free of the prior objection—and thereby produced a sequence that does not flow well. This seems to me a much more radical claim.

In sum, all dialectical argumentation begins with an apodictic law or dictum, and the dialectical argumentation analyzes that which was transmitted succinctly and concisely. In some cases the apodictic source with which the sugya begins is "obvious (*peshita*)" or can be inferred from another apodictic source, and is only articulated to raise another problem whose solution is similar to the source in some way. Sometimes the basic apodictic dictum became separated from the illustration of the problem and joined with other similar apodictic dicta, apparently by someone who did not understand the straightforwardness of the source. This subsequently puzzled a sage who was aware that the source was straightforward as to why this apodictic dictum was transmitted independently. I refer here to Sanh 10a: "Rava said: [If witnesses testify] 'So-and-so committed bestiality with an ox'..." This was questioned, "That is the same [case]!" That is, this apodictic dictum of Rava can be derived from another dictum of Rava: "[If witnesses testify], 'So-and-so [103] had intercourse with a betrothed maiden'...," so why does Rava need to tell us the same rule twice? The answer is provided: "Because he [Rava] propounded a question on it. For Rava asked: [If witnesses testify], 'So-and-so committed bestiality with *my* ox...' After he propounded it, he answered it..." In other words, originally the dictum "[If witnesses testify] 'So-and-so committed bestiality with an ox'..." was stated as the starting point for dialectical analysis of a different problem, "[If witnesses testify], 'So-and-so committed bestiality with *my* ox...'"[22]; later it was separated from this context and attached to apodictic material, and provoked the question, "That is the same [case]!"

Clearly, legal systems distinguish between court decisions and decrees on the one hand, and the dialectical argumentation that takes place prior to the verdict on the other. The former is more reliable and authoritative than the latter. Apodictic laws are better known (and easier to remember) and are taught in law schools as required texts with which all students must be acquainted. The dialectical argumentation, however, is known primarily by scholars and historians and is unnecessary for those engaged in practical law. As a result, dialectical argumentation is liable to be forgotten over the course of time, and to change, and not to be transmitted in its original form; laws and apodictic rulings, however, remain intact on account of their wide distribution and ease of preservation.

The Transmitters (Tannaim)

Did the "Reciters (*tannaim*)," those who taught Mishnah and baraitot before Amoraim, also transmit apodictic Amoraic material? Did the Reciters also transmit fixed laws that were not from the Tannaitic era? Scholars generally accept that the transmitters (*masranim*) only transmitted Mishnah and baraitot, and make no mention of brief explanations of the Mishnah. Thus J. N. Epstein writes: "The Reciters taught the Mishnah, the Tosefta, halakhic midrashim, and even the mystical baraitot," but omits mention of Amoraic explanations.[23] I believe that the Reciters attached apodictic Amoraic explanations to Tannaitic material and transmitted them to the following generations, but they did not transmit dialectical argumentation. We find, for example, in BM 27a: "The Reciter taught before Rav Nahman: 'This only applies to one who purchased from a merchant....'" Now the term "This only applies (*lo shanu*)" is Amoraic,[24] and it is utilized in explanations of the Mishnah and baraitot. Men 17a states: "The Reciter taught before Rav Yitshaq b. Abba: If he offered a handful of incense [with the intention] of eating the remainder [the next day], in the opinion of all it becomes *pigul* (unfit)." The expression "the opinion of all" does not derive from the baraita, which states instead "all agree." Mishnah Menahot 3:1 also lacks "the opinion of all," and instead [104] reads "and they agree."[25] More indicative is Bekh 59a and 60b, where the Talmud is responding to a contradiction between two baraitot. In one passage the Talmud responds: "The Reciter taught before

Rav Sheshet: Who is this? It is R. Shimon b. Yehudah, as we taught: R. Shimon b. Yehudah says..." The other passage states: "The Reciter taught before R. Yohanan: Who is this? It is R. Shimon b. Eleazar..." The expression "Who is this (*ha mani*)?" is Babylonian Aramaic and is unattested in baraitot. This formulation resembles the style of dialectical argumentation, the function of which is to resolve contradictions and which was not delivered to the transmitters. Accordingly "the Reciter taught" in this passage does not serve to resolve the contradiction between the baraitot but rather to identify the second baraita,[26] that it accords with R. Shimon b. Eleazar.[27] Either way, the Reciters in these passages transmit Amoraic explanations, and such explanations were certainly not uncommon.

However, if these are examples of Amoraic explanations, why did the Reciters not include the attributions? A similar question can be asked of an Amora who states a ruling and the ruling opens with the term "taught (*teni*)" or suchlike, for example, "Rav Yosef taught," which appears frequently in the Talmud: if it is a baraita, then how does it differ from a typical baraita introduced by the term "It was taught (*tanya*)"? But if it derives from the Amora himself, then what is the difference between "So-and-so taught" and "So-and-so said"? These issues are obscure, as our information about the transmitters is very limited. The Talmud itself says almost nothing about the transmitters, while scholars have focused primarily on the Reciters of the Geonic era, after the Talmud was committed to writing. The activity and procedures of the Reciters of the Amoraic and Stammaitic eras are unclear, and we have no choice but to speculate. The consensus seems to be as follows: Amoraic explanations of the Mishnah and baraitot reached us almost exclusively through the transmitters. Had these explanations reached us having been passed down from master to student, their formulation would not be so consistent, nor would they appear primarily in Hebrew. Rather, their formulation would reflect the language and style of individual students, and there would be many variations. Transmitters passed down the explanations from generation to generation, without the introductory term "The Reciter taught," just as baraitot were transmitted without introductory terms. The transmitters attached names of the Amoraim to their explanations; if the identity of the tradents was unknown (a relatively limited number of cases), the explanations were quoted with the addition, "The Reciter taught before R. So-and-so." And perhaps the purpose of the term, "The Reciter taught before R. So-and-so," was to alert R. So-and-so to clarify to the Reciter whether the formulation was accurate; they were especially concerned that, since the tradent of the dictum was forgotten, other parts were forgotten too.[28] Indeed, in several passages (e.g., Yev 40a, BQ 91b) R. So-and-so objects to the Reciter, who then asks him "Should I strike it out (*eisamyah*)?," that is, shall I expunge the dictum? And R. So-and-so answers "No," it is possible to emend the dictum and preserve it. At times the Amoraim themselves functioned as transmitters, and in these cases they introduced their teachings with the term, "He recited before R. So-and-so," for example, Ber 15b: "Rav Ovadiah recited before Rava (his master)." In such cases—and in all cases where "recited" appears in connection with a named Amora—we should conclude that the Amora-Reciter does not transmit his own traditions [105] (for if so, the Talmud would have used the verb "said"), but rather a baraita—which are often transmitted without the names of their tradents—or an Amoraic explanation whose tradent has been forgotten.

However, Talmudic passages that state "R. So-and-so said, and some say it was taught in a *matnita* [baraita]" introduce Tannaitic, not Amoraic, explanations, even when the language is that of the Amora and not of the baraita.** For example, Ber 57a: "Ulla said, and some say it was taught in a *matnita* [baraita]: This applies when he saw it on its stem"; Yev 107b: "Rav Yehudah said, and some say it was taught in a *matnita* [baraita]: At first they would write... when they saw that the formula was lengthy..."; Git 59a: "Rav Kahana said: 'Even seven [years old], even eight.' It was taught in a *matnita* [baraita]: 'Even nine, even ten.'" Although the language of this *matnita* is Babylonian Aramaic, and not that of the Tannaim, I still understand this expression "It was taught in a *matnita*" in its typical sense, meaning "in a baraita," despite the Amoraic language. For when a dictum has two attributions, the language is that of the first tradent, even if the second tradent lived long before him. This obtains too of several passages that state: "R. So-and-so—and some say R. Such-and-such—said." The language, style, and formulation are that of the first named sage. See, for example, Gittin 56b: "Rav Yosef—and some say R. Akiba—said: *[God] turns sages back and makes nothing of their knowledge (Isa 44:25)*. He should have said to him, 'Let them off this time.'" This Babylonian Aramaic formulation is certainly not that of R. Akiba, the Tannaitic sage who lived in the Land of Israel more than five generations before the Amora Rav Yosef.[29] Therefore it is also possible that the term "It was taught in a *matnita*" points to an authentic baraita, although the language is that of the Amora mentioned first.[30]

[106] Nevertheless, it is still unclear to me if the transmitters passed down Amoraic explanations in the name of the Amora together with the

Mishnah or baraitot. That is, when the transmitter of the Mishnah came to a mishnah-paragraph or to a baraita accompanied by an Amoraic explanation, did he combine them and teach them together, or did he pass them down as two separate traditions? That is, were there two separate transmissions, a transmission of the Mishnah and a transmission of Amoraic explanations, and the transmitter of the Amoraic explanations quoted only the pertinent clause of the mishnah or the baraita and attached the explanation to it? I cannot say for sure. However, since the Mishnah (though not baraitot; see below) was known by all sages,[31] whereas knowledge of Amoraic explanations was limited to specialists—it stands to reason that the Mishnah and its explanations were not transmitted together. Consequently, Amoraim of the Land of Israel did not know all the explanations of the Mishnah of their colleagues in the Land of Israel, and Babylonian Amoraim were not acquainted with all the explanations of their Babylonian colleagues; and therefore not all dicta of Babylonian Amoraim are to be found in the Bavli, and not all the dicta of Amoraim of the Land of Israel are to be found in the Yerushalmi—some Babylonian explanations only appear in the Yerushalmi, and some explanations from the Land of Israel appear only in the Bavli. If dicta do not appear in one of the Talmuds, then they probably were not known, because the Mishnah and the Amoraic explanations were not transmitted together, but rather each was transmitted independently; some transmitters specialized in Mishnah, while others specialized in explanations.

The Amoraic transmitters only passed down explanations that resembled fixed laws, such as "It was only taught," or "And this is a case (*vehu*)." They did not transmit explanations of the type, "What case are we dealing with (*hakha bemai asqinan*)," as well as most explanations formulated in Aramaic. These survived as part of the dialectical argumentation, and were not transmitted in an official manner. A similar, though not identical, process occurred with the Tosefta. Even if the Tosefta was not assembled and edited by R. Hiyya and R. Oshaya[32]** but rather by other early Amoraim, it was passed down by official transmitters; the rest of the baraitot were not passed down by these transmitters, but survived in the collective memory of the sages and were forgotten over the course of time: "This baraita is not known to us."[33] See *Yalqut Shimoni, Bamidbar*, #771: [107] "This [sage] teaches [the traditions] of Bar Qappara, and that one teaches [the traditions] of R. Hiyya, and that one teaches [the traditions] of our holy Rabbi [Yehudah HaNasi]." This may imply that there existed a separate transmission for each of these sages, and the Amoraic explanations were not attached to the Mishnah of R. Yehudah HaNasi or to the baraitot of Bar Qappara and R. Hiyya. It is also possible that the source of this tradition of the *Yalqut Shimoni* antedates the Amoraic period (and therefore cannot shed light on the transmission of material in Amoraic times),[34] but this requires further investigation.

Because this book focuses on the "Formation of the Babylonian Talmud," it would seem out of place, at first glance, to discuss the transmitters, the "Reciters," those who transmitted fixed laws and brief explanations accurately from generation to generation. "Formation" is synonymous with "development," while the transmitters were those who preserved the text so that it did not change. However, this view is not completely correct. The text was prone to change, and became a factor in the formation of the Talmud. Every time the Talmud states that the Amora did not in fact state what was attributed to him previously—whether it employs the term "Rather, said R. So-and-so," or "But if it was said, it was said thus," or simply "Say! (*eima*)," or "This is what he says (*hakhi qa'amar*)," or that his statement was made by inference—a change in transmission took place, and it became clear that the initial transmission was errant. The transmitter thus altered (one would assume unintentionally) the words of the Amora whose tradition he transmitted, in that he attributed to the Amora words that the Amora did not articulate. I already mentioned that when the transmitter (when, e.g., the Talmud states "the Reciter taught") learned from an Amora that his transmission was flawed, he asked the Amora "Should I strike it out?," that is, should I delete it, or will the Amora find a way to correct it and to preserve it? Never is it stated explicitly that the transmitters themselves chose to delete their traditions when an Amora informed them that they had made a mistake. However, this too probably happened in some cases when the transmitters realized they had erred.

It is also possible that in instances such as, for example, Sanh 31a, where they attribute to R. Yohanan the dictum "The law accords with Rabban Shimon b. Gamaliel," and he most likely also said "The law is not in accord with the Sages," that originally only one version was transmitted (whereas according to the Talmud, both versions were transmitted). However, some of the transmitters subsequently altered the formulation from "The law accords with" to "The law is not in accord with," or vice versa. In this case the transmitters retained both versions such that we can no longer determine which one is the original, while in other cases only one version was preserved. The contribution of the transmitters to the formation of the

Talmud was not direct, but indirect: the degree of their reliability in transmission determined the dialectical argumentation and influenced it.

The identity of the transmitters during the Amoraic and Stammaitic eras is unknown. We cannot conclude from Yev 64b, "Avin was reliable, Yitshaq the Red was not reliable," that these two were transmitters. The context of this report is not about their reliability as transmitters of laws or explanations such that we could conclude that they functioned in this capacity. This report rather only recounts that "A case came before R. Yohanan," and only regarding this case can it be said, "Avin knew when he (R. Yohanan) retracted; Yitshaq the Red did not know when he (R. Yohanan) retracted."[35] Likewise Rav Yosef's question in Git 6b, "Who can assure us [108] that R. Evyatar is reliable?" does not concern R. Evyatar's reliability as a transmitter, but rather his reliability as a source of legal traditions (e.g., the legal tradition he attributes to R. Yitshaq, which is contradicted by a baraita.) In Qid 44a R. Asi asks R. Zeira, "Is R. Avin reliable?" meaning, is R. Avin reliable to transmit exactly what he saw and heard transpire between R. Yohanan and Resh Laqish in the house of study? Rashi, however, explains: "Do you know that R. Avin can be relied upon to be punctilious about his traditions that he not forget them?" See too Ber 38b: "R. Zeira was astonished at him: What does R. Benjamin b. Yefet have in common with R. Hiyya b. Abba [that you mention them together]? R. Hiyya b. Abba is precise and learned traditions from his master R. Yohanan. R. Benjamin b. Yefet is not precise."[36] Here it is possible that two transmitters are mentioned, one punctilious about his traditions, and one not. At all events, one should not ignore the role of the transmitters in the formulation of baraitot and Amoraic dicta. However, they made less of a contribution to the Mishnah, since the Mishnah was known to many and did not depend on them as much. The reliability of their transmission also determined the accuracy of the content.

The Stammaim as "Reciters" and as Editors

Despite the role of the transmitters in formulating Amoraic dicta, they should not be placed in a separate category, as I did in my Introduction to *MM: bava qamma*, 7–12, where I designated them "Reciter-Stammaim (*stammaim tannaim*)." I attributed to them the processes of expansion, supplementation, and change,[37] and classified them as if they were the "Editor-Stammaim (*stammaim orkhim*)." Now I am of the opinion that most of the examples adduced to demonstrate that the Reciters, the transmitters, changed and altered Amoraic traditions should be attributed to the Editor-Stammaim, those who "tested and verified the explanations and rationales that brought about the formulation of dicta, and joined them together," and not to the Reciter-Stammaim, the transmitters of dicta in Amoraic times. In that Introduction, I assumed that anything connected to the original dictum without the involvement of another authority was an integral part of that dictum, such as "in what circumstances," "he holds," or the use of Aramaic following Hebrew.** Accordingly, where I identified expansion, supplementation, or change to the original dictum, I attributed the alterations to the transmitters. Now, however, I believe that when the original dictum has been expanded, supplemented, or changed, even without indication of the involvement of another authority, the "Editor-Stammaim" could be responsible. Therefore, let me briefly revisit the examples I adduced and analyze them in turn, following the same order, so as to demonstrate that they too can be attributed to the Stammaim.

(1) BQ 22a–b: The Stammaim who changed the specific issue of the Amoraic discussion, "one who occupies another's domain without his knowledge," to the general topic of "this one benefits while the other incurs no loss" could have been the Editor-Stammaim, who first explained the objection of Rava against Rami b. Hama as, "This is a case of 'this one benefits while the other incurs loss,' while the other is a case of 'this one benefits while the other incurs no loss'" (though it is possible that Rava himself made the explanation.)

(2) BM 22b: See p. 120 regarding the [109] transformation of the explanation, "Therefore Rabbah holds that a sign that is liable to be trampled [and destroyed] is not considered a sign.... Therefore Rava holds that a sign that is liable to be trampled [and destroyed] is [nevertheless considered] a sign," into "an independent tradition," namely, "Rabbah states... It is not considered a sign. And Rava states: It is considered a sign."

(3) Similarly, regarding the supplement to the question asked of Rav Sheshet in BM 112a: "Does an artisan acquire title by virtue of the improvement he makes to the article," which was also noted by the medieval authorities—there is insufficient evidence to conclude that it derives from the Reciter-Stammaim. Although it appears to be the continuation of the question, it could be a later addition.**

(4) Likewise, Hag 14b–15a: "They asked Ben Zoma: If a virgin became pregnant, is she permitted [to be married] to the High Priest? Do we take

into account [the dictum of] Shmuel.... He said to him, "That [case] of Shmuel is not common." Ben Zoma did not say "That [case] of Shmuel is not common" (as the Tanna Ben Zoma could not quote the Amora Shmuel). This is certainly an addition, and the addition could be considerably later, from the Editor-Stammaim.

(5) The case of BQ 58a is similar: "R. Yirmiah asked.... According to the one who says, 'If [damage resulted] from negligence at the beginning, but in the end [was caused] by an accident, he is exempt...'" The "one who says" here is Rav Yosef, and it is very likely that the Editor-Stammaim—and not the Reciter-Stammaim, and certainly not R. Yirmiah—integrated Rav Yosef's view with R. Yirmiah's question. Rav Yirmiah lived in the Land of Israel, and the Editor-Stammaim made it seem as if R. Yirmiah discussed the view of his contemporary Rav Yosef, who lived in Babylonia.[38]

(6) Sanh 33a: Here it is difficult to say that Rav Sheshet's solution to a contradiction between two mishnahs derives from the Editor-Stammaim: "Rav Sheshet said: 'Here it is a case when [the judge] erred regarding a law found in a mishnah; there it is a case when [the judge] erred in deciding between [opposing] opinions.'" This is because "the Editor-Stammaim were conscious of their own activity" (Introduction to *MM*: *bava qamma*, 9) and presumably knew that above, on Sanh 6a, Rav Sheshet stated only, "If he erred in a matter [found in] a mishnah, he may retract," and made no mention of deciding between opinions. Indeed, not only did Rav Sheshet not mention the issue of deciding between opposing opinions, but from the question that Rav Safra asked Rav Abba in which Rav Safra's statement is cited, it is almost explicitly clear that Rav Sheshet was not dealing at all with this issue. For if Rav Sheshet had been addressing that issue and ruled that the judge may not retract, then Rav Safra would not have asked Rav Abba, "What was his [the judge's] error?" The answer would be obvious—the judge erred in deciding between opposing opinions, and there would have been no need for Rav Abba to respond to Rav Safra. However, it is possible that Rav Sheshet's statement on Sanh 33a derives from the Reciter-Stammaim, as they "were not conscious of their own activity, and were not aware that they expanded, supplemented, completed and changed Amoraic dicta" (ibid.). Thus it is probable that over the course of time, "Rav Abba's response was unconsciously added to Rav Sheshet's dictum and transmitted together with it in Rav Sheshet's name." Indeed, the dictum is quoted in this way in Sanh 33a: "As Rav Sheshet said in the name of Rav Asi: If he [the judge] erred regarding a law found in a mishnah, he may retract; if he [the judge] erred in deciding between [opposing]

opinions, he may not retract." Here both types of error appear in the dictum attributed to Rav Sheshet—"and on the basis of this tradition of the transmitters, the Editor-Stammaim later resolved the contradiction between two mishnahs and attributed it to Rav Sheshet."

Here then is a case of an Amora resolving a contradiction in which he only stated half of the dictum; the second half of the dictum was stated by a different Amora, and over the course of time the Reciter-Stammaim combined the two halves and transmitted them in the name of the first Amora. This combination subsequently enabled the Editor-Stammaim to reconcile a contradiction between two mishnahs and also to attribute it to the first Amora.

[110] I would venture to suggest, though only as a conjecture, that the transmitters also functioned as "combiners (*metsarfim*),"[39] that throughout Amoraic times they had a dual function: as transmitters they transmitted dicta independently, while as "combiners" they combined opposing dicta and fashioned disputes, or they connected them into a single dictum in the form "both said," and they added to disputes the introductory term "it was said." Just as in the early Amoraic period, in the generation following Rav and Shmuel (see Shab 52a and my comments above), the transmitters functioned as combiners, so too in the Stammaitic era the transmitter-Stammaim functioned as combiners. However, in the Stammaitic era they not only transmitted Amoraic dicta but also transmitted and combined fragments of dialectical argumentation. Because they functioned anonymously, it is difficult to identify the combined dicta that they fashioned, and therefore their work as "combiners" was not noticed. And because the primary activity of the Stammaim was reconstructing dialectical argumentation and transforming it into sugyot—which was considerably more difficult and labor-intensive than the transmission of dicta, and also involved a greater quantity of material—it is reasonable to assume that they did not engage in both activities simultaneously, but first focused on the reconstruction, and only when the need for reconstruction decreased and became less demanding did they begin to combine traditions. Throughout the Amoraic period a single transmitter served several Amoraim. Even the great Amoraim such as R. Yohanan did not formulate so many dicta that one transmitter could not also include additional dicta of other Amoraim. A transmitter's combining activity thus began already with transmission. Not so the transmitters of the Stammaitic period: the great quantity of dialectical argumentation, especially that of the leading

Amoraim, required several transmitters, and their activity as "combiners" was not necessary until most of the sugyot had been reconstructed.

It seems that they also combined the passages in the Talmud formulated as "There are some who say" or "In Sura they teach it that way; in Pumbedita they teach it this way," which include a type of dialectical argumentation, as we never find Amoraim relating directly to these different versions. The reason we find contradictions between sugyot and even within one sugya and pertaining to a single issue is because different sources were combined by the Stammaim who lived at the end of the Talmudic period, when they could no longer change or harmonize sources,[40] and they integrated the sources as they found them despite the contradictions. (I commented on contradictions within the Talmud above, see, e.g., p. 65 ff.)

In some cases the Stammaim were not aware of the contradiction, for example, Sanh 27a: "A refutation of Abaye. This is indeed a refutation. Shall we say they disagree [in the same dispute] as the Tannaim?...As to R. Yose's opinion, there is no disagreement. As to R. Meir's opinion, they disagree. Abaye holds like R. Meir." There is no "refutation" of Abaye according to this conclusion, namely, that Abaye holds like R. Meir, while R. Yose disagrees. The baraita follows R. Yose—as we find in the Talmud: "The ruling follows Abaye. But was he not refuted? That [baraita] follows R. Yose." Thus whoever stated "A refutation of Abaye" did not state "Shall we say they disagree?" The point of departure of both passages is the dispute between Abaye and Rava, although they focus on different implications. Note that this passage should not be equated with the passages at Git 53b and Tem 25b, where the Talmud also states "A refutation. Shall we say they disagree [in the same dispute] as the Tannaim?" For in these passages the Talmud completely rejects the possibility that they disagree over the same dispute as the Tannaim, and the "refutation" therefore remains in force. In Sanh 27a, however, the "Shall we say they disagree [in the same dispute] as the Tannaim?," [111] namely the dispute between R. Meir and R. Yose, remains a possibility and functions as a response to the objection against Abaye brought from the baraita; consequently there is no "refutation." In this case we cannot say that the combiner was aware of the contradiction but lived at a time when he was not permitted to add to the Talmud and resolve the contradiction, since the Talmud itself subsequently states that there is no contradiction on Abaye, and the combiner could have quoted this section. We must say rather that the combiner integrated two contradictory sources without noticing the contradiction.**

Combiners in the Amoraic era, who dealt with Amoraic dicta, easily recognized disagreements and pointed them out in dispute-formulations between various Amoraim. Combiners in the Stammaitic era, however, who dealt with dialectical argumentation, only became aware of contradictions after careful and detailed study, so it is possible that they failed to notice various contradictions.

Forced Explanations

Because dialectical argumentation was not transmitted by the transmitters, and because the Stammaim reconstructed the dialectical argumentation hundreds of years after it was stated by the Amoraim, it is understandable that there are many forced explanations in the Talmud: when there is no reliable and accurate canonical transmission, sometimes the only choice is to offer a forced explanation of the text, as the "forced" aspect of the explanation compensates for the flaw in the transmission. In order to account for the great frequency of "forced explanations (*dehuqim*)" in the Talmud, appearing on each and every folio, we must adopt two assumptions: the Stammaim were not contemporaries of the Amoraim; and the dialectical argumentation was not transmitted in an official form—until the Stammaim came and combined it with Amoraic dicta and fixed laws. Had there been an official transmission of dialectical argumentation in an organized and edited form, it would have remained reliable even in the later Stammaitic era and would have been preserved in a complete and flawless state like the Amoraic explanations of the Mishnah and baraitot and the fixed laws of the Amoraim. And again, were the Stammaitic passages of the Talmud contemporaneous with the Amoraim, then there would not be such a great amount of forced explanations, even if the transmission was flawed. For they would have simply asked the Amoraim, the authorities of the dicta, or asked their students, to rectify the problems.

There are also forced explanations of a second kind: these are not the result of fragmentary sources which the Stammaim were forced to complete based on their own reasoning, and the best they could do was to offer a forced explanation. On the contrary—here the sources were complete and reliable, but they contradicted another Amoraic dictum or a baraita. In such cases the Stammaim preferred to give forced explanations to both sources rather than to admit that they contradicted each other. In rare cases an Amora responds, "He did not know this baraita" (Shab 19b), or was not concerned about reconciling his opinion with a baraita.[41] And Rav's disciples and their disciples were not concerned if Rav [112] disagreed with a baraita, claiming, "Rav is a Tanna and disagrees"[42] (cf. Shab 22a and parallels, "In all matters our master [Rabbah] acted in accord with Rav"). Forced explanations of the first type commonly appear in dialectical argumentation, while forced explanations of the second type are typically found in apodictic interpretations and dicta.

Let me provide a brief example of the second type from Sanh 3b (parallel in *Mekhilta, Mishpatim*, chap. 15, p. 302): R. Yonatan disagrees with R. Yoshiah and begins his statement, "The initial [appearance of the word 'judges'] is its first occurrence, and one does not interpret first occurrences." Thus they disagree on this point, namely, whether the first occurrence of a word may be used for exegetical purposes or not. The Talmud, however, rejects this explanation of the disagreement: after positing, "Let us say that they disagree over whether one interprets first occurrences," it continues, "No, all hold that one does not interpret first occurrences." Why does the Talmud reject the simple explanation of the disagreement? Apparently the Stammaim who composed this passage knew the Stammaitic stratum of the sugya below at Suk 4a, which attributes to R. Yohanan an explanation of the dispute between R. Shimon and the Sages such that both hold the principle "subtract one occurrence [as necessary] for [the precept] itself," which is somewhat analogous to "one does not interpret first occurrences." (See Rashi, Suk 6b, s.v. *legufei*.) The Stammaim of Sanh 3b did not want there to be a contradiction between the explanations of the baraitot in the two passages and preferred the forced explanation in Sanh 3b. Nevertheless, in Suk 6b still other Stammaim offer an alternative explanation of the disagreement between R. Shimon and the Sages in terms of "interpreting first occurrences"—here we have additional evidence for our claim that the Stammaitic passages in the Talmud derive from different academies.

We should realize that, as a general rule, views change over the course of time, and a text articulated on the basis of a particular view in an earlier era might be explained in a forced manner when that view changed in later times. A straightforward example is the passage from RH 16a mentioned on p. 34. The later Stammaim advanced a forced explanation of R. Yitshak's query, "'Why do we sound a sustained blast [of the shofar] on Rosh HaShana?,'' explaining it as "Rather, why do we sound the sustained blast and sound the quavering blast while seated and while standing?" This is a forced explanation as the sage never mentions standing or sitting.

However, the Stammaim explained the dictum in this way because in their time they no longer asked "Why" about commandments written explicitly in the Torah, since the straightforward explanation is "The Merciful One said to sound [the shofar]." If it is written in the Torah, that in itself is the reason. However, in R. Yitshaq's time they also wanted to know the reason for the commandment, and asked "Why" even with regard to commandments written explicitly in the Torah. This is what R. Yitshaq meant when he asked, "Why do they sound [the shofar] on Rosh Hashana?," that is, why sound the shofar at all, so there is no need for a forced explanation. The change in the sages' views of the reason for commandments caused the forced explanation of R. Yitshaq's question. And we find similar examples among other Amoraim.

The Dialectical Argumentation of the Talmud Is Not Amoraic

The traditional view claims that the Talmud's dialectical argumentation is a product of the Amoraim and was transmitted by Amoraim through the standard channels. My view is based primarily on inferences from Talmudic passages and supported by the phenomenon of forced responses found throughout the Talmud, which lead to the conclusion that the dialectical argumentation postdates the Amoraim and was not transmitted through the official channels. Is the evidence derived from inferences and forced responses sufficiently compelling to contradict a tradition dating back more than a millennium and accepted by the greatest sages? Moreover, inferences can always be explained in alternative ways, even if the alternative explanations are somewhat difficult, while the definition of a forced explanation is often subjective—[113] perhaps the editor of the text did not consider it forced? Therefore, let me again adduce three Talmudic passages as incontrovertible evidence against the traditional view and as support for my claim, and which also demonstrate that the Talmud itself was aware of the late provenance of dialectical argumentation (two of these passage were discussed above at greater length).

Sherira Gaon claims that following the death of R. Yehudah HaNasi "minds were weakened," and they had to resort to the traditional dialectical argumentation "generation after generation," in order to justify legal rulings. However, throughout the Tannaitic era there was no need for dialectical argumentation, as each Tanna could determine the legal ruling by himself: "because they had brilliant minds there was no need for explanation" (*Epistle of Rav Sherira Gaon*, 52). In my opinion, throughout the Amoraic era, just as in the Tannaitic era, they did not transmit the dialectical argumentation to succeeding generations, and only fragments remained, preserved in the memories of the audience who heard it in the house of study as a means to arrive at the final conclusion. Most of the dialectical argumentation was forgotten, and the Stammaim reconstructed it later, to the best of their ability, in order that it not be lost completely. However, because they flourished long after the Amoraim, they did not have access to all the sources, and consequently they had to resort to forced explanations and contradictions. Thus the Stammaim received material through two channels of transmission: one channel included traditions passed down from the Reciters, the transmitters of tradition, which the Amora himself had dictated to them, and which contained the Amora's words verbatim. The other channel contained material collected from the "survivals" which remained for subsequent generations, albeit without authentication and verification, and which did not necessarily reflect the original language of the Amora. The Amoraim, on the other hand, only had one channel of transmission: the tradition of the "Reciters." According to Sherira Gaon, the "Reciters" transmitted both legal rulings and dialectical argumentation; I believe, however, that the Amoraim did not entrust dialectical argumentation to the Reciters for preservation. I adduce these three Talmudic passages to demonstrate that the Talmud itself was aware of the two different channels of transmission in Stammaitic times and regarded the "survivals" as less authoritative.

(1) BQ 110b: "Rava asked: Are priests permitted to set [payment of restitution] for theft from a proselyte against [another payment of restitution of] theft from a proselyte? Do we say that the Merciful One called it 'guilt' (*asham*), and just as a guilt-offering cannot be set against another guilt-offering, so [payment of restitution] for theft from a proselyte cannot be set against [another payment of restitution of] theft from a proselyte? Or is [payment of restitution] for theft from a proselyte considered a monetary matter? He subsequently resolved it: the Merciful One called it 'guilt' (*asham*). Rav Aha b. Rava taught it explicitly (*behedya*): Rava said: Priests are not permitted to set [payment of restitution] for theft from a proselyte against [another payment of restitution of] theft from a proselyte. What is the reason? The Merciful One called it 'guilt' (*asham*)." A passage in much the same form appears above, BQ 78b.

I raised the following question concerning Rav Aha b. Rava, who taught Rava's tradition "explicitly (*behedya*)" in contrast to the previous formulation of Rava's tradition as a question followed by "he subsequently resolved it" (see *MM*, Bava Qamma, 431): Is a question, followed by "he subsequently resolved it" less "explicit" or less clear than a dictum, as in Rav Aha b. Rava's formulation? I suggested a new understanding for the term *behedya*, namely, "without doubt." Rav Aha b. Rava claimed that Rava never asked the question, never had any uncertainty as to the ruling, and had no doubt that payment of restitution for theft from a proselyte cannot be set against another payment of restitution of theft from a proselyte.

Now, however, it seems to me that *behedya* indicates that according to Rav Aha b. Rava, the dictum attributed to Rava was transmitted as a fixed ruling, in the brief and abbreviated form of fixed rulings, and was passed down by the Reciters. That is, this tradition was not transmitted with dialectical argumentation, as a question involving uncertainty on both sides, as in the transmission of the "survivals" of dialectical argumentation. Fixed rulings are called *behedya*, "explicit," because [114] they consist of the verbatim words of the Amora (see below on the term, "this was not stated explicitly [*befeirush*] but on the basis of an inference [*mikelala*])," whereas dialectical argumentation could have been reconstructed "by inference" and need not constitute the verbatim words of the Amora. Another example of this meaning of *behedya* appears in BQ 82a: "But who taught [the tradition] of the ten stipulations that Joshua stipulated? R. Yehoshua b. Levi. Rav Geviha of Be Katil taught it explicitly (*behedya*): R. Tanhum and R. Brays said in the name of a certain old man, and who was it? R. Yehoshua b. Levi: 'Joshua made ten stipulations when the Israelites entered the Land of Israel.'" According to the Stammaim, there is no explicit dictum that R. Yehoshua b. Levi said that Joshua made ten stipulations; this was only suggested as an answer to a question. According to Rav Geviha of Be Katil, on the other hand, R. Tanhum and R. Brays explicitly stated that R. Yehoshua b. Levi said "Joshua made ten stipulations."[43]

(2) Eruv 32b (I discussed this passage on p. 118): R. Hiyya b. Abba, R. Asi, and Rava b. Natan ask Rav Nahman (so it appears), "Did you fix it [= the explanation of that mishnah] in the *gemara*?" Rav Nahman responds, "Yes," and the Talmud brings a proof, introduced by the term "It was also stated," quoting "Rav Nahman in the name of Shmuel," that he explained

the mishnah in this way: "It was also stated: Rav Nahman said that Shmuel said: Here [in the mishnah] we are dealing with a tree that stands in the public domain, ten [handbreadths] high and four [handbreadths] wide, and he intends to make his Sabbath-abode below, and it is the view of Rabbi Yehudah HaNasi, who held that anything forbidden by rabbinical authority on the Sabbath (*shevut*) is not prohibited at twilight." This dictum of Rav Nahman in the name of Shmuel contains only the explanation of the mishnah, which has a form akin to that of a fixed ruling, without dialectical argumentation (recall that dialectical argumentation was not transmitted by Reciters in Amoraic times, and likewise not in the Tannaitic era), namely without the questions and answers asked by the Amoraim at the beginning of the passage: "Where was this tree standing? Shall we say that it was standing in the private domain... Rather it was standing in the public domain... How so? If one should say..." The "*gemara*," in the eyes of the Amoraim, contains only fixed laws or brief explanations, and when the Talmud brings proof in support of Rav Nahman that the explanation was indeed fixed in the *gemara*, it suffices with a condensed explanation and completely neglects to bring the accompanying dialectical argumentation.[44]

(3) In several passages (Shab 39b, Eruv 46a, Yev 60b, Git 39b), Amoraim ask "Did you hear this explicitly or on the basis of an inference?" (In three of these passages R. Zeira asks R. Yaakov b. Idi.)[45] There was doubt as to whether the authority of the dictum had really heard it from the "Reciters." Often the Stammaim ask, "And if it was through an inference—what does that matter?" The Stammaim do not always pose this question; if they have an answer, then they ask it, and if not, then they do not ask it. This question is only found in the Stammaitic stratum; it is unattested among Amoraim (see p. 17). My explanation for this divide is that the Stammaim routinely derived laws from inferences, and did not see a meaningful difference whether a ruling was stated explicitly or derived from an inference (*MM*, Megillah, 512–14). Consequently, when the Stammaim encountered traditions of Amoraim exploring whether the authority of the dictum heard it explicitly or derived it from an inference, they [115] surmised that there must have been an objection to the inference and inquired, "And if it was through an inference—what does that matter?" Not so the Amoraim: they were not accustomed to transmitting rulings derived from inferences, and when they suspected that a dictum was not originally stated explicitly, they sought clarification. To this I now

add a further explanation. The Amoraim received traditions through the Reciters, who transmitted only that which they heard explicitly from the Amoraim, and who did not transmit dialectical argumentation. "Inferences," however, found among the "survivals" of the dialectical argumentation, were not accepted by the Amoraim. Although they undoubtedly were familiar with the dialectical argumentation of their predecessors, or at least a portion of it, and presumably utilized it, they also knew how to assess the difference between the canonical and reliable fixed rulings as opposed to the reconstructed and conjectured dialectical argumentation. So when Amoraim encountered a dictum articulated in the form of a fixed ruling that they suspected had been changed from its original state, they asked about its origins, even when they did not find any objection to the inference.

The transmission of "Oral Torah" in the Talmudic era therefore can be divided into three phases. In the period of the Tannaim, traditions were passed down from generation to generation in the form of fixed rulings, some of which were assembled over time and became the Mishnah and baraita-collections. These were passed down to succeeding generations by the "Reciters" (*tannaim*), the official transmitters of tradition.

In the period of the Amoraim, they transmitted the Mishnah and baraita-collections, and also autonomous fixed rulings of Amoraim, but these were not attached to the individual mishnahs and baraitot that the Amora was explaining. Rather, these were transmitted in the form of a dictum, or as a dispute by the addition of the introductory term "it was said."[46] Only on rare occasions were concise explanations added to a mishnah or baraita, and these were preceded by the terms "this only applies (*lo shanu*)," "this is [a case] (*vehu*)," and suchlike. All of these were transmitted by the "Reciters."

In the period of the Stammaim, who flourished after the Amoraim, they did not formulate traditions as fixed rulings to be passed down to succeeding generations, even though they certainly made new rulings. They mainly concentrated on the systematic reconstruction and transmission of dialectical argumentation, which previous generations had neglected and had not preserved in the Talmud. For this reason, fixed rulings are very rare among the Stammaim. And because they were forced to rely on traditions that were commonly attributed to earlier Amoraim, there is reason to doubt the accuracy of their dialectical argumentation.

Aspects of the Methods of Reconstruction of the Stammaim

The foundation of my theory of the formation of the Talmud rests on the thesis that the Stammaim reconstructed Amoraic dialectical argumentation, and sometimes Tannaitic dialectical argumentation too, because there was no official transmission of dialectical argumentation in the Amoraic period. All my other premises—the prevalence of forced explanations in the Talmud, the late dating of the Stammaim, the absence of a comprehensive editing, and more—derive from this central and fundamental thesis. Therefore it is my responsibility to point out a few aspects of the methods of reconstruction adopted by the [116] Stammaim. To this end it will be necessary to return to some of the examples discussed above, albeit in a more abbreviated manner.

The Talmud, as is well known, is replete with Stammaitic explanation and supplementation of Amoraic and Tannaitic traditions.[47] These can appear at the beginning of the Amoraic dictum, at times in the middle,[48] and frequently at the end.[49] Because dialectical argumentation was not passed down as official transmission but survived independently, without external intervention and lacking authentication and confirmation, it was not always preserved in its entirety and is often found in a deficient state. The Stammaim were forced to get involved in the legal argumentation, to reject parts of it, and sometimes also to change the formulation of the law or to complete it after much of the relevant information had been forgotten. Centuries after the original dicta were stated the Stammaim returned to them and assessed the different contexts, inquiring, for example, "What case are we dealing with?" and suchlike, and that which did not survive they reconstructed and completed. The reconstruction differed from dictum to dictum: sometimes only the explanation, the justification, or part of it did not survive; sometimes the dictum itself was deficient; and sometimes the dictum and its explanation were intact and clear, but the context was unknown.

(1) When the explanation or justification alone did not survive, the Stammaim often distinguish their own additions with the words "What is the reason (*mai ta'ama*)?" or suchlike. And in some cases only the words "What is the reason?" are from the Stammaim, while that which comes both before and after are from the Amora himself. See, for example, BQ 110b (p. 146): "Rava said: Priests are not permitted to set [payment of

restitution] for theft from a proselyte against [another payment of restitution for] theft from a proselyte. What is the reason? The Merciful One called it 'guilt' (*asham*)." The reason, "The Merciful One called it 'guilt,'" was stated previously by Rava himself.[50]

(2) When the dictum is deficient, the explanation employs specific terminology, such as "In what circumstances?," "There is an internal contradiction (*ha gufa qashya*)?," and suchlike. However, a baraita will be followed by the term "What is he saying (*mai qa'amar*)?" Sometimes the specific terminology indicating Stammaitic intervention is lacking, but the Stammaitic provenance can be recognized because of a linguistic shift from Hebrew to Aramaic.** However, in some cases the Stammaim maintain the Amora's language and formulate the addition to his dictum in Hebrew too, and it is only possible to distinguish the Amora's statement from the Stammaitic addition by analyzing the content.[51]

(3) When the dictum survived without its context and the Stammaim themselves created the context—which they obviously formulated anonymously—then the false impression is produced that an Amora relates to anonymous material. But this is in fact not the case. For example, Pes 48a:

[A] R. Ishmael, son of R. Yohanan b. Beroqa says...
[B] But it was taught: R. Ishmael, son of R. Yohanan b. Beroqa, says....
[C] There is no difficulty. The one [statement] refers to [wheat of] poor quality. The other refers to [wheat of] good quality.
[D] Rav Pappa said: 'Learn from this that wheat of poor quality...'"

[117] It appears as if the unattributed statement "There is no difficulty..." [C] predates Rav Pappa [D], as he seems to comment on it. Not so: Rav Pappa's dictum was passed down in a truncated form, without a context, exactly as it appears in the Talmud. The Stammaim had difficulty explaining the expression "Learn from this" of Rav Pappa's dictum; they did not know what he "learned from." Therefore the Stammaim reconstructed a contradiction between two baraitot containing rulings of R. Ishmael, son of Yohanan b. R. Beroqa [A–B] and claimed that Rav Pappa referred to this contradiction.[52]

This example illustrates the difference between my method and the methods of earlier scholars. Earlier scholars would adduce this passage as proof that the Amora, Rav Pappa, engages an anonymous Amoraic tradition,[53] whereas I believe that the anonymous passage is late, and that the anonymous section that precedes Rav Pappa's statement in the text derives from the Stammaim. And this in turn relates to my different view of dialectical argumentation: I hold that argumentation was not passed down through an official transmission but reached the Stammaim in a fragmentary state hundreds of years later. They reconstructed it in much the same way as it appears before us in the Talmud. Of an Amora's dictum, the Stammaim only knew the part that they quote in his name. In this case they knew of Rav Pappa's teaching the statement "'Learn from this..." [D] alone, devoid of a context, and not responding to the claim, "There is no difficulty" [C]. It was the Stammaim who reconstructed the context, the contradiction and the solution [A–B] and placed this argumentation before the dictum, "Rav Pappa said: 'Learn from this...,'" and thereby caused his truncated statement to refer to that interchange. Earlier scholars, on the other hand, assume that the dialectical argumentation too was included in the regular transmission of tradition, and that the Amora's statement was detailed and comprehensive and also included the unattributed part that precedes it. Here they would claim that the anonymous portion of the Talmud is early; Rav Pappa therefore did not need to repeat the contradiction and its resolution, as these had been stated beforehand.

In addition, the Stammaim were punctilious to quote Amoraic dicta exactly as they were stated originally; but when they abbreviated the Amora's dictum, they sometimes quoted it anonymously and not in the name of the Amora, since the Amora had not articulated it in that way. For this reason, when the Stammaim employ such terms as "Did not the master say (*ha'amar mar*)?" or "As the master said (*kede'amar mar*)" to quote Amoraic or Tannaitic dicta, they omit attributions because they do not quote the dicta exactly as stated.** On Mak 6b the Talmud quotes Rav Pappa's question to Abaye and Abaye's response with attributions: "Rav Pappa said to Abaye: Does R. Yose accept this reasoning?... He [Abaye] said to him: It [the authority of the mishnah] is R. Yose b. R. Yehudah." However, on Mak 9b the Stammaim quote Rav Pappa's question and Abaye's response anonymously; because they abbreviated these statements, they did not retain the attributions (I commented on this phenomenon on p. 46).

In some cases the Stammaim attributed to Amoraim statements which they did not articulate, at least not with those very words. When the Stammaim explain why an Amora made a given statement rather than a possible alternative, they use the term "R. So-and-so objected to him (*matqif leih*)," before quoting his dictum. The Stammaim employ this term even when the Amora did not explicitly make this objection, and even when it is not clear that [118] it was specifically on account of this objection that the Amora made his statement.[54] Similarly, the Stammaim do not hesitate to attribute to an Amora dicta introduced by "R. So-and-so said," and then to refute them and conclude "Rather, R. So-and-so said," as if the Amora articulated all of the dicta, but they were refuted such that only the final dictum remained. However, in reality the Amora only stated the final dictum. See, for example, Yev 20b: "Rather, Rava said: A woman widowed after betrothal is also forbidden [to the high priest] by both a positive and negative commandment.... What can be said then of the case of a woman of illegitimate birth (*mamzeret*) or a *netinah*?... Rather Rava stated: A widow after betrothal is [forbidden] as a preventative measure on account of a widow after marriage.... What can be said then of the case of a woman of illegitimate birth (*mamzeret*) or a *netinah*?..." [See p. 124, where the entire passage is presented.] If the first dictum, "A woman widowed after betrothal is also forbidden...," is refuted on account of the objection "What can be said then of the case of a woman of illegitimate birth or a *netinah?*," then one ought not offer in response a dictum that is vulnerable to the same objection, "What can be said then of the case of a woman of illegitimate birth or a *netinah?*" We must conclude that these first two dicta and the objection were reconstructed solely for the purpose of creating dialectical argumentation and were rejected. Only Rava's final dictum, "The first act of intercourse [with the woman widowed after her betrothal] is [prohibited as] a preventative measure against a second act of intercourse" was clarified to be the true dictum.

If we do not want to claim that the Stammaim knew of multiple versions of an Amoraic dictum, then we must conclude that they considered the initial formulations of the Amoraic opinion as hypothetical possibilities. Even when these formulations were rejected, indicating that the Amora did not actually state them, the Stammaim still quoted them as "R. So-and-so said" and transmitted them in the name of that Amora. They formulated the explanation that they devised as "R. So-and-so said," despite the refutation. We also find, albeit rarely, that the Stammaitic completion (*hashlamah*) of an Amoraic dictum is formulated in the first person, as if expressing the exact words of the Amora, but in reality is the language of the Stammaim. I refer to BB 23a: "Was it not stated in reference to this statement, 'R. Mari says that it refers to smoke, and Rav Zevid says that it refers to an outhouse.' He said to him (Rav Yosef to Abaye): 'Because I am sensitive, these [ravens] are akin to smoke or an outhouse.'" Clearly Rav

Yosef did not respond to that which Rav Mari and Rav Zevid said, as they lived more than two generations later. His entire statement was formulated by the Stammaim. Nevertheless, they formulated it in the first person as if Rav Yosef spoke these words. The Stammaim here reconstructed Rav Yosef's answer and put the words in his mouth, as if he stands and responds in our presence.

Part IV: Compilers and Transposers

TO THIS POINT I have primarily discussed the anonymous stratum (*stammot*), the unattributed or "Stammaitic" material, and the "Stammaim" who composed it, and I concluded that their activity continued until the eighth century CE, long after the Amoraim. I made it clear that Rav Ashi was not the editor of the Talmud; that the Talmud, as a complete work, was never subjected to a general editing; and that the Stammaim were the sages who developed and transmitted to posterity dialectical argumentation, which makes up the vast majority of the text of the Talmud. The Tannaim and Amoraim had not included dialectical argumentation in the official transmission, and therefore it was neglected and forgotten—until the period of the Stammaim, who reconstructed and restored it. The core of the Talmud is the stammaitic stratum, and the Torah of the Talmud is the Torah of the Stammaim.

My account of the formation of the Talmud, however, is not yet complete. Apart from the Stammaim, "Compilers (*me'asfim*)" and "Transposers (*ma'avirim*)" also left their marks on the Talmud. Clearly "Compilers" contributed to the organization of material; for if there were no Compilers, who combined sugyot together and placed them in different contexts?** It is even possible that there were two types of Compilers: The first flourished at an earlier time and participated in the closing of the Talmud and resolved discrepancies between disparate and even contradictory sources. A second type lived later, after the closing of the Talmud, when it was no longer possible to insert one's own opinion into the text, but it was yet possible to add to a Talmudic passage from elsewhere, that is, to transfer sections of dialectical argumentation from one sugya to another. It is fitting that these two—Compilers and Transposers—take their places in the lineage of the Talmud.[1] This Part discusses them, focusing on the "Transposers," albeit not because "Transposers" were more important than Compilers. On the contrary, as we will see, "Compilers" made the larger contribution to the Talmud, which had a substantially different appearance prior to their intervention, as they bestowed on the Talmud its present form. Their influence is manifest throughout the Talmud, whereas the influence of "Transposers" is limited to the duplication of sections of sugyot in various passages.

Determining the time and source of transpositions is what makes the analysis of the Transposers difficult and requires detailed attention. Compilers, it seems, functioned in a limited period, between the Stammaitic and Saboraic eras (c. 730–770), and all activity related to the combination of sources can be assigned to that time. Transposers, however, functioned throughout the generations, and so we cannot definitively date the transposition of sections of anonymous material. That transpositions took place in different periods produced some errant transpositions due to misunderstandings or lack of information regarding the original meaning of the passage. Sections of dialectical argumentation were sometimes transferred from an appropriate context to an inappropriate context, but it is not known precisely by whom and in what era. Consequently, each and every transposition requires independent analysis, and it is particularly important to check the extent to which the material fits [120] the sugya in order to determine its source; clearly argumentation that fits the sugya neatly belongs there. Nevertheless, it is difficult to determine the time of the transposition on the basis of fit, especially when the integration is nearly perfect. Therefore, we must rely on our prior knowledge of the nature and development of the Talmud over the generations and attempt to assess the matter of transposition on that basis. However, first we need to define the specific function of Compilers and the nature of their activity by way of a brief comparison to the work of the Transposers, and by means of analysis of examples from the Talmud.

Compilers

"Compilers" gathered together the sugyot and fashioned them into a single Talmud. Prior to their activity there were many "Talmuds"—dicta and Amoraic explanations of the Mishnah and of baraitot—deriving from the different academies, and the "Compilers" combined them together. The "Transposers," however, already possessed our Talmud, in its present order, and they then transposed sections from one sugya to another, from one location to another. The Stammaim apparently were dispersed among disparate study houses; they did not always debate face-to-face, nor exchange arguments one with another, although in many places we do find a connection between the different houses of study. The absence of joint activity sometimes produced "contradictory sugyot (*sugyot muhlafot*)" and sugyot with opposing conclusions and argumentation. In addition, the degree of knowledge of earlier sources was not uniform, and sometimes one house of study knew that which a different house of study did not; a house of study, for example, that lacked knowledge of a given mishnah would offer a forced explanation. The Compilers gathered together the explanations into one passage without commenting on the contradictions between the disparate sections and the possibility of explaining the mishnah with a fitting, rather than a forced, explanation.

The Compilers apparently lived at a time when it was no longer possible to harmonize sources and remove forced explanations;[2] for it is implausible that they did not notice the prominent contradictions and forced explanations obvious to all. They left them intact, and trusted that students would understand that the passage contained differences and disagreements among the sources. When they received a fragmentary source, they added it to the end of the sugya without analysis.[3] This was their policy, for example, with baraitot introduced by the terms "It is also taught thus (*tanya namei hakhi*)," and "There is a teaching that accords with him (*tanya kevateih*)," even when these words follow an Amoraic disagreement. They did not integrate them into the dialectical argumentation and did not introduce these baraitot with the introductory term "They responded (*meitivei*)" as objections against the opposing Amoraim. For example, in Shab 40a the Talmud objects to Rav "they responded" and resolves the objection, and thereafter states "It was taught in accord with Shmuel"—without presenting that source as an objection against Rav. Similarly, in Meg 29b the Talmud objects against Rav on the basis of several baraitot, and at the end of the sugya introduces an additional baraita with the term "It was taught in accord with Shmuel," but does not use this source to object to Rav. This baraita derives from the Compilers, who were no longer able to add dialectical argumentation to the Talmud and had received no tradition of analysis of the baraita; they therefore simply added it to the end of the sugya.** And it is possible that this principle of ordering traditions explains why the sugya at Git 78a ends with the proof, "It was also taught thus (in accord with R. Yohanan): If he threw. . . . ," whereas the parallel sugya at BB 85b lacks this conclusion [121]. In BB 85b the sugya continues, and if the baraita introduced by "It was also taught thus" had been integrated there, students would not have known that it was added by the Compilers and would have used the baraita to object against the other Amoraim. Therefore the Compilers did not add the baraita to BB 85b, but only to Git 78a at the end of the sugya, as in that case all would recognize it as a later addition.

[If this reasoning is correct, then it follows that these parallel sugyot at Git 78a and BB 85b are not the work of Transposers but of Compilers, who thought that this Amoraic sugya belonged in both tractates (apart from the "It was taught thus…"), and therefore incorporated it into both. A similar case is the parallel sugya at BB 91a and Men 77a. In BB 91a the sugya concludes with the story of Rav Pappa b. Shmuel, and in Men 77a with the statement of Ravina: "Our mishnah is also precise…" This statement does not appear in BB 91a, and the story does not appear in Men 77a, which indicates that neither sugya was the result of a transposition that postdated the era of the Compilers, since after the Compilers' era there was no source of material for new additions to the Talmud.** It seems, therefore, that the Compilers judged it appropriate to include that sugya beginning "Shmuel said" twice: once in BB 81a with the addition of the story about Rav Pappa b. Shmuel, which relates to the topic discussed there; and again in Men 77a, with the addition of Ravina's statement, "Our mishnah is also precise," which is the proximate mishnah in that suyga. This seems to me more plausible than to say that the sugya at BB 91a derived from the Transposers, who transferred it from Men 77a, but refrained from transferring Ravina's statement because the mishnah to which Ravina refers is the proximate mishnah in Tractate Menahot, and consequently it is not fitting to say "*Our* mishnah" in Bava Batra but only in Menahot. For we find a number of questionable cases where Amoraim say "Our mishnah is also precise (*matnitin namei diqa*)," and it is probable that some of these references are to mishnahs of other tractates.[4] We conclude that Compilers integrated duplicate sugyot in different contexts, not only when the sugyot are contradictory and opposed, but also when they are identical but for additions of material in one that are not in the other and vice versa.]

Perhaps we should also consider as additions of the Compilers passages that contain two versions of an interchange that are generally parallel to one another, although in an inverted or contradictory relationship, and in only one version an Amora is quoted, which seemingly implies that that version is more authentic (see, e.g., Tosafot, Bets 13a s.v. *ika*). The Talmud, however, never makes this inference. If the Amoraic dictum appears at the end of the passage, we can assume that it was added by the Compilers at a time when it was no longer possible to analyze it dialectically, and they therefore left the dictum as they found it. For example, Sanh 31a–b:

[A] A certain women produced a document [of a debt between two individuals]. She said to him [Rav Nahman]: "I know that [the loan attested by] this document was repaid."

[B1] Rav Nahman believed her.

[C1] Rava said to Rav Nahman: Whose opinion does this follow? R. Yehudah HaNasi, who ruled: "Letters" (i.e., a document) are acquired through "delivery" (*mesirah*; and therefore the woman possessed the document).

[D1] He [Rav Nahman] said to him [Rava]: This case is different. Because had she wanted to, she could have burned it (so there was no reason for her to lie).

[B2] There are some who say: Rav Nahman did not believe her.

[C2] Rav said to Rav Nahman: But had she wanted to, she could have burned it!

[D2] [Rav Nahman replied:] Because it had been confirmed in a court, we cannot say, "Had she wanted to, she could have burned it."

[E2] Rava objected to Rav Nahman: "A receipt signed by witnesses is validated by the signatories. If it was not signed by witnesses, but was produced by a third-party, or was written [on a document of debt] below the signatures of the witnesses, it is valid." Therefore a third-party is believed.

[F2] The refutation of Rav Nahman is indeed a refutation.

The difficulty that Rava poses to Rav Nahman [E2] at first suggests that the second version of their interchange is more reliable [B2 vs. B1], as the difficulty only applies to that version of Rav Nahman's opinion. The Talmud itself, however, does not make this inference. This is because the difficulty was added by the Compilers at a time when they no longer added such inferences to the Talmud (but see n. 11 below). This also explains why the Talmud does not respond to Rava's difficulty and why the Talmud does not distinguish between the case of the woman who claimed that a valid document of indebtedness had been repaid [A], whom Rav Nahman did not believe (B2) [122], and the case of the third party in the baraita [E2], on which basis Rava inferred that the document is deemed valid [E2]. Rava's difficulty [E2] was added in the era of the Compilers, and at this time they no longer added objections and responses to the Talmud.

Let me return to the main subject: a fragmentary source that appears at the end of a sugya derives from the Compilers. This obtains only if the source does not appear elsewhere in the Talmud, but if it appears elsewhere, then it is more likely that it was a transposition, that the source was mistakenly transposed from one passage to another. An example of this phenomenon appears in BM 94a, commenting on mBM 7:10.

[A] mBM 7:10: "And any stipulation that can be fulfilled in the end, and that he stipulated at the beginning, the stipulation is valid."

[B1] Rav Tavla said in the name of Rav: This is the opinion of R. Yehudah b. Teima. But the sages say: Even if it cannot be fulfilled at the end, but he stipulated at the beginning, the stipulation is valid.

[B2] As it was taught: This is your divorce-document on condition that you ascend to the heaven.... If the stipulation was fulfilled, it is a [valid] divorce-document. If the stipulation was not fulfilled, it is not a [valid] divorce-document. R. Yehudah b. Teima said: It is a [valid] divorce-document. R. Yehudah b. Teima stated a general principle: Any [stipulation] that cannot be fulfilled in the end, and that he stipulated at the beginning, is only to distress her, and it is valid.

[C] Rav Nahman [b. Yaakov] said in the name of Rav: The law is in accord with R. Yehudah b. Teima.

[D] Rav Nahman b. Yitshaq said: This can also be inferred from our mishnah (*matnitin namei diqa*), which teaches: "And any stipulation that can be fulfilled in the end, and that he stipulated at the beginning, the stipulation is valid. Therefore if it *cannot* be fulfilled, the stipulation is not valid. Hear [it] from this."

Tosafot (BM 94a, s.v. *amar*) and other commentaries object: "What does Rav Nahman [b. Yitshaq] mean to tell us (by his inference at [D])? Behold, above Rav stated, 'This is the opinion of R. Yehudah b. Teima [B1].'" They answer: "One could say that [Rav Nahman b. Yitshaq] did not know of Rav's statement."[5] However, even if this is true, the Talmud itself obviously knew Rav's dictum, and should have asked what Rav Nahman b. Yitshaq added.

At first I thought that the end of the sugya, beginning from Rav Nahman [b. Yaakov]'s citation of Rav [C], was added by the Compilers. They came upon this source but could no longer add dialectic argumentation to the Talmud. Therefore, they did not raise any difficulties but simply included the dictum of Rav Nahman b. Yitshaq at the end of the sugya in its present form. Now, however, it seems to me that the Compilers had access to two different sources. The first was connected to mBM 7:10 and consisted of the dictum of Rav Tavla in Rav's name and the baraita he quotes [B1–B2]. The second source was originally based on the baraita [B2], which also appears in Git 84a, and included the dictum of Rav Nahman [b. Yaakov] [C] and the inference of Rav Nahman b. Yitshaq [D]. Thus Rav Nahman b. Yitshaq was originally commenting to Rav Nahman [b. Yaakov]'s comment on the baraita in a context such as that of Git 84a, and he made an inference from this mishnah from Tractate Bava Metsia. The sources disagree over two points: First, who said that mBM 7:10 follows the opinion of R. Yehudah b. Teima, Rav or Rav Nahman b. Yitshaq? According to the first source, it was Rav; according to the second source it was Rav Nahman b. Yitshaq. Second, the two sources disagree as to whom the law follows, R. Yehudah b. Teima or the Sages. According to the first source, the law follows the opinion of the Sages, for when an Amora (typically an early Amora) states, "These are the words of So-and-so, but the Sages say . . . ," then he generally rules according to the Sages [B1]. The second source, on the other hand, states in Rav Nahman [b. Yaakov]'s name "The law is in accord with R. Yehudah b. Teima [C]." The Compilers, in their usual way, made no comment about the disagreement between the sources, and integrated them in different contexts. They connected the first source [B1–B2] to mBM 7:10, and the second source [C–D] to the baraita in Git 84a [B2]. Subsequently, someone (mistakenly) transferred the section containing Rav's ruling [C] from Git 84a to BM 94a. Thus it now appears more likely, as Tosafot say, that "Rav Nahman [b. Yitshaq] did not know Rav's statement," rather than understanding that these are two different sources. If this explanation is correct, then Rav Nahman b. Yitshaq did not refrain from stating "This can also be inferred from our mishnah," even when the mishnah appears in a different tractate.

It should also be noted that in some cases the Compilers inserted a passage taken from elsewhere, but the original place [123] lacks the dialectical argumentation, even though that is its appropriate location. For example, the Talmud will state "and we discussed it (*vehavinan bah*)" on a mishnah quoted from elsewhere, but that original context lacks the difficulty and explanation raised in the "discussion" of that mishnah.[6] The redactor of the original passage containing the mishnah apparently did not know of the analysis introduced by "and we discussed it," and consequently did not include it. Moreover, Sanh 18b identifies particular sages with the sobriquets, "the elders of Sura," "the Amoraim of Pumbedita," "the judges of the Land of Israel," sobriquets that do not appear anywhere else in the Talmud. This implies, according to some scholars, that the Talmud in its present state is not complete. At some point these sobriquets had been in the Talmud, and the composer of Sanh 18b knew the passage in which they appeared and identified sages with the sobriquets on that basis. However, the Compilers did not know that passage, or did not collect all sugyot.[7] This is additional evidence that there was no general editor of the Talmud, and that no editor knew of the entirety of the Talmud and harmonized its different sections.

Although the activities of the "Compilers" and the "Transposers" sometimes overlapped, there are nonetheless fundamental differences between them, especially regarding their goals. Let me state here the fundamental difference, from which all other differences devolve: the Compilers—unlike the Transposers—inserted into the proto-Talmud complete and separate sugyot, and even contradictory sugyot, that originated in different houses of study. We can surmise that when the similarity between sugyot was substantive, then they combined them; if not, they distributed them throughout the Talmud. It seems that they juxtaposed versions of talmudic passages with the terms "there are some who say" or "another version," because the passages were similar in their content,[8] even if their legal rulings were incompatible. The Transposers, on the other hand, either transferred an entire sugya or completed a sugya that they considered to be deficient on the basis of a similar or identical sugya found elsewhere, which they believed to have originated in the same house of study. They assumed that, if the sugyot derived from the same source, then they had to be completely compatible, and so they transferred sections from one to the other. However, they were not completely consistent and did not always transfer material from one passage to another.

The Compilers' purview extended over the entire Talmud. Prior to their activity, the Talmud was not unified as in its current state, but was split up among different houses of study and academies. The Compilers combined the disparate sugyot into one book. The Transposers' purview, on the other hand, extended only over the passage with which they were engaged. They already had access to a "united" Talmud, a proto-Talmud, and they intervened in places that they thought required completing. The Compilers integrated different sources; the Transposers completed a truncated sugya on the basis of a complete sugya redacted in another context. The Compilers were active in a limited era whereas the Transposers were active throughout the generations; indeed sages never refrained from completing the deficient on the basis of the complete.

Now, although I claimed that passages introduced by "there are some who say" and "another version" were juxtaposed together by the Compilers, there are some exceptions in which the Compilers received the passages from earlier Stammaim already in this combined state. These are the sugyot where the alternative versions are followed by dialectical argumentation, of which some pertains to the one version, some to the alternative, without the Talmud specifying to which version each objection applies [124]. In such cases—and they are rare—the Stammaim received the two versions from Amoraic times and then arranged the objections and solutions according to a different criterion, namely, to align them with the order of the sources on which the objections were based. Let me quote an example from BB 94a: at the outset of the sugya, after citing Rav Huna, the Talmud supplies two versions: "Some say, [this is the] law, and some say, [this is a] penalty." The passage evaluates the two versions, questions them with the term "they responded (*meitivei*)," brings support with the term "come and hear (*ta shema*)," following the order of mishnahs in the Talmud, and only at the end objects on the basis of two baraitot.[9] According to the explanation of the commentaries,[10] some of the objections apply to the "law" explanation and some to the "penalty" interpretation, although the Talmud does not clarify which objection is directed to which version. The passage ends with the response of Rav Huna b. Rav Yehoshua, which is apparently predicated on the "penalty" explanation—but does not conclude that this version is correct. We find the same phenomenon elsewhere,[11] where an Amora's opinion correlates with but one of the versions, and yet the Talmud does not conclude that this version is original.

The Compilers did their work, apparently, up to the end of the Stammaitic period and close to the Saboraic age, up to the middle of the eighth century (c. 750 CE), when it was still possible to add brief explanations to improve the Stammaitic stratum but not possible to introduce substantive changes required to reconcile contradictions and eliminate forced explanations. This type of activity accounts for the fact that we find in the *She'iltot* some additions that do not appear in our Talmud, and explanations in our Talmud that do not appear in the *She'iltot*.[12] The process of integrating sources into our Talmud had not been entirely completed in the time of Aha of Shabha Gaon, author of the *She'iltot*. The medieval commentators (and the later Geonim) were sensitive to contradictions and forced explanations, and discussed them in separate works. However, as noted above,[13] they were no longer able to change the text and sometimes only succeeded in reconciling the sources by forcing the text.

To this point I have described the later Compilers, who were no longer permitted to insert their own opinions into the Talmud and therefore left disparities and contradictions between two sources as they found them. These late Compilers only added brief explanations that contained a new element, and therefore it is relatively straightforward to identify their contribution simply by thorough study of the passage. However, to trace the contribution of earlier Compilers—who contributed to the dialectical argumentation within the Talmud—and to identify their role in integrating material into the sugya often require more detailed analysis and comparison of the different parts of the passage. And sometimes extremely profound analysis is required to discern their contribution. Similarly, when the Compilers completed an earlier statement, it is difficult to distinguish the original statement from the addition and to determine which part derives from the Stammaim and which part from the Compilers. Only in cases where the addition is forced and shows signs of artificiality, and where its removal allows us to see clearly that sections of the passage do not fit well together but derive [125] from disparate and even opposing sources—these indications point to the hand of the early Compilers. Such cases are not very common, and it is difficult to categorize them accurately; nevertheless, they are frequent enough to demonstrate that the Compilers were not active at the beginning of the Stammaitic era but only after the sages had branched off into disparate academies and transmitted different and opposing views. Let me bring one example of harmonization among sources which, in my opinion, evinces forced argumentation, and points to earlier Compilers who worked prior to the final closing of the Talmud.

I refer to Sanh 16b:

[A] One may only add to the area of the city [= Jerusalem] and the courtyards [of the temple] by the authority of the court of seventy-one judges [= mSanh 1:5].

[B] Whence is this derived? Rav Shimi b. Hiyya said: Scripture states, *Exactly as I show you—the pattern of the tabernacle, and the pattern of all its furnishings—so shall you make it (Exod 25:9)*—in future generations (that is, just as the Tabernacle was legislated by Moses, who was in place of the "Great Sanhedrin," the court of seventy-one judges, so the city and courtyards in the future must be legislated by the court of seventy-one judges; see Rashi, ad loc., *s.v. ken*).

[C] Rava objected: "All the vessels that Moses made are consecrated by their anointing. Those made afterwards are consecrated by their service." But why? Let us say that, *So shall you make (Exod 25:9)* refers to future generations (which should also be consecrated by anointing, not by service).

[D] There it is different, as Scripture states, [*On the day that Moses finished setting up the Tabernacle, he anointed and consecrated it and all its furnishings as well as the altar and its utensils.] When he had anointed and consecrated them (Num 7:1)*. [Only] "*them*"—[are consecrated] by anointing; future generations [do not consecrate] by anointing.

[E] I would say [to interpret the verse this way instead]: Only "*them*"—[are consecrated] by anointing; future generations [consecrate] either by anointing or service.

[F] Rav Pappa said: Scripture states, *They shall take all the service vessels with which the service in the sanctuary will be performed (Num 4:12)*. Scripture made their [consecration] depend on their service (the imperfect, *will be performed*, refers to future generations).

[G] Why then do I need *them (Num 7:1)*? (i.e., what is the purpose of Num 7:1, invoked in section [D], which now seems to be superfluous?).

[H1] Were it not for *them (Num 7:1)*, I would have thought that future generations must [consecrate] by [both] service and anointing, since it says, *so shall you make (Exod 25:9)*.

[H2] The Merciful One therefore wrote *them*. *Them* [the vessels of Moses's time are consecrated] by anointing; but not those of future generations.

However, after Rav Pappa expounds, "Scripture made their [consecration] depend on their service" [F], one cannot claim—even without the exposition to account for the word "*them*" [H2]—that "future generations must [consecrate] by [both] service and anointing" [H1]. "Depend on their service" means that consecration depends on service *exclusively*, not service together with anointing. Why then does the Talmud say, "Were it not for *them (Num 7:1)*, I would have thought that future generations must [consecrate] by [both] service and anointing [H1]?" One can ask a similar question of the previous exposition, "[Only] *them*—[are consecrated] by anointing; future generations [do not consecrate] by anointing [D]," which also means by anointing *exclusively*, such that there is no need for service

[E].[14] Therefore no further expositions are required to rule out anointing for future generations. It appears that we are dealing with different sources that the Compilers fused together, but who could do so only in a forced way. Both sources resolve Rava's objection, "Let us say that, *So shall you make (Exod 25:9)* refers to future generations [which should also be consecrated by anointing, not by service] [C]." One source resolved it by the exposition, "*When he had anointed and consecrated them (Num 7:1)*. [Only] '*them*'—[are consecrated] by anointing; future generations [do not consecrate] by anointing" [D]. The other source, Rav Pappa, resolved it with the exposition, "*They shall take all the service vessels with which the service in the sanctuary will be performed (Num 4:12)*. Scripture made their [consecration] depend on their service" [F]. The two expositions agree that service alone effects consecration for future generations such that there is no need for anointing.[15] They disagree, however, over the source of the principle that anointing was limited to the vessels of the Tabernacle. The Compiler, however, who harmonized sources, was forced to say, first, that the exposition of "*them*" [D] does not preclude the possibility that "I would have thought that future generations must [consecrate] by [both] service and anointing" [H1], that is, that anointing is also a possibility; and second, that the exposition, "Scripture made their [consecration] depend on their service" [F] does not preclude the possibility that future generations consecrate "both by anointing and by service" [E]—but in fact this is not the case.

Now sometimes we find that after the Talmud quotes "there are some who say" or "another version" it then analyzes the two versions dialectically, referring to them as "the former version (*lishna qamma*)" and "the latter version (*lishna batra*)." Yet sometimes the Talmud simply quotes the versions "there are some who say" or "another version" without commenting at all. These versions were juxtaposed together because of their similar content, even though they present contradictory rulings. This difference appears to be a function of the time of the respective Compilers: when the Talmud reacts and propounds objections and responds with answers, the passages were juxtaposed at a time when it was still possible to add new dialectical argumentation to the Talmud. When the Talmud does not comment on the versions and offers no dialectical argumentation, then the juxtaposition probably took place when it was no longer possible to add new dialectical argumentation [126]. Of course it is possible to claim that they added no dialectical argumentation because they had nothing to add, but this possibility seems less plausible to me.

Thus there existed both creative Compilers, who produced new Talmud, and juxtaposing Compilers, who simply combined traditions. There were also the Stammaim of earlier generations, those who were engaged in creatively producing Talmudic material, namely, in the reconstruction of the dialectical argumentation, and who flourished before the disparate and contradictory sources that required harmonization had come into being. Therefore, we can distinguish three stages within the Stammaitic era: (1) The first and earliest stage (c. 550–650 CE), immediately after the Amoraic era, was replete with (fragmentary) Amoraic traditions, many of which the Stammaim incorporated. The Stammaim were centralized in one location, and internal debates were rare. Even after they dispersed into different houses of study, and disagreed among themselves, they did not attempt to reconcile the disagreements. (2) In the second stage, approximately a century later (c. 650–730), a proliferation and diffusion of houses of study took place, and the Stammaim devoted great efforts to reconcile the resulting differences of opinion. As with any reconciliation, in some cases they only succeeded in resolving the incongruities by means of forced explanations (see the example of Sanh 16b above). (3) The third stage began only at the very end of the Stammaitic era, when the reconstruction of dialectical argumentation had ended, and when the Stammaitic stratum came to a close in and of itself, near the time of the Saboraim (c. 730–770). The Compilers could still integrate brief explanations at the end of a sugya but could not add their own dialectical argumentation, nor supplement the closed Talmud—these are the cases of blatant contradictions that we sometimes find follow one another directly, without any effort to reconcile them; even if the Compilers had a resolution, they could no longer add it to the text.

In sum, we can distinguish three types of completion of earlier material. First, when the sugya is without parallel and appears in only one place in the Talmud, we must concentrate on that passage alone and investigate which part is Amoraic and which part is Stammaitic. Then we must check if the Stam's formulation and explanation of the Amoraic dicta are accurate, that is, if they are free from forced explanations—and if there is a forced explanation, we must come up with an alternative. Second, when there are two or more similar sugyot, we must assess the relationship among them. If they contradict each other, and one passage did not know of the other, then the Compilers inserted the contradictory passages in different contexts, apparently close to the Saboraic age; this is the case when there was no effort to harmonize the sources. However, if the passages are similar or identical, then we must suspect that this was not their original state but rather they originally derived from a single sugya that was later transferred to another location. It is also possible that only one of the passages was complete, while the second was fragmentary or truncated—and it was subsequently completed by the Transposers. Recall that Transposers were active both during and following the Stammaitic era. Third is the case of a single sugya that contains contradictory sources. If there was no effort to harmonize the sources, then the sugya derives from the later Compilers, when it was no longer permitted to harmonize.[16] If they did harmonize the sources, one must consider whether the harmonization was forced or not. If it was forced, then the sources derive from different and independent houses of study, and the Compilers joined them together but could only reconcile them in a forced way. If the harmonization reads smoothly, we can conclude that the Compilers found them already in the harmonized state [127].

Transposers and Types of Transpositions

The length of the activity of the Transposers exceeded that of the Compilers, as Transposers functioned throughout the periods of the Stammaim and Saboraim, and even thereafter. There are five types of Transpositions.

(a) The first is when two passages correspond identically in content, phrasing, and order, such that it is impossible to say that two different individuals formulated the exact passages independently. In such cases we are forced to conclude that one source was transposed to a second context. This type of transposition could have taken place at all times, and even in the post-Talmudic era; the Transposers did not consider the transposition to be an addition to the Talmud, which had already been closed, but simply a movement of Talmudic material from one location to another. It is difficult to date this type of Transposition. However, it would seem that such transpositions post-dated the Stammaitic era, as the Stammaim would have selected from the first sugya only that which was fitting to integrate into the second sugya and omitted that which did not belong; they would not have transferred the entire sugya as they found it. The original sugya can be determined on the basis of the content and fit with the context. For example, the sugya debating whether payment for half-damages is a fine or a monetary penalty is found verbatim in BQ 15a and Ket 41a. It probably originated in BQ 15a because it concerns damages.[17] Moreover, the first source adduced in the passage comes from Bava Qamma, and the second from Ketubot, and the Stammaim would not have started with a mishnah from Bava Qamma if its original context was in Ketubot.

(b) The second type of transposition is when the content of two passages is identical, but not the phrasing, and one passage does not fit its context perfectly. An example is when a sentence begins with "since (*she-*)," which is required in one context, but in the second context is superfluous according to normal linguistic usage.[18] Although the content is identical, the original context of the passage is the location where it fits perfectly. However, the transposition could have taken place in the Stammaitic era, or even in the Saboraic age.

[Let me note in passing that if a dependent clause beginning with "since" appears in the Mishnah, it may derive from the editor: he quoted his source verbatim even though the style did not completely fit the Mishnaic context. For example, mPar 5:5: "Only vessels with a tight cover protect [their contents from tent-impurity], since only vessels protect [their contents from impurity] in earthenware vessels." According to Yom-Tov Lippman Heller, in his commentary *Tosafot yom tov*, the word "since" introduces this statement "because of the phrasing of mKel 8:3, where it is fitting to begin the clause with 'since,' as it provides the reason for the preceding statement."[19] (Mishnah Kelim 8:3 reads: "If the [dead] reptile was in the oven, food within it [a colander] becomes impure, since only vessels protect [their contents from impurity] in earthenware vessels.") More significant is the fact that the editor of the Mishnah sometimes quoted a stock phrase [128] in which one of the words did not fit with the content of the new context: "Rav Hisda said: the 'deaf-mute' does not belong here. It was taught [in this mishnah] because of the typical phrase (yMeg 2:1, 73b)." That is, the expression, "a deaf-mute, imbecile, and minor" became a stock-phrase, and the three are mentioned together in many contexts, since most rules apply to all three. The editor of the Mishnah followed this general usage in mMeg 2:4 ("All are eligible to read the Scroll except for a deaf-mute, an imbecile, or a minor"), in a context where the "deaf-mute" did not fit, since a "deaf-mute who cannot hear and cannot speak" is not able to recite the Scroll of Esther; this too is a transposition.]

(c) A third type is when the content of a dictum is similar, almost identical, but the context in which it appears differs. If the attributions are mentioned in different sugyot—for example, "Rava asked of Rav Nahman: If he was unaware..." appears in Shab 70b, Shevu 19a, and Shevu 26a—then we assume that the Amora originally stated his dictum in all the contexts it appears. This too is the view of the medieval commentators,[20] who assume that the Talmud would not attribute a dictum or explanation to an Amora that had been derived by an inference without remarking on this process;[21] the Talmud would have used the expression, "*as* R. So-and-so said (*kede'amar*)...here too (*hakha namei*)." And see on p. 185, on the Talmud's ruling, "The same reason [applies to] the Shofar; the same reason [applies to] the lulav; the same reason [applies to] the Scroll of Esther," which Rabbah stated explicitly in all three contexts.[22]

However, in the case of a question and response attributed to Amoraim, of identical content, and found in two or more contexts, we cannot say that the Amoraim articulated these statements in the multiple contexts, because after his colleague answered him once, the interlocutor would not have asked the same question again. Consequently such cases must be transpositions. Such is the case of Zev 18b (= Yom 71b) and Taan 17b (= Sanh 22b), although there is some confusion as to the correct reading in both passages, whether "Ravina said to Rav Ashi" or "Rav Ashi said to Ravina" (see below). Whatever the correct readings, it is inconceivable that Ravina would ask Rav Ashi the same question twice, or the opposite, that Rav Ashi would ask Ravina twice, or that in one passage Ravina would ask Rav Ashi and in the other Rav Ashi would ask Ravina the same question that they had already discussed. The only reasonable conclusion is that it has been transposed.

[On the correct reading: see *Masekhet ta'anit min talmud bavli*, ed. Henry Malter (Philadelphia: Jewish Publication Society, 1928), ad loc. Yet it appears that the correct reading in Zev 18b (= Yom 71b) is "Rav Ashi said to Ravina," and the question is based on Ravina's dictum, "From here: *They shall have linen turbans on their heads (Ezek 44:18)*." (In Eruv 63a too, Rav Ashi asks of Ravina.) In Taan 17b (= Sanh 22b), on the other hand, the correct reading is "Ravina said to Rav Ashi," as found in most Talmudic passages, where Ravina asks Rav Ashi rather than the reverse. Incidentally, the first part of their interchange should read "they responded to him (*meitivei*)" rather than "Ravina responded (*mativ ravina*)," because after the term "responded (*mativ*)," the answer "*he* said to him" is not fitting, as the term indicates an individual is asking of many sages and not of a single individual.] [129]

It is difficult to determine where the passage found at Zev 18b and Taan 17b originates (certainly not MQ 5a). However, it is clear that neither Ravina nor Rav Ashi would ask the question "Who knew of this [law] before Ezekiel came?" twice, nor would either sage answer "And according to your reasoning, that which Rav Hisda said..." twice. They asked and answered once, and the second passage is a transposition that runs from "Rav Ashi said to Ravina" up to "Ravina said to Rav Ashi" (or the reverse). The switching of the names of the questioner and respondent is also unusual in transpositions. [Nor can one say, following Tosafot, Bekh 34b and Rashba"m, Pes 118b, that Rav Ashi or Ravina asked the same question on every occasion that other sages attempted to bring proof from Ezekiel: "Who knew of this [law] before Ezekiel came?" For the response, "And according to your reasoning, that which Rav Hisda said..." would not be appropriate, as the objection also would have been made directly against Rav Hisda's dictum, such that it could not be adduced as counterevidence.]

(d) A fourth type of transposition is when the contexts of the sugyot differ and the content is anonymous,[23] and the sugya fits well in both contexts. An example is the passage found in Qid 17b and BB 108b–109a beginning, "The reason [for including the son, rather than the brother] is because of this objection," and also found in part in Arakh 25b, beginning with, "Infer it from the fact that here there are two considerations." It is difficult to determine when this transposition occurred. Because the content is so similar as to rule out the possibility that we deal with independent sources, we cannot attribute it to the Compilers; had the Compilers not found the dialectical argumentation already in their source, they would not have transferred it to a second context. However, it is possible that the later Stammaim would have transferred dialectical argumentation to a new context.[24]

Indeed, sometimes the Stammaim employ an expression typically associated with a certain Amora, quoting it in that Amora's name, even in a context in which the Amora did not comment. In *MM*, Bava Qamma, 111 n. 10 I noted that in BQ 29b Rava states of Rav Ashi (and of Rav Ada bar Ahava), "Our mishnah was difficult for him," even though Rava lived before Rav Ashi. We must conclude that "the Stammaim employed an expression commonly used by Rava to explain Rav Ashi's dictum." Similarly, I claimed in *MM*, Eruvin, 231 to Eruv 88b, and *MM*, Pesahim,

311 to Pes 14a, that the phrase "Rava said: Our mishnah was difficult for him" is a transposition. Similarly, we find in Sanh 30b: "Abaye said to him: [The fact that you said] 'The law' [accords with R. Yehoshua b. Qorha] implies that [others] disagree." To whom did Abaye say this?[25] To Ulla, who is mentioned just above in the passage? There is no other instance in the entire Talmud in which Abaye speaks with Ulla. Moreover, Rav Yosef [130], Abaye's teacher, in the same passage quotes Ulla that "The law accords with R. Yehoshua b. Qorha in both land and movables." Were Abaye responding to Ulla here, he would say: "The law accords with R. Yehoshua b. Qorha in land but not in movables." Therefore, it is clear that the words "Abaye said to him: [The fact that you said] 'The law' [accords with R. Yehoshua b. Qorha] implies that [others] disagree" is a transposition from Shab 106b; and in fact several manuscripts omit "Abaye said to him" in Sanh 30b.[26]

(e) A fifth type of transposition is when two sugyot consisting of anonymous material appear in two different contexts, and the anonymous argumentation fits only one of them. For example, to mNid 2:6, "Five types of blood in a woman are impure. . . . Yellow blood: Akavya b. Mehalalel declares impure, and the Sages declare pure. R. Meir says: Even if it is not impure as a bloodstain, it is impure in regards to being a liquid. R. Yose says: It is not impure in either case," Nid 19b comments: "But this view [of R. Yose] is the same as that of the first opinion [in that mishnah, which does not consider yellow blood impure]? Behold, this informs us: Who is the first opinion? R. Yose. For whoever says a tradition in the name of the one who said it brings redemption to the world." R. Yose cannot be identified with the first opinion, the Sages who disagree with Akavya b. Mehalalel and who rule that yellow blood is pure, since R. Yose lived generations after Akavya.[27] In addition, R. Yose disagrees with R. Meir over how to explain the Sages' position: for R. Meir, yellow blood does not count as blood with respect to laws of menstrual impurity, but counts as blood with respect to the laws of impurity of liquids; for R. Yose, yellow blood also does not count with respect to the laws of impurity of liquids. The only possible explanation is that this section of Talmud was transferred from Hul 104b where it appears verbatim;[28] the original location is ascertained by the fit with the context. Dating these types of transpositions is difficult; they must postdate the Stammaitic era, and therefore date to the Saboraic age, or even to the time of Yehudai Gaon, since the Talmud contains additions from this time (such as rulings from the *Halakhot gedolot*), but not from later times.[29] Furthermore, it is unlikely that transpositions with legal implications would have been carried out after the Saboraic age.[30] The Stammaim, however, certainly would have been aware that this Talmudic passage does not fit well with mNid 2:6 and would not have mistakenly transposed it there. The Stammaim were willing to engage in forced explanations when the sources they had received were incomplete, but they did not make mistakes in understanding and distinguishing disparate sugyot, nor did they transpose traditions that did not fit the secondary contexts. Therefore, these transpositions probably took place at the end of the Saboraic period—and thus we have an example of additions to the Talmud that postdate the Stammaim.

[Let me add an observation about this transposition from Hul 104b to Nid 19b: while the comment, "But this view [of R. Yose] is the same as that of the first opinion?" fits well here in Hul 104b, which comments on mHul 8:2, the response: "Behold, this informs us: Who is the first opinion? R. Yose. For whoever says a tradition in the name [131] of the one who said it brings redemption to the world" seems slightly forced. Why does the Mishnah only reveal the identity of the first opinion here and not in other places where the opinion is anonymous? As an alternative to the Talmud's explanation, I would suggest that R. Yose's statement in mHul 8:2 was transferred from mEd 5:2, where R. Yose's opinion, without the anonymous first opinion, was included among the few laws that are atypical in that the House of Shammai expresses the lenient view and the House of Hillel the stringent view. This transfer could have taken place in the Amoraic period, such that the Stammaim encountered R. Yose's opinion in mHul 8:2, considered it integral to that mishnah, and gave a somewhat forced explanation.

Now a similar sugya appears in Ker 23a. However, this sugya is not completely anonymous. It begins with a dictum of Rava: "Rava said to Rav Nahman…He said to him: Behold, this informs us: who is the first opinion? R. Yose." At first glance, it seems more likely that the passage in Nid 19b was transferred from Ket 23a, where these names of the Amoraim appear, rather than from Hul 104b, where the passage is anonymous, and which also may have been a transposition from Ker 23a. However, I am uncertain whether the answer, "He said to him: Behold, this informs us: who is the first opinion? R. Yose," derives from Rav Nahman. The reading in ms. Munich 95 is "Rather [*ela;* אלא], behold, this informs us" instead of "He said to him [*a"l;* א"ל]"; variants between "Rather" and "He said to him"[31] are commonly found in the Talmud. If so, then it is possible that the Stammaim, and not Rav Nahman, answered Rava's question—clearly Rav Nahman had also answered Rava, but the Stammaim no longer knew his response and therefore provided their own. (The same can be said just below in the continuation of the passage in Ker 23a: "Rava said to Rav Nahman: Did R. Shimon really say this?... Rav Sheshet b. Rav Idi said: For example..."—Rav Sheshet b. Rav Idi, and not Rav Nahman, responded to Rava's query even though Rava directed his query to Rav Nahman.) Now Rava's question, "But this view [of R. Yose] is the same as that of the first opinion?" is stronger in Ker 23a than in the parallels at Nid 19b and Hul 104b. For the baraita quoted there, "But was it not taught: R. Yose says:..." (= tKer 5:8[32]) explicitly indicates that the first opinion is that of R. Yose; the formulation of the mishnah, on the other hand, suggests that R. Yose is explaining the first opinion. However, the response, "Behold, it informs us: who is the first opinion..." does not fit well, and if it is from the Stammaim, and not Rav Nahman, we could say that it was influenced by the parallels in Nid 19b and Hul 104a.][33]

Another example of this fifth type of transposition appears in Qid 61a: "'who dedicates his field.... If it contains ditches ten handbreadths deep or rocks ten handbreadths high they are not measured with it.'... Rav Uqba b. Hamma says: 'We are dealing with a case of ditches filled with water.'... Infer it also because it teaches an analogy to rocks." The inference "Infer it also..." does not fit the context in Qid 61a, as the passage subsequently cites another dictum of Rav Uqba b. Hamma regarding the selling of a field, which specifies that such ditches and rocks are not measured with it, "even if they are not filled with water." Thus Rav Uqba b. Hamma does not draw an analogy between ditches and rocks. We must conclude that this passage in Qid 61a was transferred from Arakh 25a, which does not cite Rav Uqba b. Hamma's dictum about the sale of a field, but only about the dedication of the field. Now in [132] BB 103a the ruling "even if they are not filled with water" is attributed to Rav Pappa and not to Rav Uqba b. Hamma. It is possible that Rav Uqba b. Hamma and Rav Pappa disagree whether to compare ditches to rocks, with Rav Uqba holding that one should not compare the two, and Rav Pappa's opinion was mistakenly attributed to him in Qid 61a. A mistaken attribution need not be ascribed to the Transposers but could have occurred throughout the Talmudic period, and even after the closing of the Talmud.[34]

I suggested above that transpositions that do not fit the flow of the sugya date to the end of the Saboraic period (c. 700–750). While this suggestion is generally true, there are exceptions. I have found examples where it is unlikely that the transposition is so late and cogent reasons point to an earlier date. In addition, erroneous transpositions are not all that rare in the Talmud, so it is questionable to assign them all to one period. The fact that those who follow the traditional dating of the Talmud fail to comment on this issue implies that they consider that transpositions too derive from the editing of Rav Ashi and his school, and that only a few mistaken transpositions can be attributed to a "blundering student (*talmid to'eh*)."** However, if we reject the view that the Talmud was edited by Rav Ashi and his associates, then it is implausible to claim that all the erroneous transpositions occurred in one limited era rather than accumulating over a lengthy period of time. This is especially true given that critical scholarship sometimes understands the forced explanations of the Talmud to result from erroneous transpositions of a passage, transpositions from a context where the explanation is not forced. Forced explanations are an integral component of the Talmud, and if some of them resulted from erroneous transpositions, then erroneous transpositions too must be considered characteristic of the entire Talmud. I refer not only to transpositions of a few words, which the medieval commentators already noted derive from scribal errors,[35] but also to series of objections and responses, kinds of brief sugyot that were sometimes transposed by mistake from a different context. Medieval commentators were reluctant to see objections and responses as erroneous transpositions or scribal errors because they considered them to be Amoraic material that went through an editing process. But had they not considered the Talmud to have been comprehensively edited, they would have found a much greater number of erroneous transpositions, and among them instances that cannot be dated to the post-Saboraic age and attributed to scribal errors, or at least are of uncertain date. I continue with several such examples:

(a) On p. 34 I demonstrated that the passage in Git 83b, from "As for the Sages—what do they learn from *[writ of] divorce*..." until Rava's dictum, was erroneously transferred from the parallels (Eruv 16b, Suk 24b, Git 21b), including Qid 5b: "For 'the Sages' mentioned there include R. Yose the Galilean, while in the parallel passages R. Yose the Galilean disagrees with 'the Sages,' as pointed out by the medieval commentaries." This transposition probably dates to [133] the era of the Stammaim, the composers of the Talmud, as a component of their explanations of the views of the Tannaim R. Yose the Galilean, R. Tarfon, R. Eleazar b. Azariah, and R. Akiba, who all disagree with R. Eliezer in the baraita quoted on Git 83b. (The Stammaitic explanations of the baraita are marked by such terms as "the master said [*amar mar*]" and "[Let us return to] the full text [quoted in part above] [*gufa*].") It is unlikely that the Stammaim would have neglected explicating R. Eleazar b. Azariah's view, which the transposition comments upon in its contextualization in Git 83b. Furthermore, the order of Git 83b is unusual, as it first explicates the views of R. Akiba and R. Yehoshua (who said to his colleagues, "One does not answer a lion [= R. Eliezer] after his death") before explicating the view of R. Eleazar b. Azariah, even though he is mentioned before them in the baraita. However, if this section is a transposition—and transpositions that do not fit their contexts are late, postdating the Stammaitic era—then the reason it comes at the end of the passage is clear: this is a characteristic of glosses (and a transposition dating to this late period is considered a gloss), namely, that they appear at the end of the sugya, as a supplement, and not in the middle. In sum, this passage requires further study.

(b) Another example of an erroneous transposition is Qid 25b. The Talmud quotes Rav, who expounds, "Large cattle are acquired by pulling (*meshikhah*)." When Shmuel learned that Rav expounded thusly, he asked Rav's students: "Did Rav say that 'Large cattle are acquired by pulling'? Did we not teach (in mQid 1:4) 'by delivery'? And Rav also said [that large cattle are acquired] 'by delivery'! Did he [Rav] then retract this ruling?" The passage continues: "He ruled in accord with this Tanna, as it was taught: 'Both the one (small cattle) and the other (large cattle) are acquired by pulling.'"[36] The answer, "He ruled in accord with this Tanna" is from the anonymous Talmud, serving to resolve Shmuel's astonishment at Rav's dictum. But this response itself is astonishing, because Shmuel was well aware of this baraita, as he stated "And Rav also said [that large cattle are acquired] 'by delivery'!," meaning that Rav had initially ruled in accord with mQid 1:4 (i.e., large cattle are acquired by delivery), and did not agree with "this Tanna" (i.e., by pulling). It therefore appears that this response, "He ruled in accord with this Tanna," was erroneously transposed here from BQ 11b, where it fits the context: Ulla says in the name of R. Eleazar that large cattle are acquired by pulling. The Talmud objects on the basis of mQid 1:4, which states that large cattle are acquired by delivery, and responds: "He ruled in accord with this Tanna, as it was taught: 'Both the one (small cattle) and the other (large cattle) are acquired by pulling.'" This interchange was subsequently transferred to Qid 25b.

When were such transpositions carried out? This is a very difficult question. However, the case of Qid 25b probably took place within the Talmudic era and was not a product of the medieval copyists. For if not, then the Talmud left Shmuel's question about Rav's ruling without an answer, and without noting "a difficulty" or "a refutation"[37] (which is unusual for the Bavli; the Yerushalmi, as is well known, frequently leaves objections without responses). Now, this passage in Qid 25b that aligns Rav with the ruling of the baraita contradicts the view found in BQ 96b and Arakh 29a, "Would Rav disregard the Mishnah and rule in accord with a baraita?" Thus it is implausible that Rav would give precedence to a baraita over a mishnah. However, if our analysis here is correct, then Qid 25b need not stand in tension with this view, as the explanation of Rav's ruling was erroneously transposed from BQ 11b. We are then left with the difficulty that Ulla's ruling in BQ 11b—which is not a transposition—contradicts this view that the Mishnah should not be disregarded in favor of a baraita. Perhaps we must distinguish between Rav and other Amoraim: Rav, who was "a member of Rabbi [Yehudah HaNasi]'s inner circle" (Git 59a), would not have strayed from the Mishnah that R. Yehudah HaNasi edited. Other Amoraim, however, sometimes preferred to rule in accord with a baraita rather than the Mishnah, and BQ 11b concerns the Amoraim Ulla and R. Eleazar. Nevertheless, we must conclude that these Talmudic passages disagree whether it is preferable to rule in accord with the Mishnah or a baraita [134], although they do not disagree about Rav's view on this matter, but about the views of other Amoraim. For in Suk 19b Abaye asks Rav Yosef, "Do you disregard the Mishnah and rule in accord with a baraita?,"[38] which differs from BQ 11b, which accepts such a policy. On the other hand, if the transposition to Qid 25b is erroneous, it is more plausible to date it to post-Talmudic times, and we have no way of knowing who inserted it into the Talmud. This too requires further study.

Let me also note that the following section in Hul 87b is a transposition from BB 97a: "It (= Shmuel's dictum, that all blood with a reddish appearance causes susceptibility to impurity) was only necessary [for a case] when it (= blood) was infused (*tamdu*) with rain water. But rain water too, since it was collected [in a vessel] and poured [into the blood] was intended [for that purpose, and is subject to impurity]. [Rather] it was only necessary [for a case] when they became infused (*nitmedu*) in and of themselves (= without human agency)." For it is inappropriate to use the verb "infused" (*tamdu*) or "became infused" (*nitmedu*) with "blood," which is the subject of Shmuel's dictum. The verb *TMD* does not mean "mixed" (*irvu*), as Rashi writes, but rather to place water on lees (on grape shells); "infused with rain water" means that rain water was placed upon the lees, while "became infused in and of themselves" means that rain water fell on the lees by itself. The appropriate context for this section is BB 97a, where the issue is whether water upon lees is considered as wine or water—and here the verb "infused" fits. But it does not fit Shmuel's statement about a mixture of blood and water in Hul 87b; it was transposed from BB 97a to Hul 87b.[39]

It is not completely clear, however, whether the content too in Hul 87b does not fit or only the language (the verb "infused"). In BB 97a this section relates to a statement of R. Yohanan in the name of R. Shimon b. Yehotsadaq that comments on a baraita dealing with water placed on lees of priestly tithe, levitical tithe, and temple dedications: is this water considered as wine (since it absorbed taste from the lees) and prohibited, or as water and permitted? R. Yohanan in the name of R. Shimon b. Yehotsadaq glosses the baraita, "Just as they stated [these rules] in regards to prohibitions, so they stated [the same rules] in regards to causing susceptibility to impurity." The Talmud objects that both wine and water cause susceptibility to impurity, and explains: "It was only necessary [for a case] when it was infused with rain water." Now rain water requires human intention in order to cause susceptibility to impurity,[40] and no intention took place in this case. Therefore, if the infusion is considered water then it does not cause susceptibility to impurity, but if it is considered wine then it does so. However, in Hul 87b this section relates to Rav Yehudah's statement in the name of Shmuel, "All (blood) that has a reddish appearance effects atonement (if sprinkled on the altar), causes susceptibility to impurity, and must be covered," which makes no explicit mention of water. The simple understanding of this dictum is that blood lacking a reddish color counts neither as blood nor water and does not cause susceptibility to impurity (similar to the proximate dictum of R. Asi of Neharbel in Hul 87b, "It was said of thin blood"). And the Talmud's objection, "If it is blood, then it causes susceptibility to impurity, and if it is water, then it causes susceptibility to impurity," is not a valid objection—it is neither blood nor water. Furthermore, if Shmuel meant that the blood was mixed with rain water, "that he infused it with rain water," which differs from his rulings regarding atonement and covering the blood, then he should have articulated this in the continuation of his ruling. Thus not only does the language of this section not fit the context in Hul 87b, but the content does not fit either.

The Talmud often transmits an Amoraic dictum in two different versions, such as two different formulations or as alternatives introduced by the term "another version (*lishna aharina*)." In some cases one version or the accompanying dialectical argumentation [135] reads more smoothly than the alternative version and its dialectical argumentation.[41] In such cases I assume that the smoother version is original and parts of it were transposed into the alternative version. Now it is well known that although the content of these different versions of statements can be radically different, the underlying structures remain identical to the original formulation.[42] I have accordingly claimed that it is sometimes possible to decide which version is original: one identifies the common structure and then assesses which version fits the structure better. I will present one example here from Yev 34b, where the first version of Shmuel's statement is, "And all of them (= the women listed in mYev 4:10) must wait three months [before marriage] except for a convert and an emancipated slave who were minors. However, a minor Israelite must wait." The Talmud objects to Shmuel's mention of the minor Israelite: "But Shmuel already stated this another time." From this objection it would appear (in contrast to Rashi's explanation) that the words "However, a minor Israelite must wait" are part of Shmuel's statement and not an inference made by the Talmud. But if these words are the continuation of Shmuel's statement, they are out of place, as the fact that "a minor Israelite must wait" is included in the first part of his statement: "All of them have to wait three months except" the two listed categories. However, the second version of Shmuel's statement, introduced by the term "another version (*lishna aharina*)," reads: "All of them must wait three months [before marriage] except for a convert and an adult emancipated slave, but a minor Israelite need not wait three months." Here the parts of the ruling fit well. The first part ("All of them must wait three months") and the second part ("except for a convert and an adult emancipated slave") deal with adults, and distinguish between adult Israelites, who have to wait before remarriage, and converts and emancipated slaves, who need not wait. Shmuel then adds that a minor Israelite need not wait. The first version of Shmuel's statement was a transposition from the second version, which was probably the original version, and therefore the structure of the first version was influenced by the second version. "In the time of the transposer, the forms of the dictum and the accompanying dialectical argumentation were already fixed. He changed the content—because he had received such a tradition—but did not change the form. In some cases the older form does not fit well with the new content" (*MM*, Yevamot, 41). Thus we have another category of transpositions, from one version of an Amoraic dictum to another version of that same dictum.

Perhaps too it is possible to categorize the following transposition as a different type of transposition, where the question differs in the two passages, but the response is identical, and was transposed from one passage to the other. Perhaps the opposite too, where only the identical objection was transposed to another passage, but the responses remained different. This process can be recognized even where the different objection or response appears in only one of the passages, and it is exclusively through an inference based on the language or style that we learn of its presence in the other passage.[43] Table 4.1 shows an example from Taan 17a–b (Sanh 22b).

The Talmud raises the objection: "If so, then during the present time too," that is, during the present time priests should not grow their hair long [B]. For if Ezekiel ruled *They shall not let their hair go untrimmed (Ezek 44:20)*, then in present times too they should not have long hair (see Ritb"a). The Talmud responds: "It is similar to the drinking of wine" [C], and then rejects this response [F1], since priests are permitted to drink wine when they are not serving in the temple. In respect to this point, the Talmud adduces the dispute between R. Yehudah HaNasi and the Sages [D1–D3], in which the Sages indeed prohibit priests from drinking wine: "What is the reason **[there]** [that the Sages prohibit priests drinking wine]? Lest the temple be speedily rebuilt, and we need a priest fit for service, but there be none (since they have all drunk wine)" [F1]. And therefore one could say the same of growing the hair long, that a priest should not let his hair grow long in the present time in case the temple is rebuilt and a fit priest cannot be found [F1]. The Talmud responds: "**Here** it is possible for him to cut his hair [136] and enter the temple" [G]. The parallel in Sanh 22b for the rejection of the response is: "**There** the reason is lest the temple be speedily rebuilt, and we need a priest fit for service, but there be none (since they have all drunk wine). **Here** too we require a priest fit for service (but there will be none, since they have grown their hair)" [F2]. However, the objection in this passage is "If so, then during the present time too" [B], and a response that differentiates between "there" (the issue of wine) and "here" (the issue of growing the hair long) does not fit. The difficulty is not that the one is permitted and the other forbidden, but that priests are permitted in the present time to grow their hair long in violation of Ezek 44:20. The formulation of this response in terms of "here" and

Table 4.1 Taan 17a–b and Sanh 22b

Taan 17a–b/Sanh 22b	Hypothetical original sugya
[A1] Rav Pappa said to Abaye: Perhaps the Merciful One meant that they [priests] should not grow their hair at all [with the verse *They shall neither shave their heads nor let their hair go untrimmed (Ezek 44:20)*.]	
[A2] He said to him: If it had been written…but as it is…(thus they may grow their hair, but not too long).	
[B] If so, then in the present time too! (priests should not be allowed to grow their hair long, based on Ezek 44:20, but all agree that they are allowed to do so.)	
[C] It is similar to the drinking of wine. Just as wine is forbidden only in the time they enter [for temple service], but when it is not a time that they enter [for temple service], it is permitted. So too here (in the case of growing the hair long, it is only forbidden in the time they enter for temple service).	
[D1] (Is drinking wine in the present time permitted?) Was it [not] taught: Rabbi [Yehudah HaNasi] says: I would say that priests are always forbidden to drink wine, but what can I do, as his misfortune (that the temple was destroyed) is to his advantage (that he can drink wine).	[d1] It was taught: Rabbi [Yehudah HaNasi] says: I would say that priests are always forbidden to drink wine, but what can I do, as his misfortune (that the temple was destroyed) is to his advantage (that he can drink wine).

(*Continued*)

Table 4.1 Continued

Taan 17a–b/Sanh 22b		Hypothetical original sugya
[D2] And Abaye said: In accord with whose opinion do priests drink wine in the present day? With Rabbi [Yehudah HaNasi].		[d2] And Abaye said: In accord with whose opinion do priests drink wine in the present day? With Rabbi [Yehudah HaNasi].
[D3] This implies the Sages forbid it!		[d3] This implies the Sages forbid it!
		[e] And why do the Sages distinguish between growing the hair [in the present time, which is permitted], and drinking wine [in the present time, which is forbidden?]
[F1] [Taanit 17a–b] What is the reason [**there**]? Lest the temple be speedily rebuilt, and we need a priest fit for service, but there be none (since they have all drunk wine).	[F2] [Sanh 22b] **There** the reason is lest the temple be speedily rebuilt, and we need a priest fit for service, but there be none (since they have all drunk wine).	[f] **There**, what it is the reason? Lest the temple be speedily rebuilt, and we need a priest fit for service, but there be none (since they have all drunk wine).
Here too! (The Sages should prohibit the priests growing hair lest the temple be speedily rebuilt and one need a priest fit for service)?!	**Here** too we require a priest fit for service (but there will be none, since they have grown their hair)?!	
[G1] **Here** it is possible for him to cut his hair and enter [the temple service immediately]. [G2] **There** too it is possible for him to sleep…		[g] **Here** it is possible for him to cut his hair and enter [the temple service immediately].

"there" was apparently transposed from another passage—even though no such passage survives—where the question was why priests today are prohibited from drinking wine but permitted to grow their hair long [e]. The distinction between "here" and "there" fits such a question. Presumably the original passage featured as its main issue the dispute between R. Yehudah HaNasi and the Sages over whether priests may drink wine in the present time [d1–d3], and then continued with an additional question, why the Sages permit priests to shave their heads since they prohibit drinking wine [e]. And the Talmud responded by distinguishing "here" from "there" [g]. In Taan 17a–b and Sanh 22b the dispute between R. Yehudah HaNasi and the Sages was brought up incidentally, in the course of the response, "It is similar to the drinking of wine," which meets the objection, "If so, in the present time too [that priests should not grow their hair long]." Because of this dispute the Talmud continued with the response of "here" and "there," as in the original passage, even though it does not fit this context.

Additional support for this reconstruction can be derived from the fact that in the continuation of the passage Rav Ashi meets the objection "If so, then during the present time too [B]" (in both Taan 17b and Sanh 22b) with a different response, against which they also object from the similarity between growing the hair long and drinking wine in Ezek 44:20–21 (in the end, Sanh 22b concludes with the objection intact, whereas Taan 17b offers a response). It stands to reason that Rav Ashi did not take into account the difficulty occasioned by this similarity. But this is possible only if we assume that originally he was not answering the objection "If so, then during the present time too," as this is the point to which the idea of the similarity to drinking wine is connected, and he should have been aware of the objection.

More important, the Stammaim, who reconstructed the fragments of tradition that survived from the Amoraic (and Tannaitic) periods, very rarely combined sources that were not fitting. However, the Compilers, who lived at the end of the Stammaitic era, did so frequently; for near the time of the closing of the Talmud it was no longer possible to engage in dialectical argumentation and to add to the Talmud. In order to preserve their sources the Compilers were forced to include them even when they did not fit.

I would even venture to speculate that when the Stammaim studied in the academy they did not follow the order of tractates but studied by topic. The Amoraim, however, proceeded according to the order of tractates, and when they completed their discussions, they transmitted their final conclusions to transmitters, while the dialectical argumentation, to the extent that it endured, survived without authorization. In Amoraic times the sugya was studied within its chapter of the tractate, but also as a topic, as evidenced by Rava's dictum in BM 35a, "Our chapter was *Hamafqid* (= Bava Metsia, Chapter 3)," and explained by Rashi, "We were engaged with that chapter." That is, they were studying Chapter *Hamafqid* in the house of study when the question about the appreciation of the value of the jewels was brought before Rav Nahman, Rava's master (the phrase in Nid 48a, "in our chapter *Yotsei dofen* [= Niddah, Chapter 5]," is not germane.) Not so the Stammaim—their studies were organized exclusively according to topics. The heavily reworked Stammaitic sugya resulted from this mode of study. The homogeneity of the topic binds the parts of the sugya together, and even if the connection between the different topics is loose, the connection within each topic remains strong. However, when they closed the Talmud, the Compilers redacted the sources according to the order of the tractates. Because they could no longer add dialectical argumentation and deal with contradictions and incongruities, they inserted the sources as they were found, without harmonizing them and without a tight connection between them. Whereas the Stammaim made numerous inferences on the basis of the content and arranged the order of material on that basis, the Compilers left the sources as they found them and simply combined them together, sometimes even in a state of disorder—the evidence of this is the incongruities and loose connections between passages. We find an example of this procedure in the genre of the *Yalqut* midrashim.**

Five Additional Observations

Let me conclude with a few observations regarding transpositions:

(1) My concern here is the transposition of sugyot or parts of sugyot without explicit indication that the material has been transposed, not with transpositions of Amoraic dicta. Transposed Amoraic dicta are commonly found in the Talmud and are introduced explicitly as transpositions with the term, "As R. So-and-so said . . . here too . . ." Dicta can be cited by other Amoraim or by the Stammaim. In rare cases the Talmud itself notes that a dictum was not transposed, but that the Amora himself stated it explicitly in each context. This is how I understand the passages, "The same

reason applies to the lulav...," "The same reason applies to the shofar...," "The same reason applies to the Scroll of Esther...," namely, that Rabbah stated his dictum thrice (Suk 42b–43a, RH 29b, Meg 4b). That is, Rabbah explained the three prohibitions against performing the lulav ritual, sounding the shofar and reading the Scroll of Esther when these festivals fall on the Sabbath as precautionary measures lest one carry the ritual items. If not, the Talmud would have stated, "As Rabbah said [elsewhere]." [However, in Pes 69a it is unclear if Rabbah explicitly stated, "It is a prohibition lest...," and indeed the words "Rabbah said" do not appear in ms. Oxford or in the glosses to ms. Munich.[44] However, in Bets 17b–18a Rabbah explicitly states, "It is a prohibition lest...," as Abaye "said to him," responding directly.]

(2) The prevalence of transpositions does not point to the process of editing.[45] A Transposer adds nothing of his own but simply transfers mechanically what was said in one context to another context while retaining the language of the original source. His activity was generally limited to sugyot originally found in two (or more) contexts, a lengthier version in one context and a briefer version in the other. Because he saw no reason (though he sometimes erred in this) why one sugya should be abbreviated, he added the parts not found in the other context. Transposers were active in every era, and even after the Talmudic era. I even tend to think that many of the mechanical transpositions postdate the Talmudic era (c. 780 CE); they did not consider these transpositions to violate the prohibition of adding to the Talmud, as the material was found in the Talmud itself and was simply transferred from one place to another. Of course the contribution of the editors was completely different. The editors ranged over the entire Talmud and collected ideas scattered throughout, or new ideas, in order to complete and harmonize earlier traditions, and they flourished at a time when changes and emendations could still be introduced.

(3) I have suggested—albeit indirectly—that the problem of forced explanations applies only to dialectical argumentation, which contains the explanations and elucidations of sources, and when these do not fit the language of the sources, then it is necessary to add something to, or remove it from, the source. Such explanations are not smooth but are rather difficult and forced. Regarding apodictic material and fixed laws, on the other hand, it is possible to reject the text, or to say that it does not make sense, or that it is incomplete or corrupt, but not that it is a forced and difficult law. The "forced" aspect inheres in the language, in the disjunction between the formulation of the source and the new explana-

tion proposed to elucidate it. With apodictic [138] material the language fits the law or dictum. It should be added that the problem of transpositions does not apply to apodictic material. Fixed laws are complete in and of themselves; unlike explanations, they are not predicated on an earlier source. And because they do not accompany an earlier source, one cannot say that they were transposed from one source to another. In the explanatory material we find, for example, "There are some who teach this [explanation] on this [source]." The explanation is predicated on the source, and the two versions dispute what that source was. Those responsible for the second possibility (introduced by "There are some who say") would claim that the first version was a transposition. Fixed laws, however, do not depend on a source; they are independent, in the sense of not context-dependent, and cannot be transposed from one source to another. Now it is possible—and we have many such examples—that someone changed a fixed law under the influence of another source. Yet this is not a transposition but rather an emendation; like any emendation it can be correct or incorrect.

(4) The general impression is that the Transposers identified a good explanation in one passage and transposed it from that context to a second passage. In cases where the original passage can be determined, namely, the passage where the explanation fits best, it is assumed that the secondary passage, where the explanation fits less smoothly, is later than its source, and that the transposition was carried out at a later time by someone else. But this is not always the case, and in some cases one must consider whether the passage was transposed by the same sage who explained the source. He repeated his earlier explanation in another context, even though it did not fit the secondary location well; because he had already given that explanation in connection with one source, he was drawn to it and stated it again despite the poor fit. Thus a Transposer may have been influenced by his own prior explanation. For example, in mSanh 2:3 the Sages say to R. Yehudah: "That was only to appease the people," and therefore one cannot take the case of King David following the bier of Avner (2 Sam 3:31) as a precedent that a king who so wishes is permitted to accompany a bier. Now the Sages say the same thing to R. Yehudah in a baraita in bSanh 20a, but in a different context, namely, whether women precede or follow the bier (see Table 4.2):

The Sages' answer makes good sense in mSanh 2:3 [c], namely, that a king is not obligated to accompany the coffin, but that David followed after

Table 4.2 Mishnah Sanhedrin 2:3 and Sanh 20a

mSanh 2:3	baraita, Sanh 20a
If a king suffered a death [in his family], he may not go beyond the entrance of his palace.	
[a] R. Yehudah says: If he wishes to follow after the bier, he follows.	[A] R. Yehudah says: Women must always precede the bier.
[b] For we find that [King] David followed after Avner's bier...	[B] For we find that [King] David followed after Avner's bier...
[c] They (the Sages) said to him: That was only to appease the people.	[C] They (the Sages) said to him: That was only to appease the people. And they were appeased.
	[D] For David was going out from among the men and entering among the women, and then going out from among the women and entering among the men...

Avner's bier to appease the people. In the baraita, however, the answer is not so easy to understand [C]. We must add that in order to appease the people, David was also walking among the women. Yet from the fact that King David followed the bier one cannot really prove that the women were not walking there (since King David would not have walked among women)—and conclude rather that they were walking in front of the bier, as R. Yehudah argues [A]. In addition, the language reads more smoothly in mSanh 2:3: "that," for example, David walking after Avner's bier [c], "was only to appease the people." However, in the baraita, "that" apparently refers to David walking after the bier rather than before it [B]—and it was only "to appease the people." This formulation is not clear—the sages could omit "that was only to appease the people" [C] and answer R. Yehudah simply, "For David was going out from among the men and entering among the women, and then going out from among the women and entering among the men" [D], and then add "in order to appease the people." But they do not respond in this way.

Therefore, it appears that the Sages' response in the baraita is a type of transposition from the Sages' response in mSanh 2:3. The Sages themselves were influenced by their previous reply and repeated it in a context where it is not sufficiently clear and does not read smoothly. Now we find on several occasions that the Talmud raises a contradiction between rulings attributed to "the Sages" who disagree with R. Yehudah in one source and "the Sages" who disagree with R. Yehudah in another source. The Talmud accordingly assumes that in the absence of considerations to the contrary, "the Sages" who disagree with a certain Tanna are always the same sages.[46**] (In Shab 120b, the Talmud even emends the baraita and states, "The mishnah has an omission and he teaches thus" in order that 'the Sages' disputing with R. Yehudah in the mishnah not contradict 'the Sages' disputing with R. Yose in the baraita.) [139] If in our case of mSanh 2:3 and the baraita of Sanh 20a we are dealing with the same "Sages" disagreeing with R. Yehudah, then we have an example of a transposition (or type of transposition) that was carried out by the Sages themselves.

However, this reconstruction remains uncertain. It is possible that originally the Sages of the baraita stated only, "For David was going out from among the men and entering among the women, and then going out from among the women and entering among the men" [D], and subsequently someone added, "That was only to appease the people. And they were appeased" [C], by transposing a line from the mishnah.

(5) And perhaps it would not be superfluous to add that I am dealing here with deliberate transpositions, where the Transposers knew the transpositions were not part of the Talmudic passage, and nevertheless added them on their own authority. I am not concerned here with glossators and scribes who believed that the transposition was originally part of the Talmudic passage but had mistakenly dropped out over the course of time. The latter process occurred in every era, including the glossators of the late middle ages. These glossators were self-consciously emending the Talmud and removing mistakes, and did not believe that they were adding to it.

By Way of Conclusion

My general argument has been stated implicitly and explicitly: that one cannot understand the text of the Talmud unless one knows how the text was transmitted to us, by whom, and what the stages of its formation were. Not only did the sages who provided the content of tradition influence the formation of the Talmud, such as the Tannaim, Amoraim, and Stammaim, but also other sages who specialized in various activities, and whose specific contributions were incorporated among its pages in different eras, impacted the formation of the Talmud. I refer to the transmitters, combiners, Compilers, and Transposers.

(1) The "transmitters"—the *tannaim* or Reciters—transmitted fixed laws in the Tannaitic era, and in the Amoraic era also explanations of the Mishnah (and of baraitot); in the Stammaitic era they transmitted the dialectical argumentation too. They devoted themselves completely to memorization. They transmitted that which the Tannaim, the Amoraim, and the Stammaim instructed them to transmit, and they functioned as "living encyclopedias." Accordingly, we find that at times the Amoraim corrected the traditions which the Reciters had memorized. In addition, the Reciters themselves sometimes were uncertain about the accuracy of a specific tradition and suggested to an Amora to erase it, "delete it" (*eisamyah*; e.g., BB 77b). Similarly, the Talmud on occasion states, "but if it was said, it was said thus," indicating that the tradition as stated previously is inaccurate. Their share in the formation of the Talmud is small and also cannot be identified. The changes they made to the traditions entrusted to them occurred by accident, not as a result of examination and research. They flourished in all generations and were contemporaries of the sages who transmitted the traditions to them. Information about them is very sparse; see p. 133.

(2) The "combiners (*metsarfim*)" combined Amoraic opinions into disputes (in the form "It was said [*itmar*]"), even when the Amoraim did not disagree face-to-face and even when they were not contemporaries. When it was no longer known who held which opinion [140], they formulated the dispute in the form, "One said . . . the other said . . ." This occurred even at a time close to that of the disputants, for example, in Shab 52a, where Rav Yosef, who lived two generations after Rav and Shmuel, already did not know who held which opinion and opined, "You can conclude (*tistayem*) that Shmuel was the one who held . . ." Sometimes later Amoraim and Stammaim observe, "and they do not disagree (*vela pligei*)," namely, that the combination is inaccurate, and that in fact the Amoraim do not dispute that issue. Combiners were active until the end of the Stammaitic era. Disputes between Rav Aha and Ravina (the Second), accompanied by extended dialectical argumentation including several strata, are almost always introduced by "One said . . . the other said . . ."; see p. 47, Part I, "Combination of Different Opinions into a Dispute."

(3) The "Compilers" juxtaposed the disparate sources and set them in order within the appropriate tractate. They lived near the time of the

closing of the Talmud, when it was no longer acceptable to add new dialectical argumentation within the Talmud. Therefore they could not resolve contradictions and work out incongruities but had to include sources as they found them; see p. 156.

(4) The "Transposers" transferred material from one passage to another. They lived in all periods and even (perhaps primarily) after the Talmudic era. The nature of the transposition and the degree of originality, that is, whether there is any new understanding of the passage from which it was taken, depend to a large extent on the period in which the transposition took place. After the Talmudic era they could only transpose antecedent traditions in a mechanical way. There are many types of transpositions, and the extent to which the transposition fits the secondary location varies from case to case; see p. 168 ff.

Part V: Postscript

The Anonymous Stratum (setam) of the Mishnah, Yerushalmi, and Halakhic Midrashim in Comparison to that of the Bavli

[141] In the Introduction to *Meqorot umesorot: bava metsia* (2003) I argued that the Stammaim were the first to attribute independent value to dialectical argumentation and to preserve it for posterity. While this claim is true in general, it can lead to the mistaken impression that the attitude of the Stammaim toward dialectics arose suddenly and without connection to earlier rabbinic activity. This attitude to dialectics was in fact the product of historical development, although its ultimate and most mature expression was realized in the Stammaitic period of the Bavli. This mistaken impression can result from a comparison of the Bavli, which is mostly dialectical argumentation, with the Mishnah, which almost exclusively contains apodictic law, suggesting that prior to the Stammaim there was no effort to preserve the argumentation. However, if we compare the Bavli to the halakhic midrashim or to the Yerushalmi, compilations that precede the Bavli, we see that the conscious effort to preserve dialectical argumentation did not transpire suddenly, and we realize that the Stammaim were not the first to engage in the enterprise. In the era prior to the Stammaim some brief and simple dialectical argumentation was preserved. But the Stammaim were the first to transform dialectics into an independent pursuit, to explore all possible avenues of investigation, to pursue subtle and complex analysis, and to propound objections and solutions—which far surpassed anything seen previously. They created the sugya and, indirectly, produced new legislation.[1] I stated this thesis in slightly different words above at the outset of Part III, but because of the importance of this issue it is appropriate to revisit it here, to elaborate on certain points, and to discuss the anonymous stratum of the Bavli in comparison to that of other compilations.

Accordingly I briefly address here the issue of anonymous material of the Bavli in comparison to that of the Mishnah, to the Order of Damages of the Yerushalmi, to the other tractates of the Yerushalmi, to Tractate Nedarim of the Bavli (and by extension to the other "unusual" tractates—Nazir, Temurah, Keritut, and Meilah), and to the halakhic midrashim. Each contains anonymous material, though the reasons differ from case to case, and likewise the quantity and degree of development vary until its climax in the Bavli. In the "unusual" tractates too the extent of the development of the anonymous stratum varies [142].

The Anonymous Stratum of the Mishnah

The Mishnah is totally oriented toward halakhah; it lacks aggadah (except for a few sections[2])**, exhibits very little dialectical argumentation,[3] and contains a few brief explanations, such as "because (*mipnei*)," and "since (*she-*)," though these are rare. There are a few interpretations of scriptural verses such as "the verse teaches (*talmud lomar*)," "as it is said (*shene'emar*)," and suchlike, and even these are not distributed uniformly among the tractates. The dependence of these interpretations upon attested midrashim is evident from the many times that a mishnah is excerpted from a midrash, and is also confirmed by the fact that a mishnah sometimes cannot be understood without reconstructing the underlying midrash.[4] In the Mishnah an anonymous formulation (*setam*) is a sign of authority. The more a mishnah lacks attributions, the greater the authority. The authority of an anonymous mishnah exceeds that of a mishnah stating "the Sages say" or "these are the words of the Sages," and the authority of these formulations exceeds that of an individual opinion. The editor selected these formulations, and he expressed his legal judgment by the way he quoted the opinions, whether anonymous or attributed, and whether attributed to an individual or to the majority. This was the editor's major contribution to the Mishnah, in addition to the choice of topics, which he apparently was responsible for selecting to include or omit.[5] When the editor was unable to decide the law and quoted two individual opinions, the law was decided by recourse to principles of adjudication (*kelalim*), such as when R. Meir and R. Yehudah disagree, the law follows R. Yehudah.[6] These principles also helped the student determine the law in cases where the Mishnah contradicts itself. (Even the context of a ruling, namely, the tractate in which it appears, influences the adjudication of the law. See, e.g., Ber 27a: "Rav Kahana said: The law follows R. Yehudah, since the teaching in Tractate Edduyot [*behirta*] accords with him.") The Mishnah was intended as a book of law.

The Mishnah's legislative purpose also explains why we do not find disagreements among the Tannaim formulated as "one said... and the other said...," a common Talmudic formulation for presenting disagreements among Amoraim. In these types of disagreements, later authorities knew that earlier masters had disagreed but no longer recalled who said what. In such cases, one cannot decide with which sage the law accords, because in cases of disagreement the law was decided according to the principles of adjudication, which were based on the attributions and not on the content (e.g., the principle of adjudication noted here, that when R. Meir and R. Yehudah disagree, the law follows R. Yehudah). If they were uncertain as to the attributions, they would have had difficulty deciding between the views and determining the practical law. Therefore, the Mishnah omits disputes of this type [143].

The Anonymous Stratum of the Yerushalmi

I have already mentioned that there was no difference between the Tannaitic and Amoraic eras regarding the transmission of tradition. In Amoraic times, as in Tannaitic times, they only transmitted apodictic formulations, namely, the final legal decisions, through the official transmission. Dialectical argumentation, on the other hand, was not preserved after the final conclusion had been reached; it was abandoned and forgotten. Only apodictic law was passed down by "Reciters," the official transmitters. The dialectical argumentation that ultimately reached us, on the other hand, is that which happened to linger in the memory of the students who had heard the discussions. But because it was not formulated for official transmission it became fragmented and forgotten with the passing of time—until the advent of the Stammaim who reconstructed it.

However, when the editor of the Yerushalmi redacted the legal rulings of the Amoraim, he appended the explanations of mishnahs and baraitot that underpinned their rulings. He may have done this so as to prevent the confusion of Amoraic with Tannaitic tradition. At this time, the reasons underlying Amoraic explanations of Tannaitic sources (and of earlier Amoraic traditions) had not been completely preserved, as they constituted an element of the dialectical argumentation. Consequently, the editor had to complete and supplement them himself. Although the editor believed that the Amoraim based their rulings on the reasons and explanations that he provided, he did not formulate them with Amoraic attributions, because he did not have an explicit tradition that the Amoraim articulated those words. Rather, he formulated them anonymously so that students would know that they derive from him. In this way there developed anonymous units of dialectical argumentation accompanying the apodictic, a phenomenon absent from the Mishnah.

These editorial supplements were originally terse and simple, as found in Yerushalmi Neziqin (edited c. 300–350 CE).** After about 100 years (c. 400 CE), they were enhanced and expanded, and sometimes became complex and difficult to understand. Yet they remained appendices to Amoraic explanations, the purpose of which was to elucidate the Amoraic rulings. Only after another 150 years in Babylonia did the dialectical argumentation become an endeavor in and of itself, and indirectly became a significant source of new law too.

In this respect, Bavli Tractate Nedarim resembles the Yerushalmi. There too—in contrast to the other tractates of the Bavli—the anonymous supplements are brief and simple, and function mostly to flesh out the rationale for Amoraic explanations of Tannaitic sources, and sometimes for Amoraic legislation. In Nedarim dialectical argumentation is not an end in and of itself. It does not contain multiple layers of propositions and rejections but rather a minimal amount of give-and-take, without nested sequences of objections and solutions. As is well known, because Nedarim commonly features distinctive linguistic forms, scholars assign it a late date, arguing that it was redacted after the other Bavli tractates, and in a different place.[7] They find support for this theory in the medieval tradition attributed to Yehudai Gaon to the effect that Tractate Nedarim was not studied in his academy, to which Epstein added "perhaps it had not been studied before then."[8] Indeed, such was the case! [144] It was not studied much before the time of Yehudai Gaon, not because it postdated other tractates, but on the contrary, because it predated the rest of the tractates. It originated in early Stammaitic times before the full development of their method, which ultimately came to its full expression in other Bavli tractates. The stages in the development of the anonymous stratum, from a thin overlay to the essence of the sugya, is therefore Yerushalmi Neziqin (mid fourth century),[9] the other Yerushalmi Tractates (end of fourth century), Bavli Nedarim (about the seventh century, two generations before Yehudai Gaon), and the other Bavli tractates (mid eighth century).

Now scholars have observed that the dialect of the "unusual" tractates—Nedarim, Nazir,[10] Temurah, Keritut, and Meilah—is similar to that of the

Geonim, and adduce this as proof that these Tractates were redacted in Geonic times, which, in their view, postdate the other Bavli Tractates. They opine that Tractate Nedarim and these other "unusual" tractates were composed after the other Talmudic tractates, in the times of Geonim who postdate Yehudai Gaon, because we have Responsa literature from that era, which allows for comparison of dialects. Until the time of Yehudai Gaon, however, we have almost no Geonic literature that would make such comparisons possible.[11] Yet according to my view that the Stammaim flourished during Geonic times, it is eminently possible that Tractate Nedarim originated in the early Stammaitic era, which antedated Yehudai Gaon.[12] The Stammaim of all tractates flourished during Geonic times—as opposed to the traditional view that all tractates, with the exception of the "unusual" ones, date to the Amoraic era. Admittedly, it is not clear why these "unusual" tractates reflect the Geonic dialect more than the other tractates of the Bavli. Nevertheless, the linguistic evidence of these tractates in relation to the other tractates and to the dialect of the Geonim has not been clarified sufficiently and cannot be used to determine priority and posteriority.[13] The character of the anonymous stratum seems to me to be a more reliable measure. This matter, however, requires additional study.

The Anonymous Stratum of the Halakhic and Aggadic Midrashim

This account of the nature of the anonymous strata and the process of their composition applies to halakhah alone; the nature of anonymous strata in the realm of aggadah, however, differs both qualitatively and quantitatively. For example, the halakhic midrashim contain a great deal of anonymous aggadah. So too anonymous aggadah is commonly found in the early portions of *Midrash Rabbah* (*Genesis Rabbah* and *Leviticus Rabbah*). [145] But anonymous aggadah is not common in the Bavli. The halakhic anonymous stratum of the Bavli is dialectical, whereas that of the aggadah is exegetical or declarative. In halakhah, as is well known, a Tanna may not disagree with an Amora, whereas he may do so in aggadah. Likewise regarding scriptural exegesis, "the Amoraim were not scrupulous about disagreeing with baraitot as long as the difference had no bearing on the law."[14] Aggadah is less authoritative, and therefore less hierarchical. However, the anonymous aggadah found in the halakhic midrashim, like that of the Mishnah and the anonymous halakhic portions of these halakhic midrashim, possesses a kind of exegetical authority (this is less the case in the later midrashim). An anonymous aggadic tradition when interpreted by many scholars has greater authority than when interpreted by a single scholar.

Yet these observations do not fully explain the entire difference between the aggadah of the anonymous stratum and that attributed to individuals. Perhaps the obligation to preserve the original source in its *ipsissima verba* applied less to aggadah than to halakhah. In halakhah one is not permitted to change the content, and one is always obligated to quote one's master exactly. In aggadah, a sage apparently was permitted to change the content, and when he did, he did not mention his source by name. A modicum of evidence for this point emerges from Ber 31a and Eruv 64a: "One should not part from his colleague except after exchanging words of halakhah, for in this way he will remember him." If he parted from his colleague after words of aggadah, however, he might not remember his fellow sage, for he might change the content and omit the attribution.[15] Still, it is unlikely that a sage was permitted to omit the name of an aggadic authority if he preserved the tradition exactly and repeated precisely what was said. If all this is correct, it explains why halakhah was fixed to a greater degree than aggadah. The prohibition against changing the content and the obligation to repeat the tradition in the name of the speaker preserved halakhah so that it would not be forgotten.

This consideration explains why there is so much anonymous material among the halakhic midrashim. Despite the name "halakhic" midrashim, these midrashim mostly contain aggadah (with the exception of the Sifra, which is entirely legal until *Parshat Behuqotai*), and the sages were not meticulous about preserving attributions of aggadic traditions. In distinction to halakhah, one cannot say of aggadic traditions, "this Tanna is authoritative" (i.e., the law accords with his opinion) and "this Tanna is not authoritative," or "this Tanna is reliable but that one is not reliable,"[16] and therefore it makes little difference who said what. The content is of decisive importance, not the attribution. As a result, the attributions of a great deal of aggadah were gradually forgotten and aggadic traditions became anonymous. On the other hand, the purpose of the anonymous formulation of halakhic traditions of these midrashim differs little from that of the Mishnah—it too is a sign of authority. Consequently, a great number of legal traditions of the halakhic midrashim were transferred to the Mishnah after being reformulated in Mishnaic style, which differs from that of the midrash, for example, with respect to order. The midrashim interpret the words of a verse according to their order in the verse, followed by the term "this teaches (*melamed*)," and then the law or lesson. The order is reversed in the Mishnah, which first provides the law, then the term "as it is said (*shene'emar*)," and finally the verse. (See, e.g., mSanh 10:1: "The house of stoning was outside the court, as it is said, *Take the blasphemer outside the camp [Lev 24:14]*." Compare *Sifra, Emor*, Chapter 19:1 [ed. Weiss, 104b]: "*Take the blasphemer outside the camp [Lev 24:14]*—this teaches that the court was inside and the [146] house of stoning was outside.")

Now we know that the Amoraim[17] possessed "books of aggadah" and consulted them (even if some sages opposed this practice),[18] but we never find mention of "books of halakhah."[19] Yet no mechanism preserves a text better than to render it in writing.[20] If a text is written, then even if an aggadah is totally or partly forgotten, one can consult the book and thereby restore it to one's memory. But this cannot be done with halakhah, which was not written down, making it difficult to refresh one's memory. The degree of permanence bestowed by writing is superior to the mnemonic advantages of halakhic texts, namely, the advantage that law is determined by means of the attributions and according to the general principles of adjudication; the advantage that they preserved an individual opinion in order to be able to take into account his halakhic stature so as to know whether to rule according to his opinion or not; and even the advantage that they transmitted halakhic traditions verbatim together with the sources and tradents. Remembering the names of the tradents and their language does not guarantee that content be preserved, whereas writing preserves everything accurately.

We must accordingly clarify why the sages did not write "books of halakhah" when they wrote "books of aggadah." Consider Git 60a:

[A] Rabbah and Rav Yosef both said: One may not read from a Book of Haftarahs on the Sabbath.

[B] What is the reason? Because it is not permitted to write them down (i.e., to write the Haftarahs only, as excerpts from the Bible).

[C] Mar bar Rav Ashi said: "It is also forbidden to carry them."

[D] What is the reason? Because it is not permitted to read them.

[E] But this is not so! It is permitted to carry them and it is permitted to read them.

[F] R. Yohanan and Resh Laqish looked at books of aggadah on the Sabbath.

[G] But it is not permitted to write them down (since oral traditions should not be written)!

[H] But [just as elsewhere we say]: "Because it is impossible [otherwise], *It is a time to act for God; they break the law (Ps 119:126).*"

[I] Here too: "Because it is impossible [to remember them], *It is a time to act for God; they break the law (Ps 119:126)*"—and they wrote down books of aggadah.

Here the Talmud mentions that R. Yohanan and Resh Laqish looked at books of aggadah on the Sabbath even though it was not permitted to write such books (since "you may not recite oral traditions from a text") [F–G]. The Talmud concludes that writing down aggadah must have been a type of special dispensation due to the difficulty sages confronted in memorizing the corpus of aggadah: "because it is impossible [to remember them otherwise], *It is a time to act for God; they break the law (Ps 119:126)*—and they wrote down books of aggadah" [I]. The Talmud does not conclude that it is permitted to write down books of halakhah, since at the time of the sage who composed this tradition—namely, the Stammaitic tradent of the statement challenging the claim about Books of Haftarahs, "but this is not so, it is permitted to carry them and it is permitted to read them" [E][21]—the Mishnah and Talmud had not yet been reduced to writing, and the only written books [147] were "books of aggadah."[22] Why were there no halakhic books? Presumably, as I have observed repeatedly, the Tannaim and Amoraim transmitted to posterity legal decisions alone, without the dialectical argumentation and for the most part without the reasoning—such that it was easy to remember them orally, and there was no need to write them down. This was not the case with aggadah. Aggadah cannot be divided into apodictic and dialectical components, nor can it be transmitted in an abbreviated manner such that a more developed version can be reconstructed. All of it, in all of its parts, is transmitted to posterity, which increased the danger that it be forgotten. Therefore they permitted writing down aggadah on the basis of the principle, "*It is a time to act for God; they break the law (Ps 119:126).*"

Now according to the tradition quoted by Judah b. Barzillai in his *Sefer ha'ittim*,[23] Natronai b. Hakhinai Gaon wrote out the Talmud (for the first time?) from his memory for the Jewish community of Spain.** Natronai lived after Yehudai Gaon, after the Talmud had been completed by the Stammaim and Saboraim, and after dialectical argumentation had been added (c. 780). At this point the dispensation on the basis of "*It is a time to act...*" was also applied to halakhah. As halakhah too became difficult to memorize and the danger of forgetting increased, the sages permitted writing down halakhah and studying it from written texts,[24] just as they permitted studying aggadah from written texts toward the end of the Tannaitic period.[25]**

Nevertheless, it is hard to judge whether it is more difficult to memorize the dialectical argumentation of halakhah than the details of aggadah. And in aggadah too it is necessary to distinguish between exegetical and ethical traditions, on the one hand, and historical traditions, on the other. Historical traditions are more similar to halakhah, and sometimes [148] contain a type of dialectical argumentation. There are many genres of aggadah and each genre has many distinctive aspects, such that it is difficult to generalize as to what is more difficult to memorize.

At all events, aggadic texts are no more fixed than halakhic texts despite the existence of books of aggadah and the absence of books of halakhah. Halakhah did not require additional modes of preservation, but was preserved by its apodictic and fixed form.

Addendum

[The Introduction to *Meqorot umesorot: sanhedrin* (2012)]

The explanations in this volume, *Meqorot umesorot* to Tractate Sanhedrin, like the explanations in the previous volumes of my commentary, are based on three fundamental assumptions concerning the editing of the Babylonian Talmud.

(1) The composition of the Talmud did not cease with Ravina and Rav Ashi in the fifth century CE but continued for centuries thereafter by the Stammaim, who transmitted their traditions anonymously. The anonymous stratum of the Talmud postdates the stratum of attributed traditions, and the Stammaim postdate the Amoraim.
(2) The Amoraim did not transmit dialectical argumentation but only fixed laws, and therefore a significant part of their dialectical argumentation was forgotten to some degree, and the little that remained survived on its own.
(3) The Talmud was never edited. In Talmudic times no one went over the entire Talmud in order to elucidate, clarify, or improve it (paraphrasing Hyman, *Toledot tannaim ve'amoraim*, s.v. "Rav Ashi"), and to eliminate contradictions and incongruities from within the sugyot themselves. Talmudic sugyot overall were not edited, but were explicated by the Saboraim who lived after the Stammaim, and then were assembled

> together by the Compilers. Some Saboraim lived near the end of the eighth century CE, when the Talmud was almost closed, and it was no longer acceptable to add dialectical argumentation or to harmonize its disparate sources.

I argued these points in detail in the Introduction to *MM: bava batra*, p. 65 ff. and pp. 85 ff., above, and there is no need to elaborate here.

However, I would like to clarify the explanation of the Talmudic dictum "Rav Ashi and Ravina—the end of *hora'ah* (BM 86a)," which has been adduced, since the time of Sherira Gaon, as proof that Rav Ashi and Ravina edited the Talmud (although Sherira Gaon himself does not say this explicitly). I have no doubt whatsoever that *hora'ah* does not mean Talmud (*gemara*), but rather "legislation" or "fixed law" and likewise that "end" (*sof*) does not refer to editing, but rather "conclusion, finish." However I did not provide a satisfactory explanation or compelling analysis of the Talmudic concept "the end of *hora'ah*." I was correct to point out that the term "it was said (*itmar*)," which precedes Amoraic dicta and Amoraic disputes over fixed laws, is not found with Amoraim who postdate Rav Ashi and Ravina (Part II, n. 39).[26] However, from a linguistic perspective one cannot understand "the end of legislation" as the end of the use of the term "it was said (*itmar*)." My explanation that this dictum "does not express an historical fact, but rather the adulation of a student who thought that the death of his celebrated master brought an end to legislation"[27] is possible, though it does not fully capture the meaning of "the end of legislation" (above, p. 4). Here I would like to propose a new solution: "the end of legislation" means the end of the *transmission* of legislation. But before I flesh this out I need to say a few things about the transmission of the justifications of fixed laws.

According to Sherira Gaon and to those who follow his line of thought, a radical change took place at the beginning of the Amoraic era; whereas in the Mishnaic era they only transmitted fixed laws, as evidenced by the Mishnah and baraita-collections, in the Amoraic era they transmitted the justifications of the rulings (including dialectical argumentation) together with the laws. Sherira Gaon claims that both the dictum and its justification derive from Amora himself. One can accept or reject this position, but there is no denying that Sherira Gaon makes this claim. He also opines that in the Amoraic era, in contrast to the Mishnaic age, "the minds weakened" (= a kind of "decline of the generations"), such that students could no longer derive the reasoning on their own and required the Amora himself to provide it. I disagree with this and believe that the Amoraim continued to employ Reciters (*tannaim*), and transmitted the laws alone, without the justifications. Over the course of time, even the transmission of laws deteriorated, and thus the quantity of traditions of the form "one said... the other said" increased—a term unattested in the Mishnah or baraita-collections—because they no longer knew who stated which opinion. And little by little the activity of transmitters (Reciters) stopped completely. This occurred at the end of the Amoraic era, and henceforth, in the Stammaitic period, laws and dialectical argumentation were intertwined, and these were transmitted by the Stammaim themselves together with their explanations of Tannaitic sources. When we find sections of dialectical argumentation attributed to an Amora— for example, when an Amora states "what case are we dealing with?" after an extended dialectical exchange—these sections were not transmitted through the official chain of transmission but survived by themselves.

In other words: in Amoraic times the "Reciters" transmitted fixed laws and brief explanations; sometimes they transmitted the explanations separately, and sometimes together with the laws using the forms "because (*mipnei*)," "since (*lefi*)," "for the reason that (*mishum*)," but without dialectical argumentation, as is characteristic of the Mishnah and baraita-collections. This manner of transmission of the Tannaitic era actually continued into the Amoraic era, and one can understand the nature of Amoraic transmission on the basis of that of their predecessors. However, a change occurred in the Stammaitic era such that everything was transmitted by the Stammaim themselves (including dialectical argumentation) and supplemented by their own innovative explanations. The Amoraic contributions to dialectical argumentation, on the other hand, were not transmitted by the "Reciters," but remained in the memories of students and disciples.

To return to "the end of *hora'ah*." As noted above, in the Tannaitic and Amoraic eras, fixed laws were passed down by "Reciters," the transmitters of tradition, who were distinguished for their prodigious memories, and who with great precision transmitted orally the traditions of earlier sages. Anyone who wanted to know a particular law turned to them. They were, in essence, legislative authorities (*ba'alei hora'ah*), since we can only access Tannaitic and Amoraic opinions through them. Now they received laws from the Tannaim and Amoraim without the dialectical argumentation; in that age, as I have noted, the reasoning and the argumentation was not preserved for future generations. Subsequently, in the Stammaitic era, when dialectical argumentation was preserved for future generations, it was not transmitted by the Reciters, but rather the Stammaim themselves reconstructed and transmitted the traditions. To preserve dialectical argumentation with all its detailed complexities and nuances demands more than a phenomenal memory. One must be a great scholar (*talmid hakham*) with profound knowledge and consummate analytical ability. The Stammaim were now the only sages of the academy (as there were no longer professional Reciters), and they integrated and transmitted fixed laws and dialectical argumentation together. They did not transmit fixed laws independently but wove them into the dialectical argumentation. In other words, the Stammaim created the sugya; Amoraim formulated and transmitted fixed laws, while the Stammaim formulated and produced sugyot. In the few places that fixed laws appear in the anonymous stratum of the Talmud, Rashi observes that these derive from the "scholars of the academy (*bnei hayeshivah*)."[28**]

This is the meaning of the statement that Rav Ashi and Ravina were the end of legislation, that in their days they stopped transmitting fixed laws (= legislation, *hora'ah*) to "Reciters," and the sages themselves transmitted them and integrated them with dialectical argumentation.

The fact that Rav Ashi and Ravina are the last Amoraim of whom it is stated "The Reciter repeated before Rabbi So-and-So (*tanei tanna qameih*)" provides additional evidence that the official transmission to "Reciters" ceased in their time. (For Rav Ashi, see Sanh 78a in ms. Karlsruhe [the comments of Rabbinowicz, *Diqduqei soferim*, ad loc., n. *vav*, require further examination]; for Ravina, see Bets 17a, 29b). This term was not used thereafter, since the sages no longer transmitted fixed laws to "Reciters."

These three assumptions have significant pedagogical implications, which I will illustrate here:

(1) In keeping with the first assumption, that the Amoraim and Stammaim lived in different eras, the student of Talmud must know how to distinguish between attributed Amoraic traditions and the anonymous Stammaitic material. The use of language, Hebrew or Aramaic, sometimes helps. This distinction is of paramount importance, not only for historical purposes, to become acquainted with the corpus of tradition of different eras, but also because that which is identified as Amoraic can be accepted or rejected, but not contradicted. The explanation of Amoraic dicta of the anonymous Talmud, however, is sometimes of questionable veracity; if it becomes clear that the explanation is incorrect, then one can suggest an alternative explanation. A large percentage

of the explanations proposed in the volumes of my commentary are alternative explanations.

(2) The disparity between the time of the origin of dialectical argumentation in the Amoraic era (and also in the Tannaitic era) and its reconstruction and transmission to posterity, which according to our second assumption occurred many years thereafter in the Stammaitic era, resulted in the Stammaim sometimes lacking the sources in their entirety. Consequently, they had to explain the sources in a forced manner or complete them in a way that does not fit well with the flow of the sugya. My goal in these volumes is to find alternatives to these forced explanations and problematic reconstructions; the parallel passages are usually a crucial resource for this endeavor. The better part of my commentary consists of these types of alternative explanations, and this assumption is decisive in most cases.

(3) Inasmuch as there was no general editing of the Talmud, as noted in our third assumption, no authority harmonized internal contradictions and smoothed over difficulties. Therefore, the Talmud contains contradictory content and variations in style and in thought processes, which resulted from the combination of disparate sources. Had there been a general editor, he would have removed the contradictions and imposed a more-or-less consistent style. Now the medieval commentators, despite recognizing that the Talmud contains "contradictory sugyot" (see, e.g., Tosafot, Men 58b, s.v. *ika*), generally attempt to reconcile contradictions, as if the Talmud was all of one cloth. In their view, had there been substantive contradictions, the editor or editors would have removed them or harmonized the sources. I leave contradictions and incongruities intact, because I attribute them to different sources. I trace the development of the contradictions and of changes in style and thought in order to determine their origin and point of departure. I explain them but do not reject them.

Finally, I wish to add that according to my claim that the Stammaim postdate the Amoraim, it is impossible that an Amora responds to an anonymous statement. However, we do find many passages where an Amoraic dictum appears to be predicated on anonymous material. But this is not in fact the case. The Amoraic dialectical argumentation was not passed down in the official transmission but "survived (*nisredah*)" in the memory of students (I call this "survivals [*seridim*]"). When such Amoraic traditions reached the Stammaim in fragmentary state, the Stammaim themselves supplemented them wherever they appeared to be deficient, whether in the dictum's beginning, middle, or end—whatever was necessary. When the supplement precedes the dictum and functions to provide "context" for the Amoraic statement, it appears as if the Amora refers to the anonymous stratum, though in fact he did not.

While the formulation of Stammaitic material is late, postdating the Amoraic era, the content can be early and can accurately reflect the words of the Amoraim themselves. We can assume that most Stammaitic supplements correctly express the ideas of the Amoraim if not their exact words. This means that not all Stammaitic material is late. To argue for a late dating requires additional evidence.

Scholars wonder at the fact that we have no information about the historical era between the last of the Amoraim (550 CE) and Yehudai Gaon (c. 750), a period of approximately 200 years. And because no traditions survived from this period, it seems to be completely obscure. But this is not so. In fact, many traditions of all sorts derive from this period; however, they are anonymous, appearing in the unattributed stratum of the Talmud, which is the largest stratum. The names of some of these sages, those who served as Heads of the Academies of Sura and Pumbedita, are mentioned in the *Epistle of Rav Sherira Gaon*. But their literary activities can only be discerned by analysis of sugyot, and then only in the most general terms. Namely, the sages of the first part of this era (550–700) mainly dedicated themselves to completing Amoraic dialectical argumentation with their own argumentation, with a predilection for dialectics (to proliferate the back-and-forth) and rhetoric (spurious objections), and almost without any of their own fixed rulings. When these sages finished completing the argumentation, their successors devoted themselves to the interpretation and explanation (and perhaps also editing) of the completed argumentation (this is the generation of "Saboraim," 700–750). Their successors compiled and edited all traditions known to them; this era is accordingly known as the period of the Compilers (730–770; and perhaps most transpositions derive from this era). This era continued, with some final glossing and editing, until after the Talmud was closed, and they added material without any dialectical analysis. All the details of these processes are found in the Introduction to *MM: bava batra*.

Notes

TRANSLATOR'S INTRODUCTION

1. Leib Moscovitz's *Talmudic Reasoning* (Tuebingen: Mohr Siebeck, 2002), a comprehensive analysis of Talmudic legal science, conceptualization, and abstraction, is a rare and welcome exception.
2. Ephraim Urbach, *Hazal: pirkei emunot vedei'ot* (Jerusalem: Magnes, 1969); Yaakov Sussman, *Ephraim Elimelech Urbach: A Bio-Bibliography* (Jerusalem: World Congress of Jewish Studies, 1993), 79 (Hebrew).
3. On Halevy, see O. Asher Reichel, *Isaac Halevy, 1847–1914: Spokesman and Historian of Jewish Tradition* (New York: Yeshiva University Press, 1969); Julius Kaplan, *The Redaction of the Babylonian Talmud* (New York: Bloch, 1933), 19–25.
4. *Meqorot umesorot: yoma–hagigah* (Jerusalem: Jewish Theological Seminary, 1975).
5. Shamma Friedman also developed the theory that the anonymous stratum postdates the Amoraic stratum. His initial publication appeared as "Pereq ha'ishah rabbah babavli [A Critical Study of *Yevamot X* with a Methodological Introduction]" *Mehqarim umeqorot*, ed. H. Dimitrovksi (New York: Jewish Theological Seminary, 1977), 277–441. Friedman's brilliant and prodigious contributions to the study of the Bavli in this and numerous subsequent publications deserve independent recognition and comprehensive evaluation.
6. A very modest challenge to the late dating of the anonymous layer has recently been advanced by Robert Brody, "Setam hatalmud vedivrei ha'amoraim," *Iggud—Selected Essays in Jewish Studies* 1 (2008), 213–32. Brody's arguments have been soundly refuted by Shamma Friedman, "Al titmah al hosafah shenizkar bah shem amora," *Talmudic Studies: Investigating the Sugya, Variant Readings and Aggada* (New York and Jerusalem: Jewish Theological Seminary, 2010), 57–135.
7. Kaplan, *Redaction*, 195–233. Hyman Klein published his ideas in a series of articles: "Gemara and Sebara," *JQR* 38 (1947), 67–91; "Gemara Quotations in Sebara," *JQR* 43 (1953), 341–63; "Some Methods of Sebara," *JQR* 50 (1959), 124–46; "Some General Results of the Separation of Gemara from Sebara in the Babylonian Talmud," *Journal of Semitic Studies* 3 (1958), 363–72. Avraham Weiss, *Hatalmud*

habavli behithavuto hasifrutit (Warsaw, 1937); idem, *The Development of the Talmud as a Literary Unit* (New York: Alexander Kohut Memorial Foundation, 1943) (Hebrew). On the contribution of these scholars, see Friedman, "Pereq ha'ishah rabbah babavli," 293–301.

8. Confidence in source-criticism, it should be noted, is diametrically opposed to the views of Jacob Neusner, who has also produced a type of grand synthesis of the development of rabbinic Judaism and the Bavli's place in this history. Because Neusner rejects the possibility of source-critical study of the Bavli (other than the Tannaitic traditions incorporated into the text), he attributes the entire Bavli to the final editors in c. 600 CE. There is thus an interesting parallel between Neusner and the trend in scholarship mentioned previously that resists addressing these larger issues. Both abandon serious attempts to analyze the text in order to find evidence on which to base answers due to the complexity of the material. Whereas other scholars leave the questions unanswered, Neusner arbitrarily attributes everything to the final editors in order to simplify the task.
9. See p. 85 ff.
10. See p. 4 and the annotation thereto.
11. Introduction to *MM: yoma–hagigah*, 7,10; *Midrash, Mishnah, and Gemara*, 76.
12. *Midrash, Mishnah, and Gemara*, 140 n. 1. The end of the period, it should be noted, is also constrained by Sherira Gaon's dating of the Saboraic period, as at this point Halivni believed the Stammaim preceded the Saboraim, which put an upper boundary at somewhere in the sixth century.
13. Introduction to *MM: bava metsia*, 12.
14. Though perhaps not fully "emancipated." In the Introduction to *MM: Sanhedrin* (Jerusalem: Magnes, 2012), included here as an "Addendum," Halivni returns to this tradition and offers an alternative explanation that contains a degree of historicity.
15. Introduction to *MM: bava metsia*, 12–13.
16. See, e.g., n. 14 above.
17. See p. 23 and the annotations thereto for references to some recent work on the Stammaitic contributions to aggadah.
18. See the recent collection of essays *The Talmud in Its Iranian Context*, ed. C. Bakhos and R. Shayegan (Tuebingen: Mohr-Siebeck, 2010), and studies of Yaakov Elman including "Middle Persian Culture and Babylonian Sages: Accommodation and Resistance in the Shaping of Rabbinic Legal Tradition," *Cambridge Companion to the Talmud and Rabbinic Literature*, ed. C. E. Fonrobert and M. S. Jaffee (Cambridge: Cambridge University Press, 2006), 165–97. See too Shai Secunda, "Reading the Bavli in Iran," *JQR* 100 (2010), 310–42; Geoffrey Herman, "Ahasuerus, the Former Stable-Master of Belshazzar, and the Wicked Alexander of Macedon: Two Parallels between the Babylonian Talmud and Persian Sources," *AJSR* 29 (2005), 293–97.
19. See p. 198.
20. See Martin Jaffee, *Torah in the Mouth: Writing and Oral Tradition in Palestinian Judaism, 200 BCE-400 CE* (Oxford: Oxford University Press, 2001); idem, "Oral

Tradition in the Writings of Rabbinic Oral Torah: On Theorizing Rabbinic Orality," *Oral Tradition* 14 (1999), 3–32; Yaakov Elman, "Orality and the Redaction of the Babylonian Talmud," *Oral Tradition* 14 (1999), 52–99; Talya Fishman, *Becoming the People of the Talmud* (Philadelphia: University of Pennsylvania Press, 2011).

21. *Thesaurus of Talmud Manuscripts*, ed. Y. Sussman (Jerusalem: Ben Zvi Institute, 2012).
22. E.g., Eruvin 32b, a critical passage for understanding the process of transmission of tradition in the Amoraic age, exhibits problematic textual variants. See p. 118 and the references in the annotation.
23. See p. 61.
24. Halivni does not mention these persecutions explicitly in his account (except in the Preface, n. 1). He intends the "years of persecution and sufferings" mentioned in *Epistle of Rav Sherira Gaon*, ed. Lewin, 99, "at the end of the rule of the Persians," which corresponds to 550–589, judging by the context in Sherira's narrative. Sherira states that the sages of Pumbedita came to the "outskirts of Nehardea, to the city of Peroz-Shapur" at this time, which might also imply that the Pumbedita academy was destroyed.

AUTHOR'S INTRODUCTION

1. The proportion of forced explanations is large, even if we take into account the persecutions (of the Sasanian King Yazdegard) that took place between 469 CE and c. 589 CE and in later times too, as well as plagues, and the destruction of academies (by the Persians), which all contributed to the loss of tradition—but not to the extent we find in the Talmud.**
2. *MM*, Taanit, 456 ff.
3. Ibid.

PART I

1. While one generally cannot discern that the Talmud's dialectical argumentation is incomplete except through detailed analysis, in some cases this fact is immediately clear. I will quote a few examples from those I discussed in *MM*, Rosh Hashanah, 401 ff., my first remarks on this topic. In several Talmudic passages an Amora objects ("He said to him," indicating a face-to-face conversation) to another Amora (Shab 50a, Eruv 88b, Suk 33a–b, Suk 35b, Ket 18a, Ket 73b). And yet due to the force of the objection the Talmud states, "But if it was said, it was said thus (*ela i itmar hakhi itmar*)," proposing an explanation different from that which was stated previously—an explanation according to which the Amora's objection makes no sense. We have no choice but to conclude that "in all of these cases they had received a tradition about the objection alone, but not about the response. They knew the Amora raised an objection, but did not know the response, and the anonymous Talmud later conjectured that the other Amora had responded by revising his initial position because of the objection. The change in his position

was expressed with the term 'if it was said, it was said thus.'" Similarly in RH 27b–28a, Rabbah states: "If he heard part of the [shofar] blast in a pit and part at the rim of the pit—he fulfills his obligation. If he heard part of the [shofar] blast before dawn breaks and part of the [shofar] blast after dawn breaks—he does not fulfill his obligation." Abaye objects: "What is the difference...?" After some further discussion, the Talmud concludes: "Rabbah speaks [only] of a case where he sounds [the shofar] for himself as he rises [from the pit]." However, if Rabbah deals with such a case, what was Abaye's objection? Therefore "The anonymous Talmud knew that Abaye objected to Rabbah, 'What is the difference...?' but did not know what Rabbah responded. At first the Talmud thought that Rabbah responded, 'The latter case is at night, which entails no obligation whatsoever [to hear the shofar].' But after this explanation was rejected, the anonymous Talmud concluded that, 'Rabbah speaks [only] of a case where he sounds [the shofar] for himself as he rises [from the pit],' i.e., this is what Rabbah actually responded to Abaye." In all such cases the dialectical argumentation was incomplete, and only a portion of it was known to the anonymous Talmud.

Another type of fragmentary passage features an Amora making an inference from a mishnah or baraita with the formulation "Is this not a case of [*mai lav*]..." (without explaining why that Amora chose these circumstances), and the Talmud rejects the inference with the formulation "No..." In some cases the "No..." is then followed by a continuation of the discussion, "If so (i.e., if the 'No...' is correct)." In such cases the Amora arrived at his explanation, which he expressed by the formulation "Is this not a case of...," because of the consideration raised by the "If so..." This implies that the "If so..." was part of the original Amoraic dialectical argumentation, and it was the redactor who interrupted the Amoraic statement in the middle by adding "No..." However, in cases where the continuation of the discussion lacks the "If so...," one has to ask why the Amora chose the explanation introduced by "Is this not a case of..." "The Amora certainly had a reason why he chose to explain the source that way and not as proposed in the rejection" (citation from *MM*, Bava Metsia, 263). Why was this reason not quoted in the Talmud? Because it was not known. The Talmud knew his inference, but not his reasoning. On the other hand, when the entire passage is anonymous, including the "Is this not a case of...," but the continuation lacks an "If so..." response, then we are dealing with a rhetorical question and answer, as is commonly found in the anonymous stratum (but not among the Amoraim; see below, p. 16), and the purpose of the interchange is simply to show that there are two possible ways to explain the source.

2. It should be noted that where the Stammaim quote Amoraic argumentation that appears to be complete or semi-complete, it is no guarantee that the original Amoraic sources have been preserved. As noted, dialectical argumentation in the Tannaitic and Amoraic periods was not transmitted in an official form through the chain of tradition but was absorbed by those who heard it, and then transmitted in an unsystematic and unauthorized manner, which subsequently resulted in it being overlooked and forgotten. In some cases, supplements that did not fit well were

nevertheless added to earlier argumentation. Because the argumentation was passed from teacher to teacher without supervision, it picked up some components that do not belong. The Stammaim, however, subsequently treated these components as an integral part of the argumentation and attempted to explain them, which resulted in forced interpretations. See, e.g., my comments in *MM,* Bava Batra, 253.

3. Isaak Halevy, *Dorot harishonim* (Berlin, 1923), vol. 3, chapters 3–5, and in the supplements to vol. 2, emends the text of Sherira Gaon and dates the death of the second Ravina earlier in order to extend the Saboraic period another twenty-odd years. See B. M. Lewin, *Rabanan savora'ei vetalmudam* (Jerusalem: Aviezer, 1937), 4–5.
4. In the Introduction to *MM: bava metsia,* 12, I suggested on the basis of Git 59a and the parallel at Sanh 36a, that "This student can be identified as Rav Aha b. Rava." This suggestion is elaborated upon below, p. 87, where I conclude that the Stammaim did not consider Rav Ashi to be the "end of *hora'ah*" to the same degree as Rabbi Yehudah HaNasi (vis-à-vis the Mishnah), or they would not have compared him to Huna bar Natan in these passages. Now Rav Aha b. Rava certainly did not refer to the second Rav Ashi and the second Ravina (as the historian H. Graetz interprets Sherira Gaon,) nor to (the first) Rav Ashi and the second Ravina (as explained by Halevy, *Dorot harishonim,* 3:18, disagreeing with Graetz), because Rav Aha b. Rava slightly preceded them, and this assessment of Rav Ashi and Ravina was probably articulated after their deaths and not while they yet lived. However, according to Sherira Gaon, Rav Aha b. Rava died eight years before Rav Ashi, which would entail that the adulatory statement, "from the days of Rabbi [Yehudah HaNasi] until Rav Ashi . . ." was articulated when Rav Ashi was still alive.
5. His name does not appear in the extant manuscripts. However, in *MM,* Megillah, 547, I claimed: "When one textual tradition mentions an Amora and the other textual tradition is unattributed, we prefer to say that the original text had an attribution which was later omitted than to say the reverse, that originally there was no attribution and it was added later. For who would gratuitously invent an Amoraic attribution" (unless there were some particular reason for mentioning that Amora)? Therefore, the original reading seems to be that of R. Hananel (and Sherira Gaon)—for who would invent the name Rav Revai of Rov which appears in no other source? This name was later deleted, either because they did not know of such a sage, or because they considered him to be one of the Stammaim and not an Amora. However, because Revai of Rav lived a long time—Sherira Gaon states that he "lived many years" (*Epistle of Rav Sherira Gaon,* ed. B. M. Lewin [Haifa, 1921], 70 [Hebrew])—it is possible that he was mentioned in the Talmud in his youth but was already considered as one of the Stammaim in his old age. In this case, the Stammaitic period would begin earlier than the middle of the sixth century.
6. See my comments in *MM*, Bava Batra, 278–79.
7. See Menahem Meiri, *Seder haqabbalah,* ed. S. Z. Havlin (Jerusalem and Cleveland: Ofek, 1995), 113: "This generation was midway between the Amoraim and the Saboraim. Some of these scholars were among the sages of the Talmud, while others were Saboraim, even though they lived in the same generation."

8. See "Preface," p. xii.
9. See the Introduction to *MM: yoma–hagiga*, 7, n. 11.
10. See below, p. 144.
11. See, e.g., BB 38b: "Rav expounds the reasoning of our Tanna, but he does not subscribe to it." Other examples are collected in J. N. Epstein, *Mavo lenusah hamishnah* [henceforth: *MLH*] (Jerusalem: Magnes, 1964), 176. And see Rashi, Hul 95b, s.v. *rav*: "Regarding the principle, 'The halakhah follows Rav in matters of ritual law,'—this applies to disagreements with Shmuel, but not to [Rav's] disagreements with a Tannaitic source." And see Tosafot, Hul 41a, s.v. *uvashuq* (in the Yerushalmi the phrase "a Tannaitic source disagrees" is also applied to other Amoraim), and see too my comments in *MM*, Bava Qamma, 5 and Sukkah, 176.

    It should be noted that there are occasions, such as Bets 31a and BB 79b, where the Talmud resolves a contradiction between a mishnah and an Amora by claiming that the mishnah reflects an individual opinion with which the Amora disagrees (in some cases the Amora is not even among the earlier Amoraim, such as Rav Yosef and Rava.) In these cases too we must conclude that the Amora disagrees with the mishnah, or at least with that opinion being formulated anonymously. While the editor of the mishnah formulated this Tanna's opinion anonymously to establish it as the halakhah, the Amora ruled in accord with the opponent of that Tanna, who was not mentioned in the mishnah. So too when an Amora rules according to an individual opinion in the mishnah (e.g., in Suk 19b Rav Yosef rules according to R. Eliezer's opinion against the view of the sages; in Meg 18b "Shmuel takes note of an individual opinion," an opinion recorded in the Mishnah), this opposes the Mishnaic principle, "Where an individual disagrees with a majority, the law follows the majority," and the majority opinion includes cases in which a ruling in the Mishnah is attributed to "the Sages" or a similar plurality (i.e., even if not formulated anonymously). However, these considerations do not decisively establish that the Amoraim intended to disagree with the Mishnah, since we find that the Amoraim will say of a mishnah, "These are the words of Rabbi So-and-so. But the sages say..."
12. As to Rav appearing in a baraita, see Nathan b. Yehiel of Rome (1035–1106), *Arukh hashalem*, ed. A. Kohut (New York: Pardes, 1955), 237–38, s.v. *rav*, quoting Hai Gaon.
13. See Hayyim Yosef David Azulai (d. 1806), *Shem hagedolim* (Lemberg, 1856), s.v. Rav Ahai. He states this in connection with the well-known comments of Rashba"m (cited in Tosafot, Ket 2a, s.v. *pashit* and Zev 102b, s.v. *parikh*) that Aha of Shabha Gaon was one of the Saboraim. Nevertheless, Aha of Shabha need not be identified with Rav Ahai mentioned in the Talmud.
14. However, Tosafot, BM 22b, s.v. *tiuvta*, apparently believed this term derives from Abaye and Rava.
15. See my comments in *MM*, Bava Batra, 218–220, to BB 119b.

16. See, e.g., Tosafot, Ber 37b, s.v. *leshon h"g*; Ber 43a, s.v. *ve'al.*
17. The absence of explicit testimony that passages from, e.g., Saadia Gaon (892–942) entered the Talmud indicates that Geonic material ceased being added to the Talmud during the approximately 100 years between *Halakhot gedolot* and Saadia Gaon. Nevertheless, this should not be taken as an absolute. See, e.g., Qid 4b: Shmuel b. Hofni Gaon (d. 1034) lacked the section "And according to Mar bar Rav Ashi..." (See *Otsar hageonim,* ed. B. M. Lewin [Haifa, 1928–62], ad loc., p. 4). This section was either added after that time, or just before that time such that he did not know it. It is also possible that after Saadia Gaon, glosses were added to the Talmud unintentionally and haphazardly, in contrast to the earlier practice. Cf. *MM*, Taanit, 427: "It is more likely that Sherira Gaon lacked this entire passage."
18. The characteristics that Halevy, *Dorot harishonim,* 31–32, attributes to the Saboraim who postdated Rav Ashi and Ravina apply to this period. It is also possible that "the final rabbis" (*rabanan desiuma)* lived during this period and adjudicated law. See *Otsar hageonim,* Berakhot, Responsa, p. 128 n. 11. This matter requires further study. See too David Rosenthal, "Rabbanan desiuma uvnei siumei," *Tarbiz* 49 (1979), 52–61.
19. I agree with Sherira Gaon that the Saboraim flourished after the Talmudic era, after the Talmud was almost closed, and that they added but brief explanations, mainly to the anonymous material. But I disagree with him over the dating. According to Sherira Gaon, the Talmud, including the anonymous material, concluded with the second Ravina at the end of the fifth century CE, and the Saboraic era began then, whereas I claim that the Stammaim flourished between Ravina and the Saboraim. The Saboraic era—which was limited in both length and productivity—occurred after the Stammaitic era, or, to be more precise, at the end of their era, in the eighth century.
20. Some scholars attribute to the Saboraim anonymous sugyot, especially those appearing at the beginning of a tractate or a chapter. I have found no evidence that this is the case, and no characteristics that distinguish these sugyot from other anonymous sugyot that would indicate that the sugyot originate in disparate times (despite the various attempts of several scholars). I have my doubts even regarding the sugya at the beginning of Tractate Qiddushin that Sherira Gaon attributes to the Saboraim. It is true that the section concerning whether the word *derekh* is masculine or feminine seems to be very strange (Qid 2b). But strangeness does not indicate that it derives from the Saboraim. Zecharia Fraenkel already sensed as much; see *Monatsschrift fuer Geschichte und Wissenschaft des Judentums* 11 (1861), 265. **
21. See below, p. 194, in connection to Tractate Nedarim.
22. "Retraction" does not mean that I changed my mind, but rather that over the course of time I am less influenced by the traditional view. And see later in this chapter.
23. See *MM*, Bava Batra, 242–43.

24. Only the view that the Stammaim flourished long after the Amoraim accounts for the phenomenon that the Talmud almost always cites disagreements between Ravina and Rav Aha, late Amoraim, in the style "one said x and one said y," indicating that they no longer recalled who said what. Moreover, in a few places the Talmud contains earlier and later strata that deal with such disagreements, and in these passages there is uncertainty about other aspects of the opinions of these Amoraim (see below, p. 92 ff., where I deal with some of these cases in depth). If the period of the Stammaim (and Saboraim) lasted but two or three generations and ended in 589 with R. Hanan of Ashiqiyya, as accepted by the traditional view—then these uncertainties must have cropped up a relatively short time after these Amoraim lived. But how could it be that the proximate generations did not know their opinions accurately?
25. Thus the fact that the Geonim (especially Hai Gaon) attribute statements appearing in the *She'iltot* or in *Halakhot gedolot* to the Saboraim (or employ similar terminology) is not evidence that the *She'iltot* or the *Halakhot gedolot* quote the Saboraim without mentioning them by name. They themselves are Saboraim. See, e.g., J. N. Epstein, "Seridei sheiltot," *Tarbiz* 6 (1934), 460 = *Studies in Talmudic Literature and Semitic Languages*, ed. E.Z. Malamud (Jerusalem: Magnes, 1988), 2:378 ff (Hebrew). See too S. Assaf, *Qiryat Sefer* 10 (1933–34), 345: "In their responsa, Rav Sherira and Rav Hai sometimes attribute to the Saboraim and the early Geonim statements that also appear verbatim in *Halakhot gedolot*. But they (the Saboraim and early Geonim), however, neglected to mention it (*Halakhot gedolot*)." See too my comments in *MM*, Yoma, 134, n. 3*. Accordingly, one should not reject on principle (as do I. Halevy et al.) the opinion of Rashba"m that the Talmudic expressions "Rav Ahai objected" and "Rav Ahai solved" refers to Rav Ahai (= Aha) of Shabha, author of the *She'iltot* (see Tosafot, Ket 2b, s.v. *pashit*, and Zev 102b, s.v. *parikh*.) Now the words "Rav Ashi said" that follow "Rav Ahai objected" in Nid 33a were added by Rav Ahai, and are not evidence that Rav Ashi responds to an earlier sage (in the parallel passage at Ket 2b, ms. Munich and the Geniza fragments omit "Rav Ashi said"). Rav Aha adopted the Stammaitic practice and completed Rav Ashi's statement (which was not sufficiently clear) by adding an objection before Rav Ashi's answer. And the reason his name appears in the Talmud is because he lived after the Stammaim, at the very end of that period. See too n. 13, above.
26. The title *savora* also appears in yQid 3:2, 63d with a slightly different meaning—a man adept at reasoning (*sevara*) who will admit to the truth and not stubbornly oppose it.
27. A good example of this phenomenon, appearing in numerous places throughout the Talmud, are explanations proposed by the term "they assumed (*savruha*)," where later Stammaim explain and complete (see the end of this footnote) the words of earlier Stammaim. (However, in Taan 4a, the term "they assumed" explains a statement of Rava [and Abaye], and in Zev 27a it explains a statement

of Shmuel.) In several places Rashi comments to the term "they assumed": "the rabbis of the academy," and in Pes 77a he comments "the Amoraim of the academy," and in Sanh 6a, "the Amoraic sages of the academy." Rashi does not connect these sages to Rav Ashi, as he does, e.g., in Suk 3b, s.v. *hayta*: "[This tradition derives from] all the sages of the academy, who were in Rav Ashi's study house." Apparently Rashi believed that the sage who provided the explanation introduced by "they assumed" lived after Rav Ashi, after "the end of legislation," and in Rashi's opinion, the Talmud was already completed (!). See too Rashi, Hul 49a, s.v. *ve'ain*: "The Talmud makes this ruling, and these laws were adjudicated in the later academies." However, it is not clear why the authors of these passages employed the term "they assumed," inasmuch as there are other places where they "assume" (*sover*), but do not acknowledge that it is an assumption. Moreover, what is the difference between "they assumed" and "you might have thought (*salqa da'atakh*)," e.g., Eruv 15a, Bets 2a, BM 92b, etc? Perhaps the term "you might have thought" provides a brief explanation, which those responsible for the earlier tradition did not deem important enough to mention, whereas the term "they assumed" completes that which was missing from an earlier tradition: the tradent should have provided the explanation, but failed to do so. In those cases where it appears that "they assumed" also provides but a brief explanation (e.g., BB 68a, "they assumed that *shelahim* means....,") we must say that the rejection of the "they assumed" (in BB 68a, "do you think...") also derives from the later Stammiam; and even without the "they assumed" we would have known this to be the case. This issue needs further investigation.

28. See *MM*, Bava Batra, 133–34, where I discuss the different types of "Which [ruling of] R. So-and-so?"
29. See *MM*, Eruvin, 109 n. 6.
30. This dating depends to a considerable extent on the evaluation of forced explanations in the Talmud. The primary purpose of my Talmud commentary *Meqorot umesorot* is to provide alternatives to the forced explanations prevalent throughout the Talmud. These volumes follow the order of the Talmud focusing on forced explanations and attempting to replace them with more satisfactory interpretations (*peshat*). But why are forced explanations so common in the Talmud? Because—as I explain in the Introductions—the anonymous stratum of the Talmud, which contains the forced explanations of the Amoraic dicta, postdates the Amoraim by many years and did not possess complete versions of the Amoraic sources. However, according to the medieval commentators, who refused to recognize the existence of forced explanations in the Talmud, at least not to the same degree, there was no need to think that the anonymous stratum was late.
31. The quantity of forced explanations is so great that one cannot claim that they are not the responsibility of the editor but rather derive from an "errant student" whose comments entered from the margin into the body of the text; see Part III,

p. 143 in "Forced Explanations." Explanations differ from legal rulings, as apodictic rulings can be accepted or rejected but cannot be changed, inasmuch as they constitute what a Tanna or Amora stated. However, if one disagrees with an explanation, he can replace it with a different explanation. The purpose of scrutinizing legal rulings is to determine whether the Amoraim (and the Tannaim) actually stated that which is attributed to them; the function of examining explanations is to determine if the explanation is correct or not.

32. See the Introduction to *Meqorot umesorot: seder nashim*. We find the same phenomenon among the Amoraim—and sometimes the Talmud itself notes this fact—though not to the same degree as attested among Stammaim.
33. See p. 51.
34. I first commented on this matter in *MM*, Yevamot, 30, and periodically added further observations.
35. See *MM*, Bava Batra, 226–27.
36. See *MM*: *yoma–hagiga*, Introduction, 9: "How would it occur to anyone... and to object on that basis...; it is more likely that the assumption and the answer... are rhetorical and do not represent real views."
37. One should not take the "to him" as unambiguous evidence that the interchange was face-to-face. Scribes did not always distinguish between "to it" and "to him," and they confused the two.
38. This term ("objected [*matqif*] to him") is not found in the Yerushalmi, nor among the first generations of Amoraim. See *MM*, Pesahim, 469, n. 1.
39. See the index to *MM*, *eruvim-pesahim*, s.v. "*matqif*" (4).
40. Zecharia Fraenkel noted this fact, *Mavo hayerushalmi* (Breslau: Schletter, 1870), 35a. See too *MM*, Pesahim, 454–55, and the indices to the other volumes of *MM*, s.v. "*mena amina*."
41. See *MM*, Rosh Hashanah, 407 n. 5, on the difference between "whence shall I prove it (*mena amina lah*)?" and "whence do you know it (*mena teimra*)?"
42. In *MM*, Sukkah, 246 n. *5, I stated: "Every 'whence shall I prove it' has the presumption of Amoraic provenance until proved otherwise."
43. See below, p. 59.
44. See the comments of Tosafot, ad loc.: "Rashi explains that the Talmud was unable to provide explicit evidence that the ruling accords with R. Yehudah. But the fact that it (the anonymous Talmud) gave a forced interpretation with the objection 'But those two honeycombs are *muqtsot* [D]'—and did not rather state that the ruling [A] accords with R. Shimon—implies that the Talmud held that the ruling accords with R. Yehudah."
45. See n. 1.
46. See the section titled "Compilers" (*me'asef*) in Part IV, and p. 157, on the terms "there is a teaching that accords with him (*tanya kavateih*)," and "we also taught thus (*tanya namei hakhi*)."
47. See too, p. 18: "The Stammaim typically place the strongest objection last."

48. Clearly the opinions expressed in the "anonymous *gemara*" do not have the status of "consensual agreement" and have no more authority than individual opinions (unlike the Mishnah, where the law follows the anonymous mishnah). The anonymous stratum rather consists of late argumentation of post-Amoraic provenance. It is possible that anonymous opinions in fact are less authoritative (see the Introduction to *MM: shabbat,* 12 n. 24 on Maimonides's treatment of the anonymous Talmud), and there was no need for the Stammaim to identify their contribution, as the anonymous formulation itself attested to its provenance.
49. See the indices to the volumes of *MM*, s.v. *retorikah.*
50. See *MM*, Shabbat, 301 n. 1, and Bava Batra, 118–19, and elsewhere.
51. One must assume that the Stammaim relied a great deal on inferences to reconstruct the dialectical argumentation.
52. In *MM,* Eruvin, 76, I connected this difference—whether to ask "what [difference does it make] if stated on the basis of an inference?" or not—to that which Rav Yosef said to Rav Menasheh b. Shagubli: "May the Merciful One forgive Rav Menasheh b. Shagubli: I told it to him with respect to the mishnah, but he said it about the baraita (Eruv 29a)." I suggested that they disagreed whether one is permitted to transfer a teaching from one source to another in cases where there is no legal impact. The medieval commentators also debate this issue. Rashb"a states: "If Rav said it explicitly about the mishnah and not the baraita, how could Rav Menasheh b. Shagubli say that Rav said 'and so too for the *eruv*?,' about the baraita, when Rav did not say this? Certainly he [Menasheh] must atone [for this error]." Ritb"a, however, states: "It seems to me that it was stated either on the mishnah or the baraita . . . and even if he heard Rav explicitly state it about the mishnah, one need not worry if it is applied to a baraita."
53. See *MM*, Bava Qamma, 162 n. 1.
54. See *MM*, Pesahim, 457–58.
55. See *MM*, Bava Qamma, 130 n. 5.
56. *MM*, Eruvin, 52.
57. Ibid.
58. Ibid., 151.
59. Ibid., 185.
60. Ibid., 194 n. 2.
61. *MM*, Pesahim, 408.
62. Tosafot, Meg 19b, s.v. *dilma.* Let me point out, in passing, that what is so forced (*dohaq*) about the Talmud's emendation in this passage and in the parallel at Ber 15b is not the presence of the phrase "for R. Yehudah rules a minor fit" after the mishnah has already stated "these are the words of R. Yehudah." It is not uncommon that a mishnah or a baraita states "these are the words of R. So-and-so, for R. So-and-so says." Rather what is forced is the use of "perhaps it [the mishnah] has an omission and he teaches thus. When does this apply? . . ."

Near the end of Part II, in the section titled "The Editor of the Mishnah and his role in Editing," I analyze the expression "for R. So-and-so would say…" and distinguish three types. According to our taxonomy, the "For R. Yehudah says…" in Ber 15b and Meg 19b is of the third type, which neither supplies a reason nor provides a source, but rather preserves the original language: R. Yehudah articulated both statements, and the editor of the Mishnah quoted them as he found them. But all this is forced, as noted, since it is unnecessary; the straightforward reading of the mishnah is clear.

63. Tosafot, Shab 102a, s.v. *rav*. See too Qid 44b: "It has an omission and he teaches thus" and Tosafot, BM 113a, s.v. *vehasorei*. Accordingly, I must slightly correct my comments in *MM*, Shabbat, 284 n. 2.
64. I collected some of them in *MM*, Ketubot, 136 n. 4.
65. See below, p. 196.
66. Accordingly, I must slightly revise my claims in the Introduction to *MM*: *shabbat*, 17, and accept more readily Bacher's claim that "With the death of Rav Ashi the fountain of aggadah in Babylonia ceased" (Willhelm Bacher, *Die Agada der babylonischen Amoräer* [reprint; Hildesheim: Georg Olms, 1967], 147).
67. Accordingly, I amend what I stated in the Introduction to *MM*: *yoma-hagiga*, 17.
68. In Shab 4b–5a Rav Yosef states, "Who is [the authority who stated] this [tradition]? It is Rabbi," and the Stam asks, "Which Rabbi?," but fails to find an answer to this question, raising objections to each possible response. Other explanations that disagree with Rav Yosef are noted: an explanation attributed to R. Zeira, "Who is this? Others"; an explanation attributed to R. Abba, "For example, if he caught it in a basket"; and an explanation ascribed to Rava, "A man's hand is considered for him as an area four cubits by four cubits." It is not clear whether R. Zeira (the second) and R. Abba (the second or third) knew Rav Yosef's answer, and only because of the objections articulated here by the Stammaim made their alternative explanations, i.e., these Amoraim already knew of those objections; or whether they did not know the objections (and we are dealing with the first R. Zeira and R. Abba), and the objections derive from the Stammaim. (Rava, a leading student of Rav Yosef, presumably knew the objections.) In either case, the identification of the tradition of Rabbi was not included in the official transmission along with Rav Yosef's words, "Who is [the authority who stated] this [tradition]? It is Rabbi," and later sages therefore did not know which tradition of Rabbi's that Rav Yosef referred to. This too demonstrates that during Amoraic times dialectical argumentation was not included in the official transmission.
69. See *MM*, Pesahim, 348 n. 2, referring to Naz 32a: "Rava said to Rav Nahman: 'As for you, who claim…' Rav Shimi bar Ashi said…" Rav Nahman certainly had a response to Rava's question from the mishnah. Why then did he not respond to Rava directly? One cannot say that Rav Shimi bar Ashi was present when Rava asked Rav Nahman, as "There is no other passage in which Rav Shimi bar Ashi

appears in the presence of Rav Nahman. Rather, Rav Nahman's answer was not preserved by the Talmud." See too Ker 23a: "Rava said to Rav Nahman: 'Did R. Shimon really say...' Rav Sheshet b. Rav Idi said... ." Rav Nahman apparently responded to Rava, but the Talmud did not know his response, and therefore quoted a different response attributed to Rav Shehet b. Rav Idi, who postdated Rav Nahman. However, in Git 28b: "Rav Ada bar Matneh said to Rava...Rav Yehudah of Disqarta said...Rav Mesharshia objected...Rather Rava said..." Here we have to say that Rav Ada bar Matneh, Rav Yehudah of Disqarta, and Rav Mesharshia were present when Rava provided the final response. Rav Ada bar Matneh objected to Rava, Rav Yehudah of Disqarta answered the objection, and Rav Mesharhiah then objected to the answer of Rav Yehudah of Disqarta. Thus Rav Ada bar Matneh's objection remained in force, requiring Rava to modify his response. All this apparently took place in Rava's presence. (This same objection attributed to Rav Mesharshia in Suk 26a was transferred there from this passage in Git 28b. R. Yohanan did not make his statement in Suk 26a ["Rather, Rabbah b. bar Hannah said R. Yohanan said..."] on account of Rav Mesharshia's objection, as Rav Mesharshia lived long after him.)

In some cases, however, the Stammaim respond to an objection that an Amora made directly to his colleague. This helps us understand passages which first have "he said to him (an objection)..." and then, following this objection, the Talmud claims "but if it was said, it was said thus (*ela i itmar hakhi itmar*)," revising the dictum against which the objection was directed (*MM*, Rosh Hashana, 402). After the revision of the dictum ("but if it was said, it was said thus...,") the direct objection made in the Amora's presence is no longer intelligible. Consequently I suggested: "In all these places there was a tradition as to the objection but no tradition as to the response. It was known that an objection was made against the Amora's dictum, but his response to that objection was not known. The Stammaim later assumed that the Amora responded that he had decided to change his dictum because of the objection and they expressed the revised dictum with the term 'but if it was said, it was said thus.'" In other passages the Stammaim suggest that the Amora made another response, but did not revise his dictum. For additional examples, see *MM*, Betsah, 355 n. 20.

70. And see Sanh 28b: "Rav Yehudah said, Shmuel said, the law follows R. Yose." Rav Yosef quotes this dictum for a leniency, that the law follows R. Yose permitting one's brother-in-law to testify. Abaye said to him: "How do we know that [Shmuel refers to] the [opinion of] R. Yose mentioned in the mishnah, who permits the brother-in-law, perhaps [he means] R. Yose of the baraita, who disqualifies the brother-in-law?" Clearly the original dictum of Rav Yehudah in the name of Shmuel only transmitted, "the law follows R. Yose"—and no more. It did not include whether he permits or disqualifies a brother-in-law. But it is also unlikely that Rav Yosef originally heard only "the law follows R. Yose." Rather, it is reasonable to assume that Shmuel originally explained what he meant, but that his

dictum was attached to the end of the dialectical argumentation, after they had adduced several traditions attributed to R. Yose. As a result they became uncertain about the words, "The law follows R. Yose." Because the dictum followed dialectical analysis of R. Yose's rulings in both the mishnah and the baraita (such baraitot were taught "in conjunction" with the mishnah [see my comments in *MM*, Pesahim, 445, and see Sanh 32b: "and according to your reason the mishnah poses a difficulty..."]), they were not sure which one was meant, R. Yose in the mishnah or R. Yose in the baraita, and Rav Yosef and Abaye disagreed on this issue. The key point is that even Rav Yosef, who was a leading student of Rav Yehudah, no longer knew the referent of Rav Yehudah's tradition citing Shmuel. However, the continuation of the passage, "as Shmuel said, 'For example, Pinhas and I...,'" does not derive from Rav Yosef and Abaye but from the Stammaim, and it is not the continuation of the statement that Rav Yehudah quotes in Shmuel's name. This must be the case as here it states only "Shmuel said" and not "Rav Yehudah said Shmuel said"; also the language "the law follows R. Yose" does not correspond to "For example, Pinhas and I." This is a truncated dictum, which apparently was part of the dialectical argumentation and was subsequently forgotten—therefore, we do not know what it means.

71. Any qualms about disagreeing with the view accepted since the time of Sherira Gaon—and perhaps even prior to his time (the author of *Seder tannaim ve'amoraim* antedated Sherira Gaon), the widespread view held by all students—should be alleviated by a quick review of the issue of whether the Bavli knew the Yerushalmi. Sherira Gaon in a responsum (*Sefer hamakhri'a*, #42), and his son Rav Hai (*Teshuvot hageonim*. ed. S. Assaf [Jerusalem, Darom, 1929], p. 125) and several other medieval commentators believed that the Bavli knew the Yerushalmi. This claim is explicitly found in Alfasi, at the end of Tractate Eruvin: "We rely on our Talmud (= the Bavli), since it is later, and they were more proficient in their knowledge of the Talmud of the Westerners (= the Yerushalmi) than we are." However, the great scholars of the Yerushalmi of the previous generation concluded with certainty that the Bavli did not know the Yerushalmi. See the commentary on the Yerushalmi, *Ahavat tsion veyerushalayim*, by Baer Ratner (12 vols. reprint; Jerusalem, 1967), Sukkah, 79: "With apologies to the honor of the sages mentioned above, this is not the case. He who studies the Bavli and Yerushalmi realizes from each and every page that the Bavli did not know the Yerushalmi and the Yerushalmi did not know the Bavli. And this is as clear as day." Similarly, Epstein states in his "Introduction to the Talmud Yerushalmi" (included in *Mevo'ot lesifrut ha'amoraim*, 291): "Anyone who compares the Bavli with the Yerushalmi—even a superficial comparison—immediately sees that the Bavli did not know the Yerushalmi and the Yerushalmi did not know the Bavli." So too Zeev Wolf Rabinowitz, in his commentary to the Yerushalmi, concluded: "It is proven that the Bavli did not know the Yerushalmi" (*Sha'arei torat erets yisra'el* [Jerusalem, 1940], 519).** Granted their evidence

against the accepted view of the Bavli's knowledge of the Yerushalmi is stronger than my evidence concerning the dating of the anonymous portions of the Talmud. And granted that it is possible to say that Sherira Gaon, who lived many years after the redaction of the Talmud (according to his view), understandably no longer knew whether the Bavli had access to the Yerushalmi. However, Sherira lived only about 200 years after the Stammaim, according to my view, so how is it that he knew nothing about them? Nevertheless, the traditional view appears to be an idealization of the Bavli, namely, that the Bavli is more authoritative because it had access to, and rejected, the Yerushalmi (a type of application of the principle "the law follows the later authorities"**). Part of the appeal of this view is the association of the Bavli's authority with Rav Ashi, who served as the Head of the Academy for sixty years** and instructed many disciples, and can be seen as the editor and compiler of the Talmud, since his persona symbolizes authority far more than the anonymous sages, the late Stammaim.

Perhaps I should mention in this context the question of whether or not the Mishnah was written in the time of Rabbi Yehudah HaNasi (and the Bavli in the time of Rav Ashi). The *Epistle of Rav Sherira Gaon*, "Spanish" version, which is the superior text according to many scholars, states several times that the Mishnah was written in the time of Rabbi Yehudah HaNasi. (See B. M. Lewin's Introduction, 24b ff.) However, contemporary theory holds that the Mishnah and Talmud were not written down at the time of their completion; see Saul Lieberman, *Hellenism in Jewish Palestine* (New York: Jewish Theological Seminary, 1950), 87: "Since in the entire Talmudic Literature we do not find that a book of the *Mishna* was ever consulted in cases of controversies or doubt concerning a particular reading we may safely conclude that the compilation was *not published in* writing, that a written *exdosis* of the *Mishnah* did not exist." Epstein, on the other hand, who determined that the superior version of Sherira Gaon's Epistle was the "French" version (*Mevo'ot lesifrut ha'amoraim*, 610 ff.), which does not mention that the Mishnah was written down, claimed that the Mishnah was indeed written (*MLH*, 270). Either way, Sherira Gaon's view was not accepted.**

72. According to *Sefer haqabbalah* of Abraham ibn Daud, the Saboraic age lasted until 689 CE (see the end of Chapter 5). Similarly, Halevy, *Dorot harishonim*, 3:12–32, postulates a lengthy period of activity. But this does not follow from the *Epistle of Rav Sherira Gaon*, 97, which states: "Most of the Saboraim died within a few years."
73. In rare cases anonymous material appears in the form of apodictic law, e.g., "If there were nine heaps of matzah..." (Pes 9b), and "If it (the sukkah) was taller than twenty cubits..." (Suk 3b). Note that Rashi comments in Pesahim, "These are legal rulings," and in Sukkah, "These are legal rulings known to all the scholars in the academy that were in the school of Rav Ashi, who edited the

Talmud"; (and see Rashi, Suk 4a, s.v. *savar abaye*, which suggests Abaye knew of that ruling). Rashi sensed that unattributed legal rulings are unusual. See too BB 69b: "If he says to him, 'Land and date trees. . . ,'" to which Rashba"m comments, "The Talmud exposits."

74. Halevy and his followers are mistaken to claim that Rabbah Tosfa'a was so called because "He added (*mosif*) to the Talmud and completed it," arguing that "'Tosfa'a' is neither the name of a city nor a family name" (*Dorot harishonim*, 3:10).** "Tosfaya" is a city northeast of the Tigris. See Israel Lewy, *Qeta'im mimishnat abba shaul* (Berlin, 1876), 94, and the commentary to Tractate Moed Qatan of R. Shimon b. Hayatom.
75. See p. 44.
76. See p. 151.
77. See *MM*, Bava Batra, 123–24.
78. I wish to correct that which I wrote in the Introduction to *MM*: *yoma–hagiga*, 5: The Talmud assumes that the baraita cannot be consistent with R. Yehudah because it holds that one may not take the priestly tithe from [fresh] figs for pressed figs in a place where it is not customary to press figs, even though fresh figs are more valuable, and R. Yehudah goes according to what is more valuable. I erred in writing that "it easily can be said" that the baraita is consistent with R. Yehudah.
79. [A long note is omitted here, in which Halivni systematically quotes and rejects all the passages adduced to prove the existence of "early anonymous passages" by Halevy, *Dorot harishonim*, vol. 2, chapter 86, and H. Albeck, *Mavo latalmudim* (Tel Aviv: Dvir, 1969), chapter 10, 576 ff.—JR.]
80. Abraham ibn Daud, *Sefer haqabbalah*, Chapter 5, claims that the Saboraic period concluded at the end of the seventh century. According to this view, we have seventh century material within the Talmud and also extra-Talmudic material from that time, namely, Saboraic responsa and explanations quoted by the Geonim.
81. It is possible that the Talmud, due to its immense scope, nurtured and enlightened the subsequent generations. They depended upon the Talmud and left their contributions within it—and we find the same phenomenon following the production of other major compositions. Nevertheless, we should find at least fragments of their literary works. Nahmanides and Ritb"a, in their commentaries to the beginning of Qiddushin, claim that the first folios of the tractate are from Huna Gaon, who lived in the middle of the seventh century. Thus this period was not completely forgotten.
82. Avraham Weiss already sensed this (I refer to his book *The Literary Activities of the Saboraim* [Jerusalem: Hebrew University, 1953 [Hebrew]); however, he attributes the teachings of the Saboraim to this period. I have emphasized that one must be skeptical about the historical accuracy of any claim that cannot be substantiated on the basis of the Talmud itself, that is, by analysis predicated on the

internal evidence of the Talmud, but rather that derives from inference or conjecture originating from dated theories that were once widespread but never confirmed (and for this reason I base my claims on the anonymous material than pervades the Talmud). The Saboraim are not mentioned in the Talmud at all, and though their existence should not be doubted, since their names are preserved among the Geonim and later authorities, their period of activity should be limited. See p. 8.

83. See *MM*, Qiddushin, 628 n. 6.
84. See *Otsar hageonim*, Qiddushin, p. 2.
85. See too Git 83b.
86. Perhaps the authors of the passage were reluctant to correlate the disagreement between Abaye and Rava with a Tannaitic dispute.
87. See *MM*, Shabbat, 65–66, and *MM*, Bava Batra, 155–56.
88. Z. H. Hayyot (Chajes), in his glosses to RH 16a, observes: "Although our Sages of Blessed Memory regularly investigate the reasons for the commandments"—(here he collects some examples; he was anticipated by Solomon b. Tsemah Duran [Tashba"ts], vol. 3, #135–36, as referenced by Yosef b. Yehudah Engil in his glosses to RH 16a)—"the text should have stated, '*mipnei mah*' (for what [reason]) do we sound the Shofar. The word '*lamah*' (literally, 'why') is not appropriate for instances of investigating the reasons for commandments," and this is why the Talmud expresses astonishment at his query. However, I noted in *MM*, Rosh Hashanah, 380 n. 6, that in *Halakhot pesuqot* of Yehudai Gaon (the attribution to Hai Gaon in that note is an error) and also in *Halakhot gedolot*, Laws of Rosh HaShana, the reading is indeed "*mipnei mah*" (for what [reason]), hence Hayyot's explanation is not persuasive.
89. "Because you have to return her pledge every evening, and from the fact that you are always coming and going, in the morning to take the pledge and in the evening to return it, you bring her into disrepute among her neighbors" (Rashi to Qid 68b, s.v. *darish*).
90. Contradicting the Talmud. This point is addressed by Shmuel Ashkenazi in *Responsa Meqom Shmuel*, #32 (noted by Z. H. Hayyot [Chajes] in his glosses to BM 115a). At first, "It occurred to me that Maimonides here conforms to his general approach...of always ruling in accord with the anonymous Mishnah and not deferring to the dialectical argumentation of the Talmud. Talmudic argumentation at times attempts to interpret the Mishnah in a forced manner to cohere with a particular teaching. However, we do not rely on such forced answers for legal decisions. This is because this kind of answer is only to uphold the ideas of the sage who objected, but we do not rely on such arguments when seeking the true understanding. In *Mishneh Torah*, Laws of Neighbors, Chapter 2, Maimonides himself explained this ruling, as he wrote [elsewhere]...to the sages of Lunel, that the teaching in the Talmud [concerning R. Yehudah's understanding of the verse] is simply a hypothetical answer but does not accord with

the law. It functions only to respond to an objection, and is actually the opposite of the truth.... And we regularly find this approach among the writings of Maimonides and the compositions of the other Geonim—that we do not base legal rulings on forced answers. (References to forced interpretations among the Geonim and medieval jurists were collected by Shraga Abramson, *Peirush rabbenu hananel latalmud [R. Hananel's Commentary to the Talmud]* (Jerusalem: Weiss, 1995), 183 ff., although he neglected some examples, e.g., Rashi to Hul 95b: "Rav Huna holds like his teacher Rav, who forbade [meat] in a case when it disappeared from sight [*ha'alamah*], but we do not rule according to him, but rather in accord with the mishnah. Although they interpret.... these are forced interpretations." Rashi does not rule in accord with Rav, even though BM 24b states that the law follows Rav's opinion, because Rav's interpretation can only be reconciled with the mishnah by means of a forced explanation.) R. Shmuel Ashkenazi does not accept this understanding of Maimonides ("It is very forced to say this,") and he explains Maimonides according to the view of Tosafot, Sot 14b, s.v. *kedi*, that R. Yehudah will "interpret the reason of a verse" provided that it does not contradict the simple explanation of Scripture. The simple explanation of this commandment is that it applies to both wealthy and poor widows, so R. Yehudah also provides a reason for the commandment. However, this does not follow from the Talmud (see Yom 42b, Sot 8a, Sanh 16b). As to the difficulty that without Ashkenazi's explanation then Maimonides's interpretation contradicts the Talmud—scholars have already noted other places where Maimonides, in his *Commentary to the Mishnah*, deviates from the Talmud's explanation. See *MM*, Eruvin, 50 n. 8 and Pesahim, 539 n. 13, and elsewhere. I have expatiated on this point because it is germane to the methodology of my Talmudic commentary.

91. Similarly, the parallel sugyot of Git 48b and BQ 6b originate in BQ 6b because the content fits better there, since "the best of his land" appears in Scripture in the context of damages. Moreover, this section appears in Git 48b between Abaye's and Rava's explanations of the mishnah. Had the sugya originated in Git 48b, it would have been organized more appropriately, with the explanations of the mishnah stated first, and then the incorporation of this section with a term like "*gufa* ([Let us return to] the full text [quoted in part above"]).
92. Despite the claims of Epstein, *MLH*, 37 n. 2.
93. Cf. Albeck, *Mavo latalmudim*, 592 n. 15.
94. See n. 71.
95. See Epstein, *Mevo'ot lesifrut ha'amoraim*, 274.
96. See *MM*, Yoma, 134 n. 3*; Sukkah, 209 n. 2*; Bava Batra, 73–74.
97. See too Bets 21a: "That is a difficulty. And if you prefer I will say..." I thank my son Ephraim Betsalel Halivni for this reference.
98. I discussed the best methods of distinguishing between them in the Introduction to *MM: bava qamma*.

99. See p. 143, on the topic of forced explanations.
100. On the Saboraim, see p. 8 and cf. n. 82.
101. See Solomon Luria, *Hokhmat shlomoh*, to the beginning of Bava Metsia.
102. See the indices to the volumes of *MM*, s.v. "*amar abaye*" (Abaye said).
103. The Florence manuscript also attributes the tradition to Rav in Bekh 52b. See *Melekhet shlomoh* to mBekh 8:10: "However, here the anonymous Talmud (*setama detalmuda*) states it . . . , and even according to the text which includes the emendations of Betsalel Ashkenzai." See too Albeck, *Mavo latalmudim*, 580.
104. See Pes 89b: "He objected with all these objections (that appear previously in the anonymous stratum) and he responded to him as we responded (the anonymous responses above)." One need not say that Rav Huna b. Rav Yehoshua repeated the same objections found in the anonymous stratum, and hence the anonymous stratum antedates him. For if so, why did he bother to raise these objections after the responses were already known? But in this case even the phrase "as we responded" is from the Stammaim, and although the content is similar, the context differs. The Stammaim respond to the question "It was asked of him," while Rav Huna b. Rav Yehoshua relates to the occasion when he "shared bread" with Rav Pappa. To improve the order of traditions the Stammaim first brought the section with the question "It was asked of him . . . " and then quoted the account of Rav Huna b. Rav Yehoshua and Rav Pappa in abbreviated form (i.e., without detailing all the objections and responses), because the section with "It was asked of him . . . " fits the mishnah more closely than does the account of the sages. In addition, some textual variants lack "He objected with all these objections and he responded as we responded" and read, "He objected 'One who appoints . . . ' (= one of the objections mentioned above). He said to him, 'Characters differ' (= the response above)." (See *Diqduqei soferim*, ad loc. n. *yod*; however, according to Tosafot, s.v. *de'ot*, Rav Pappa would not have answered "Characters differ" but rather "This case differs, as one cannot say 'Behold, you accepted me [into your fellowship],'" and Rav Huna b. Rav Yehoshua would never have objected on the basis of the mishnah. To this one could argue that he preferred to say "Characters differ," because the mishnah explicitly states "One who appoints another to his portion," whereas "Behold, you accepted me" is the language found in the Talmud's query "It was asked of him.") However, in Bets 18a one cannot say that the objections are from the Stammaim; rather, Abaye raised all the objections twice, once to Rabbah and once to Rav Yosef (he wanted to see how Rav Yosef would respond after he heard the responses from Rabbah). The Stammaim, conforming to their standard organization of traditions, put Rabbah before Rav Yosef, detailing the objections to Rabbah and his responses, and referring to them in abbreviated form with Rav Yosef. I discussed other cases of "as we taught" (or "as we rejected") in *MM*, Yoma, 108 n. 2. See too *MM*, Rosh HaShanah, 358 n. 4 and 363 n. 1.

105. See my comments above, p. 45, about Suk 50b–51a and Arakh 11a. In Yev 61a and Sanh 19a the dictum "they prohibited the first intercourse on account of the second intercourse" is anonymous, whereas in Yevamot 20b it is attributed to Rava. But in this case the lack of attribution was not due to the Stammaim quoting the dictum in an abbreviated form, but rather because Rava retracted his opinion in Yev 20b, stating "What I said is not a [valid] statement" [see p. 124 for translation and detailed analysis of these passages.] In Yev 61a the Talmud does not accept Rava's retraction and remains with the refutation of his opinion (also found in Yev 20b). This implies, incidentally, that these parallel passages, Yev 61a and Sanh 19a, did not read "Rav Ashi" (i.e., "Rava—and some say Rav Ashi—said") in the retraction of the opinion in Yev 20b. Indeed, in its other instantiations, the phrase "What I said is not a [valid] statement," is said by the same sage who provides the alternative, but here Rav Ashi is not mentioned earlier in the passage. (While the medieval commentaries suggest that the Talmud's objection to the retraction of the opinion in favor of an alternative, namely, "the refutation," follows the reading of "Rav Ashi" in the retraction, this suggestion cannot be accepted without textual evidence [see p. 126, sections O, P, Q].) Thus Yev 61a and Sanh 19a accepted Rava's dictum but not his retraction.

106. It is interesting that even when the Talmud subsequently states "You can conclude... *(tistayem)*," and identifies who said which opinion, it retains the original dispute form "one said...and one said..." Similarly, even after stating: "R. Yitshaq b. Nahmani and someone who was with him disagreed about it. And who was it? R. Shimon b. Pazzi. And some say R. Shimon b. Pazzi and someone who was with him [disagreed]. And who was it? R. Yitshaq b. Nahmani," the Talmud nevertheless retains the "and someone who was with him," as if the sage's identity is in doubt (Meg 23a, Sanh 10b). Here too the original form was not revised.

107. Even the term "the two of them said," is not conclusive evidence that both sages together stated the dictum. See, e.g., Men 5a: "R. Yohanan and Resh Laqish, the two of them said: 'Even when the Temple stood...' And that [dictum] of Resh Laqish was not stated explicitly but inferred"; and it is likely that the claim "And that [dictum] of Resh Laqish..." is Amoraic. There are also instances of the term "the two of them said" that date to a time very close to that of the disputing Amoraim. Rav Yehudah was the leading student of Rav and Shmuel, so much so that the Talmud sometimes says of his dicta that "It is from Rav" or "It is from Shmuel" (see Yev 18a–b, and Tosafot, s.v. *d'i*; and elsewhere too). Yet Rav Yehudah combines the opinions of Rav and Shmuel (or he encountered them already having been combined) and quotes them with the term "the two of them said" (Eruv 40b). The same is found of the term "and so said R. So-and-so." And perhaps this is the Talmud's meaning when it objects "If that is the case, let him state it too," and Rashi explains, "Let him

state his dictum among those Amoraim," meaning, why were the dicta of the Amoraim not combined together (Men 30b)?** However, it is doubtful whether the Talmud is consistent in this respect, since in several other passages it does not raise this objection. See Halevy, *Dorot harishonim*, vol. 2, chap. 86, p. 557.

108. So too we find in Nid 53b: "Resh Laqish said: In a case where she checked... and R. Yohanan said: 'Even *(af)*'..." However, in BM 22b the Talmud begins with Rabba's dictum, "And even..." before quoting the comment of his student Rava, "this was only stated..." See too n. 124, and *MM*, Bava Metsia, 187 n. 1.

109. Epstein deals with this issue at length in *MLH*, 1007–1032.

110. The Talmud at Sanh 24b resolves this query on the basis of Rava's dictum, as Rava too holds that the dispute between R. Meir and the Sages was after the verdict had been issued. If so, then Rava too disagrees with the combiner, or else Rava antedated him. However, the Talmud's resolution of the query on the basis of Rava's view is not necessary, for it is possible to say that Rava was expressing his own view and not that of R. Yohanan. Cf. Rashi and Tosafot, ad loc., and the counterarguments of Meir b. Todros Abulafia, in *Yad rama"h*.

111. In Shab 31b Ulla is mentioned before R. Yohanan. This may be because in the places where the Talmud discusses the disagreement between R. Yehudah and R. Shimon over the issue of "labor that is not needed for its own sake" (see the marginal references in Shab 73b), R. Yehudah is mentioned before R. Shimon. And because Ulla explains the mishnah in accord with R. Yehudah and R. Yohanan in accord with R. Shimon, Ulla is mentioned before R. Yohanan. Sanh 20b is similar: Shmuel is mentioned before Rav because in the baraita (introduced by the term "[the dispute is] similar to a Tannaitic dispute"). R. Yose, who holds like Shmuel, is mentioned before R. Yehudah, who holds like Rav.

112. See *MM*, Bava Qamma, 457.

113. I first commented on this phenomenon in *MM*, Yevamot, 30. However, in some cases the Saboraim were unable accurately to reconstruct the question that troubled the Amora. See, e.g., the Talmud's attempts to reconstruct the motivation for R. Yohanan to say "the opinions are reversed (*muhlefet hashita*)" in Bets 9b.

114. For example, "Rav Matneh said, and some say Rav Ahadboy bar Matneh said in the name of Rav Matneh"—Shab 60a. See too Ber 68b: "Rav Nahman said: Ulla became confirmed in his error [by accepting the tradition] of R. Binyamin," and Rashi's comment: "Ulla, who quoted R. Yohanan above [that the blessing for boiled vegetables] is 'by whose word [all things exist],' learned and adopted this errant tradition from R. Binyamin such that it became entrenched in his mind to the point that he stated it in the house of study in the name of R. Yohanan." In other words, Ulla, who stated "in the name of R. Yohanan that one blesses 'by whose word [all things exist]' on cooked vegetables," did not mention that he heard of R. Yohanan's dictum from R. Binyamin b. Yefet. He

simply stated the dictum in the "name of R. Yohanan." Had Ulla stated that he heard the dictum from R. Binyamin b. Yefet, he would have rendered it less reliable. Why is a dictum attributed to R. Binymain b. Yefet in the name of R. Yohanan less reliable? It is possible that any dictum in the form "R. So-and-so said in the name of R. So-and-so" is less reliable, and it is also possible, as the Talmud notes, "R. Binyamin b. Yefet was not punctilious (in learning traditions of R. Yohanan)." Now if the formula "in the name of R. Yohanan (*mishmeih d'rabbi Yohanan*)" means that he himself did not hear from R. Yohanan directly, but rather from another sage who heard it from R. Yohanan, then we should rather say that the second possibility is correct: Rav Nahman meant that R. Binyman b. Yefet was not punctilious in learning R. Yohanan's traditions.

115. Ms. Munich and other mss. read "Rabbah bar Zevada said in the name of Rav" in Sanh 22b too, and not only in Taan 17a.

116. That is, why did they not mention the Stammaim explicitly, for there are hints? I noted in the Introduction to *MM: bava metsia*, 7 (and see above, p. 9) that Sherira Gaon's description of the Saboraim better fits the Stammaim. I conjectured that originally his description was indeed about the Stammaim, but it was subsequently transferred to the Saboraim, after "Rav Ashi and Ravina—the end of *hora'ah*" was interpreted in terms of the editing of the Talmud, including the anonymous stratum. And perhaps (as also suggested above, p. 9) they transferred not only the description but also the name "Saboraim"; originally this name was used of the Stammaim, but after they attributed the anonymous stratum to Rav Ashi as a function of his role as editor, they switched the name to the Saboraim.

117. See p. 133 ff., concerning the transmitters (the "Reciters" [*tannaim*]). They too were almost forgotten, and are not mentioned as a group but only as individuals. Perhaps this is because the chroniclers wanted the authority of the Talmud to depend on Ravina and Rav Ashi completely, and not on anonymous individuals whose names are not known and whose individual opinions were not transmitted.

118. Joseph ibn Verga (*She'erit yosef; Netiv peirush, Derekh hamesader* (Warsaw, N. Sokolov, 1909 [Adrianople, 1554]), 53), puts it this way: "Accordingly, there are two types of anonymous Talmud. One derives from the sages of the academy, and one from Rav Ashi. This is the view of the holy Rabbi Yonah." See too the Responsa of Mahari"q (Joseph Colon b. Solomon Trabotto; 1420–1480), # 169.

119. Asheri does not mention Ravina whose name is mentioned together with Rav Ashi as "the end of *hora'ah*" (BM 86a). Perhaps this is because Rav Ashi was a greater sage than Ravina. I. H. Weiss, in his edition of *Darkhei hagemara* by Isaac Campanton (d. 1463; Vienna: M. Knoepflmacher, 1891), 12, comments to a remark by Campanton, "Ravina? Why would Campanton mention Ravina

here?" and proceeds to explain, "Perhaps he considered Ravina to be the anonymous Talmud" (But why did he not also attribute it to Rav Ashi?) If Weiss's explanation is correct, then perhaps in that generation, the generation preceding the Spanish exile, they identified the anonymous Talmud with Ravina; but see n. 38.

120. In *Seder hadorot* (of Yehiel b. Solomon Heilprin, 1660–1746), s.v. Rav Ashi, n. *vav*. "He (Rav Ashi) composed (*hibber*) the Babylonian Talmud."

121. See too Asheri's comment in *Pisqei haro"sh* to Sanhedrin, chapter 4, section 6: "In the Talmud which Rav Ashi and Ravina edited (*sidder*)."

122. See Asheri, ibid.: "Because one is allowed to dispute and change and even reject all rulings of the Geonim that are not explicated in the Talmud edited by Rav Ashi and Ravina." In other words, the authority of Rav Ashi and Ravina extends to everything included in the Talmud.

123. It should be noted that according to the first version of the passage in BQ 10a it appears that Rav Pappa responds to, and disagrees with, the anonymous stratum. But one need not interpret the passage this way; see *MM*, Bava Qamma, 28. Moreover, one can say that the second version is more authoritative.

124. In Sanh 24b Rav Sheshet did not state "Anything of this type is not an *asmakhta* ('stipulation')" in contradistinction to Rami b. Hamma, who postdated him; see too *MM*, Qiddushin, 701 n.1. However, it is unclear to me why this passage mentions Rami b. Hamma before Rav Sheshet. I doubt it is because of his explanation "Anything of this type...," and that if Rav Sheshet had been placed first, it would not have been possible to say this. Cf. Ket 32a, "Ulla said..." and on the next folio, "R. Yohanan said: You can even say..." However, in this case we have the word "even," and in many cases involving a clause with "even," the latter Amora's statement is provided first; see p. 48. In Sanh 41a Rami b. Hamma appears before Rav Yosef; however, in that case the content necessitates this order. Now ms. Florence of Sanh 24b reads "Rav Ashi" in place of Rav Sheshet, and ms. Munich omits "Anything of this type..."—I suspect that these are emendations.

125. Epstein, *Mevo'ot lesifrut ha'amoraim*, 55, commented on this case, but his conclusion is by no means necessary. Moreover, the medieval commentaries go even further in attributing the dicta of the anonymous stratum to the Amoraim on account of the proximity of the two. See, e.g., Tosafot, Sot 15a, s.v. *savar*, who object to Shmuel's statement in Naz 2b–3a, that according to R. Eleazar Hakappar a pure Nazirite is not considered a sinner, on the basis of Shmuel's statement in Taan 11a, that he is considered a sinner. Yet in Naz 2b–3a this is not stated by Shmuel; Tosafot have attributed to Shmuel the words of the anonymous stratum because they follow immediately another statement of Shmuel ("[a case] where he takes hold of his hair"), thinking that they too were said by Shmuel. I did not adduce above a similar example

from Sanh 23a: "But did not R. Eleazar say: This was only taught of the creditor, but as for a borrower, they compel him [to appear] and to be judged in his [the creditor's] town," whereas on Sanh 31b this dictum appears as Amemar's explanation of R. Eleazar's statement ("Rav Ashi said to Amemar, 'Did not R. Eleazar say, They compel him [to appear] and to be judged in his [the creditor's] town...,'" and Amemar answers, "This rule [that they compel him to go to the place of assembly] applies when the borrower demands it of the creditor, but as for the creditor..."). In this case some manuscript variants lack, "They compel him [to appear] and to be judged in his [the creditor's] town," and therefore one could take the words "This rule applies..." as part of Rav Ashi's statement, and explain that Rav Ashi came to this conclusion because of R. Eleazar's question to R. Yohanan, "He who lends his fellow a *maneh*, must he spend another *maneh*?," which fits the creditor and not the borrower. This conclusion follows from the words "this was only taught," which are based on R. Yohanan, i.e., that R. Eleazar claims that this ruling of R. Yohanan, "they compel him to go to the place of assembly," was taught only of the creditor, but "as for a borrower, they compel him [to appear] and to be judged in his [the creditor's] town." See the commentary *Nimuqei hagriv* (in the Vilna printing of the Talmud) to Sanh 23a, who refers to a similar explanation of Rashb"a, Shab 50b, though there too the analysis depends on the variant readings. See *Diqduqei soferim* to Shab 50b, n. *samekh*; see too Avraham Weiss, *Leheqer hatalmud* (New York: Feldheim, 1954), 263, who cites other examples. (However, those cases where the Talmud states "as R. So-and-so said" [*de'amar* or *kede'amar*] rather than "R. So-and-so said" can be explained in the sense of "R. So-and-so thought"; see Ker 10a and Bekh 47b, and see too BM 24a.)

126. See Part II, "The Editing of the Talmud," n. 107.
127. See Taan 12b; tTaan 1:6, yTaan 1:4, 64c.

PART II

1. See below, nn. 9 and 45.
2. See above, p. 30 ff.
3. See Aharon Hyman, *Toledot tannaim ve'amoraim* (London, 1910), s.v. Rav Ashi, and n. 86 there.
4. See Even-Shoshan's Hebrew Dictionary, s.v. *orekh* ("editor").
5. See Part IV, "The Compilers," p. 156.
6. Well known are the words of the author of *Seder tannaim ve'amoraim* (ed. Kalman Kahana [Frankfurt, 1935], 9), that the Saboraim set "all teachings" in their proper order.
7. Good examples of this phenomenon can be found in *MM*, Sukkah, 181 ff.

8. See *MM*, Bava Batra, 124b (and the indices to the volumes of *MM*, s.v. *tseiruf meqorot* ("combination of sources") and *tseiruf qeta'im* ("combination of passages"). For example, Tosafot, BM 94a, s.v. *amar*, object to Rav Nahman b. Yitshaq, "What does he inform us? . . . Behold, Rav said it above," and respond, "One could say that he (Rav Nahman b. Yitshak) had not heard of Rav's statement." The Talmud itself ought to have raised this difficulty, since it had previously cited Rav's dictum. Apparently Rav Nahman b. Yitshaq's statement was included at a time when they no longer added dialectical argumentation to the Talmud. Similarly, sometimes such terms as "it is also taught thus (*tanya namei hakhi*)" and "there is a teaching that accords with him (*tanya kevateih*)" are added at the end of the sugya and not incorporated into the middle of the sugya together with an objection such as "they responded (*meitivei*)" against the opposing opinion. And see p. 156 above.
9. J. N. Epstein seems to contradict himself (*Mevo'ot lesifrut ha'amoraim*, 12). If Rav Ashi and Ravina "collected all the material that preceded them, for the most part in its original form, explicated it, completed it, and arranged it," how did it happen that "each and every tractate is a self-contained book? . . . There are contradictions and inconsistencies within a tractate, between different chapters and among different issues, and there are also duplications within one tractate." The contradictions and inconsistencies are too numerous to say that the editors did not notice them.

   For this reason it appears that the Bavli never went through a general editing process, in the sense that someone checked over the entire Talmud to render it internally consistent: to examine, refine, and harmonize all the parts of different sugyot (and not only within the same sugya), to see if they indeed cohere with one another, such that there remain no contradictions and inconsistencies among them. No editor made sure that obscure traditions be interpreted on the basis of explicit ones, or that traditions be rendered in a consistent style. The lack of harmonization proves that the sugyot were taught separately, each one independently of the others, without connection to the entire tractate. Accordingly, the difference between the Bavli and the Yerushalmi is not—as Isaak Halevy claims in *Dorot harishonim*, vol. 2, chap. 65—that the Bavli went through an editing process while the Yerushalmi did not—but that the composers of the anonymous stratum of the Yerushalmi added only a thin layer necessary to connect the words of the Amora (their meaning and justification) with the source (mishnah, baraita) [see too below, p. 194]. The anonymous stratum of the Yerushalmi does not aspire to do more than this; moreover, its composition ceased soon after it began, at the end of the fourth century CE. The composition of the anonymous stratum of the Bavli continued for more than 200 years, and it aspires not only to provide minimal explanations of Amoraic dicta but also to investigate, analyze, and penetrate to the heart of the issue, to elaborate on the details, and to explore the different possibilities so as to create the sugya. Nevertheless, the anonymous stratum of the Bavli cannot be compared to a unified composition, as it only succeeded in reworking sugyot. (The medieval commentaries, however, subsequently tried to achieve that goal, but they could not rewrite the Talmud completely.)

Given the lack of comprehensive editing, one can assume that there existed more than one version of the Talmud throughout the Stammaitic period, even at its end, that is, in the Saboraic age. Indeed, we find in the *She'iltot* some passages that do not appear in our versions of the Talmud (see J. N. Epstein, "Sridei she'ilot," in *Studies in Talmudic Literature and Semitic Languages*, ed. E. Z. Melamed [Jerusalem: Magnes, 1988], 2:384 ff.). Nevertheless, gradually one version prevailed and became dominant, which Eliezer Shimshon Rosenthal calls "the vulgate"—and it is approximately our version (see his *Talmud Bavli, Masekhet Pesahim: Ketav-Yad Sasson-Luntzer* [London: Valmodanna Trust Library, 1984]).**

10. See Tosafot, Men 58b, s.v. *ve'ika*. This term appears frequently among the medieval commentaries in several tractates. This material has been collected recently by Yehonatan Etz-Chayim, in the introduction to *Sugyot muhlafot bemasekhet neziqin* [Contradictory *sugyot* in The Nezikin Tractates] (Lod: Mekhon Haberman Lemehkere Sifrut, 2000 [1976]). See especially p. 19.

11. If Rav Ashi and his academy engaged in the editing of the Talmud for two or three generations—as described by Halevy, *Dorot harishonim*, 3:64 ff.: "The Generation of Rav Ashi"—surely they would have cleansed the Talmud of all contradictions.

12. I am uncertain whether there is a contradiction between Bets 9a, where the Talmud objects to Rav Hanan b. Ami based on a statement of Rav, and Sanh 25a, where Rami b. Hama disagrees with R. Yehoshua b. Levi and R. Yohanan, and the Talmud expresses a kind of astonishment, "Do you oppose one Amora (literally, "man") with another Amora (*gavra agavra ka rameit*)"? (To Bets 9a Rashi explains, "Even though Rav was an Amora [and in theory of equal authority to Rav Hanan b. Ami], they object on the basis of his statement because he was the master of all sages of the diaspora in his generation, with the exception of Shmuel"; and Tosafot comment, "Even though Rav was an Amora, this is nevertheless a valid objection, because Rav was the greatest sage of his generation and the Head of the Academy for all Jews except for Shmuel, so it is unreasonable that Rav Hanan b. Ami would disagree with him" [see too Tosafot, BM 46b, s.v. *trei*, as referenced by R. Akiba Eger in the marginal glosses there, and Tosafot, MQ 2b, s.v *hayyav*.])

Now in the parallel passages that use the term "Do you oppose one Amora with another Amora (*gavra agavra ka rameit*)?" it is two contemporaneous Amoraim who dispute: (a) in Eruv 82a, R. Yehoshua b Levi and Shmuel disagree (Nahmanides to BB 2b states that they raise an objection based on Shmuel's statement because "Shmuel possessed great skill" [Nid 64b] and Rashb"a comments, "Shmuel is different [from other Amoraim] as he was elderly, and close to the Tannaim, and they object from his statements [against an Amora] just as they object from any of the Tannaim"; but cf. Sanh 112b: "and this disagrees with Shmuel [*upliga deshmuel*]," and Rashi comments, "this [statement] of Ravina [disagrees] with Shmuel." Ravina is mentioned before Shmuel because Shmuel's dictum is not explicit); (b) in Taan 4b, R. Asi and R. Yohanan and R. Eleazar disagree (and the Talmud calls R. Eleazar "the master of the Land of Israel" in three places: Yoma 9b, Git 19b, and Nid 20b); (c) in BQ 43b Resh Laqish disagrees with Rav Dimi, in the name of R. Yohanan; (d) in Sanh 6a R. Abbahu and Shmuel disagree; (e) in Sanh 30b "R. Abba and R. Iddi" disagree with Ulla; (f) later on that same folio Rav Yehudah and Rav Hisda disagree, (g) and in Hul 52a R. Illa and Rav disagree (see the glosses of Betsalel Rensburg there, and *Diqduqei soferim* n. *nun*).

These disagreements take place between Amoraim who were near contemporaries, whereas Rami b. Hama lived almost 100 years after R. Yehoshua b. Levi and R. Yohanan, and if Rav Hanan b. Ami (he was a student of Shmuel, and there is no need to conjecture that there was a second sage of that name; see Hyman, *Toldot tannaim ve'amoraim*, under his entry) is not permitted to disagree with Rav, then Rami b. Hama should not be allowed to disagree with R. Yehoshua b. Levi and R. Yohanan. One could raise a similar objection against Sanh 24a, "Rava stated his own reason," and Rashi explains, "He disagrees with both of them," namely, with Shmuel and R. Yohanan. Would Rava disagree with Shmuel and R. Yohanan? It is no help to suggest that one cannot compare Amoraim with one another, that in Babylonia they had greater respect for Babylonian Amoraim, and therefore it is possible that later Babylonian Amoraim such as Rava would indeed disagree with the R. Yehoshua b. Levi and R. Yohanan, Amoraim from the Land of Israel, but not with Rav—since we have Rava disagreeing with Shmuel, a Babylonian. Perhaps Amoraim would not disagree with Rav alone, for it is said of Rav (and of R. Hiyya, BM 5a), "He is a Tanna, and disagrees (*tanna hu upaleig*),** but not of Shmuel (see *Yad malakhi*, #552)—but they would disagree with Shmuel. This matter requires further investigation.

However, I have grave doubts about the correctness of the explanations of Rashi and Tosafot to Bets 9a, as to why the Talmud did not want to say that Rav Hanan b. Ami disagreed with Rav. In some cases the Talmud objects to an Amora on the basis of another Amora solely to determine whether the Amoraim indeed disagree among themselves; and subsequently the Talmud explains their statements such that they do not disagree (see Git 81a, "Did not Rav Ashi say..."; Ket 50a, "Did not Rav say to Rav Shmuel b. Shilat..." [although here one might say that "They decreed at Usha" refers to Tannaitic decrees]). So too in Bets 9a the Talmud objects to Rav Hanan b. Ami based on a statement of Rav not because Rav Hanan b. Ami cannot disagree with Rav but rather to ascertain whether we are dealing with two different opinions; and in the end the Talmud states that they do not disagree and so there is only one opinion. Similarly in Eruv 81b–82a Rav Aha b. Rava makes an objection to Rav Ashi on the basis of the fact that R. Yehoshua b. Levi disagrees with Shmuel, and according to some readings Rav Ashi responds to him, "Do you oppose one Amora with another Amora"; and in Taan 4b R. Zeira objects to Rav Ashi based on the fact that R. Yohanan disagrees with R. Eleazar, and Rav Ashi answers him, "Do you oppose one Amora with another Amora"; and in BQ 43b, Abaye objects to Rav Dimi in the name of R. Yohanan based on a statement of Resh Laqish, and Rav Dimi answers him, "Do you oppose one Amora with another Amora"; and in Sanh 6a Rava objects to Rav Nahman based on Shmuel's disagreement with R. Abbahu, and Rav Nahman answered him, "Do you oppose..."; and in Sanh 30b Abaye objects to R. Hiyya b. Avin and to Ulla based on statements of R. Abba in the name of Rav Huna in the name of Rav and of Rav Iddi b. Avin, and they answer him, "Do you oppose one Amora..."—and in all these cases did the Amoraim not know that Amoraim are permitted to disagree with one another? Rather, they wanted to know if it is necessary to say that there was a contradiction. (Similarly, when the Talmud objects to an explanation of a mishnah on the basis of an Amoraic dictum, it wants to know how the Amora explained that mishnah, as it certainly did not mean to direct an objection against a mishnah on the basis of an Amoraic dictum; cf. Eliav Shochetman, "Gavra agavra ka rameit," *Sidra* 6 [1994], 93–107.)

A second possibility, though less likely, is that the objection against Rami b. Hama based on the statements of R. Yehushua b. Levi and Shmuel and the response "Do you oppose one Amora with another Amora" in Sanh 25a were transferred there from Eruv 82a, despite the fact that in Eruv 82a R. Yehudah states, "In what circumstances does this apply?" so that the objection does not stem from R. Yohanan's statement, whereas in Sanh 25a R. Yehudah states, "When does this apply?" such that the objection also follows from R. Yohanan's statement. Cf. Sanh 26b, "R. Abbahu said that Eleazar said: The law follows R. Yehudah"..."'The law' implies that they disagree." Incidentally, if we conclude that the Talmudic passages, i.e., the anonymous strata, of Bets 9a and Sanh 25a contradict each other, it stands to reason that Bets 9a is the latter, since in later times they were more reluctant to say that an Amora would disagree with the greatest master of his generation. This issue is unclear and requires detailed study.

13. In Ned 10a Abaye states that "Shimon the Righteous and R. Shimon and R. Eleazar HaKappar all hold the same opinion (*shita ahat*) that a Nazirite is a sinner." Now Shimon the Righteous and R. Shimon believe that a pure Nazirite is a sinner too. Nevertheless, Abaye's statement does not prove that R. Eleazar HaKappar also believed that a pure Nazirite is a sinner. The "same opinion" (*shita*) need not be the same in all respects, as the medieval commentaries note ad loc.
14. Rashi, Ker 26a, sensed this, and explained that a pure Nazirite presents no difficulty, seeing that "he is able to bring it [the sacrifice] and stipulate that if he

were not a Nazir now, he will subsequently become a Nazir." But one could still ask whether he is exempt from bringing the sacrifice if he failed to stipulate and then Yom Kippur intervened.

15. In Ker 25b–26a, Rav Hoshaya responds to an objection directed against the interpretation of R. Eleazar. However, in no other Talmudic passage do we find Rav Hoshaya—even the second Rav Hoshaya—responding to R. Eleazar.
16. The response in Shevu 8a, "He [R. Eleazar HaKappar] holds like R. Shimon…" does not fit the sugya in Ker 26a. However, the response in Ker 26a fits the sugya in Shevu 8a, as the medieval commentaries have noted.
17. In Shevu 8a the Talmud twice states, "He holds that it may be deduced from the passage itself (*mimeqomo hu mukhra*)." The first time this is said of R. Shimon, that "he rules in accord with his own opinion (*leta'amei*)," Ra"n indeed objects, "What occurred to him to say this?" as this response is obvious. However, the second time this is said of R. Eleazar HaKappar, but it is illogical to explain that his opinion accords with that of R. Shimon, as it is equally possible to explain that he also rules in accord with the anonymous authority of the mishnah, who disagrees with R. Shimon according to the Talmud's response in Ker 26a. We are forced to conclude that according to the Shevu 8a, the response of Ker 26a does not fit.
18. Note that Sot 15a states, "He [R. Shimon] holds like R. Eleazar HaKappar who said that a Nazirite too is a sinner." Tosafot and other commentaries point out that R. Shimon himself says that a Nazirite is called a sinner in Ned 10a, and hence the Talmud could have attributed this opinion to R. Shimon himself, rather than stating that he holds like R. Eleazar HaKappar. They explain that the Talmud does this on account of the prevalence of the dictum in R. Eleazar HaKappar's name. We find many such cases throughout the Talmud. See the indices to *MM*, s.v. *baraita*.
19. In *MM*, Sukkah, 197, I observed that the Stammaitic composers of the sugya at Yev 80b knew the dictum of R. Shimon b. Gamaliel ("any human birth that survives thirty days cannot be considered a miscarriage") in a truncated form, without the conclusion "as it says, *its redemption is from one month (Num 18:16)*"—which speaks of the typical case of a full term baby. For this reason they apply the dictum to a baby born at seven months.
20. See Tosafot, BM 94a, s.v. *amar*; and see too *MM*, Bava Metsia, 250.
21. Some versions do not read "a great matter in its literal sense." Moreover, the meaning of this phrase is not entirely clear. See *Yad rama"h* and *Hiddushei hara"n*, ad loc.
22. R. Akiba Eger in his marginal glosses to Sanh 16a refers to Sanh 18b and concludes, "This requires much further analysis"; he was anticipated by the author of *Torat hayyim*.
23. Cf. Rasha"l, *Hochmat shlomoh*, ad loc., and Solomon Algazi, *Halikhot eli*, 67b, *s.v.* "*Tana'ei hi.*" The *Yad rama"h* had an odd reading here: "Do we require a verse [be

carried out] as written? He said to him: 'Yes, as we learned...,'" and he comments that Mar Qashisha asked Rav Ashi a general question, and not about a contradiction between sources. Rav Ashi answered, "Yes" and quoted proof from the mishnah, "If one of them [his parents] was without hands...," and then Mar Qashisha rejected Rav Ashi's proof from the mishnah and said, "There [the case of the stubborn and rebellions son] it is different, as the entire verse is superfluous." I have not found this reading attested elsewhere, and I suspect that it was created in order to resolve the difficulties that plague this sugya, including the objections raised by Tosafot.

24. The same phrasing is found in Qid 25b and AZ 71b.
25. Some readings omit "Why." However, this does not change the meaning of the following line, which is an objection.
26. The reading in ms Vatican 130 is reversed: the first part of the sugya reads, "Why," and the second part, "Do you infer from this?"
27. Nahmanides and Ritb"a and others argue on the basis of BM 67b that this issue was resolved: "Mar Zutra said in the name of Rav Pappa: "In a case of mortgaged property...And according to the one who holds that vessels of a purchaser in the domain of the seller acquire [possession] on behalf of the purchaser, even..." In the words of Ritb"a: "Because the late Amora Rav Pappa holds this opinion, we rule according to him." However, it is possible that the phrase "And according to the one who holds..." are no longer the words of Rav Pappa but of the anonymous stratum.
28. Resh Laqish's remark in BB 85b, "[As long as the basket is] tied to her, even if it is not hanging," is based on the statement of R. Eleazar in the name of R. Oshaya (the first R. Oshaya), "For instance, if the basket is hanging from her" found in Git 78a and in some manuscripts of BB 85b.
29. Rasha"l in *Hochmat shlomoh*, ad loc., sensed this, but did not appreciate the difficulty posed by "But did not Rav Shizvi say that Rav Hisda said..."
30. See above, p. 15, on "Rav Uqba of Meshan said to Rav Ashi," Bets 36a.
31. I first commented on this phenomenon in *MM*, Yevamot, 17.
32. See *MM*, Rosh Hashanah, 409–10.
33. See too *MM*, Bava Batra, 55.
34. See below, p. 134, on "The Editor of the Mishnah and his Role in Editing."
35. See below, p. 156 ff., "Compilers and Transposers."
36. *MM*, Sukkah, 194 n.1.
37. See *MM*, Gittin, 573 for the reason I discuss Tem 25b rather than the similar case found in Git 53a.
38. The name of Ravina is sometimes omitted; see, e.g., Maimonides, in his introduction to the *Mishneh torah*: "Ravina and Rav Ashi were the last of the Talmudic sages, and Rav Ashi composed the Talmud." See too Rashi, Sanh 30a, s.v. *amar lan*: "The passage mentions Rav Ashi because his court was the high court in the days of Ravina, and the two of them edited the *gemara* of the Babylonian

Talmud, as stated there in BM 86a, 'Rav Ashi and Ravina—the end of *hora'ah.*' During his (Rav Ashi's) time these matters were stated and fixed in the Talmud." Cf. Part I, n. 119.

39. See my comments in the Introduction to *MM: bava metsia,* 20 ff., and the following footnote. This claim finds some support in the fact that among all quotations of Amoraim with the term "it was said (*itmar*)," one never finds Amoraim that postdate Rav Ashi and Ravina (the first Ravina, except for Rafram in Yev 27a [although some texts read Rafram b. Pappa who preceded Ravina and Rav Ashi], and Rav Ashi and Ravina in three places: Yev 11a, BM 95a, AZ 26b. See below, p. 92 on Rav Aha and the second Ravina.)

40. J. N. Epstein claims, against Rashi, that beginning with the words, "Rabbi [Yehudah HaNasi] and R. Natan—the end of Mishnah," the passage no longer quotes the "Book of the Primordial Adam" but is the anonymous Talmud (*Mevo'ot lesifrut hatannaim,* 200 n.1). But if so, what is this tradition doing there? What is the connection between this tradition and that which precedes it, the connection to the healing of R. Yehudah HaNasi. etc.? However, if these words are from the "Book of Primordial Adam," why are they written in Hebrew, while the rest of the quotation is Aramaic? Perhaps the words "Mishnah" and "*hora'ah*" are nouns that were also used in Aramaic (on *hora'ah,* see the previous note; *hora'ah* can be considered a kind of Amoraic baraita, a collection of apodictic Amoraic laws.) As to the word *simanakh* ("your mnemonic" in the passage: "Rav Ashi and Ravina—the end of *hora'ah.* And your mnemonic is . . ."), it is unclear when mnemonics were introduced into the Talmud, both the mnemonics preceding Amoraic dicta that the Talmud subsequently quotes (see Hyman, *Toledot,* 17–28) and the mnemonics for dicta previously quoted, as in our case. In passing it should be noted that there is no other place where Shmuel interacts with R. Yehudah HaNasi (the reading in Git 66b–67a, "Shmuel said that Rabbi [Yehudah HaNasi] said" is questionable). Thus from a historical perspective the tradition is dubious.

41. See above, n. 39.

42. See, e.g., Halevy, *Dorot harishonim,* 3:23: "That which happened in the time of Rabbi [Yehudah HaNasi], so it happened exactly in the time of Rav Ashi."

43. Despite the exertions of Halevy, *Dorot harishonim,* 3:26 ff.

44. See, e.g., Tosafot and Ro"sh, Shab 9b, s.v. *betisporet,* where they deal with the anonymous Talmud that explicates a mishnah or baraita. However, when the unattributed anonymous material explicates an Amoraic dictum, they typically attribute it to the Amora himself.

45. I have not defined sufficiently the role of the editor. And Isaak Halevy—whose views in *Dorot harishonim* I dispute—does not call Rav Ashi the editor of the Talmud. (However, some of his successors do employ the term "editor": see, e.g., M. Margulies, *Encyclopedia of the Sages of the Talmud and the Geonim* [Tel Aviv: Joshua Chachik, 1970), (Hebrew)], s.v. Rav Ashi.) Nevertheless, in several

places Halevy describes Rav Ashi's activity in a manner that is very similar to the contemporary sense of an "editor." To quote one example: "Rav Ashi ordered (*sidder*) and sealed (*hatam*). Now it is clear that there already was an order to the entire Talmud prior to Rav Ashi. However, Rav Ashi added the ordering (*siddur*) related to the sealing of the Talmud, and to the determination of the law on the basis of the sugya, and to the clarification of widespread doubts...about the interpretation of the Mishnah and baraitot (*Dorot harishonim*, 3:210)." This idea is expressed more clearly in Hyman, *Toledot*, 252, s.v. Rav Ashi: "The Talmud had been set in order by each and every generation, and so Rav Ashi found the entire Talmud set in order. Nevertheless, he and his important colleagues sealed it (*hatmuhu*) and revised it, and clarified it thoroughly...to clarify and elucidate each and every tradition, and to be exacting about the identity of the tradent, and all this was done by Rav Ashi and his contemporaries." When I say that the Talmud had no editor, I mean that "the Talmud had no set order (*seder*) before Rav Ashi." The Amoraim had no Talmud (just as the Tannaim had no Talmud), that is, no dialectical argumentation in set order, and transmitted though an official transmission, such that Rav Ashi added to it what Halevy calls "the ordering (*siddur*) related to the sealing of the Talmud." Amoraic knowledge of dialectical argumentation was partial and incomplete, because—unlike apodictic laws—they did not receive dialectical argumentation through the "Reciters" (*tannaim*) who learned it "mouth to mouth" from the Amoraim themselves. Rather, Amoraim knew only that which happened to be remembered by those who heard it, and this was not always reliable. The Stammaim took upon themselves the task of reconstructing and completing the dialectical argumentation, but they too did not edit it with a uniform and consistent editing. Efforts to find indications that Rav Ashi had some role in the editing of the Talmud have produced no solid evidence. (See I. H. Weiss, *Dor dor vedorshav* [Vilna, Romm, 911], 3:210; and see the moderate view in Julius Kaplan, *The Redaction of the Babylonian Talmud* [Jerusalem: Makor, 1933]). Rav Ashi's role was no greater than that of other Amoraim. So too references to "the discussions of Rav and Shmuel (*havayyot derav ushemuel*)" (Ber 20a and parallels), and "the discussions of Abaye and Rava" (Suk 28a) do not imply that they edited the discussions, but only that they distinguished themselves therein—and distinction does not necessarily involve editing. "The determination of the law on the basis of the sugya," and "clarification of doubts" were not limited to Rav Ashi; all the Amoraim engaged in these activities. Because Rav Ashi was the Head of the Academy for sixty years and had many disciples, he made more legal decisions and clarifications than others—but this does not make him an editor.

46. Cf. above, p. 15, concerning Rav Uqba of Meshan's question to Rav Ashi in Bets 36a.
47. See the *Responsa of Israel Bruna* (1400–1480), #29: "Because during the age of Tosafot they engaged in dialectical analysis of inferences and fine distinctions, which was not in accord with the true meaning." The earlier medieval

commentaries sometimes reject the Talmud's explanation on the grounds that it is a forced explanation, "forced teachings (*shinuyei dehiqei*)," (especially Alfasi and R. Hananel and apparently Maimonides too—albeit less often—see, e.g., Rashi to Hul 95b, s.v *rav huna*). See too Yev 91b and BB 135b: "Should we rely on a [forced] explanation?" These cases are collected by Shraga Abramson, *Peirush rabbenu hananel latalmud* (Jerusalem, Weiss, 1995), 183 ff.; and one could add other examples, e.g., *Responsa of Maimonides,* ed. A. Freimann (Jerusalem: Meqitsei Nirdamim, 1937 [Hebrew]), 2:530, #8 (= ed. J. Blau, p. 673): "That teaching is just for the sake of argumentation, and is not in accord with the law."

48. The Stammaim endeavored to reconstruct texts that they received in incomplete form, and sometimes abandoned the simple explanation when it impeded their efforts, and therefore explicated the texts in a forced manner. They suppressed their sensitivity for the simple explanation in the interests of completing the text. (This tendency is evident today among editors of texts, for example, the Dead Sea Scrolls, when the text is extremely fragmentary.) However, after the Talmud was closed and there was no longer any need to complete the text, especially during the period of the medieval commentaries, sensitivity to the simple explanation returned and increased, and the commentators frequently made observations about the forced explanations of the Talmud. Because the Talmud was treated as a canonical work by this time, they could not propose explanations that differed from those of the Talmud, and had no recourse, when explicating the difficulties found in the stammaitic stratum, other than to claim that the Stammaim meant something different. In this way they transfer the difficulty from the text explicated by the Stammaim to the Stammaim themselves.

    After the medieval commentaries recognized that the Talmud contains forced explanations, later commentaries concluded that it was acceptable to propound forced explanations themselves. In the Introduction to *MM: seder nashim,* 10 n. 9, I quoted Hatam Sofer (Moses Schreiber [Sofer], 1762–1839): "Forced explanations are for the most part true. However, logical contrivances are mostly lies, which obscure the truth." And R. Israel Salanter (1810–1883) in the introduction to the journal *Tevuna* states: "What is the truth? The truth does not live in simple explanations alone, for simple explanations are only one aspect of the modes of proof, and generally substantive difficulties surface to attack the simple explanations and to reject them, as we see in the interpretations of the Talmud." The Stammaim resorted to forced explanations in order to reconstruct the text, whereas the medieval commentaries resorted to forced explanations to preserve the text. See too my comments in *Peshat and Derash* (New York: Oxford University Press, 1991), 1–52, on modes of interpretation throughout the generations.

49. I. Halevy emends Sherira Gaon's language, resulting in a fifty year period between Rav Ashi and the second Ravina.

50. Quoting *MM*, Nedarim, 326.

51. Indeed, the sugya in Ker 25b continues with objections based on a suspected adulteress of doubtful status and the beheaded heifer (which are answered by Abaye and Rava), which do not appear in Shevu 8a. This may be because the goat for Yom Kippur does not atone for them either.
52. I do not completely reject the possibility that Shevu 8a did not know of Rav Ashi's statement, and for this reason it does not appear there. It appears that Shevu 8a knew more tannaitic material—it knew the complete versions of the baraitot of R. Eleazar HaKappar and R. Shimon b. Yohai, whereas Ker 25b knew more Amoraic material. That sugya is extremely lengthy, and includes an Amoraic continuation, "If this is so, then a suspected adulteress of doubtful status...," "If this is so, then a beheaded heifer...," which does not appear in Shevu 8a. It should be noted that this continuation appears at the end of the sugya, after an anonymous sugya (except for the statement of Rav Ashi, which does not belong there, and the statement of Rav Hoshaya, which belongs in Shevu 8a, as noted above), even though it is Amoraic. Ker 25b begins with a passage similar to that of Shevu 8a, and only then does it add material without parallel there.
53. This difficulty weakens the explanation of Tosafot and Rashb"a.
54. See the medieval commentaries, ad loc.
55. A paragraph has been omitted here, which deals with another aspect of that sugya at the beginning of Tractate Gittin, but does not contribute to the flow of the book's argumentation. It can be found in the annotations.**
56. Cf. S. Albeck, "Sof hahora'ah va'ahoranei ha'amoraim," *Sinai* 41 (1958; Jubilee Volume), 59 ff.
57. It is implausible to explain that the editors in fact knew who said what, but subsequent generations forgot, and that our Talmud reflects the later situation.
58. The issue of disagreements between Rav Aha and Ravina is addressed at length in *MM*, Sukkah, 181–84, and n. 8. I noted that R. Meshulam Behr (*Divrei meshulam* [Frankfurt: David Droller, 1926], 79) already suggested that the Ravina who disagrees with Rav Aha is the second Ravina. He quotes *Halakhot gedolot* (Warsaw, 1875), 52c and 57a, which states that the law follows Ravina when he opposes Rav Ashi because "Rav Aha and Ravina both postdate Rav Ashi." Subsequently Albeck (*Mavo latalmudim*, 442 n. 459) quoted *Yihusei tannaim ve'amoraim* (ed. Y. Maimon [Jerusalem: Rav Kook, 1963], 100), who also claimed that it is the second Ravina who disagrees with Rav Aha.**
59. Quotation from *MM*, Sukkah, 182.
60. *MM*, Sukkah, 183.
61. In Stammaitic times the academies were concentrated in Sura and Pumbedita, and had "Compilers." In Amoraic times, by contrast, there were local academies (as in Tannaitic times, as suggested by Sanh 32b: "*Justice, Justice you shall pursue [Deut 16:20]*—to R. Eliezer in Lod, to R. Yohanan b. Zakkai in Beror Hayyil"), and the Amoraim taught in their various localities (e.g., Qid 53a: "R. Zeira expounded in Mahoza: A convert may marry a *mamzeret*. The entire people pelted him with their citrons. Rava said: Who would [be so foolish as to] expound

such a tradition in that place where converts are common?!") But there were no centralized institutions. See B. Cohen, "Yeshivot mekomiot bebavel betekufat hatalmud," *Zion* 70 (2005), 447 ff.**

62. The term "It stands to reason (*mistabra*)" is not limited to the Saboraim (as suggested by various scholars). See B. M. Lewin, *Rabanan savora'ei vetalmudam* (Jerusalem: Aviezer, 1937), 15. This term is also found among the Amoraim.
63. The rest of the sugya is entirely anonymous and very similar to the anonymous discussion that follows Rav Aha's statement above. It would appear that these anonymous passages are based on the dispute whether a wounded animal is capable of giving birth or not. I will return to this point elsewhere.
64. I do not understand Halevy, *Dorot harishonim*, 3:43: "Both Rav Aha and Ravina received from Rav Ashi an unspecified (*setam*) dictum of Amemar's together with Rav Ashi's objection based on Mishnah Edduyot, and each arranged the sugya according to his own view." How does "unspecified" apply here? Either Amemar stated "eggs of a wounded (bird, *tereifah*)," that is, a wounded bird whose status was certain (so Rav Aha), or he stated "eggs of a wounded (bird) of doubtful status" (so Ravina). If he stated "eggs of a wounded (bird) of doubtful status," there is no way one could err and think that he meant a wounded bird whose status was certain. And if he said, in response to Rav Ashi, "That is a case of [the bird becoming pregnant through] friction with the ground" (so Rav Aha), there is no way one could mistakenly think that he said: "That applies only to the first clutch" (so Ravina). The "unspecified dictum" to which Halevy refers is a dictum that can be interpreted according to different opinions which do not disagree about the wording of the dictum itself but only over its interpretation (see p. 59 where I cite examples from Berakhot and Ketubot). In this case, however, Rav Aha and Ravina disagree over the wording of the dicta, and consequently one of them transmitted that which Rav Ashi and Amemar never articulated. If they participated together in the editing of the Talmud, why did they not clarify all this by asking Amemar and Rav Ashi?
65. Rav Ashi too was not among the editors of the Talmud. The fact that he served as Head of the Academy for sixty years, that he reviewed his "learning" twice, a "first cycle" and a "later cycle" (BB 157b), and that many Amoraim studied under his aegis, more than attested among other Amoraim (because of his lengthy tenure as Head of the Academy)—these facts should not lead us to conclude that he was the editor of the Talmud. On the contrary, given that Rav Ashi reviewed his learning in two cycles, had he been the editor, he no doubt would have eliminated contradictions and forced explanations from the Talmud. See, e.g., Tosafot, Hul 58b, s.v. *keman*: "Perhaps Rav Ashi did not know that baraita" (found in Pes 27a, and also did not know some of the argumentation there). And see too Tosafot, BM 94a, s.v. *amar*: "If you should ask what Rav Nahman comes to tell us [with this statement], as Rav already said [the same thing] above? One could say that he did not know of Rav's statement." Why did Rav Ashi, as

editor, not remark that Rav Nahman b. Yitshaq's dictum had already been stated by Rav? See too Nahmanides, *Milhamot*, Pesahim, #787: "The Talmud does not resolve all details of that baraita, whether it accords with Ravina or Rav Ashi . . . And it is possible that the Talmud explains it in this way and Rav Ashi objects to that explanation." Thus Nahmanides, too, did not consider Rav Ashi to be the editor of the anonymous Talmud. The medieval jurists, however, were not consistent in their views of the formation and editing of the Talmud (just as they were not consistent in citing variant readings; see *MM*, Nedarim, 302 n. 10), and one should not attribute to them a particular view based on their comments in one passage. See too the summary in Kaplan, *The Redaction of the Babylonian Talmud*, 70. Had Kaplan studied the Bavli in depth and analyzed sugyot in a critical manner, he would not even have found "weak arguments" that Rav Ashi was the editor of the Talmud.

66. Indeed, according to Alfasi, the one who says "[The buyer must] accept [ten casks of sour wine for every hundred]" explains mBB 6:1 as dealing with a case when the seller said "I sell you this cellar," without any further specification, and without the buyer mentioning that he needs the wine for a dish. But this does not follow from the Talmud itself. Apart from the explanation of the mishnah with the term "The mishnah has an omission and he teaches thus," the Talmud, after quoting the disagreement between Rav Aha and Ravina, does not quote the same passage that is quoted above. See too Maharsh"a, who quotes Alfasi, and then states, "Nevertheless, Tosafot's astonishment is appropriate." And see too the *Shita mequbetset*.
67. It is not clear if this addition derives from Rav Zevid or from the "School of R. Oshaya."
68. If the reading "our Mishnah" is correct, then he does not disagree with mBB 6:1 but rather explains it. But there are some texts that do not read "in our Mishnah," and it is possible that Rav Zevid refers to an older mishnah and disagrees with mBB 6:1 over the explanation of the older mishnah.
69. Cf. mHag 1:7: "R. Shimon b. Menasia says . . . " He lived slightly after R. Yehudah HaNasi. See the chapter appended to Avot, 6:9.
70. In *MM*, Pesahim, 400 ff., I demonstrated that the Talmud contains a few instances of "Rav Ashi objected to it (*matqif lah*)" which appear to relate to the anonymous stratum—but this is in fact not the case.
71. On the difference between "Rather, said R. So-and-so (*ela amar*)" and "But if it was said, it was said thus (*ela i itmar hakhi itmar*)," see Tosafot, Shab 50a, s.v. *ela*, and my comments in *MM*, Shabbat, 146 ff. (In some cases "the Talmud knew only the objection that was raised, but not the response," and later conjectured the response. Thus "Rather, said R. So-and-so" does not necessarily derive from the Amora himself, but possibly from the Stammaim.)
72. Perhaps in Qid 32b the use of "But if it was said, it was said thus" suggests even more uncertainty. Rav Ashi had stated, "Even the one who says (i.e., Rav Yosef)

that if a master renounces his honor, his honor is renounced, [he agrees that] if a Nasi renounces his honor, his honor is not renounced." The students of the academy (of the succeeding generation) objected to this statement from a baraita that the Nasi Rabban Gamaliel arose and served drinks to R. Eliezer and R. Yehoshua at his son's banquet. Consequently they changed Rav Ashi's dictum, as if he said: "Even the one who says (i.e., Rabban Gamaliel, in that baraita) that if a Nasi renounces his honor, his honor is renounced, [he agrees that] if a king renounces his honor, his honor is not renounced." This version is quoted in the parallel Talmudic passages; however, it appears that we are dealing with different sources (although see the medieval commentaries ad loc.): in Sot 41b and Sanh 19b the response (to the objection concerning the case of a king apparently renouncing his honor) is "[the performance of] a commandment is different"; in Ket 17a the response is "it was an intersection." The different responses derive from different academies, and this difference did not occur immediately, but after several generations.

Yet it is doubtful whether the Talmud's reconstruction of Rav Ashi's dictum is accurate. We find no authority who disagrees with Rabban Gamaliel and holds that a Nasi cannot renounce his honor. In the baraita R. Eliezer simply asked R. Yehoshua: "What is this, Yehoshua? Rabban Gamaliel is standing and serving while we sit?" R. Yehoshua explained to him that Abraham too acted thus, and R. Eliezer accepted the explanation. Those who reconstructed Rav Ashi's dictum endeavored to render the reformulation in the same style as the first formulation, and therefore added, "Even the one who says that if a Nasi renounces his honor, his honor is renounced," although it is not appropriate here; they chose not to formulate his ruling in apodictic style: "If a king renounces his honor, his honor is not renounced." Nor did they wish to reconstruct Rav Ashi's dictum as "Even the one who says that if a master renounces his honor, his honor is renounced, [he agrees that] if a king renounces his honor, his honor is not renounced," as the disparity between a master and a king is too great to compare them together, and I doubt that it would be accurate. However, if the Talmud was completed in the generation that followed Rav Ashi, it is difficult to imagine that this type of development with uncertainty as to the dicta occurred in Rav Ashi's academy or even a generation or two thereafter.

73. See Tosafot, MQ 22b, s.v. *ulesimhat*; and Tosafot, Bekhorot 36b, s.v. *i"k ve'od*.
74. See, for example, BB 88a, where the sugya ends with Rava's statement; and see *MM*, ad loc.
75. These points were anticipated by A. Weiss, *Leheqer hatalmud* (New York: Feldheim, 1954), 93. Cf. Kaplan, *The Redaction of the Babylonian Talmud*, Chapter 5, "The Anonymous Parts of the Talmud," and see n. 84r.
76. See Hul 92a: "Three excellent officials.... The Sages turned their eyes to Rabbana Uqba and Rabbana Nehemia, the sons of the daughter of Rav."
77. As noted by Halevy, *Dorot harishonim*, 3:91.

78. "In any such case" [B]—such as the deed of acknowledgement of Ravina. Rava lived prior to the second Ravina, and could not refer to him. It is possible that Rava did not state the words "in any such case," but rather mentioned a specific case, and Rav Natan b. Ami added "in any such case" in his response to Ravina.
79. See too Tosafot, Sanh 3a, s.v. *lerava.*
80. See *Yad rama"h, Hiddushei hara"n* and *Shita mequbetset* (in the name of "*Hashita*") to Ket 22a.
81. Contemporaries of Rav Ashi did not always rule in accord with him. See Shab 129a: "Ravina said to Mereimar: Mar Zutra rules leniently and Rav Ashi rules strictly; with whom does the law accord? He said to him: The law accords with Mar Zutra." (But cf. Yev 25b: "Rav Zuti at the school of Rav Pappi taught in accord with the one [Rav Ashi] who says, 'If one married her, he need not divorce her.'" However, unattributed cases of "the law is (*vehilkheta*)" generally accord with Rav Ashi. (See Qid 79b, "The law is in accord with Rav"; BB 41a: "The law is that we do not concern ourselves with this"; and see too Men 34a, and Tosafot, BM 67b, s.v. *ravina.*)
82. "Rabbana" appears in Geonic sources as a title even for sages who were not exilarchs. See *Seder tannaim ve'amoraim,* section A: "Rabbana Sama b. Rabbana Yehudah." And see *Epistle of Rav Sherira Gaon,* ed. Lewin, p. 2: "Rabbana Sherira"; p. 95: "Rabbana Avina b. Rav Huna"; pp. 96–98: "Rabbana Amemar b. Mar Yanuka," "Rabbana Samma b. Rabbana Yehudai"; p. 117: "Rabbana Saadia." And see *Seder rav amram gaon,* ed. D. Hedegard (Lund: Lindstedt, 1951), 2: "Rabenu Yaakov b. Rabbana Yitshaq." See too *Responsa of R. Natronai Gaon, Yore de'ah,* #157: "My teachers Rabbana Natan and Rabbana Yehudah." And see Aha of Shabha Gaon, *She'iltot,* #1 and #125: "Moshe Rabbana."
83. See, e.g., *MM,* Bava Batra, 256–57. In *MM,* Rosh Hashanah, 380 n. 2, I noted that "I" or "We" does not necessarily mean that the tradent is the author of the dictum. The tradent could be quoting the dictum from earlier authorities. Thus there is no evidence from, e.g., Rav Ashi's dictum in Hul 2b, stating "*I* have a difficulty with..." (See Tosafot, s.v. *ana*), that Rav Ashi was the editor of the Talmud. On the contrary, because the objection was already extant in the time of Rava and Abaye, the "I" simply indicates that Rav Ashi quoted the same objection articulated by Rava and Abaye. See Mahara"m, ad loc.
84. It is important to note that there is a substantive difference between traditional explanations and those proposed by critical study. Traditional explanations eliminate difficulties pertaining to the Talmud itself and attribute them to the reader's insufficient understanding: if only one understood the passage correctly, there would be no difficulty. Critical study, on the other hand, leaves the difficulties intact—the passage is difficult and problematic—but inquires after the historical developments that, over the course of time, produced textual difficulties. Moreover, traditional study denies the existence of contradictions and

forced explanations in the Talmud (with the exception of a few "contradictory sugyot" and suchlike), whereas the raison d'être of critical study is to explain how difficulties originated. Traditional study assumes that the transmission of Talmudic tradition was accurate and reliable from early times, from the beginning of the Amoraic era, and also subjected to a comprehensive and thorough editing by Ravina and Rav Ashi. Critical study, however, assumes that throughout the Tannaitic and Amoraic eras dialectical argumentation was not passed down as part of the official transmission and that it consequently remained in a fragmentary state lacking order and authority. This situation continued until the Stammaim reconstructed the argumentation and transmitted it to future generations—however, they did not subject it to a comprehensive editing that removed all contradictions. Because the Stammaim were not contemporaries of the Amoraim but flourished centuries thereafter, they sometimes lacked comprehensive information of the textual changes and other transformations that impacted the text under discussion. Without this knowledge they could only reconstruct the sugya by resorting to forced explanations and problematic reasoning. Disjointed ordering of traditions was also caused by the fact that in some cases the Stammaim did not finish reconstructing the sugya, and then, near the time of the closing of the Talmud, the "Compilers" amalgamated the parts in their current state.

85. Recently David Goodblatt and I. Gafni disputed this issue: see David Goodblatt, "New Developments in the Investigation of the Babylonian Yeshivot," *Zion* 46 (1981), 13–38 (Hebrew).**
86. I am not referring here to the "assembly months (*yarhei kallah*)" that took place at set times, at which the Talmud implies that a great multitude was present, and not only professional students.
87. Amoraim were dispersed among different villages, whereas the Geonim were concentrated in two cities, Sura and Pumbedita.
88. See Epstein, *Mevo'ot lesifrut hatannaim,* 200 ff.
89. In BB 79b Rava states (according to some manuscript variants) of the anonymous mishnah, "He who sold a cistern has sold its water" (mBB 5:3), that "It is an individual opinion, and we do not hold by it." He evidently rules in this way because it is the opinion of R. Natan, and the disputant of R. Natan is often R. Yehudah HaNasi, and R. Yehudah HaNasi disagrees with him here too—and Rava rules according to R. Yehudah HaNasi even where R. Yehudah HaNasi disputes an anonymous mishnah. This explanation is preferable than to suggest that Rava ruled according to the anonymous baraita against the anonymous mishnah.
90. See *MM*, Bava Metsia, 148.
91. The simple meaning of this passage is that R. Yehudah HaNasi rendered the opinion in the words of "the Sages," and not, as Albeck claims "that the Reciters who taught laws (prior to R. Yehudah HaNasi) ruled in this way, and R. Yehudah

HaNasi then formulated the anonymous opinion in accord with their ruling" (Hanokh Albeck, *Mavo lamishnah* [Jerusalem: Bialik, and Tel Aviv: Dvir, 1959], 276). Cf. ySot 3:6, 19b: "He said to him, 'R. Yehudah HaNasi agreed with the view of R. Eleazar b. R. Shimon etc.'" Similarly, on p. 275 Albeck attempts to prove his case from mGit 5:6: "If he purchased it from the husband and then purchased it from the wife, the transaction is void," to which the Talmud states, "R. Yehudah HaNasi formulated the anonymous opinion . . . in accord with R. Yehudah" (Ket 95a), even though the end of mGit 5:6 states explicitly, "This was the earlier mishnah." Albeck concludes, "Behold we have an ancient mishnah that was not formulated anonymously by R. Yehudah HaNasi." However, I seriously doubt whether the phrase "This was the earlier mishnah" refers to the clause, "If he purchased it from the husband," and not to the clause, "If he purchased it from the *siqariqon*," since the continuation of that clause is, "A later court stated: If he purchased from the *siqariqon* . . . " and it is to that datum about the later court that the phrase "This was the earlier mishnah" relates.

92. The Stammaim, especially later Stammaim—unlike the Amoraim, and especially the early Amoraim—are reluctant to say that the editor of the Mishnah altered the language of his sources.
93. I retract my comments on this issue stated in the Introduction to *MM*: *shabbat*, 22. See too my article, "Mishnas which Were Changed from Their Original Forms [*Mishnot shezazu mimqoman*]," *Sidra* 5 (1989), 63–88.
94. See Shevu 4a; and *MM*, Qiddushin, 544.
95. See *MM*, Gittin, 570.
96. This is not the place to address at length the issue of the differences between the language of the Mishnah as opposed to baraitot. Let me note only this difference, that when a sage adduces a mishnah in abbreviated form, he knew the mishnah in its entirely. (For example, the term "It was stated above [*amar mar*]"; literally, "the master stated," when referring to a mishnah, quotes only a portion of that mishnah; see Epstein, *MLH*, 904 ff.) However, in some cases a sage who adduces a portion of a baraita did not know more of the baraita than what he quotes. I mentioned a good example above, Naz 3a, where the Stam claims that R. Eleazar HaKappar holds that a Nazirite is called a "sinner" only when he has become impure, but a pure Nazirite is not called a sinner. The Stam evidently did not know the continuation of R. Eleazar HaKappar's statement that the Nazirite is called a sinner because "he deprived himself of wine," which includes the pure Nazirite. Parts of baraitot were sometimes taught separately (I noted this on several occasions; see the indices to *MM*, s.v. *baraita*), and students sometimes knew only a part of a baraita but not the entire source. In BB 79a the original baraita contained two laws pertaining to trespass (*me'ilah*): the first clause states "one does not trespass" and the last clause states "one trespasses," and the disputing opinion "reverses" and holds that the first clause should state "one trespasses" and the last clause "one does not trespass." Apparently over the

course of time the first part of the baraita became separated from the latter part, and the disputing opinion was taught not in terms of "reverses" but as "R. So-and-so rules: one trespasses." As a result, one Amora proffered an interpretation to which another Amora objected based on the complete baraita. The complete baraita originally read: "If he dedicated them empty, and they were subsequently filled, the law of trespass applies to them but not to their contents. If he dedicated them filled, the law of trespass applies to them and to their contents. R. Eleazar b. R. Shimon reverses [the rule]." Later the first part became separate, and R. Eleazar b. R. Shimon's opinion was formulated as "The law of trespass also applies to their contents" rather than as "reverses [the rule]." Rabbah knew this version, and therefore he stated that the disagreement only applied to a field and tree. Abaye then objected to him on the basis of the full baraita: "If this applies to a field and tree, why does he reverse [the ruling]?" (BB 80a). This reconstruction is more plausible than the opposite, that originally these two laws were taught independently, and Rabbah knew them in this form, and subsequently they were combined and integrated into one baraita by adding the opinion of R. Eleazar b. R. Shimon with the expression "reverses." The two laws complement one another, and it stands to reason that they were originally taught together. This version was also known to tMeil 1:19; see *MM*, Bava Batra, 149–50.

97. *MM*, Yevamot, 115.
98. *MM*, Pesahim, 377.
99. *MM*, Peshaim, 379–80. See too *MM*, Shabbat, 260–61; *MM*, Ketubot, 217 n.1. It subsequently came to my attention that the Gaon of Vilna already noted this point in *Shenot eliahu*, to yHal 1:6, 58a.
100. The distinction was perhaps transferred from BB 20b; see *MM*, ad loc.
101. This explanation is attractive when the first opinion appears as the "anonymous mishnah" which reflects the view of the editor; the editor deemed only part of the dissenting opinion worthy to include in the Mishnah, and omitted the part which he considered completely lacking in merit. However, when the first opinion of a mishnah is attributed to an individual, according to which we generally do not rule, one cannot say that the editor of the Mishnah omitted a part of the dissenting opinion because he considered it completely lacking in merit. (This is especially true when ruling against the first opinion accords with the general principle, "[In disagreements between] R. Yehudah and R. Yose, the law follows R. Yose," [Eruv 46b, and in several places in the Yerushalmi, including the end of Tractates Terumot and Niddah].) For if so, we would not know how to rule on that issue: we would not rule in accord with the first opinion, since it is an individual opinion, nor in accord with the dissenting opinion, since that part of it is not mentioned at all. Based on this reasoning, we can determine that the correct version of mMeil 3:6 is that which omits "the words of R. Yehudah" as the authority of the first opinion, which renders the

first opinion that of the "anonymous mishnah." And one can therefore claim that when R. Yose disagrees about the field and tree in BB 79a—implying that he agrees concerning the cistern and dove-cote—this implication results from the editor's decision not to include R. Yose's opinion about the cistern and dove-cote in the Mishnah, because he did not consider this opinion to have any merit. However, R. Yose originally disagreed about the cistern and dove-cote too, as is implied by R. Yehudah HaNasi's statement: "R. Yehudah's opinion is to be accepted regarding the cistern and dove-cote, and R. Yose's opinion regarding the field and tree" (baraita, BB 79a). However, the second baraita, "I do *not* accept the opinion of R. Yehudah regarding the field and tree" (also on BB 79a; a similar formulation is found in tMeil 1:19) disagrees with that first baraita. (The version of the baraita at Bets 39a, cited above, also conflicts with that found in the Tosefta; see Lieberman, *TK*, Yom Tov [= Betsah], 1008).

However, if the editor of the Mishnah utilized the general principles for adjudicating disputes between Tannaim mentioned in the Talmud, such as "[In disputes between] R. Yehudah and R. Shimon, the law follows R. Yehudah" (see the citation above), and especially the principles stated by R. Yohanan, the student of R. Yehudah HaNasi (see p. 192, where I stated that such is indeed the case, and that for this reason we do not find expressions such as "one said x and the other said y" in the Mishnah), then it is possible to make sense of the reading "these are the words of R. Yehudah" for the first opinion of mMeil 3:6. In this case we would accept the reading for the second opinion as "R. Shimon says," in place of "R. Yose says," as found in our attestations of the Mishnah. And we could explain that the editor of the Mishnah omitted the cistern and dove-cote from R. Shimon's statement because he ruled according to the principle that in disputes between R. Yehudah and R. Shimon, the law follows R. Yehudah. However, in the cases of the field and tree he gave some weight to the opinion of R. Shimon and included it as an individual opinion, whereas in the cases of the cistern and dove-cote he accorded R. Shimon's opinion no weight at all. See *MM*, Bava Batra, 150–51.

102. The Mishnah has a predilection for brevity (and perhaps it was on account of the persecutions following the Bar Kochba rebellion that they condensed the Mishnah to "a single volume" so that it would be easier to memorize, and they omitted dialectical argumentation, aggadah, and legal justifications**). Most of the laws included in the Mishnah lack justification, and the justifications included are extremely brief. The Talmud has a predilection for verbosity and rhetoric, exploits every opportunity in legal analysis, and is also rich in aggadah. Perhaps these tendencies were due to the fact that the Stammaim, from the time of the first Gaon, R. Hanan of Ashiqiyya, c. 589 CE, lived in an age of relative peace, and therefore permitted themselves to engage in dialectical argumentation at length, and to include all subjects. Well known is R. Levi's dictum in *Song of Songs Rabbah* 2:16 (ed. Vilna, 15a; on the verse *Sustain me with raisin*

cakes, refresh me with apple, Song 2:5): "In the past, when money was abundant, they would yearn to hear a teaching of Mishnah, law or Talmud; but now that money is not abundant, and especially since they are suffering from subjugation [to Rome], they only aspire to hear [words of] blessing and consolation."

103. See *MM*, Ketubot, 246; *MM*, Bava Metsia, 253 etc.

104. See, e.g., mBB 5:8: "One who sells wine or oil to his fellow. . . . [A] and [after emptying the measure] he must let three more drops drip out. [B] If he overturned it and drained it, [the drops] belong to the seller. [C] The shopkeeper is not obligated to let three more drops drip out. [D] R. Yehudah says: At twilight on the Sabbath eve he is exempt." The Talmud (BB 87a), based on a baraita, explains that R. Yehudah disagrees with the middle clause of the mishnah [C], ruling that *only* on the eve of the Sabbath is the shopkeeper exempt, but not at other times. Samuel b. Joseph Strashun (Rasha"sh), however, refers to Shevu 38a, where the Talmud objects "Why mention [the case in which] he concedes to him?; rather let him mention [the case in which] he disagrees with him." Similarly, here R. Yehudah should have mentioned the point on which he disagrees with the Sages (that the shopkeeper *is obligated* at other times), not the point on which he agrees (that the shopkeeper is exempt on the Sabbath eve).

Therefore it seem that R. Yehudah's opinion originally appeared in a baraita which was lacking this middle clause of the mishnah [C], and R. Yehudah added to the opinion of the Sages [A]. He mentioned twilight on the Sabbath eve, when one is exempt from letting drops drip out, and disagreed with the Sages on this point. In the mishnah, however, there is an additional clause about the shopkeeper [C], and so the editor should have altered R. Yehudah's dictum. But he kept the dictum exactly as it appeared in the baraita—and this produced the disjunction.

It goes without saying that the phenomenon illustrated here, that the editor of the Mishnah omitted and added phrases in the Mishnah, is not limited to cases where we find disjunction. However, it is difficult to discern the contribution of the editor in cases where disjunction is not evident.

105. See *MM*, Bava Batra, 153–54.

106. See, e.g., mGit 5:1: "A creditor is paid from land of medium quality, and the wife's *ketubah* from land of the worst quality. R. Meir says: Also (*af*) the wife's *ketubah* [is paid] from land of medium quality." Yet a baraita in Git 49b states: "The wife's *ketubah*—[is paid from] land of the worst quality—these are the words of R. Yehudah. R. Meir says: 'From land of medium quality.'" Either the editor of the Mishnah added the word "also" to R. Meir's dictum after including the case of the creditor together with the wife's *ketubah* (this seems most likely), or the editor of the baraita omitted the word "also" from R. Meir's dictum after he separated the case of the *ketubah* from the case of the creditor. Epstein, *MLH*, 1007 ff., discussed the word "also (*af*)" at length. (However, his comments on p. 1016 about this example are incorrect.)

107. I commented on this phenomenon on several occasions. Let me cite here the example from *MM*, Ketubot, 175 ff. Mishnah Ketubot 3:3 states: "A maiden who was betrothed and divorced: R. Yose the Galilean says: No fine is incurred for [seducing] her. R. Akiba states: A fine is incurred for [seducing] her, and she gets her fine." At first glance there is no reason to doubt that the phrase "and she gets her fine" was stated by R. Akiba. However, the baraitot quoted on Ket 38b demonstrate that R. Akiba stated only "A fine is incurred for [seducing] her" (in contrast to R. Yose the Galilean's ruling that no fine is incurred), and the editor of the Mishnah added "and she gets her fine," on the basis of his own opinion. The editor of one of the baraitot disputed this point and added "and her father gets her fine" on the basis of his own view. Neither ruling was stated by R. Akiba; rather both derive from the editors.

108. The comments of Solomon Edni, in his Mishnah commentary *Melekhet shlomoh* to mBer 1:3, suggest that he did not have the words "Did we not learn: 'It once happened that the elders of the House of Shammai and the elders of the House of Hillel went to visit R. Yohanan HaHorani'" in his version of the Yerushalmi. See too the commentary of the *Pnei moshe* to ySuk 2:8, 53b.

109. See my article "Mishnas which Were Changed from Their Original Forms," 63.

110. The editor of the Mishnah could have disclosed that R. Yehudah also disagrees over "an equal measure" without adding words to the first opinion. He could have formulated the disagreement without specifying a quantity, e.g., "He who makes wine from grape-skins is exempt [from tithing it]. And R. Yehudah declares him liable," and we ourselves would realize that the first opinion exempts even a quantity greater than "an equal measure," and R. Yehudah obligates "an equal measure." Or he could have added to the words of R. Yehudah, "even for 'an equal measure'" (i.e., "He who makes wine from grape-skins is exempt [from tithing it]. And R. Yehudah declares him liable even for 'an equal measure'"), and we would understand that the first opinion also exempts a quantity greater than "an equal measure." Because the editor of the Mishnah did not formulate the dispute in this way, it stands to reason that his purpose was not to "inform you of the extent of R. Yehudah's [opinion]."

111. David Weiss Halivni, "Shehayah rabbi ploni omer bamishnah uvabaraita," *HUCA* 31 (1960), 15–22.

112. However, in Shab 133a the question about the redundancy is not directed to the Mishnah, as the mishnahs deal with different laws; Shab 133a deals with circumcision and Pes 61a concerns Passover. Rather, the objection is against the dictum of Rav quoted by Rav Yehudah, as noted by Tosafot, ad loc., s.v. *utsrikha*, who bring proof from Men 96a, where it also says, "R. Akiba stated a general rule," and yet there too the Talmud does not object, "Why do I need this?" Therefore the Talmud in Shab 133a answers, "It is necessary" (i.e., that Rav Yehudah quoting Rav had to say it twice). However, in Sanh 36b the question

pertains to the Mishnah itself, concerning the ruling there and repeated in Nid 49b, and therefore the question is phrased with the term "We learned on another occasion." However, Tosafot, ad loc, s.v. *tanina*, claim that there too the objection cannot be directed against the Mishnah.

113. *MM*, Ketubot, 183 n. 6. I was uncertain whether the Talmud's explanation that the clause of mKet 4:1 ("The seduced maiden . . .") was connected to the second clause ("If she stood in judgment . . .") is correct (Ket 42a–b). Let me also note that R. Shimon and the Sages disagree there over the case of "if she stood in judgment," and they both belong to the school of R. Akiba.

114. In Sanh 20b the language of the Mishnah is almost identical in both places (mSanh 1:5, mSanh 2:4), and there too the Talmud objects, "We learned on another occasion." However, in this case the repetition informs us that it is the king who initiates a discretionary war; the first mishnah (mSanh 1:5) does not make it clear who initiates this war. Now one could say that the second mishnah would have sufficed in and of itself, and there is no need for the first mishnah. But perhaps the first mishnah teaches that if there is no king, then the Sanhedrin of 71 alone can initiate a discretionary war.

115. The Yersuhalmi, however, does not ask this type of question; see *MM*, Shabbat, 75.

116. See Tosafot, Pes 83b, s.v. *rabbi shimon*, and the marginal references there.

117. Now there are cases of "R. So-and-so states . . ." that do not appear within disputes. See the list in *Tosafot yom tov* to mBik 3:5 (although some of these are debatable). However, the vast majority appear within disputes. Indeed, the early Amoraim (Eruv 82b, Sanh 24b–25a) disagree whether Tannaitic dicta introduced by the words "In what circumstances?" and "When?" disagree with the previous dictum or explicate it. This implies that when a dictum is not introduced by these terms that it disputes the previous statement. See the comment of *Tiferet yisrael* (near the end of Mishnah Arakhin, "This implies that the general principle of earlier authorities is not accurate, namely that wherever we find in the Talmud 'R. So-and-so states' he disagrees with the previous opinion, and wherever we find 'Said R. So-and-so (*amar rabbi ploni*)' he does not disagree." And see above, p. 107, on the term "The entire mishnah is [the opinion of] R. So-and-so."

118. See p. 47, Part I, "Combination of Different Opinions into a Dispute."

119. Because there are no extant Amoraic Mishnah or baraitot, and the (apodictic) Amoraic dicta were not transmitted by way of an editor, these dicta at first glance would appear to be more reliable than the Mishnah. But this is not necessarily the case. When Amoraic dicta were combined into dispute forms, such as "It was stated (*itmar*)" and two attributed opinions quoted, the dissenting opinion was abbreviated. The process of abbreviation involves a type of editing. See below, p. 133 on "transmitters."

120. The plague struck at the beginning of the sixth century, which was the beginning of the Saboraic period according to Sherira Gaon, and coincided—

according to his view—with the end of the Amoraic period. (The plague is attested in non-Jewish sources; see Procopius, *History of the Wars*, 2:22–33. I am grateful to my student Jeffrey L. Rubenstein for bringing this source to my attention.)

121. See above, Part I nn. 15, 17.

122. I retract that which I stated in the Introductions to *MM: yoma–hagigah*, 7, and *MM*: *shabbat*, 17.

123. In this respect too the Talmud differs from the Mishnah. The Compilers of Stammaitic traditions (below, p. 156) lived in an age when it was no longer possible to add to the Talmud, and certainly not to change it. However, the compiler of the Mishnah (who was, apparently, the editor) sometimes changed earlier mishnahs, even if it is also true that "the mishnah was not changed from its original form (*mishnah lo zazah mimqomah*"; see above, p. 108.)

124. I explained the passage, "*Talmud*—there is no [occupation] more meritorious than this. One should always run to Mishnah more than to Talmud (BM 33a)," as follows (*MM*, Bava Metsia, 113): that the Mishnah contains both biblical verses and law, and the Talmud contains biblical verses, law, and also dialectical argumentation; therefore, nothing is more meritorious than the study of Talmud. "But for practical reasons they stated, 'One should always run to Mishnah more than to Talmud,' since Mishnaic tradition is more reliable than Talmudic tradition. And R. Yohanan added (in BM 33a): 'This teaching was taught in the days of R. Yehudah HaNasi,' because his Mishnah alone was so reliable that its study was considered more meritorious than Talmud study, even though Talmudic tradition is richer.** However, this does not apply to mishnah-collections other than that of R. Yehudah HaNasi." Later generations knew the sources of the traditions contained in "Our Mishnah," and it was still possible to identify them. Even if in some cases the original language of the sources had been changed, in most cases sources were transmitted as they were received. In Talmudic times, on the other hand, even in the period of the baraitot, they had no direct tradition of the dialectical argumentation, which was reconstructed in the rabbinic academies and depended to a great extent on conjecture. The Mishnah is therefore more faithful to its sources than the Talmud. See too *MM*, Shabbat, 22–25.

125. See Tosafot, Shab 131b, s.v. *i*: "In some cases [the Talmud] makes this inference, in other cases it does not make this inference"; Tosafot, Shevu 5a, s.v. *bishevu'ot*: "In some cases the Talmud does not state this." See too Tosafot, Ber 22b, s.v. *venehzei*: "In many places the Talmud does not object in this way," and Tosafot, Shab 12b, s.v. *rabbi*: (I am grateful to my son Ephraim Betsalel for this reference.)

126. See the Responsa of the Rashb"a, vol. 2, #403. This is perhaps related to "He taught [some matters] and omitted [others]." See Shabtai Hakohen (c. 1621–1663), *Nequdot hakesef* to Yoreh Deah, #133.

127. *Halikhot olam*, beginning of Section 3. However, Joseph Karo in his *Kelalei hagemara*, ad loc., disagrees and claims: "In my opinion there are contradictory views in BQ 63a; when the Talmud has an answer, it asks this question (i.e., 'All—what does this add?'), and when it has no answer it adopts the alternative interpretation (that 'All' introduces a general principle)." The author of *Yavin shemuah*, ad loc, noted that there is no contradiction between the two alternative interpretations in that passage as to whether "All" is to be expounded or not.

128. See BQ 43b, "Perhaps he taught [some matters] and omitted [others]," and in BQ 62b the Talmud does not ask, "What [else] did he omit [besides] this omission?," whereas in 10a and 16a it asks. Nor does the Talmud ask in Qid 49a and Mak 21b. See the marginal references provided on Suk 54a. See too Yev 73b, and cf. *Halikhot olam*, Section 3, chapter 2: "In all places that it states, 'He taught [some matters] and omitted [others],' it is asked: 'What [else] did he omit [besides] this omission?'" It is worth noting that some medieval commentators consider "He taught [some matters] and omitted [others]" to be a "forced explanation," and they do not attend to whether the Tanna omitted an additional item or not. See Rava"d, in *Shita mequbetset* to BQ 15a; Rashb"a ad loc. and in *Shita mequbetset* to Ket 46b; Nahmanides to the first chapter of Qiddushin, cited in Joseph Karo, *Kelalei hagemara*, ad loc.

129. See p. 17.

130. See Tosafot, MQ 22b, s.v. *ulesimhat*; and Tosafot, Bekh 31b, s.v. *im ken*, etc.

131. I commented on this issue on many occasions. See *MM*, Shabbat, 354 and Bava Batra, 224.

132. There is a respectable number of contradictions in the Mishnah, such as the contradiction between mSuk 5:4, "When they arrived at the tenth step, they sounded a lengthy blast, and a quavering blast, and a lengthy blast," and mSuk 5:5, "[They sounded] three blasts at the altar." For tSuk 4:10 states explicitly: "The one who says [that they sounded blasts] 'at the altar' does not say [that they sounded blasts] 'on the tenth step'; the one who says [that they sounded blasts] 'on the tenth step' does not say [that they sounded blasts] 'at the altar'"; this dispute is between R. Eleazar b. Yaakov and the Sages. This Toseftan passage is quoted in Suk 54a and ySuk 5:6, 55c. See my article, "Mishnas which Were Changed from their Original Forms," 87.

133. Rashb"a and Ritb"a, to BQ 102a, s.v. *ela*. In my article mentioned in the previous note I suggested reversing the hierarchy, such that an anonymous opinion that follows a dispute between an anonymous and an individual opinion is *less* authoritative than an anonymous opinion without any dissenting opinion, because an anonymous mishnah that lacks any dissenting individual opinion is more authoritative than an anonymous mishnah that includes a dissenting individual opinion. See too Tosafot, Bes 2b, s.v. *gabei*.

134. See my article, "Mishnas which Were Changed from Their Original Forms."

PART III

1. In the earlier generations "Their minds were great and they only needed [to learn] the basic principles." However, the situation changed in Amoraic times such that "Their minds became weak, and they had to collect their [various versions of] Talmud, and to recite them, and to add other methods to understand their learning and to memorize it and they included . . . the explanation of difficult matters, regarding which the earlier ones, whose minds were great, did not need explanations" (*Epistle of Rav Sherira Gaon*, 52).** I disagree with this view, as will be seen below. See too Menahem Meiri, "Introduction" to Tractate Avot, the section on R. Hananel.
2. The consensus of scholars since Leopold Zunz, *Die Gottesdienstlichen Vorträge Der Juden, Historisch Entwickelt* (reprint; Hildesheim: G. Olms, 1966 [1832]), 45–53, places the editing of the halakhic midrashim in the middle of the third century CE. Similarly, Saul Lieberman claims that the editing of *Sifre* to Deuteronomy took place in the middle of the third century CE (See "Roman Legal Institutions in Early Rabbinics and in the Acta Martyrum," *JQR* 35 [1944–45], 27 n. 173.) I am inclined to believe that the editing was later; I hope to return to this issue in a future publication.
3. See *Midrash, Mishnah, and Gemara*, chapter 3.
4. Legal cases (*uvdot*) were also not conveyed to the official transmitters. Accordingly several Talmudic passages claim, "This [ruling] was not said explicitly but on the basis of an inference" and continue with the expression, "He who saw [the event] thought"—he who was present at the time of the event transmitted the legal case. See the Introduction to *MM: bava metsia*, 24.
5. See *MM*, Eruvin, 91 ff. Perhaps the Talmud refers to this distinction between apodictic and dialectical argumentation when it states, "Some formulate this [objection] in the form of a contradiction (*ve'ika deramei lahu mirma*)." Now the alternative formulation of the objection preceding the "Some formulate . . ." version also involves a contradiction, which is introduced by "and it was taught." However in this version the Amoraic statement is an apodictic dictum, while in the "Some formulate . . ." version, which employs the term "there is no difficulty," it is in the form of dialectical argumentation. (Instantiations of "Some formulate this [objection] in the form of a contradiction" are listed in the marginal gloss of Akiba Eger to RH 27b, though he omits Ket 27a [note that in the second version there, which includes the expression "some formulate this (objection) in the form of a contradiction," Rava is not mentioned at all, so how did he come to be quoted in the first version?]; BQ 16a [twice; the first case requires further study], and Arakh 27b. On the various types of "Some formulate this [objection] in the form of a contradiction," see *MM*, Bava Batra, 16).
6. "And thus it received all the qualities and characteristics of writing"; Lieberman, "The Publication of the Mishnah," *Hellenism in Jewish Palestine*, 88.

7. Perhaps this explains why dialectical argumentation contains so much rhetoric (explanations, responses, and objections with obvious answers). These suggestions are advanced not as real possibilities, but only to enhance the interchange.
8. See *MM*, Bava Metsia, 22.
9. See the indices to *MM*, s.v. *meimrot.*
10. Shab 54a, Ket 11b, Nid 58b are examples of a different phenomenon.
11. See the Introduction to *MM: bava qamma,* 14, and below, p. 120.
12. See Rashi, Nid 29a, s.v. *be'anpei*. Cf. Rashi, Nid 58b.
13. See BB 130b, and Rashba"m ad loc., and yPeah 2:2, 17a.
14. See too Ber 9a, Men 5b.
15. According to Judah b. Barzillai, *Sefer ha'ittim* (Berlin: Y. Fisher, 1903), 2:267, Natronai b. Hakhinai Gaon was the first to have written down the Talmud on behalf of the Kairouan community.** If this dating of the writing of the Talmud is correct, and if he was permitted to write it down (see, e.g., Git 60b) because it was too vast to commit to memory, in particular on account of the growth of dialectical argumentation in later generations (apodictic material is easier to remember)—this provides additional evidence that the Talmud was not completed in the sixth century CE. Were it already complete at that time, it ought to have been written down close to the end of the Amoraic period. Yet Natronai Gaon was a student of Yehudai Gaon, who was among the last Saboraim, those who lived at the end of the Stammaitic period.
16. Nevertheless, the reconstructed material of the Stammaim can be graded hierarchically according to its character: (1) When the dialectical argumentation is completely anonymous and it functions as an explanation of a mishnah or baraita or Amoraic dictum, then the Stammaim had no tradition (or fragmentary tradition) whatsoever of the original dialectical argumentation—it is all reconstructed. (2) When an Amora is mentioned in the sugya—typically at its end—and states, for example, "When is this the case...?," and his words can be related directly to the mishnah, baraita, or Amoraic dictum that he is explaining—in such a case the explanation indeed derives from Amoraic tradition, but the reasoning derives from the Stammaim. (3) However, when the Amoraic dictum cannot be related to the source that it ostensibly explains except by means of the Stammaitic dialectical argumentation—then we have to say that the Stammaim reconstructed the sugya including the sources to which the Amora purportedly relates. For example, in BB 97a, Rav Pappa's statement, "[This is a case] of a cow which drank [the mixes] one after another" can only be related to R. Yohanan's statement, "[The same rules] that they stated about prohibitions apply to the issue of rendering fit [for receiving impurity]," by means of the Stammaitic interchange that follows R. Yohanan's statement ("It [R. Yohanan's dictum] is necessary for a case when it became a mixture [*tamad*] in and of itself," and as a response to the objection against this solution). Now seeing as an Amora never relates to a

Stammaitic passage, we must say that here the Stammaim lacked the complete sources to which the Amora related, and they utilized dialectical argumentation to reconstruct them. This awareness accounts for almost all the places in the Talmud where an Amora seems to relate to the Stammaitic stratum; originally the Amora was not relating to the Stammaitic stratum, and the juxtaposition is simply a product of the unattributed supplement added by the Stammaim who dialectically debated the issue—and they lived long after the Amora.

17. See Qid 64a: "Rav Ashi said: Do you really think that . . . ?" Even the authority who stated above, "The first clause is a case when it is in his power, the latter clause is a case when it is not in his power" could not think otherwise, as "It is obvious." And see p. 13.
18. Rashb"a and other commentaries claim that the "Subsequently. . . . said [O]" refers to Rav Ashi, in line with the "Others say Rav Ashi" version. However, this suggestion is forced and moreover, if correct, then it could be proven that the more authentic tradition is the attribution to Rav Ashi (i.e., the "Others say Rav Ashi" rather than the "Rava said"). But there are no cases where the "What I said was not a [valid] statement" does not pertain to that same Amora. According to the "Others say Rav Ashi" tradition, the passage should have stated, "Rav Ashi stated: The first act of intercourse [with the woman widowed after her betrothal] is [prohibited as] a preventative measure . . ." (at [M]).
19. Similarly, I wrote in *MM*, Pesahim, 400, that "In Pes 44b ff., it is possible that the names of Abaye and 'a certain sage' were subsequently omitted because of the objection raised in Naz 37a." In this way an Amoraic dictum was turned into an anonymous passage, and it appears as if the Amoraim relate to the Stammaitic stratum—but this is not the case.
20. However, some interpreters hold that the Talmud's objection, "If so, [all negative commandments] throughout the entire Torah, can be considered both positive and negative commandments, as it is written, *You shall sanctify yourselves (Lev 11:44)*" [J], contradicts Rava's first answer [H], and that we are dealing with confusion between two verses, between *You shall sanctify yourselves (Lev 11:44)* and *You shall be holy (Lev 19:2)*.
21. Perhaps the original objection to Rava's first response [H], was that the verse, *They shall be holy to their God (Lev 21:6)* [I], only pertains to the context of that biblical passage (about impurity), which does not contain the prohibition of the high priest marrying a widow, as the medieval commentators suggest here and at BM 30a.
22. It is likely that the dialectical argumentation originally was longer than that which is quoted in the Talmud here, and included the reasons that Rava "answered it"; however, these discussions were omitted and replaced by the response to the objection, "That is the same [principle]."
23. Epstein, *MLH*, 688, including references to the primary sources, which all derive from the Geonic period after the Talmud was written down (his reference

to the *She'iltot* does not appear in the manuscripts). See too Lieberman, "The Publication of the Mishnah," 88: "A regular oral *ekdosis*, edition, of the *Mishnah* was in existence, a fixed text recited by the *Tannaim* of the college"; and see Y. Sussman, "Manuscripts and Text Traditions of the Mishnah," *Proceedings of the Seventh World Congress of Jewish Studies*, vol. 3, *Studies in Talmud, Halakha and Midrash* (Jerusalem: World Union of Jewish Studies, 1981), 238 n. 9 (Hebrew): "The main function of the Reciters in the Babylonian Geonic academies was the accurate and authenticated preservation and transmission of the text of the Mishnah."

24. The analogous Tannaitic expression is "In what circumstances? (*bameh devarim amurim*)," or "When? (*eimatai*)." An exception appears in Git 18a: "R. Eleazar b. R. Tsadoq said: This only applies when they are not busy..."
25. *MM*, Pesahim, 3.
26. Cf. Lieberman, "The Publication of the Mishnah," *Hellenism in Jewish Palestine*, 97: "Such *Tannaim* did not incorporate their short notes in the body of the *Mishnah*, they only added it as a kind of oral marks."
27. However, the continuation of the passage is clearly Stammaitic; see Rashi, Yev 59b, s.v., *hi hanotenet*: "The editor of the Talmud..."
28. See Hag 22b: "You recalled to me Rabbah b. Avuah's statement."
29. Similarly, Yom 69b, "Rav—and some say R. Yohanan—said: Alas, alas, is he (the evil inclination) who destroyed the temple and burned the sanctuary..." This is probably the formulation of Rav and not R. Yohanan. Taan 14b: "R. Zeira—and some say R. Shmuel b. Nahmani—objected to him: If it had said, 'Joshua'...."—this formulation was not from R. Shmuel b. Nahmani.
30. According to Halevy, *Dorot harishonim*, 2:69 ff., the term "it was taught in a *matnita*" does not introduce an authentic baraita, but rather an Amoraic explanation attached to Tannaitic sources. However, his evidence is wholly without basis. His proof on p. 138 from Pes 110b—"Ulla, according to his reason," which implies that the passage is Amoraic—does not appear in the manuscripts; Halevy ought to have consulted *Diqduqei soferim* (for reasons that are unclear to me, he never cites *Diqduqei soferim*). On p. 142 he expresses surprise at the Talmud's proof on Yev 24b, based on the baraita stating "R. Yehudah HaNasi says: Since...," that the sages disagree with R. Yehudah HaNasi and that Rav holds in accord with the Sages. He comments, "This is very strange, as the Talmud never explicitly states that the Sages disagree with R. Yehudah HaNasi." Yet the Talmud and the medieval commentaries often assume that when a passage quotes an individual opinion, the majority disagree. See, e.g., Nid 52b: "These are the words of R. Shimon b. Yehudah." The Talmud then asks, "And the Sages? (i.e., what is the opinion of the Sages who disagree with him?) Rav Hisda said...." And sometimes the Talmud quotes an individual opinion and then asks, "Do the Sages disagree with him or not disagree?" The Talmud asks this question when it has evidence, or it thinks it has evidence, for one side or

the other. See too, for example, Tosafot, Shab 4a, s.v. *aval lemata*: "Since R. Zeira stated: 'Whose opinion is this? It is the opinion of "The Others,"' this implies that the Sages disagree with him." I discuss this issue at length in *MM*, Shabbat, 302 n. 2, and see the references there. I have already rejected Halevy's claim on p. 144 based on BQ 82a in *MM*, Bava Qamma, ad loc., and below, p. 147. His statement on p. 123, "Because Bar Qappara is not mentioned in the Yerushalmi (at the beginning of *Ketubot*)"—is incomprehensible, as twice it says there "As Bar Qappara taught."

I have gone into detail to reject Halevy's evidence regarding the term *matnita*, because it is a component of his general view that the early Amoraim such as R. Hiyya, R. Oshaya, and Levi did not compose baraitot, and when the Talmud utilizes the verb "taught (*tanna*)" with respect to their activity, it refers to explanations that accompany baraitot. (As to Levi, let me observe in passing that of him alone the Talmud says in eight passages, "Levi said, and thus Levi taught in his *matnita*.") I disagree with this; early Amoraim too composed and taught baraitot; however, apart from the Tosefta, these baraita-collections were not transmitted to succeeding generations by the transmitters, the Reciters. But unlike the dialectical argumentation—which was also not passed down by transmitters—these baraitot were not reconstructed by the Stammaim who lived long thereafter in Babylonia, and therefore in Stammaitic times only fragments of them survived. The Talmud states of these baraitot: "Any baraita that was not taught in the school of R. Hiyya and R. Oshaya is unreliable, and one does not adduce it for refutations in the house of study" (Hul 141a). Elsewhere the Talmud states of this type of baraita: "Who can assure us that it is reliable? Perhaps it is corrupt!" (Pes 99b, Shab 121b). However, Amoraim sometimes state: "If it was taught, so it was taught." That is, the Amora did not know the baraita beforehand, and had he known it, he would not have stated his dictum. See especially Zev 96b: "If I found a Tannaitic teaching (*matnita*)." And see *Shita mequbetset* to Zev 15b: "If it was taught, so it was taught—and I will retract." This is apparently said of the baraitot of R. Hiyya and R. Oshaya too (in Hag 19a–b, the expression "If it was taught, so it was taught" refers to a baraita found in tMikv 3:4). Nevertheless, it was still easier to memorize baraitot—even the unreliable ones—than dialectical argumentation, and therefore they were better known.

31. However, see Tosafot, MQ 5a, s.v. *la'atoyei*: "If so, then the one who made this objection was not well versed in the Mishnah and did not know..." And see pseudo-Rashi, Naz 63a: "Rami b. Hami, to whom this question was posed, did not know this Mishnah." Cf. Epstein, *MLH*, 771–76: "The Proficiency of the Amoraim in the Mishnah."
32. See H. Albeck, *Mehqarim biveraita uvetosefta* (Jerusalem: Rav Kook, 1944), 137.
33. Shab 19b, and the marginal references. And see n. 31 above.
34. See too S. Emmanuel, "Teshuvot hai gaon: al tannaim ve'amoraim biyeshivot hageonim," *Tarbiz* 69 (2000), 115, "We have two explicit testimonies that the

Reciters (*tannaim*) also recited the Talmud," and N. Danzig, "From Oral Talmud to Written Talmud: On the Methods of Transmission of the Babylonian Talmud and Its Study in the Middle Ages," *Bar-Ilan Annual* 30–31 (2006), 85 ff. (Hebrew). This evidence, however, derives from the post-Talmudic Geonim.

35. Rashi comments: "Avin was always in R. Yohanan's presence. If R. Yohanan retracted... Avin would hear and retract too." It seems that this was stated by Rava, not the anonymous Talmud. However, I doubt whether the continuation is from Rava: "Moreover, it might be said that that they disagree only about circumcision. Do they [also] disagree about marriage?" Because if it is from Rava, then we have to say that Rava did not know the baraita quoted in that same passage, "If a woman married one husband who died...," which was known to Avimi of Hagronia in the name of Rav Huna. (The ensuing passage, "Rav Yosef son of Rava said to Rava...," and the discussion of the dispute between R. Yehudah HaNasi and Rabban Shimon b. Gamaliel in the baraita could have been stated after Rava's interlocutor responded to him, "Yes, thus it was taught," as Rava had not known the dispute before this interchange.) In addition, who responded to Rava, "Yes, thus it was taught"? For it is not stated that Rava addressed another sage who could be the respondent.
36. See Part I, n. 114.
37. In that same Introduction I define these terms at length.
38. In Sanh 31b the statement of R. Yohanan was truncated such that all that the Editor-Stammaim knew of his statement was: "And R. Yohanan says: He indeed holds like R. Shimon"—but no more. They subsequently added to his words, "as Rav Himnuna said...," although Rav Himnuna postdated R. Yohanan. Accordingly, Rava's statement, "This can also be inferred..." must be based on Rav Himnuna's dictum rather than that of R. Yohanan.
39. On the "combiners," see above, p. 47.
40. On p. 157, I attribute to this period the terms "It is also taught thus (*tanya namei hakhi*)" and "There is a teaching that accords with him (*tanya kevateih*)" that appear together with Amoraic disputes in cases where the Talmud does not raise objections from these baraitot against the Amoraim.
41. As is well known, the Yerushalmi does not go to great lengths to reconcile an Amoraic dictum with a contradictory baraita, and sometimes allows the conflict to remain. It is possible that this was also the policy of the Babylonian Amoraim, and it was the Stammaim who later insisted that Amoraic dicta must be reconciled with baraitot, even if this could only be accomplished in a forced manner.
42. See Yom 43b; on R. Yohanan, see Tosafot, Ket 8a, s.v. *rav*.
43. This is also Rashi's point, ad loc., s.v. *sham*. The question of Halevy, *Dorot harishonim*, 2:144, is out of place: "If so, what is the difference between the anonymous Talmud and the statement of R. Geviha of Be Katil that follows." See too *MM*, Bava Qamma, 306.
44. See *MM*, Eruvin, 91 ff.

45. In this case they were uncertain as to whether the sage heard the dictum directly from the Reciters, as opposed to the term, "This was not stated explicitly but on the basis of an inference," which indicates that they were certain that the dictum had not been stated explicitly. Sometimes the Stammaim use this term (Rav Pappa regularly employs it), as they apparently had a tradition that the dictum was based on an inference, despite its having been passed down as a fixed ruling, the standard form of the Reciters.
46. See *Tosafot yeshanim*, Yoma 57b, s.v. *de'itmar*.
47. In the Introduction to *MM: bava qamma*, 14 ff., I classified these Stammaitic interventions in four categories, namely, "expansion (*harhavah*), supplement (*hosafah*), completion (*hashlamah*), and alteration (*shinui*)," and provided examples of each. Here, I concentrate more on the method of reconstruction rather than its typology. Clearly my analysis there sheds light on this discussion.
48. On the "phenomenon of the Stammaim intervening in the middle of the statement of an Amora and adding an explanation in his own style," see *MM*, Pesahim, 477–80.
49. See the Introduction to *MM: shabbat*, 6 ff.
50. See *MM*, Pesahim, 477 n. 11*.
51. The reverse occurs too; see, e.g., Rashi, Sanhedrin 36a, s.v, *haniha*: "The conclusion is the words of Rava." Rashi seems to have inferred from Rava's dictum below, "not only according to the one who says...," that the statement "this is well" in this case is not part of the anonymous stratum. But this conclusion does not necessarily follow, as one could argue that the statement "not only according to the one who says..." too is anonymous.
52. See p. 28. Similarly, one can suggest that when an Amora says, "Thus people say (*haynu de'amrei inshei*)," and the context is not known, that the Stammaim reconstructed the context later (Suk 22b; as to Git 30b, AZ 22b, see *MM*, Pesahim, 412 n. 1). On the basis of the present analysis I should correct that which I wrote there concerning Pes 48a.)
53. See p. 27.
54. See p. 14.

PART IV

1. See p. 164. On transposition in halakhic midrashim, see Epstein, *Mevo'ot lesfirut hatannaim*, 605 ff. And see Albeck, *Mavo latalmudim*, 452–54.
2. However, expressions such as "We learned there (*tenan hatam*)" are from the Compilers (see, for example, Shev 30a "Whence do I know this? [*mina hani milei*]"). The sugya was originally found elsewhere, and these expressions inform us that it was transferred to its present location.
3. See Part I, n. 46.

4. For examples of how the term "Our mishnah is also precise" functions, see Shab 57b, where the mishnah referenced by this term is from that same chapter; in Eruv 51b, the mishnah is from the next folio; in Suk 3a, the sugya was originally connected to mSuk 2:7, which is mentioned previously. Likewise, Bets 27a first mentions mBekh 4:3 and then refers to it with "Our mishnah is also precise." So too in Zev 91a, mPes 7:3 is cited previously. Cf. AZ 10a (could RH be its original location?) And see *Diqduqei soferim* to Shevu 29b, n. *nun*.
5. But see the continuation of Tosafot's comment.
6. See Tosafot, Yev 30a, s.v. *lemai*, and BB 169b, s.v. *behazaqa*; and see *Yad Malakhi* #246.
7. The medieval commentaries sometimes ask why the Talmud did not resolve a question on the basis of an Amoraic dictum, and answer that the Talmud did not want to provide an answer from an Amoraic source (see Tosafot, Shab 72a, and the marginal glosses there). But perhaps it did not know those Amoraic dicta.
8. See, for example, Tosafot, Bets 13a, s.v. *ika*. "We never find a case of 'there are some who say' which is the opposite of the first version."
9. The objection raised by Ravin bar Nahman is actually based on mBB 7:2. See Tosafot, BB 94b., s.v. *detani*: "The reason that mishnah is not quoted...."
10. See *MM*, Bava Batra, ad loc. (p. 172 ff), where I discuss the commentaries at length.
11. See, e.g., Qid 8a: "Rav Yosef said: Whence do I know this?" and Tosafot, ad loc., s.v. *mina*: "He brings proof in accord with the first version." And see my comments in *MM*, Qiddushin, 521 n.3.
12. See Epstein, "Seridei She'iltot," *Tarbiz* 6 (1935), 460; and in his *Studies in Talmudic Literature*, 378 ff. See Robert Brody, "Sifrut hageonim vehateqst hatalmudi," *Mehqerei talmud* 1, ed. Y. Sussman and D. Rosenthal (Jerusalem: Magnes, 1990), 245 ff., on explanations found in the *She'iltot* but not in our Talmud.
13. See p. 61.
14. See Rashi, Yom 12b, s.v. *meshihatan*: "As we say in Tractate Shevuot: '[Only] *them*—[are consecrated] by anointing'"—and no other way.
15. There is also a manuscript variant in Sanh 16b and Shevu 15a that reads: "either by anointing or service" in both the exposition of *them (Num* 7:1*)* and the exposition of *will be performed (Num* 4:12*)*. These are equivalent.
16. We have already referred several times to Tosafot, BM 94a, s.v. *amar*.
17. Similarly, the identical sugyot concerning the "best quality of land" at Git 48b and BQ 6b originate in BQ 6b, because this issue of "best quality of land" is more fitting in Tractate Bava Qamma. Moreover, the sugya appears in Git 48b in the middle of the explanation of the mishnah that precedes Ravina's dictum. So too the identical sugyot in Eruv 15b, Suk 24b, and Git 21b (83b) originate, apparently, in Suk 24b, since R. Yose the Galilean's dictum appears in the proximate mishnah. See above, p. 30, on these sugyot. Hence passages that state

"We learned there" which are identical, presumably originated in the "there" context, since they begin with a source that is only found "there."

18. See *MM*, Betsah, 269 nn. 4–5 on the formulation in mBets 1:2: "Since the ashes of a stove may count as prepared."
19. In cases without an appropriate parallel, the *shin* functions as a *vav*, meaning "and" and not "since." Yom-Tov Lippmann Heller, in his Mishnah commentary *Tosafot yom tov*, remarks on this phenomenon on several occasions (for further references see *MM*, Betsah, ad loc.). However, the proof Heller cites in his commentary to mDem 1:4 citing Tosafot, Pes 51a, is spurious. The scribe simply erred (following Hul 18b) and wrote "we act" instead of "they act." See Rashb"a and Ra"n (and the glosses of the Ba"h and Rasha"sh) ad loc. In mss. Columbia and JTS 162327 the text reads: "Since we are subservient to them, [this is] not [the case]."
20. See, for example, Tosafot, Bekh 34b, s.v. *be'a*. Some scholars suggest that Rav Pappa said "Therefore we say them both" once, and the other instances of his dictum, which appear in Ber 59a, Meg 20a, and Taan 7a, are transpositions. But I am not sure about this.
21. Halevy's observation, that "They took great care to attribute a statement to [him] who spoke it, including dicta derived by inference," is astonishing (*Dorot harishonim*, 8, 508). See too, p. 17, on the phrase, "And if it was through an inference—what does that matter?"
22. In *MM*, Eruvin, 78 ff., I suggested that the passage "Rav Kahana objected to him... Rava said to him" in Mak 3b is a transposition from Eruv 29b. For if not, "We would have to conclude that he (Rav Kahana) forgot an explicit mishnah." In addition, Rava need not have answered Rav Kahana, as he himself subsequently observes, "There is no difficulty; this one accords with R. Yohanan b. Nuri; that one accords with the Sages." The difficulty with this explanation is that in Eruvin the response, "There..." is unattributed, and in Makkot it is attributed to Rava—whence did the Transposers get the name of Rava?
23. In the main text I refrained from citing the example from BB 48b: "Mar b. Rav Ashi said... he acted unjustly... and the sages nullified his betrothal. Ravina said to Rav Ashi: This is fine if he betrothed her with money..." Obviously Ravina did not ask Rav Ashi about the ruling of his son Mar, and therefore his dictum must have been transposed from the parallels (listed in the marginal glosses). However, several manuscripts omit "Mar b." Yet it is possible that the scribes emended the text in this way because in no other passage does Mar b. Rav Ashi disagree with Amemar, although we find Rav Ashi disagreeing with Amemar (e.g., BB 145a).
24. In some cases two passages appear in similar contexts, and both passages fit their context, but in one passage a few dicta and sometimes even the names of the Amoraim are omitted, making it appear as if the passage derives from the Stammaim. If an Amora subsequently relates to a section of that passage, it

appears as if the Amora is predicated on anonymous material—but this is not the case. See *MM*, Pesahim, 8.

25. If one should claim that Abaye objects against the statement of R. Hiyya b. Avin quoting Rav, "The law follows R. Yehoshua b. Qorha," on the basis of the statement of R. Abba quoting Rav Huna quoting Rav, "The Sages concede . . . ," then the Talmud's subsequent comment, "Do you oppose one [Amora] with another [Amora]," would be used here in a case of "two Reciters disagree about the opinion of Rav"—but this is unattested. See Maharash"a, s.v. *berashi*; Rabbinowicz's comments in *Diqduqei soferim*, ad loc., n. *heh* are correct.
26. Thus Ulla did not say to Abaye in Sanh 30b, "Do you oppose one [Amora] with another [Amora]," as Abaye himself knew that Amoraim sometimes dispute with one another. In Taan 4b R. Zeira thought that R. Eleazar would not disagree with his master R. Yohanan (see Yev 96b: "R. Eleazar your student sits and expounds without attribution, but all know that it is your [tradition]"; and in yBer 1:1, 2a: "All know that R. Eleazar is the student of R. Yohanan"). Rav Ada b. Rava, who objects on the basis of R. Yehoshua b. Levi's dictum against Shmuel in Eruv 91b, and did not simply say that they disagree, perhaps thought that no one would disagree with R. Yehoshua b. Levi's general principle.**
27. See the commentary of David Pardo (d. 1790), *Shoshanim ledavid*, to mNid 2:6: "This explanation is very problematic, since Akavya b. Mehalalel lived many years earlier. . . . So how can [the Talmud] explain that the Sages who disagree with Akavya are to be identified with R. Yose?"
28. Another example: I pointed out (see the annotation to Part II, n. 55, p. 288) that the statement in Git 5b, "and he was not mentioned out of respect for R. Shimon," is a transposition from RH 22b.
29. See p. 8.
30. In *MM*, Eruvin, 76 (to Eruv 29a), I noted that there is a dispute between Rav Yosef and R. Menashia b. Shagubli in a case with no legal implications. Rav Yosef told R. Menashia b. Shagubli that he must atone for transposing the words of Rav from a mishnah to a baraita. The medieval commentators also struggle with this question. Rashb"a states: "If Rav spoke explicitly of a mishnah and not a baraita, how could Rav Menashia say that Rav said 'And so for the *eiruv*' about a baraita, when Rav did not say this; certainly he requires atonement." But Ritb"a disagrees.
31. I first commented on this issue in *MM*, Qiddushin, 687 n. 5.
32. However, the formulation differs slightly in tKer 5:8. In place of "R. Yose says" it states, "And R. Yose concedes." The formulation "R. Yose concedes" does not necessarily mean that he expressed his opinion in those very words.
33. Influences from parallel passages can take different forms. See, e.g., BB 105b: "But rather 'this' implies that he [Shmuel] does not hold the [opinion] himself."** As the medieval commentaries note, the Talmud could have responded, "'This' implies that he holds the [opinion] himself." And, as Tosafot, ad loc., s.v.

ela, state, this case differs from "the case of the tenant, stated above (BB 105a; because) it can be said here that he (the owner) retracted, or it can be said that he (the owner) was explaining (his first statement with his second)." However, the parallel passage in BM 102b lacks that which is stated in BB 105a (which can be explained in two ways), and therefore BM 102b does not offer this response (that "this" implies that he does hold the opinion himself). The Stam in BB 105b—even though it is preceded by the response in BB 105a—was influenced by the Stam in BM 102b and also did not provide that response on 105b (that Shmuel does hold the opinion himself), but rather the response that "'this' implies that he [Shmuel] does not hold [the opinion] himself." These types of influences probably occurred in the Stammaitic era.

34. See *MM*, ad loc.
35. I provide some references in *MM*, Qiddushin, 714 n. 11. It should be noted that sometimes the transpositions have been deleted from our Talmud following the comments of the medieval commentaries (and especially Rashi). See, e.g., Rashi's comment to Qid 53a: "[The words] 'Do not *aid the wronged (Isa 1:17)*' should not be read here but rather in BQ (46b), with reference to the issue of the source of the principle that one first deals with the claim of the plaintiff (before the counterclaim of the defendant)." These words indeed are wanting in texts of our Talmud and also do not appear in ms. Vatican 111, which was influenced by this comment of Rashi. However, in Hul 74b, Rashi deletes "The fat of what?" which still appears in our text of the Talmud, though not in ms. Munich 95. See too Rashi to Sanh 94a. Additional examples can be found in Albeck, *Mavo latalmudim*, 471 ff. It is unclear why he omits this example from Qid 53a.
36. See p. 106 on this mishnah and baraita.
37. However, there is reason to believe that the terms "That is a difficulty (*qashya*)" and "A refutation (*tiuvta*)" are not from the Stammaim, but from a later hand, who wished to point out that here—atypically—the Stammaim provided no response to the objection. See *MM*, Bava Batra, 213–14.
38. I assume that Abaye asked the question "Do you disregard the Mishnah and rule in accord with a baraita?," as the response begins "He said to him (Rav Yosef said to Abaye)." However, as is well known, one should not place much weight on "He said to him," as medieval scribes routinely added it on the basis of their own understanding. See *MM*, Bava Qamma, 356 n. 5.
39. See Tosafot, Hul 87b, s.v. *shenitmedu*: "The Talmud could have said that [Shmuel's dictum was necessary] for the case where he infused blood with fruit juice, which does not cause susceptibility to impurity." But one cannot say this in BB 97a. The inferior wine (*tamad*) made from soaked grape husks cannot be said of fruit juice, so Hul 87b was transposed from BB 97a.
40. See the medieval commentaries, ad loc.
41. I have commented on this phenomenon on several occasions; see the indices to the volumes of *MM*, s.v. *leshonot*.

42. See, e.g., Tosafot, Bets 13a, s.v. *ika*.
43. See p. 161, that not all Talmudic passages were transmitted to us.
44. So too, apparently, Rashi's text lacked these words. See *Diqduqei soferim*, ad loc., n. *mem*. Also, the words, "And because he taught him...," were possibly transposed from AZ 46b.
45. In the Introduction to *MM: seder nashim*, 17 n. 26, I included "reworking (*ibud*)" and "influences (*hashpa'ot*)" among the types of transposition (which I defined as "the editor was aware of another sugya and utilized its material"). This type of transposition involves a kind of editing, albeit local editing. See too *MM*, Taanit, 441 n. 18.
46. In *MM*, Shabbat, 325 n. 4* I assumed that this issue was disputed by the Amoraim, and that Rabbah and Abaye, "who did not concern themselves with Rava's objection, 'R. Yehudah contradicts himself, but the Sages do not contradict themselves?'," believed that it was not appropriate to raise a contradiction between different sources attributed to "the Sages" (See Pes 11a, Men 68a, Ket 24a, Sot 8a, Sanh 45a, and Git 46b).

PART V

1. See Epstein, *Mevo'ot lesifrut ha'amoraim*, 274: "As a rule, here (in the Yerushalmi) there are no lengthy sugyot (with a few exceptions), nor highly edited sugyot which connect one statement to another and one response with another, thus constructing a dialogue, a lively give-and-take of the form found in the Bavli."
2. Such as mPeah 8:9, mRH 3:6, mSot 7 ff. (and at the end of Tractate Sotah), mSanh 10.
3. See, e.g., mPes 6:1–3, mKer 1:6 (and 3:10), mYad 4:3 (taken from a midrash halakhah).
4. See, e.g., mSuk 4:8, which asks: "The Hallel and the Rejoicing (*simha)*—eight days. How so?" And answers: "This teaches that one is obligated in [the recitation of] the Hallel and in Rejoicing and to give the honor [due to the Festival of Sukkot] on the final festival day." The response "This teaches..." does not answer the question "How so?" Moreover, before the term "This teaches..." there should be a verse that does the "teaching," in the manner of a midrash halakhah. In *MM*, Sukkah, 242, I conjectured that "this mishnah has been abbreviated. The editor of the Mishnah omitted (from the midrash halakhah) the section that defines the eight days of Hallel and Rejoicing," and also omitted the verse (that precedes "this teaches..."), from which they derived "one is obligated in [the recitation of] the Hallel and in Rejoicing and to give the honor [due to the Festival of Sukkot] on the final festival day."
5. See my English book, *Midrash, Mishnah, and Gemara*, chapter 3, pp. 38–65.
6. These principles of adjudication did not originate with the editor of the Mishnah, or at least not all of them. See Git 67a: "Isi b. Yehuda used to recount the merits

of the Sages..." They probably determined the law on the basis of these merits. And this seems to be the implication of that Talmudic passage.

7. See Epstein, *Mevo'ot lesifrut ha'amoraim*, 54 ff., and Rabinowitz, *Sha'arei torat erets yisra'el*, 299 ff. See too B. De-Vreis, *Mehqarim besifrut hatalmud* (Jerusalem: Rav Kook, 1968), 230, and N. Danzig, *Mavo lesefer halakhot pesuqot* (Jerusalem: Jewish Theological Seminary, 1993), 150 ff., who summarize the views of contemporary scholars.
8. See Nahmanides, the end of *Hilkhot nedarim* (published in the Romm edition of the Talmud, p. 28); Rabenu Nissim to Ned 22b s.v. *amar rava; Otsar hageonim*, Nedarim, Responsa, #63 etc.
9. See Saul Lieberman's introduction to "The Talmud of Caeserea" *Tarbiz* 1 (1931), Supplement 2 (Hebrew). He conjectures that Yerushalmi Neziqin was edited in the middle of the fourth century in Caeserea and not in Tiberias, as were the other tractates.
10. On Tractate Nazir, see Epstein, *Mevo'ot lesifrut ha'amoraim*, 72 ff.
11. See S. Assaf, *Tequfat hageonim vesifrutah* (Jerusalem: Rav Kook, 1955), 136: "The responsa which have come down to us from the Geonim who lived...until the time of Rav Yehudai Gaon are very few in number, and do not even add up to fifty."
12. See A. Weiss, *Hithavut hatalmud bishleimutah* (New York: Kohut Foundation, 1955), 57 ff., and the explanation of Danzig, *Mavo lesefer halakhot pesuqot*, 150 ff.
13. De-Vreis, ibid.: "The Aramaic language of these tractates is not evidence of their more recent composition, and the same is true of terminology. It is difficult to determine the provenance of their distinctive aspects. Moreover, our texts are not consistent, so it is hard to know what is original and what is the product of later editors or copyists, and even who originally devised the terminology."
14. See my comments in *MM*, Sukkah, 241, n. 10*.
15. But see *MM*, Eruvin, 169–70.
16. See yHor 3:8, 48c: "*But God does not permit him to enjoy it (Qoh* 6:2)—this refers to the master of aggadah, for he neither forbids nor permits, neither rules impure nor rules pure."
17. Not only Amoraim, i.e., rabbinic scholars, but laymen too possessed "books of aggadah." Thus "Rava appropriated scissors for cloth and books of aggadah from the orphans"; BM 116a and parallels.
18. See yShab 16:1, 15c: "R. Yehoshua b. Levi said: Never in my life did I look at a book of aggadah." But see BB 9b: "R. Yehoshua b. Levi said: Whoever regularly performs acts of charity merits having sons...who are proficient in aggadah." And in yPeah 2:6, 17a; yHag 1:8, 76d: "R. Yehoshua b. Levi said: *[The Lord gave me the two tablets of stone inscribed with the finger of God, and on them were] all the words (Deut* 9:10)...From this we learn that Scripture, Mishnah, Talmud and aggadah, and even that which a distinguished student would innovate before his master in the future, was already given to Moses at Sinai." Apparently they

only opposed writing down the aggadah. See too yShab 16:1, 15c: "R. Yehoshua b. Levi said: As for aggadah—he who writes it down has no portion [in the next world]." In yMaas 3:10, 51a: "R. Zeira reprimanded those [teachers] of aggadah, and called them books of witchcraft." See S. Lieberman, *Hayerushalmi kifeshuto* (Jerusalem: Darom, 1934), 194. These issues are well known.

19. Sanh 57b states: "R. Yaakov bar Aha found it written in a book of aggadah of the school house (*be rav*) that a gentile may be sentenced to death by one judge"—and that is indeed the halakhah.

20. See yBer 5:1, 9a: "R. Yohanan said: It is an established covenant that one who learns aggadah from a scroll (*sefer*) will not quickly forget it."

21. Halevy, *Dorot harishonim*, 3:138, disagrees with S.Y. Rappoport, who suggested that the phrase "but this is not so (*velo hi*)," which responds to Mar bar Rav Ashi, who was among the last Amoraim, therefore postdates the Amoraic period (corresponding to the Saboraic period in their view). Halevy rejects this and wonders why it is not possible that it derives from, e.g., the second Ravina who lived after Mar bar Rav Ashi. (He was anticipated by Tzvi Hirsch Hayyot [Chajes] who found it problematic: if Rav Ashi himself edited the Talmud, then who could say of Rav Ashi's answer "it is a mistake [*baduta*]." Hayyot explains: "Rav Ashi's contemporaries and the members of his school assessed his pronouncements, and said of those which they did not consider to be accurate 'it is a mistake.'" [Responsa of Mahra"ts, #20].) My theory has no need for such an explanation; unattributed statements indicate the post-Amoraic period, and therefore the phrase "but this is not so" is also from the post-Amoraic period.** However, the sharp language implies that the statement originated in the early Stammaitic period when they considered themselves of almost equal status to the Amoraim such that they dared to speak in this way.

22. This provides ineluctable proof that the Mishnah and Talmud were not written in Stammaitic times. As is well known, early medieval jurists of Spain and France already disagreed on this point, which is reflected in some of the textual variants of the "Epistle" of Rav Sherira Gaon. B. M. Lewin provides detailed analysis in his Introduction to *Epistle of Rav Sherira Gaon*, "The Epistle of Rav Sherira Gaon, Spanish and French Recensions," p. 24a. Cf. Epstein, *Mevo'ot lesifrut ha'amoraim*, 610. Contemporary scholars have revisited this issue. See the detailed article by Y. Sussman, "Torah shebe'al peh," *Mehqerei Talmud* 3, ed. Y. Sussman and D. Rosenthal (Jerusalem: Magnes, 2005), 343 ff. But in my opinion this Talmudic passage is decisive. See too Part I, n. 71.

23. 2:267.

24. As is well known, in Geonic academies they continued to study orally even after the Talmud was written down. See *Otsar hageonim*, Yevamot, Responsa, #170, p. 71, citing Aharon Sargado: "Most (sages of the academy) have never seen a book." This material has been collected by Uziel Fuchs in his dissertation, *The Role of the Geonim in the Textual Transmission of the Babylonian Talmud* (Hebrew

University, 2003), 20–21, 124–42 (Hebrew). Fuchs also demonstrates that medieval jurists, and sometimes the latter Geonim too, who learned from written texts, changed quotations of earlier authorities by substituting "technical terms of writing for technical terms of oral transmission," such as "[oral] textual tradition (*girsa*)" to "text (*nusha*)," and "there are texts (*nusha'ot*)" to "there are books (*sefarim*)," and suchlike. But previously—even after the dialectical argumentation was added to the Talmud—they did not feel it necessary to study from written texts. All the more so the Tannaim and Amoraim did not need recourse to writing, as the transmission of tradition during their times was limited to apodictic laws and brief explanations.

25. R. Ishmael b. R. Yose and R. Hiyya, yKil 9:3, 32b and yKet 13:3, 35a: "At that time I cast my eyes through the entire scroll (*sefer*) of aggadah on Psalms."
26. With the exception of Rav Aha and the second Ravina, whose disagreements are introduced by the term "it was said (*itmar*)." Yet disagreements between these two are always quoted in the form "one said…and the other said…," which implies that their disagreements were collected long after the time of the original dispute, when they no longer knew who said what. Perhaps this resulted from the fact that they lived after Ravina and Rav Ashi, after the transmission of halakhah to Reciters was abandoned; see below.
27. I identified this student as Rav Aha b. Rava, who said of Rav Ashi "From the time of Rabbi [Yehudah HaNasi] until Rav Ashi Torah and prestige (*gedulah*) were never found in the same place" (Git 59a, Sanh 36a); see p. 87.
28. See, e.g., Suk 3b, "If a sukkah…" although in this passage too there are some explanations. And see Pes 9b, "Nine heaps of matzah…"; Yev 37b, "If the [son of] doubtful [parentage] and the levir…." But cf. BB 69b, "If he says to him: I sell you the land and the palm trees." In all of these passages the laws are in Aramaic.

Translator's Annotations

The following shorthand is used for references to the text: III.4 = Part III, page 4; IIn73= Part II, note 73.

AUTHOR'S INTRODUCTION XXXI

The phrase "on one foot" derives from the famous story of the prospective proselyte who approaches Hillel and asks to be taught the entire Torah while standing "on one foot." Hillel replies: "What is hateful to you, do not do to your fellow. That is the entire Torah. The rest is commentary. Go and learn" (Shab 31a).

I.4

There were two well-known sages named Ravina, the first, a younger contemporary of Rav Ashi, presumably died around the same time as Rav Ashi, 427 CE (according to *Epistle of Rav Sherira Gaon*), and the second (sometimes called the "latter Ravina"), Ravina bar Rav Huna, among the last sages mentioned by name in the Talmud, died c. 500. When the first Ravina lived, and which Ravina is meant in this Talmudic tradition about the "end of *hora'ah*," have long been sources of confusion. Avinoam Cohen has now convincingly argued that there was in fact an even earlier Ravina, a disciple of Rava, who predeceased Rav Ashi. The Ravina of "the end of *hora'ah*" tradition is the contemporary of Rav Ashi, and the "latter" Ravina lived still later. See *Ravina and Contemporary Sages: Studies in the Chronology of Late Babylonian Amoraim* (Ramat Gan: Bar-Ilan University Press, 2001), 23–134 (Hebrew).

I.4

Sherira Gaon discusses the Saboraim immediately after mentioning the death of Ravina and R. Asi (or Yose) and the "end of *hora'ah*," that is, the end of the Amoraic era, which he dates to 499/500: "In his (= R. Asi's/Yose's) days was the end of *hora'ah*, and the Talmud was closed. Then followed the Saboraim, and most of them died within a few years, as the Geonim detailed in their historical archives" (*Epistle of Rav Sherira Gaon*, 97; for an English translation of the "Spanish" recension, see Nosson Rabinowich, *The Iggeres of Rav Sherira Gaon* [Jerusalem: Moznaim, 1988], 118–19.) "R. Asi" (in the "French" recension) or "R. Yose" (in the "Spanish" recension) is apparently how Sherira understands the "Rav Ashi" of the Talmud's "end of *hora'ah*" tradition, reading the *shin* as a *sin*. For if the Ravina here is the latter Ravina, he cannot be a contemporary of Rav Ashi, who died in 427. (Sherira's understanding of the "end of *hora'ah*" tradition, however, is problematic, as he also refers to it earlier in connection with Rav Ashi, p. 69.) Sherira dates the first Gaon, R. Hanan of Ashiqiyya, to 589 CE. So the Saboraic era, in his view, dates from 500–589 CE. And see In72, and II.86. Other Geonic sources, however, offer a different dating, and the precise contours of the Saboraic age is to this day an unresolved question. See Robert Brody, *The Geonim of Babylonia and the Shaping of Medieval Jewish Culture* (New Haven: Yale University Press, 1998), 4–11. All relevant Geonic sources are translated in David Goodblatt, *Rabbinic Instruction in Sasanian Babylonia* (Leiden: Brill, 1975), 13–34.

I.5

Some might view this periodization, where no new era can begin until the previous one completely concludes, as excessively rigid and not reflecting the messy historical reality. See, for example, the comments of Shamma Friedman, "Al titmah al hosafa shenizkar bah shem amora," *Talmudic Studies: Investigating the Sugya, Variant Readings and Aggada* (New York and Jerusalem: Jewish Theological Seminary, 2010), 72. (And see p. 25, where Halivni raises the possibility of dating the start of the Stammaitic period to the death of the second Ravina [500 CE]).

I.5

Halivni refers to this tradition again, p. 145, and IIIn1 (and in his Addendum, p. 200). It is found in *Epistle of Rav Sherira Gaon*, 20 (ed. Rabinowich, 16–17), where Sherira quotes Eruv 53a, "The hearts [= minds] of the earlier [sages] are like the entrance to the great hall (of the Temple, which was 20 cubits wide), but the hearts of the later [sages] are like the entrance to the sanctuary (which was 10 cubits wide) and ours are like the eye of a thin needle." On this tradition, other such Talmudic traditions and Sherira's views, see Menachem Kellner, *Maimonides on the "Decline of the Generations" and the Nature of Rabbinic Authority* (Albany: SUNY Press, 1996), 5–21.

I.6

According to the hierarchy of rabbinic authority, an Amora cannot contradict a Tanna (unless supported by another Tannaitic source). Yet Rav, a first generation

Amora, in rare cases seems to disagree with Tannaitic sources. Unlike almost all other Amoraim, the Talmud accords him a quasi-Tannaitic status and does not refute his opinion on that basis; see, for example, Zev 32b, Eruv 50b, and others. Halivni argues that the fact that Rav's traditions never entered the Mishnah, despite his possessing (almost) Tannaitic authority, is evidence that the sages themselves took pains to avoid mixing up rabbis of different historical eras. The Stammaim would have done the same and expressed themselves anonymously so as to avoid confusing their own traditions with those of the Amoraim. See too IIn12.

I.10

The quotation "reasoning that is close to legislation" like the quotation above, "providing explanations that are close to legislation," derives from Sherira Gaon's description of the Saboraim. The former is the formulation of the "French" version of the Epistle, the latter of the "Spanish."

I.13

In the next subsection, pp. 13–16 were added later and somewhat interrupt the flow of the main argument in that they tend to presuppose the principle that an Amora cannot respond to a Stam. They supply additional evidence that the Amoraic and Stammaitic periods were distinct, as they are characterized by differences in terminology and formulation. The main argument about the late dating of the Stammaim resumes thereafter.

I.21

Baraitot introduced by "we have also taught thus (*tanya namei hakhi*)" generally state verbatim what an Amora had stated earlier (often disputing another Amora) and tend to appear at the end of the sugya. They are not considered authentic baraitot, and seem to be of Amoraic provenance. Thus a baraita that supports the Talmud's "emendation" does not provide Tannaitic evidence that such was the correct reading of the source. See Simcha Goldsmith, "The Role of the *Tanya Nami Hakhi* Baraita," *HUCA* 73 (2002), 133–56, and the references there.

I.22

That is, in this case the emendation is correct, as the scribe, or Reciter, mistakenly skipped from the first to the second appearance of the word. The baraita as initially quoted on Git 54a reads: "If he ate impure priestly tithe (*terumah*), **he pays** restitution in pure, ordinary food (*hullin*)." Rava emends the baraita to read: "If he ate impure priestly tithe, **he pays** <restitution in any kind (of food). If he ate pure priestly tithe, **he pays**> restitution in pure, ordinary food (*hullin*)." The scribe/Reciter mistakenly omitted the words between the angular brackets.

1.23

Recent scholarship, including the work of the present translator, has suggested that the Stammaim made widespread and substantive conclusions to the aggadah of the Talmud. See, for example, Jeffrey L. Rubenstein, *Talmudic Stories: Narrative Art, Composition and Culture* (Baltimore: Johns Hopkins University Press, 1999), and *The Culture of the Babylonian Talmud* (Baltimore: Johns Hopkins University Press, 2003). See too the essays collected in *Creation and Composition: The Contribution of the Bavli Redactors (*Stammaim*) to the Aggada*, ed. Jeffrey L. Rubenstein (Tuebingen: Mohr-Siebeck, 2005), especially "Criteria of Stammaitic Intervention in Aggada," pp. 417–40. And see Joshua Levinson, *The Twice-Told Tale: A Poetics of the Exegetical Narrative in Rabbinic Midrash* (Jerusalem: Magnes Press, 2005), 278–307 (Hebrew). Some Bavli stories, in particular, show signs of extremely late reworking, perhaps well into the Geonic period. See, for example, Daniel Sperber, "On the Unfortunate Adventures of Rav Kahana: A Passage of Saboraic Polemic from Sasanian Persia," *Irano-Judaica*, ed. S. Shaked (Jerusalem: Ben Zvi Institute, 1982), 83–100; Isaiah Gafni, "The Babylonian *Yeshiva* as Reflected in Bava Qamma 117a," *Tarbiz* 49 (1980), 192–201 (Hebrew). That the Stammaim contributed so extensively to the aggadah ultimately supports Halivni's claim that most of the Talmud is of Stammaitic provenance.

1.23

The term "*shita* (system)" is commonly used by the medieval commentaries for passages where the Talmud claims that a number of Tannaim "all hold (*kulhu sevira lahu*)" a certain opinion or subscribe to a common principle. (The term is used in this sense in Ned 10a; cf. BM 69a). For detailed study, see Leib Moscovitz, "Kulhu sevira lahu," *Studies in Talmudic and Midrashic Literature—In Memory of Tirzah Lifshitz*, ed. Arye Edrei (Jerusalem: Bialik 2005), 309–47. And see 232n13.

1.24

Halivni believes that this is the latter R. Abbahu, not the more frequently appearing R. Abbahu of the second-third generation. This R. Abbahu responds to Rav Ashi in BQ 117a; see Hyman, *Toledot*, 1:72.

1.28

See p. 51 for discussion of questions that precede Amoraic dicta.

1.36

Yom 42b discusses mPar 3:7: "If the [red] heifer refused to go forth, we do not bring forth a black one with it, so that people not say that they slaughtered a black one, nor a red one, so that people not say that they slaughtered two. R. Yose says: It is not for this reason, but because it is written, *And he brings it forth (Num 29:17)*—alone." The Talmud claims the anonymous first opinion is R. Shimon, because of the reason provided. However, because R. Yose voices the dissenting opinion, not R. Yehudah, it appears that R. Yehudah actually agrees with R. Shimon. Sanh 16b quotes a baraita that prohibits proscribing a city near the border of the Land of Israel "lest the gentiles come and destroy [the whole land]." The Talmud suggests this can be derived by scriptural exegesis, and then claims that the authority of this teaching must be R. Shimon. Here too there is no evidence that R. Yehudah would disagree. In Sot 8a, R. Yehudah disagrees with the anonymous first opinion: "They do not make two suspected adulteresses drink [the bitter waters] at the same time, so that one not become defiant on account of the other [and refuse to confess her sin]. R. Yehudah says: It is not for this reason, but because Scripture states, *The priest shall adjure her (Num 5:19)*—her alone." In this case R. Yehudah agrees that this reason underpins the law but claims that it is explicitly articulated by Scripture, and consequently no inference is needed here, though elsewhere he would be willing to determine the reasons for the law. The first opinion (which the Talmud identifies as R. Shimon) claims that the reason derives from the rabbis.

1.42

An example of a "scriptural support (*asmakhta*)" to which Halivni refers is found on Ber 35a. The Talmud proposes that Lev 19:24 is the basis for the ruling of mBer 6:1, but subsequently, after extensive argumentation, rejects the attempt to derive the ruling from the verse and concludes that it derives from "logic (*sevara*)." Tosafot, s.v. *ela*, claims that the verse is simply an *asmakhta*, a scriptural support, that is, not the true source of the law.

1.43

The quotation is from Eruv 13b regarding the heavenly voice that settled disputes between the Houses of Hillel and Shammai by declaring, "These and those are the words of the living God, but the law is according to the words of the House of Hillel." For this view of the truth of conflicting textual variants, see the similar comment by Saul Lieberman, *Studies in Palestinian Talmudic Literature*, ed. D. Rosenthal

(Jerusalem: Magnes, 1991), 566 (Hebrew): "We must distinguish between absolute-historical truth and the truth of the text. There is one and only one historical truth, but the truth of the text is specific to that text; each and every text and its truth—according to the source upon which it is based."

1.46

In this case, even without the parallel passage at Arakh 11a, one could well assume that the "And do you really think so..." was not part of Rav Pappa's original dictum but was added by the Stammaim, as it begins a new thought and is very verbose. However, Halivni believes that the fact that Rav Pappa states "Do they not differ (*mai lav*)" implies that he was aware of an alternative; hence the "And do you really think so," which then supplies that alternative, might appear to be the continuation of his dictum.

1.46

Where an Amora says "as we taught (*kedeshaninan*)" or "as we rejected (*kededahinan*)," he refers to that which was stated previously and applies the same teachings or responses to a different issue. The "content" is therefore not identical. See the example quoted in In104.

1.47

The expression "R. So-and-so explained it in accord with R. So-and-so's view (*targema rabbi ploni aliba derabbi ploni*)" is used when a sage responds to an objection against his opponent's opinion, which implies that they debate face to face. (References are provided in the marginal gloss to Shab 52b).

1.49

It should be noted that in this case it seems that R. Meir knew of R. Yehudah's ruling, because they disagree explicitly in the baraita (although it is also clear that the editor of the Mishnah added "even [*af*]" to R. Meir's statement.) However, in other such cases when the editor added *af*, it is not clear that the Tanna knew of the opposing opinion.

1.49

That is, in this case the debate would have been formulated as follows: "R. Yohanan said: They (R. Meir and the Sages) disagree after the verdict has been issued, but before the verdict has been issued, all agree that he may retract. And Resh Laqish said: They disagree before the verdict has been issued, but after the verdict has been issued, all agree that he may not retract."

1.55

The quotations are from the (fictional) story at Hor 13b–14a: R. Shimon b. Gamaliel retaliates against R. Meir and R. Natan, who tried to depose him, by commanding that the traditions of these sages not be ascribed to them, but formulated as "Others say" and "Some say." Years late R. Shimon, son of R. Yehudah HaNasi, objects to this practice on the grounds that "we drink their waters," that is, learn their Torah, "but do not know their names" –which applies beautifully to the Stammaim.

1.57

For recent studies on Sherira's sources and the reliability of his chronology, see Isaiah Gafni, "On Talmudic History in the Epistle of Sherira Gaon: Between Tradition and Historiography," *Zion* 73 (2009), 271–96 (Hebrew); and Robert Brody, "On the Sources for the Chronology of the Talmudic Period," *Tarbiz* 70 (2000), 75–107 (Hebrew).

1.57

Other scholars appear to derive "Saboraim" (*savoraim*) from the *pe'al* form of the root SBR, "to think, hold the opinion," rather than the *afel*, "to explain," and call them "Reasoners" or "Thinkers." Brody, *Geonim*, 4, translates "Opiners."

11.64

The contradiction between Yom 72a and Sanh 21a is pointed out by R. Akiba Eger in his marginal gloss to Yom 72a. There the suggestion that the verse *The hem for the priestly garments not be torn (Exod 28:32)* be understood as "make a hem *such that* it not be torn" (as opposed to "do not tear the hem") is rejected on the grounds that the verse does not explicitly state "such that." But in Sanh 21a the verse *He shall not have many wives and his heart not go astray (Deut 17:17)* is understood as "He shall not have many [wives] *such that* his heart not go astray" and the Talmud does not object that the verse does not explicitly state "such that." In Sanh 113a the Talmud claims the rabbinic edict at issue, which concerns a law of the second tithe, was only enacted as long as the walls of Jerusalem are intact, but not if they have fallen. BM 53b states that "the rabbis did not distinguish" whether the walls are intact or not, therefore the edict applies in both cases. See Tosafot, ad loc., s.v. *lo*.

11.70

Rav Matneh comments to the clause of mSanh 1:5 that rules that a tribe that sinned must be judged before the court of seventy-one. The Talmud finds it difficult to understand what sin an *entire* tribe might commit. Rav Matneh therefore interprets the mishnah's mention of a tribe in terms of the head of the tribe who sinned, applying Rav Ada b. Ahava's interpretation of *"great matter" (Exod 18:22)* as "great man" to the head of the tribe. Halivni's point is that Rav Ada b. Ahava only applied the verse to the high priest, to explain why mSanh 1:5 rules that a high priest must be judged by the court of seventy-one, but Rav Matneh applied it also to another "great man," the head of the tribe.

11.72

In other words, it looks like Mar Qashisha [C1] objects to the claim of [B1]. But [B1] is anonymous, and is immediately rejected at [B2]. One never finds Amoraim objecting to anonymous material, and certainly never when the claim (= the "initial assumption") is rejected. Halivni suggests that in fact Mar Qashisha objects to the baraita cited in [B1], that is, the original baraita, and not as it is now contextualized as an anonymous objection to Shmuel [A1]. In addition, Halivni claims that Mar Qashisha must not have known the answer given at [B2], as it would resolve his question adequately, again proving he did not know the previous sugya. Nor did the Stammaim who composed the second sugya [C1–C2] know the answer of [B2], or they could have applied it to Mar Qashisha's question. So we have two independent sugyot that did not know each other, even though it looks like Mar Qashisha continues the discussion based on Shmuel's dictum [A1] of the "first" sugya [B1–B2].

11.72

Halivni conjectures that Rav Ashi's original response to Mar Qashisha was what appears in [B2]. The response the Talmud attributes to Rav Ashi [C2] contradicts Rav Ashi's dictum in Sot 27a. But if Rav Ashi gave the response of [B2], there is no contradiction.

11.82

For detailed study of the editing process of baraitot in the Tosefta (and of the editing of the Mishnah), see Shamma Friedman, *Tosefta atiqta: pesah rishon* (Ramat Gan: Bar-Ilan University Press, 2002).

11.83

The conclusion "It is a refutation" is generally the final word in a sugya, conclusively rejecting one opinion, whereas the suggestion that the Amoraic dispute parallels "a dispute among Tannaim" defends both opinions. The juxtaposition suggests two separate sources have been combined. Similarly, the declaration "[The question] stands (*teiqu*)," typically concludes a sugya, so to follow with "Come and hear," which continues the analysis, points to a different source.

11.85

It should be noted that the aggadic context is rather odd: "[BM 85b] Shmuel the Yarhina'ah [Moon-Expert?] was Rabbi [Yehudah HaNasi's] physician. Rabbi suffered an eye ailment. He [Shmuel] said to him: 'I will make you a salve [for your eye].' He said to him: 'I cannot [bear the pain of administering it].' He said to him: 'I will mix you an ointment.' He said to him: 'I cannot bear it.' He placed a vial with drugs under his pillow and he was healed [from the vapor]. Rabbi was anxious to ordain him [Shmuel], but could not do so because of the circumstances. He [Shmuel] said to him: 'Master, do not be upset. I saw the "Book of Primordial Adam" and there is written in it: "Shmuel Yarhina'ah [86a] will be called 'Sage' but will not be called 'Rabbi,' and the healing of Rabbi will be done by him. Rabbi and R. Natan—the end of Mishnah. Rav Ashi and Ravina—the end of *hora'ah*. And your mnemonic is: *Till I entered God's Sanctuary (miq***dashi***) and reflected (***avina***) on their fate (Ps 73:17)*."'" Thus the tradition is presented as a sort of esoteric or occult lore, which to my mind seriously undermines any claims to historicity.

11.87

The Talmud never states explicitly that Rav Ashi was Head of the Academy for sixty years. This notion, which Halivni and many other scholars take as fact, derives from Sherira Gaon's reading of BB 157b, which refers to "a first cycle" and a "second cycle" of Rav Ashi, apparently a cycle of reviewing the Talmud. Sherira claims that the sages reviewed two tractates per year, making a sixty year tenure (*Epistle of Rav Sherira Gaon*, 98; ed. Rabinowich, 115). See too pp. 55, 98.

11.89

Rav Ashi is presented as emending mNed 8:5: "[If he says] '*Qonam* if I taste wine this year,' and the year was intercalated, he is forbidden during that year and its intercalated month." Rav Ashi states that "this year (*hashanah*)" should be taken as "year (*shanah*)," apparently deleting the letter *heh*. Halivni suggests that Rav Ashi had לשנה in his version of the Mishnah (a reading attested in some Mishnah manuscripts), which he explained (rather than emended) as "for a year."

II.92

This dictum of Rav Ashi appears in the first sugya of Tractate Gittin, a long and highly developed passage. It begins with a dispute between Rabbah and Rava over the reason for mGit 1:1, which rules that one who brings a divorce document from the diaspora to Israel must state that is was written and signed in his presence. Rabbah rules that the reason is because they are not familiar with the requirement that a divorce document be written "for her name," that is, specifically for the woman, whereas Rava explains that the reason is that it is difficult in such cases to find witnesses to verify the signatures. After several folios of argumentation over these opinions, the Talmud (surprisingly) claims on Git 4b that in fact Rabbah accepts Rava's reason. However, on 4a Rav Ashi attempts to explain the Mishnah on the assumption that Rabbah does not accept Rava's reason, that the issue in mGit 1:1 is in fact that the document must be written and signed "for her name." Clearly then, Rav Ashi did not know the anonymous Talmud's claim that Rabbah conceded to Rava.

II.93

On the identity of Ravina in all these passages, see Cohen, *Ravina and Contemporary Sages* (and see above, annotation to I.4).

II.93

These three passages adjudicate disputes between Rav Aha and Ravina without quoting this general principle, namely, that in such disputes the law accords with Ravina for leniency. Thus AZ 33b concerns wine-flagons of idolators that have the pitch removed by having burning wood-chips placed inside them: "Rav Aha and Ravina disagree: one forbids and one permits. And the law is as the one who forbids." The passage neither rules leniently nor adduces the general principle.

II.94

In fact, there are no extant sugyot of "the second tradition." The sugyot at Sot 25a, AZ 33b, AZ 75b, Yev 29b, Hul 8b, and Hul 46b do not quote the principle; they belong to the "first tradition." But Pes 74b and Hul 93b already have the two traditions combined, quoting the principle as well as ruling "the law is..."

II.94

For the view that the Babylonian rabbinic academies (as opposed to disciple-circles) first arose in post-Amoraic times, see David Goodblatt, *Rabbinic Instruction in Sasanian Babylonia* (Leiden: Brill, 1974); Jeffrey L. Rubenstein, "The Rise of the

Babylonian Rabbinic Academy: A Reexamination of the Talmudic Evidence," *Jewish Studies, an Internet Journal* 1 (2002), 55–68, and the survey in David Goodblatt, "The History of the Babylonian Academies," *The Cambridge History of Judaism, Volume 4: The Late Roman-Rabbinic Period* (Cambridge: Cambridge University Press, 2006), 821–39. For the lack of academies in Amoraic Palestine, see Catherine Hezser, *The Social Structure of the Rabbinic Movement in Roman Palestine* (Tuebingen: Mohr-Siebeck, 1997).

11.94

Halivni refers exclusively to the *Halakhot pesuqot, Halakhot gedolot,* and *She'iltot.* See Brody, *Geonim,* 180 and n. 32 for further references.

11.97

The phrase "your guarantor needs a guarantor" is adapted from Git 28b and Suk 16a, where it is used to reject the possibility of relying on another person to guard against something happening. Like many other Talmudists, Halivni enjoys such adaptations of Talmudic phrases.

11.97

The Talmud sometimes responds to an objection concerning the formulation of a source (mishnah, baraita, or even biblical verse), that a latter clause does not refer to a different case, but rather explicates the previous case. For example, mBQ 9:3 reads: "One who gives a vessel to artisans to fix and they ruined it—they are liable to pay. One who gives a carpenter a box, chest or cupboard to fix and he ruined it—he is liable to pay." In the course of the Talmudic commentary (BQ 98b) the objection is raised that the second clause deals with the case of an artisan ruining an object given to him to fix, and therefore the first clause must deal with a different case (such as an artisan given raw materials to build an object). The Talmud counters the objections by suggesting that "[the latter clause] comes to explain [the earlier clause]." In other words, the mishnah should be understood: "One who gave a vessel to artisans to fix and they ruined it—they are liable to pay. *For example,* One who gives a carpenter..." In some cases the Talmud then asks about the superfluity: Why do you need both clauses? In other cases it does not pursue the issue.

11.98

That is, some Amoraim only appear in the Talmud in passages where they pose questions to Rav Ashi. Hyman, *Toledot,* 256, provides a list.

II.98

That Nehemia and Uqba, Rav's grandsons, were exilarchs rests on shaky literary evidence. Modern scholars, following Geonic sources, make this claim, all based on Hul 92a (see IIn76). For discussion of the evidence, see Jacob Neusner, *A History of Jews in Babylonia. Vol.* 2 (Leiden: Brill, 1968), 53–58. Geoffrey Herman, *The Exilarchate in the Sasanian Era* (Dissertation; Hebrew University, 2005), 63–64 (Hebrew), concludes that the evidence is insufficient to deem them exilarchs. If so, then there is more uncertainty over the significance of the title "Rabbana" that Halivni addresses, and less reason to take it as evidence that Rav Ashi was the editor of the Talmud.

II.102

On the nature of rabbinic schools in Amoraic and Geonic times, see annotation to II.94. On the functioning of the Geonic academies, see Brody, *Geonim*, 43–49. Besides the "itinerant" students Halivni mentions, there clearly were some students who studied "full-time" in the Geonic academy. Thus it is arguable whether the Amoraic schools, which most scholars now believe to have been disciple-circles rather than institutionalized academies, were more "academic" than the Geonic academies. Nevertheless, Halivni's point that Amoraic schools were numerous and decentralized, as opposed to one or two dominant academies in Stammaitic times, seems eminently plausible and provides a cogent explanation for why reconstruction could only be undertaken in post-Amoraic times. See also Rubenstein, *The Culture of the Babylonian Talmud*, 22–23.

II.103

Some of these "principles of adjudication" appear in the Talmud, such as "In a dispute between R. Meir and R. Yehudah, the law follows R. Yehudah" (Eruv 46a). Halivni conjectures these or similar such principles existed in the time of the Mishnah so that the practical law was known. And see p. 192 and IIn101.

II.104

R. Yohanan refers to mHul 5:2 (a disagreement between R. Shimon and the Sages) and mHul 6:2 (a disagreement between R. Meir and the Sages). He claims that "the Sages" in mHul 5:2 is R. Meir's opinion, and "the Sages" in mHul 6:2 is R. Shimon's opinion. R. Yehudah HaNasi formulated these opinions as "the Sages" because he agreed with those rulings.

II.107

An example of this phenomenon is the Talmudic commentary to mBB 8:5 at BB 130a: "One who says 'So-and-so will be my heir' when he has a daughter, or 'My daughter will be my heir' when he has a son—he has said nothing, for he has stipulated against that which is written in the Torah. R. Yohanan b. Berokah says: If he spoke of one who is fit to inherit from him, his words are valid; if of one who is not fit to inherit from him, his words are not valid." The Talmud proposes emending the mishnah as follows: "One who says 'So-and-so will be my heir' when he has a daughter, or 'My daughter will be my heir' when he has a son—he has said nothing, for he has stipulated against that which is written in the Torah. *But if he said that a certain daughter from among his other daughters, or a certain son from among his other sons, 'will inherit all my property'—his words are valid, for* R. Yohanan b. Berokah says: If he spoke of one who is fit to inherit from him, his words are valid; if of one who is not fit to inherit from him, his words are not valid." Halivni suggests that one need not emend the mishnah; the entire mishnah can be attributed to R. Yohanan b. Berokah with the understanding that the editor of the Mishnah formulated the first part without attribution, since he considered it authoritative, but attributed the second part to R. Yohanan b. Berokah, because he did not deem it worthy of the same degree of authority. The Talmud, however, assumes that the first part, as currently formulated, cannot be the opinion of R. Yohanan b. Berokah, whose ruling follows.

II.108

The numerous debates between the Houses of Hillel and Shammai that appear in the Mishnah typically present the opinion of the House of Shammai first. Halivni claims that this ordering is the responsibility of the editor of the Mishnah.

II.109

Halivni briefly explains this principle, "The mishnah was not changed from its [original] form," p. 104. To clarify his claim here: Yev 30b comments on mYev 3:6 and 3:7, which present similar cases, and concludes that mYev 3:7 is superfluous, as mYev 3:7 can be inferred from mYev 3:6. The Talmud explains that mYev 3:7 was taught first and mYev 3:6 added later. But the editor retained mYev 3:7 intact, that is, "The mishnah was not changed from its [original] form." Halvini suggests that the sequence of these rulings can be explained according to another common pattern, indicated by the term "this and there is no need to say that (*zo ve'ein tsarikh lomar zo*)." Often a series of cases is presented with the most novel first (3:6), proceeding to the most obvious (3:7). The crucial point is that Halivni sees the editor of the Mishnah as far more active and interventionist than the principle "The mishnah was not changed from its [original] form" implies. He therefore explains that originally the principle had a much more limited scope, and we should not think it characteristic of the Mishnah as a whole.

II.109

The dispute over the leper relates to the ruling in mYom 3:3, that everyone has to immerse, even if he is clean, in order to enter the temple court. In Yom 30a, Ben

Zoma and R. Yehudah disagree over the purpose of the immersion; Ben Zoma holds that it is because he moves from non-consecrated ground to holy ground, whereas R. Yehudah holds that this immersion serves as a reminder, and if it is omitted the sacrificial acts are still valid. In the course of the discussion a baraita is cited: "A leper immerses and stands at the Nicanor gate. R. Yehudah says: he need not immerse, as he has already immersed the previous night (as part of the purification ritual that ends the ritual impurity)." Abaye's question is whether the Sages (= the unattributed ruling in the baraita), who disagree with R. Yehudah, and rule that a leper needs immersion on the eighth day, agree with Ben Zoma, who holds that everyone needs immersion (according to biblical law) before entering the temple. And the reason that they formulated their ruling in the case of a leper specifically (rather than stating, in more general terms, that "Everyone should immerse and stand at the Nicanor gate" or suchlike), was to inform you of the extent of R. Yehudah's opinion, that even lepers need not immerse. Or do the sages disagree with Ben Zoma, and hold only that the leper requires immersion because he is "accustomed to his state of impurity." He has been impure for an extended period of time such that he would not notice if he became impure after the immersion on the previous night. But other people, who have immersed for the sake of entering the temple, would notice if they subsequently became impure, and therefore do not have to immerse again on the morning before entering the temple.

II.III

The following two paragraphs are a minor digression. The focus shifts from "The Editor of the Mishnah and His Role in Editing," the topic of this section, to later Amoraic and Stammaitic assumptions concerning the editing of the Mishnah.

II.113

The "baraitot of R. Hiyya and R. Oshaya" are mentioned in Tan 21a and Hul 141a (see IIIn30), and on this basis one finds both traditional and modern scholars who attribute to them the compilation of the Tosefta. Halivni refers here to Tannaitic compilations that apparently preceded or coexisted with the Mishnah.

II.113

The notion that persecutions were the dominant factor in causing the end of the Amoraic period, which Halivni derives from Sherira Gaon, has been a staple of modern scholarship and is sometimes invoked as the cause of the redaction of the Talmud itself. See, for example, Kaplan, *Redaction*, 253–58, and see Halivni's comments on the development of Mishnah-form, p. 23. Difficulties with this view are summarized by David Goodblatt, "A Generation of Talmudic Studies," *The Talmud in Its Iranian Context*, ed. C. Bakhos and R. Shayegan (Tuebingen: Mohr-Siebeck, 2010), 16–18. Interestingly, Yaakov Elman infers from the *lack* of explicit mention in the Bavli of the devastating plague described by Procopios that the main redaction of the Bavli must have been completed prior to 542 CE. See "The World of the 'Sabboraim': Cultural Aaspects of Post-Redactional Additions to the Bavli," *Creation and Composition*, 383–84.

III.118

Saul Lieberman, "The Talmud of Caeserea," *Tarbiz* 1 (1931), Supplement 2 (Hebrew), famously argued that the "Order of Damages" of the Yerushalmi, that is, Yerushalmi tractates Bava Qamma, Bava Metsia, and Bava Batra, evinces stylistic and other differences and is generally terser and less developed, when compared to the rest of the Yerushalmi. He proposed that it was edited in Caeserea, rather than Tiberias, at an earlier date. For summary of his evidence, see Herman J. Blumberg, "Saul Lieberman on the Talmud of Caesarea and Louis Ginzberg on Mishnah Tamid," in *The Formation of the Babylonian Talmud*, ed. J. Neusner (Leiden: Brill, 1970), 115–22. This view has been questioned by Catherine Hezser, *Form, Function and Historical Significance of the Rabbinic Story in Yerushalmi Neziqin* (Tuebingen: Mohr Siebeck, 1993), 362–77. See too p. 194 and Vn9.

III.118

Eruv 32b is a critical (and unique) passage for all scholars seeking to understand the forms in which traditions were transmitted and the nature of the Talmud itself. (Thus Halivni returns to this passage again, p. 147). The passage begins with an Amoraic dialectical analysis of mEruv 3:3: "Where was this tree standing? Shall we say that it was standing in the private domain... Rather it was standing in the public domain. Where does he intend to make his Sabbath-abode. Shall we say above [ten handbreadths]?... Rather, below [ten handbreadths]. How so?... But the truth is that it stand in the public domain, and he intends to make his Sabbath-abode below, and the authority of this mishnah is Rabbi [Yehudah HaNasi] who holds..." The passage continues with the dialogue and the *gemara*-form of the tradition that Halivni quotes. Thus we have a window into the process by which Amoraim analyzed sources dialectically but transmitted the conclusion alone in apodictic form. This passage, however, is not without textual difficulties: see Albeck, *Mavo latalmud*, 576–78 and *MM*, Eruvin, 91–94.

III.121

Typically a dictum that is not "explicitly stated" but derived from an "inference" is based on the (incorrect) analysis of the Amora's actions or his ruling concerning an incident (see, e.g., p. 121). In this singular case in Shevu 21a, however, R. Abbahu attributed to R. Yohanan the opinion that a false oath that concerns the past, for example, "I swear I have eaten" or "I swear I have not eaten," is considered a "false oath (*sheker*)" and not a "vain oath (*shav*)." Rav Pappa claims that R. Abbahu derived this from a complicated inference based on another statement of R. Yohanan concerning culpability for vain and false oaths, that the "false oath" to which R. Yohanan refers in that dictum is an oath concerning the past. Thus we have an apodictic ruling that was not articulated by the Amora himself.

III.122

That the Bavli and Yerushalmi sometimes preserve different versions of an Amora's dictum is analogous to the phenomenon found within the Bavli itself, that the Bavli sometimes provides two different versions of an Amoraic dictum or even a sugya introduced by the terms "There are those who say," and "Another version." In all these cases one version cannot preserve the original words of the Amora.

III.123

On the transmission process of Amoraic dicta, including changes to content, form, and terminology, see Shamma Friedman, *Talmud Arukh:* BT *Bava Mezi'a VI* (New York and Jerusalem: Jewish Theological Seminary, 1996), 1:7–23.

III.123

Jacob Neusner, as is well known, has expressed extreme skepticism of the reliability of attributions. See, however, Yaakov Elman, "How Should a Talmudic Intellectual History Be Written? A Response to David Kraemer's 'Responses,'" *JQR* 88 (1999), 371–86, for the case that most attributions are reliable to a considerable degree.

III.127

The point is that a baraita introduced by the term "It was also taught thus (*tanya namei hakhi*)" always provides an *additional* source to support an Amora's claim. But here the baraita introduced by "It was also taught thus" [N] is the same baraita on the basis of which Rava made his inference in the dialectical part of the sugya [G2]. So it is not an additional source ("also taught") but the same teaching, apparently added by someone who was unaware of the preceding part of the sugya.

III.132

In other words, Rava never gave those first two answers. The Stammaim created the whole sugya to explain why he did not offer either of those hypothetical answers, namely, that neither of them satisfies the case of the woman of illegitimate birth and the *netinah*.

But the flow of argumentation does not read smoothly because this same objection is raised against those two answers, and because the second answer addresses a case (the widow after betrothal) that *is* resolved by the first answer.

III.135

The issue here is the term *matnita*, which literally means "teaching" or "Tannaitic teaching," and typically refers to a baraita. In these cases the "teaching" appears in a formulation that seems to reflect uncertainty as to its provenance: "R. So-and-so said, and some say it was taught in a *matnita*." Halivni argues that even if the *matnita* appears in Aramaic ("the language of the Amora") and not Hebrew, it still refers to authentic baraitot. This view is disputed by some scholars; see, for example, the reference to Halevy in IIIn30.

III.136

See the annotation to II.113.

III.139

Separation of the original dictum from later explanations or glosses can be very difficult. The scholarly consensus holds that these terms ("in what circumstances," "he holds"), and especially the shift from Hebrew to Aramaic, supply additions to the original dictum. Friedman, "Pereq ha'ishah rabbah babavli," 301–8, provides fifteen criteria for distinguishing the original Amoraic dictum from the Stammaitic additions.

III.139

The question posed to Rav Sheshet at BM 112a is this: "[A] A contractor—does one violate the prohibition against 'holding wages overnight (*bal talin;* see Lev 19:13)' or not violate the prohibition (since he is not technically a laborer, but receives a fee for the work specifed)? [B] Does an artisan acquire title by virtue of the improvement he makes to the article, such that [his pay] counts as a loan, or does an artisan not acquire title by virtue of the improvement he makes to the article, such that [his pay] counts as wages? [C] Rav Sheshet said: One violates [the prohibition]." As the medieval commentaries point out, the question to Rav Sheshet consisted only of [A]; [B] is a later gloss, not strictly entailed by [A], which leads to some difficulties. See the parallel at BQ 99a and Tosafot, ad loc. s.v. *besheliha.*

III.143

Even though these late combiners "were not permitted" to add to the Talmud, they need not have left intact the conclusion that Abaye was rejected, because they could have quoted the Talmud's own admission later on that there was no contradiction. These combiners may have accepted contradictions, but not blatant untruths, namely, the rejection of Abaye when there was a response. This means they did not know of the passage that coordinates Abaye's view with a Tannaitic opinion.

III.151

See the annotation to III.139.

III.152

Thus the Stammaim do not provide the name, "Did not R. So-and-so say?" or "As R. So-and-so said" because they are not quoting the dictum verbatim. They therefore state "Did not the Master say?" or "As the Master said" to indicate that an excerpt of the original dictum is being quoted.

IV.155

The role of such "Compilers" has been sorely neglected in modern scholarship, perhaps understandably, due to the dearth of information. For some general comments on the process of the formation of units of tradition, see Martin Jaffee, "Rabbinic Authorship as a Collective Enterprise," *The Cambridge Companion to Rabbinic Literature*, ed. C. Fonrobert and M. Jaffee (Cambridge: Cambridge University Press, 2007), 28–35.

IV.157

Halivni touches on the late provenance of baraitot that follow what seems to be the conclusion of the sugya elsewhere; see pp. 176, 229n8.

IV.158

The point is that after the era of the Compilers, there were no independent Amoraic or Tannaitic traditions circulating that had not been incorporated into the proto-Talmud. At this point the Transposers were dealing exclusively with the redacted proto-Talmud, and operated by transferring material from one place to another.

IV.175

A "blundering student (*talmid to'eh*)" is a stock apologetic device. When the work of a great authority is found to have an error or heterodox claim or any problem from the point of view of a later writer, the problematic passage is attributed to the "blundering student" who misunderstood or incorrectly copied his master's words.

IV.184

That is, the editor of, for example, *Midrash yalqut shimoni* collected many interpretations of each biblical verse, and sometimes several talmudic sugyot that contain the verse, and simply juxtaposed them together. He made no efforts to address contradictions and inconsistencies.

IV.188

When an individual Tanna disagrees with "the Sages," the identity of those "Sages" is not completely clear. While it is generally assumed that they include all the other rabbis, it is possible that "the Sages" in these contexts simply refers to a majority of the sages who disagree with that individual opinion. The question then is whether "the Sages" in two disputes with the same Tanna (in this case, R. Yehudah) must be consistent or can contradict, as different rabbis could be involved in each case. Clearly, a transposition of this type, a kind of self-quotation, entails that we are dealing with the same authorities.

V.192

On the aggadah of the Mishnah, see the comprehensive study of Yonah Fraenkel, "The Aggadah in the Mishnah," *Mehqerei Talmud* 3, ed. Y. Sussman and D. Rosenthal (Jerusalem: Magnes, 2005), 655–83 (Hebrew).

V.194

See annotation to III.118.

V.198

There are different traditions as to when and by whom the Talmud was first written down, besides this account from the *Sefer ha'ittim* of Judah b. Barzillai (eleventh–twelfth century) that credits Natronai b. Hakhinai. See Brody, *Geonim*, 163; Talya Fishman, *Becoming the People of the Talmud* (Philadelphia: University of Pennsylvania Press, 2011), 72 and nn. 63–66.

V.199

The issue of orality has been much discussed in recent scholarship. See Yaakov Elman, "Orality and the Redaction of the Babylonian Talmud," *Oral Tradition* 14 (1999), 52–99; Martin S. Jaffee, *Torah in the Mouth: Writing and Oral Tradition in Palestinian Judaism, 200 B.C.E.–400 C.E* (New York: Oxford University Press, 2001);

Sussman, "Torah shebe'al peh," 209–384; Fishman, *Becoming the People of the Talmud,* 20–64. Shlomo Naeh, "The Structure and Division of Torah Kohanim (A): Scrolls," *Tarbiz* 66 (1997), 504–9 (Hebrew), adduces strong evidence that the *Sifra,* and perhaps other halakhic midrashim, were written, and that the prohibition of writing applied only to Mishnah (and Talmud), not midrash. (Despite Sussman's comments, 373–75, this claim has yet to receive due scholarly attention.)

ADDENDUM, 202

On these anonymous fixed laws, see In73.

ANNOTATIONS TO FOOTNOTES

AUTHOR'S INTRODUCTION, N.1

Halivni refers here to persecutions mentioned in post-Talmudic sources, especially the *Epistle of Rav Sherira Gaon,* 96–97, 99 (ed. Rabinowich, 118, 124). Sherira refers to persecutions in c. 470 CE in which the exilarch and other rabbis were arrested and executed, and other persecutions at the end of the sixth century. The plague is not mentioned by Sherira but by the Byzantine historian Procopious. See p. 113 and IIn120. The nature and extent of these persecutions is unclear, as is the identity of the Sasanian ruler responsible. See Jacob Neusner, *A History of the Jews in Babylonia, Vol.* 5. (Leiden: Brill, 1970), 60–69.

IN20

The classic study arguing that sugyot at the beginning of tractates (and sometimes chapters within tractates) are of Saboraic provenance is that of Avraham Weiss, which Halivni cites in In82. Halivni analyzes part of this sugya, Qid 2a–3b, on p. 30 ff. For a detailed study of this sugya, see Avinoam Cohen, "Le'ofiya shel hahalakhah hasavora'it," *Dinei Yisrael* 24 (2007), 161–241. See too Elman, "The World of the 'Sabboraim,'" 385–88, who suggests the "highly unusual" grammatical interest of this passage may reflect the influence of Muslim grammarians; this would support the late, "post-redactional" provenance of the sugya.

IN71

Interestingly, some recent scholarship suggests that the Bavli may in fact have known the Yerushalmi, at least certain tractates. See Alyssa Grey, *A Talmud in Exile: the Influence of Yerushalmi Avodah Zarah on the Formation of Bavli Avodah Zarah* (Providence: Brown Judaic Studies, 2005), and the review of literature, pp. 9–15; and Martin S. Jaffee, "The Babylonian Appropriation of the Talmud Yerushalmi: Redactional

Studies in the Horayot Tractates," *New Perspectives on Ancient Judaism*, vol. 4, ed. Alan J. Avery-Peck (Lanham, Md.: University Press of America, 1989), 23–24.

IN71

"The Law follows the Later Authorities" is a principle of adjudication, first mentioned in geonic responsa, that when an earlier and later authority dispute, the law follows the latter. This principle gained great currency among medieval jurists. See Israel Ta-Shema, "The Law Follows the Later Authorities," *Shenaton hamishpat ha'ivri* 6–7 (1979–1980), 405–23 (Hebrew).

IN71

On the source of Rav Ashi serving sixty years as the Head of the Academy, see the annotation to II.87.

IN71

On the writing down of the Mishnah and Epstein's view of this issue, see Sussman, "Torah shebe'al peh," 209–384, especially 300–318.

IN74

Rabbah Tosfa'ah (d. 474) is mentioned in *Epistle of Rav Sherira Gaon*, 95, among the last Amoraim, immediately before the latter Ravina (ed. Rabinowich, 116). Some scholars have conjectured that "Tosfa'ah" is a sobriquet of sorts deriving from *lehosif*, "to add," or *tosefet*, "addition," and refers to some type of editing activity or historical condition. See, for example, Kaplan, *Redaction*, 294–95 and n. 34: "The decline of Sura during the administration of Rabbah may perhaps account for his surname *tosfa'ah*.... After that the academy represented only a shadow of its former self, a feeble lingering, a *tosefet*, a mere addition of secondary quality."

IN107

In Men 30b the Talmud first quotes rulings of R. Hananel and Rabbah b. Bar Hannah, and then a ruling of R. Hanina, that the law follows R. Shimon of Shezur, but is uncertain as to which ruling of R. Shimon of Shezur he refers. The Talmud then proposes that he refers to the same case as R. Hananel and Rabbah b. Bar Hannah, but rejects this suggestion on the grounds that, had R. Hanina been referring to that case, his dictum would have been combined with the dicta of R. Hananel and Rabbah b. bar Hannah: "Let him state it too," that is, in combination with the other similar dicta.

11N9

On the question of different recensions of the Talmud in the early Geonic era, and of the version of the Talmud reflected in the *She'iltot*, see Robert Brody, "Geonic Literature and the Talmudic Text," *Mehqerei Talmud I*, ed. Y. Sussman and D. Rosenthal (Jerusalem: Magnes, 1990), 237–303 (Hebrew); and idem, *The Textual History of the She'iltot* (New York and Jerusalem: Academy of Jewish Studies, 1991) (Hebrew).

11N55

This paragraph was omitted from the body of the text, p. 72:

Initially I thought that the passage at the conclusion of that sugya (Git 5b), "[As for the case of] R. Shimon b. Abba: there was another man with him, and he was not mentioned out of respect for R. Shimon [b. Abba]," contradicted Rav Ashi's statement in RH 22b, which would provide additional evidence that Rav Ashi did not edit the Talmud. For in RH 22b Rav Ashi could have explained "another witness was with him, and he was not mentioned out of respect for R. Nehorai," but he does not do so and offers an alternative reason. It follows that Rav Ashi rejected the answer given in Git 5b, "[As for the case of] R. Shimon b. Abba: there was another man was with him, and he was not mentioned out of respect for R. Shimon." Subsequently I realized that this was not the case, as it is extremely likely that the statement "and he was not mentioned out of respect for R. Shimon" in Git 5b was transferred from RH 22b, because it is not strictly necessary for the argumentation in Git 5b. The crucial point in Git 5b is R. Yehoshua b. Levi's ruling that it was only required to state "it was written and signed in my presence" throughout the earlier generations, which were not proficient in the principle of "for her name" (*lishmah*; that a bill of divorce must be written specifically for that woman). Because R. Shimon b. Abba obtained this ruling from R. Yehoshua b. Levi when he brought a bill of divorce before him ("R. Shimon b. Abba once brought a bill of divorce before R. Yehoshua b. Levi," Git 5b) and asked him "Am I required to state, 'It was written in my presence and signed in my presence?,'" his name was mentioned in the passage. However, in RH 22b the crucial point is that one also violates the Sabbath in order to testify to the reliability of the witness (who saw the new moon), provided that there was already another witness who could testify as to the reliability, and therefore something additional (*hiddush*) would have been learned by mentioning the other witness's name, and it should have been mentioned. Why was it not mentioned there? Out of respect for R. Nehorai. Hence, Rav Ashi, who disagreed with this explanation in RH 22b, need not have disagreed in Git 5b.

11N58

On the identity of the Ravina who debates with Rav Aha, see Cohen, *Ravina and Contemporary Sages*, 247–60.

IIN61

On recent research on the lack of academies in Amoraic times in Babylonia, see the annotation to II.94. Halivni's reference to the lack of "centralized institutions" is consistent with the current consensus of scholarship, which would refer to Amoraic "schools" or "disciple circles" rather than academies.

IIN85

For analysis of the Gafni-Goodblatt debate, see Jeffrey L. Rubenstein, "The Rise of the Babylonian Rabbinic Academy: A Reexamination of the Talmudic Evidence," *Jewish Studies, an Internet Journal* 1 (2002), 55–68.

IIN102

Halivni develops the notion that the shift to mishnaic form and the production of the Mishnah were partially responses to the destruction of the temple and the persecutions following the Bar Kochba rebellion in *Midrash, Mishnah, and Gemara: The Jewish Predilection for Justified Law*, 4–5, 54. As the title implies, the Jewish "predilection" is to justify law on the basis of Scripture, that is, midrash and midrash-form. Mishnah-form is briefer, easier to memorize: "The destruction of the Temple in 70 C.E., with its attendant trauma, no doubt heightened the fear that another tragedy would wipe out learning and cause the law to be forgotten. Simpler means of remembering the law had to be devised" (54). This view does not seem to have gained much of a following among contemporary rabbinic scholars.

IIN124

This difficult and self-contradictory passage on the merits of Talmud and Mishnah in BM 33a has received many different interpretations. Recently Aharon Amit, "The Homilies on *Mishnah* and *Talmud* Study at the Close of Bavli *Bava Metsi'a* 2 and Yerushalmi *Horayot* 3: Their Origin and Development," *JQR* 102 (2012), 163–89, has provided a compelling solution to this crux by showing that the passage is really a Babylonian pseudo-baraita constructed from different sources. By "age of baraitot" Halivni means the years when the collections of baraitot were edited, c. 250 CE.

IIIN1

See the annotation to I.5.

IIIN15

See the annotation to V.198.

IVN26

Halivni explains here why these passages are *not* counterexamples to the standard response when an Amoraic tradition is adduced as an objection against another Amora's opinion, "Do you oppose one [Amora] with another [Amora]?" These cases are exceptions, involving a master and his disciple and suchlike. On this term, see p. 80, IIn12.

IVN33

On BB 105a Shmuel states of mBB 7:3: "This is the opinion of Ben Nannas, but the Sages say…" The Talmud at BB 105b claims that this formulation implies that Shmuel disagrees with Ben Nannas.

VN21

The expression "but it was not so," a strong rejection of the preceding statement, is considered by scholars to introduce a late comment, perhaps Saboraic (though exactly how late is debated). For references, see Friedman, "Pereq ha'ishah rabbah," 286 n. 14.

Selected Bibliography

Abramson, Shraga. *Peirush rabbenu hananel latalmud*. Jerusalem: Weiss, 1995.

Albeck, Hanokh. *Mavo latalmudim*. Tel Aviv: Dvir, 1969.

——. *Mehqarim biveraita uvetosefta*. Jerusalem: Rav Kook, 1944.

Brody, Robert. *The* Geonim *of Babylonia and the Shaping of Medieval Jewish Culture*. New Haven: Yale University Press, 1998.

Cohen, Avinoam. *Ravina and Contemporary Sages: Studies in the Chronology of Late Babylonian Amoraim*. Ramat Gan: Bar-Ilan University Press, 2001. Hebrew.

*Creation and Composition: The Contribution of the Bavli Redactors (*Stammaim*) to the Aggada*. Edited by Jeffrey L. Rubenstein. Tuebingen: Mohr-Siebeck, 2005.

Danzig, Neil. *Mavo lesefer halakhot pesuqot*. Jerusalem: Jewish Theological Seminary, 1993.

De-Vreis, Benjamin. *Mehqarim besifrut hatalmud*. Jerusalem: Rav Kook, 1968.

Elman, Yaakov. "The World of the 'Sabboraim': Cultural Aspects of Post-redactional Additions to the Bavli." In *Creation and Composition*. Pp. 383–416.

Epistle of Rav Sherira Gaon. Edited by B. M. Lewin. Haifa, 1921. Reprint; Jerusalem: Makor, 1972.

Epstein, Jacob N. *Mavo lenusah hamishnah*. Jerusalem: Magnes, 1964.

——. *Mevo'ot lesifrut ha'amoraim*. Jerusalem: Magnes, 1962.

——. *Mevo'ot lesifrut hatannaim*. Edited by E. Z. Melamed. Tel-Aviv, Dvir, 1957.

——. *Studies in Talmudic Literature and Semitic Languages*. Edited by E. Z. Melamed. Jerusalem: Magnes, 1988. Hebrew.

Fishman, Talya. *Becoming the People of the Talmud*. Philadelphia: University of Pennsylvania Press, 2011.

Fraenkel, Zecharia. *Mavo hayerushalmi*. Breslau: Schletter, 1870.

Friedman, Shamma. "Pereq ha'ishah rabbah babavli [A Critical Study of *Yevamot X* with a Methodological Introduction]." In *Mehqarim umeqorot*. Edited by H. Dimitrovksi. New York: Jewish Theological Seminary, 1977. Pp. 277–441.

Goodblatt, David. *Rabbinic Instruction in Sasanian Babylonia*. Leiden: Brill, 1974.

Halevy, Isaak. *Dorot harishonim*. Berlin: B. Hirts, 1923.

Halivni, David Weiss. *Meqorot umesorot: bava batra*. Jerusalem: Magnes, 2007.
——. *Meqorot umesorot: bava metsia*. Jerusalem: Magnes, 2003.
——. *Meqorot umesorot: bava qamma*. Jerusalem: Magnes, 1993.
——. *Meqorot umesorot: eruvin–pesahim*. Jerusalem: Jewish Theological Seminary, 1982.
——. *Meqorot umesorot: seder nashim*. Tel Aviv: Dvir, 1968.
——. *Meqorot umesorot: shabbat*. Jerusalem: Jewish Theological Seminary, 1982.
——. *Meqorot umesorot: yoma–hagigah*. Jerusalem: Jewish Theological Seminary, 1975.
——. *Midrash, Mishnah, and Gemara: The Jewish Predilection for Justified Law*. Cambridge: Harvard University Press, 1986.
——. "Mishnas which Were Changed from Their Original Forms." *Sidra* 5 (1989), 63–88.
Hyman, Aharon. *Toledot tannaim ve'amoraim*. London, 1910.
Kaplan, Julius. *The Redaction of the Babylonian Talmud*. New York: Bloch, 1933.
Lewin, B. M. *Rabanan savora'ei vetalmudam*. Jerusalem: Aviezer, 1937.
Lieberman, Saul. *Hayerushalmi kifshuto*. Jerusalem: Darom, 1934.
——. *Hellenism in Jewish Palestine*. New York: Jewish Theological Seminary, 1950.
——. *Tosefta kifshutah: A Comprehensive Commentary on the Tosefta*. 11 vols. New York: Jewish Theological Seminary, 1955–88.
Mekhilta d'Rabbi Ishmael. Edited by H. S. Horowitz and I. A. Rabin. 2nd ed. Jerusalem: Wahrmann, 1970.
Otsar HaGeonim. Thesaurus of the Geonic Responsa and Commentaries following the order of Talmudic Tractates. Edited by B. M. Lewin. 13 vols. Haifa and Jerusalem, 1928–43.
Rabbinovicz, Raphaelo. *Diqduqei Soferim: Variae Lectiones in Mischnam et in Talmud Babylonicum*. 12 vols. Reprint; New York, 1960.
Rabinowich, Nosson. *The Iggeres of Rav Sherira Gaon*. Jerusalem: Moznaim, 1988.
Rabinowitz, Zeev Wolf. *Sha'arei torat erets yisra'el*. Jerusalem, 1940.
Rubenstein, Jeffrey L. *The Culture of the Babylonian Talmud*. Baltimore: Johns Hopkins University Press, 2005.
Sifra. Edited by Isaac Hirsch Weiss. Reprint; New York: Om Publishing, 1947 [Vienna, 1866].
Sifre Deuteronomy = *Sifre devarim*. Edited by Louis Finkelstein. New York; Jewish Theological Seminary, 1983.
Sokoloff, Michael. *A Dictionary of Jewish Babylonian Aramaic*. Ramat Gan: Bar-Ilan University Press; Baltimore: Johns Hopkins University Press, 2002.
Sussman, Yaakov. "Torah shebe'al peh." In *Mehqerei Talmud* 3. Edited by Y. Sussman and D. Rosenthal. Jerusalem: Magnes, 2005. Pp. 209–384.
Weiss, Abraham. *Leheqer hatalmud*. New York: Feldheim, 1954.
Weiss, I. H. *Dor dor vedorshav*. Reprint; Berlin: Romm, 1922.

Source Index

MIDRASHIM

Subject Index